PROVENÇAL

L I G H T

Also by Martha Rose Shulman

LIGHT BASICS COOKBOOK

MEXICAN LIGHT

MEDITERRANEAN LIGHT

ENTERTAINING LIGHT

FAST VEGETARIAN FEASTS

THE VEGETARIAN FEAST

LITTLE VEGETARIAN FEASTS

FEASTS AND FÊTES

THE CLASSIC PARTY FARE COOKBOOK

GREAT BREADS

GOURMET VEGETARIAN FEASTS

THE SPICE OF VEGETARIAN COOKING

PROVENÇAL
LIGHT

Martha Rose Shulman

WILLIAM MORROW AND COMPANY, INC.

NEW YORK

PROVENÇAL LIGHT

Copyright © 1994 by Martha Rose Shulman
First published in hardcover in 1994 by Bantam Books,
a division of Random House, Inc.

It is the policy of William Morrow and Company, Inc., and
its imprints and affiliates, recognizing the importance of
preserving what has been written, to print the books we
publish on acid-free paper, and we exert our best efforts to
that end.

Library of Congress Cataloging-in-Publication Data

Shulman, Martha Rose.
Provençal light / Martha Rose Shulman. — 1st ed.
p.   cm.
ISBN 0-688-17465-5
1. Cookery, French—Provençal style.   2. Low-fat diet
Recipes.   I. Title.
TX719.2.P75S53   2000
641.5944'9—dc21   99-39649
                                                          CIP

Printed in the United States of America

First Edition

1 2 3 4 5 6 7 8 9 10

BOOK DESIGN BY DONNA SINISGALLI
Map of Provence on pages xx–xxi designed by
Laura Hartman Maestro

www.williammorrow.com

For
Frances McCullough,
who started me off and keeps me going.
Thank you.

CONTENTS

ACKNOWLEDGMENTS

In a way I've been writing this book ever since I came to France in 1981. Certain people have made it possible for me to carry on a continuous love affair with Provence. They are Christine Ruiz Picasso and Lulu Peyraud, who have been my hostesses through the years. *Je vous remercie toutes les deux.* Thanks also to Patricia and Walter Wells, who have also been wonderful hosts through the years at their beautiful house, Chanteduc, in Vaison-la-Romaine. I don't think I've ever been at Chanteduc without discovering a new wine from the neighboring Côtes du Rhône-Villages.

Thanks to my reliable and talented assistant, Anne Trager, for her infallible recipe testing.

Thanks to Peter and Jenny Mayle for their many leads while I was working on this book and especially for helping me find the house I rented near Gignac in 1992.

Thank you to David and Joy Willers, owners of Les Buis, for renting me the house.

Special thanks to Andrew and Lizzy Corpe for their hospitality and help while I was working on this book and especially for the 100-gram truffle they gave me as a Christmas present in 1992.

Special thanks also to Monsieur Martin at the restaurant La Mère Besson in Cannes and to the Sordello brothers and Serge Philippin at Le Restaurant du Bacon in Cap d'Antibes, for letting me spend time observing and learning in their restaurants and especially for showing me how to make bouillabaisse.

Thanks to Sabine Boulongne for sharing her recipes for Tomato Soup and Chilled Zucchini Soup, and for being such a fun companion in Provence.

As always, my agent, Molly Friedrich, and my editor, Frances McCullough, get a heartfelt thank-you for their continuing support, especially at the inception of this book.

And, of course, I am as always grateful to my loving husband, Bill Grantham, for being there.

Salut, empèri dóu soulèu que bordo
Coume un orle d'argènt lou Rose bléuge!
Empèri dóu soulas, de l'alegrìo!
Empèri fantasti de la Prouvènço
Qu'emé toun noum soulet fas gau au mounde!

Greetings, empire of the sun, bordered
Like a silver edge by the glistening Rhône!
Empire of pleasure and of joy,
Wondrous empire of Provence, who
Enchants the world with your name alone.

FROM LOU POUÈMO DOU ROSE BY FRÉDÉRIC MISTRAL

PREFACE

VOUS ETES EN PROVENCE. The sign never fails to thrill me. It's about 350 miles south of Paris, just after the Montélimar Nord exit on the A7, the Autoroute du Soleil, which links the south of France with Paris. I've been averaging 75 miles an hour since leaving Paris six hours ago; I've made the drive countless times, in winter, spring, fall, and summer. Yet that moment, when the sign tells me I am in Provence, always makes me want to celebrate and sing that Charles Trenet song, "Route Nationale 7," about the state highway that existed (and still does) long before the autoroute, the "vacation route" that goes from Paris to the shores of the Midi and "makes Paris a little suburb of Valence."

Oh, I'd sensed I was in Provence ever since the quality of the light began to change, becoming brighter after Valence; ever since I saw those signs on the autoroute picturing apricots and cherries. French autoroutes don't have billboards; they have brown-and-white symbols of gastronomy. As you approach Lyon, 250 miles south of Paris, there is a picture of a chef's toque. South of Lyon, as you drive through the Rhône Valley, you start to get pictures of fruit, with laconic, dream-inspiring phrases like *"les fruits de la Vallée du Rhône"*; or, as you near Cavaillon, southeast of Avignon, *"les melons de Cavaillon"*; as you approach Bandol, east of Marseille on the Mediterranean coast, *"les vins de Bandol."*

Once you are in Provence, exit from the autoroute, and no matter where you are you'll find yourself on a road bordered by orchards, vineyards, agricultural crops of one sort or another. This is where the sky is blue in France; this is where the fruit, vegetables, and olives grow. The cuisine here is France's cuisine of the sun.

I discovered Provence in July, the most intense time of year in the region. The sun is at its brightest, the weather is incredibly hot and dry, and the markets are as colorful as they get (mind you, the color doesn't fade until mid-October). I had a dream: I wanted to rent a house in Provence for the summer. I didn't exactly know what that meant, because with the exception of a quick drive-through or two, I'd never properly been to the region. But I found a big house to rent and friends to share it with.

With pictures of the house in hand and directions on how to get there, I set out with my friend Elizabeth in a yellow right-hand-drive Volkswagen Rabbit from a very cold, gray, rainy London at the end of June 1980. We stopped for a night in Paris (cold and gray but wonderful as always) and for another night in Vienne, just south of Lyon (still gray but warmer). Then we drove on and exited from the autoroute, as instructed by our landlady, at Avignon Sud. Now it was sunny; the sky was intensely blue, and it was hot. We followed signs for Apt, driving through pear and apple orchards until we reached the N100, which would take us to the Route du Pont Julien, which leads to a hilltop village called Bonnieux. Our house was between the turnoff and the village.

As we drove along, we began to notice something extraordinary: purple fields—the most intense purple I'd ever seen, and they were everywhere. It was lavender. Lavender is the unexpected magic of Provence in the summer. I remember bringing friends to Provence years later and watching them experience their first sight of the lavender fields as we drove the beautiful back road from Bonnieux to Apt. "What is that?" said the New Yorkers (they looked panicked). When I told them, they squealed with surprise and delight. Nothing prepares you for this sight. The lavender fields dot hillsides and valleys all over northern Provence, where it is a major crop. The flowers are used for sachets, and the essence of the flowers is distilled and used in soaps, perfumes, and household products. The bees profit for their honey (the buzzing of lavender fields in summer is deafening), and we profit from the bees. Lavender honey is my favorite; it manages to have a flavor that is both distinctive and mild. It doesn't assert itself as stronger honeys do, yet it adds depth to whatever it sweetens. The flowers begin to show their colors in June and flourish into August when they are harvested. The color becomes more and more vivid through the month of July. Then, before you know it, the purple fields begin to fade and the flowers are cut and bundled.

Our rented house that first summer in Provence was a typical stone farmhouse, called a *mas*. The walls were very thick, and there were no windows on the north side so that the powerful north wind, called the *mistral* (the word means "master" in the ancient langue d'oc), couldn't penetrate the house. As hot as those summer days were, the house was always cool inside. The kitchen was the main room, with ceramic tile floors and a soapstone sink and counter.

We were in a part of Provence called the Luberon, after a low, beautifully sculpted mountain range that runs east to west from Cavaillon (in the French department of the Vaucluse) to just west of Manosque (department of the Alpes-de-Haute-Provence). It's a region filled with picturesque medieval villages (Bonnieux, Lacoste, Menerbes, Gordes, Roussillon) sculpted out of mountains that flank a fertile valley. In 1980 our landlady complained that the region, which had always been rather isolated, was just being discovered by Parisians and was becoming their summer playground ("Eet eez zeir Nantucket now"). Now, in the nineties, the Luberon is no secret at all, and it's not just Parisians who come in droves in the summer. Since 1982 Avignon has been only a four-hour train ride from Paris, with the inauguration of the fast train called the TGV. Luckily, the area is a designated national park, so building permits are hard to come by and the region remains unspoiled.

I spent the summer of 1980 going to markets and cooking. Monday was market day in the town of Cavaillon; the sprawling market at Aix-en-Provence, on the other side of the Luberon mountain chain, was on Tuesdays, Thursdays, and Saturdays. Friday the whole of Carpentras, about a half hour north of us, became a market; Saturday was Apt, the nearest real town (about 7 miles away), and Sunday was Isle-sur-la-Sorgue, where there was a wonderful flea market in addition to the fruit and vegetable market.

We would fill our Provençal market baskets daily with vegetables and fruit, with olives of all kinds, with different olive oils and herbs. At home we used up garlic by the braid. It was succulent, the skin pink, the cloves big, fat, and sturdy. It went into ratatouilles, tarts, gratins, soups. The eggplants were blacker than any I'd ever seen, the tomatoes sweet, juicy, and red. Rosemary and thyme grew wild all around the house. We bought huge potted basil plants with small, peppery leaves; in addition to their culinary properties, the plants were thought to ward off flies, a constant bother in Provence (the strong garlic mayonnaise called aïoli has the same reputation). We couldn't believe how succulent the little round melons from Cavaillon were. And then there were the big, ripe figs. We learned about goat cheese and Provençal wines. I had my first Bouillabaisse, at Domaine Tempier, a winery in Bandol that has become one of my many "homes" in Provence.

When July came to a close and we drove north, my life had changed irrevocably. Provence was now part of it, and the ties would grow stronger over the years.

I ended up moving to Paris a year later and had barely unpacked my bags when I headed south. It was September 21, and the harvest had begun at Domaine Tempier. I had arranged with Lulu Peyraud, the proprietress, to come and pick grapes and write about the harvest, so I drove to Bandol in one day, arriving well after dark after more than nine hours on the road. I worked in the vineyards for a few days but quickly realized that where I really wanted to be was in the kitchen with Lulu, helping her make her amazing lunches for all of the *vendangeurs* (grape pickers). I stayed at the Domaine for three weeks, getting up early every morning to accompany Lulu to the market in Bandol or Toulon, then helping in the kitchen in the morning and afternoon. I learned an amazing amount about cooking fish and Provençal food, that is, Lulu's Provençal food. Now renowned in food and wine circles all over the world, Lulu is one of the best cooks I have ever met. Everything she cooks is simple, fresh, and wonderfully seasoned. Lulu knows how food should taste. I visit the Domaine several times a year, and I don't think there has ever been a visit when I haven't been introduced to a new dish.

The other person who has allowed Provence to be a constant part of my life is my dear friend and former Paris landlady, Christine Ruiz Picasso. Her spectacular farm, Cavalier, is my Provençal home away from home; I have been there at every season, every month of the year. Located high on a plateau facing the Luberon, which continues to be my favorite part of Provence, it is a working paradise of a farm. The crops are grain crops—wheat and barley—and Christine has her own private lavender field, right near the swimming pool (where the bees and I meet regularly in summer). Here is where Christine first made me Artichauts à la Barigoule (page 322), the famous Provençal artichoke dish that has hundreds of versions, none as good as Christine's. I have eaten my weight in Cavaillon melons and figs over the years, on blazing summer afternoons under the shade of an umbrella at an outdoor table. And here's where I had my first black truffles, in December, in Christine's wonderful truffle soufflé.

Christine's friends stay in the huge *mas* where she lived before her own private house was built. We come during our summer vacations, certainly, but at other times of year as well: when we are tired of polluted city air, when we have work to do and need uninterrupted calm, when we just want sun on our faces and a visit with Christine. Cavalier is where I sit now, looking out the window on a sunny day in early March. The almond tree is flowering, there hasn't been a freeze for a couple of nights; spring is arriving after a cold winter, and the birds, a constant distraction, are flirting with one another. In a while I'll go to the market, where I'll buy artichokes and garlic, olives and greens, wild asparagus, and goat cheese.

I've always shared Provence with my friends. Especially my first year in Paris, when I didn't know that I'd still be in France 12 years later, I would always plan a trip to Provence for out-of-town guests. With this book I hope to share Provence with all of my hungry readers. Provençal cuisine is so basic, so tied to the earth and the sea, that it's easy to be transported when you cook and eat these dishes. Testing a pumpkin gratin or a hearty stew in my Paris kitchen in the winter, I could easily imagine the *mistral* at the door and felt all the warmer when I sat down to eat. Spring and summer dishes—grilled fish with sweet uncooked tomato concassée, ratatouille, vegetable ragouts, garlicky salads—washed down with cool rosé from Bandol or the Luberon fill my heart with Provençal sunshine. I hope these wonderful dishes will do the same for you—that a huge, colorful Aïoli Monstre (page 232) will make you feel as festive as a Provençal holiday, that a fish soup will transport you to a quaiside bistro on the Côte d'Azur. Take a pissaladière (page 304), a pan bagnat (page 80), some tapenade (page 56), and a tomato omelet (page 245) on a summer picnic, and you might just feel for a minute that you are looking down over the olive groves from the heights of Les Baux or into the glistening Mediterranean from the *calanques* at Cassis. I hope so. But even if this doesn't happen to you, I won't feel that I've failed. For at any rate, you will have eaten heartily, healthily, and well.

Martha Rose Shulman
Cavalier, March 1993

SOME PROVENÇAL SAYINGS
AND PROVERBS

Filhos d'hoste et figuo doou camin:
Se noun soun toucado à la vesprado va soun lou matin.

Daughters of innkeepers and roadside figs:
If they're not touched in the evening, they are the next morning.

Voou mies de pan à la pannièro
qu'un bel homme à la carrièro

Better to have bread in the cupboard
than a handsome man in the street.

Noun pouedoun se couneisse ben
bouen meloun et fremo de ben.

It's hard to know a good melon
or a wealthy woman.

Manjo toun pèis aro qu'es fres.
Marido ta filho aro qu'es jouvo.

Eat your fish while it's fresh.
Marry off your daughter while she's young.

Manjo la marlusso qu'en brandado.

He eats salt cod only in brandade (i.e., he's a gourmand).

Es gounfle coumo un perus.

He's swollen-headed as a pear.

Pluio d'aous
douno d'ooulivo eme de mous.

August rain
brings olive oil and wine.

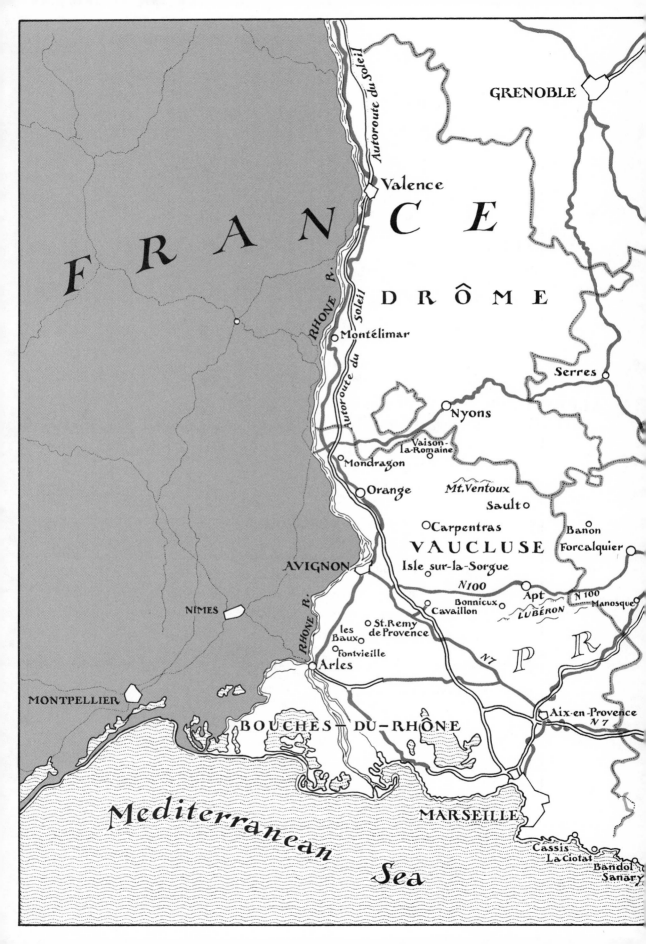

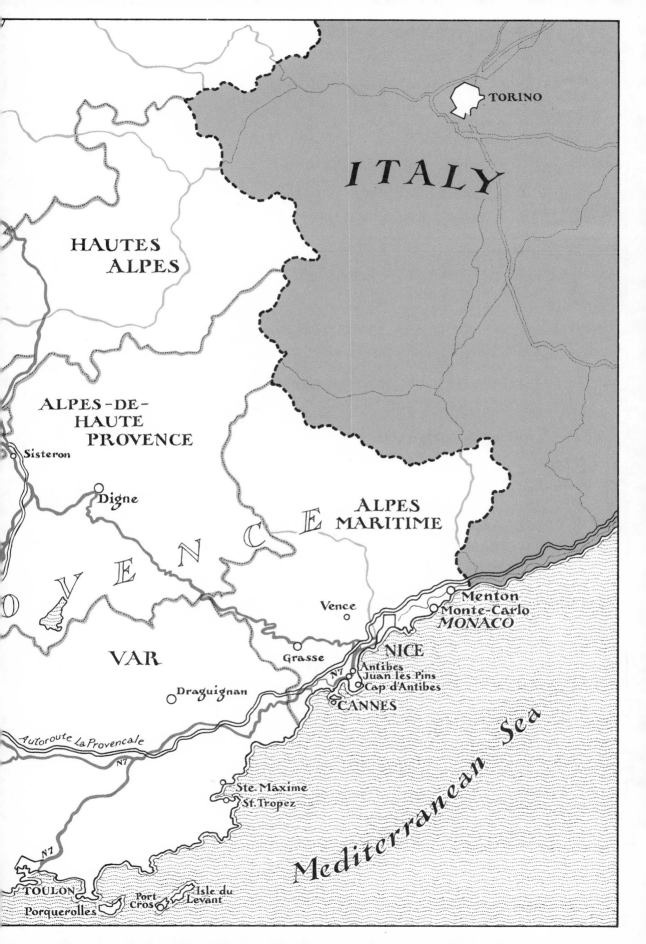

PROVENÇAL

LIGHT

INTRODUCTION

THE FOOD OF
PROVENCE

Provençal cooking is based on garlic. The air of Provence is impregnated
with the aroma of garlic, which makes it very healthful to breathe.

Provence juts up from the Mediterranean at its eastern end into rugged mountains, rolls up into gentler hills and then climbs into mountains in the middle, and spreads into the flat plains of the Rhône delta, the Camargue, and the higher country of the Rhône Valley in the west. It is a compelling place, shaded by sycamores, chestnut trees, cypresses, parasol pines, and oaks, scented with lavender here, pine there, and everywhere, it seems, with rosemary and thyme. People want to go there and do, for its sunlight, for its coastal cities and perched mountain villages, for its natural beauty and way of life, and for its food.

Anyone who studied Latin in high school remembers Julius Caesar's first line in *De Bello Gallica*: *"Gallia est omnis divisa in partes tres."* "All Gaul is divided into three parts." What Julius Caesar, proconsul in the Roman "Provincia" from 58 to 49 B.C., was describing extended far beyond the borders of what is today Provence. But these words come to mind because they evoke for me the gastronomy of this French region, an enormous area encompassing six French administrative *départements* (Vaucluse, Var, Bouches-du-Rhône, Alpes-Maritimes, Alpes-de-Haute-Provence, and Hautes-Alpes). Gastronomically and culturally speaking, only a small bit of the Hautes-Alpes could be considered Provençal. But if we are talking gastronomy, we must also include the southern part of the department of the Drôme, where Nyons and its olives are. Some—including my Michelin map #245 of Provence / Côte d'Azur—would insist on parts of the Ardèche and the Gard, but I'm sticking with the French administration here and using the Rhône as Provence's western limit.

You can get away with saying "the food of Provence," but as far as cuisine is concerned, you would have to use the plural. The cuisines of Provence are as varied as the landscape. Very roughly speaking, the *partes tres* are the cuisines of the coast, the interior, and the mountains (there is a draw here in my personal classification: the *partes tres* could also be the cuisines of the coast, the interior including the mountains, and Nice). The coastal cuisine is characterized, naturally, by its many fish dishes, including the famous fish stew called bouillabaisse (ah, but some would insist that this dish is strictly Marseillaise and that the city, sometimes referred to as "the Phoecian city" because it was colonized by a Greek tribe called the Phoecians around 600 B.C., has its own cuisine). With the exception of salt cod and anchovies,

INTRODUCTION

you find very little seafood in the cuisines of the interior (some would say this area is the real Provence), but oh so many wonderful, gutsy vegetable dishes. This cuisine changes considerably as you go north/northeast into ever more rugged mountains; olive oil eventually gives way to walnut oil, butter, and lard. The cuisine of Haute-Provence is hearty, less ebullient than the cuisines down the mountain, yet not without interest. Then there is the food of Nice and its environs, the *comté de Nice*. Originally a Greek settlement like Marseille, then the titular head of the Roman province of the Alpes-Maritimes, Nice was under the protection of the count of Provence until the end of the eighteenth century, when it became part of the Italian House of Savoy. It bounced back and forth between France and Savoy until 1860, when it voted to become part of France. Its cuisine, however, retained many Italian/Ligurian elements: from Menton to Cannes, but especially in Nice, you find marvelous pasta (ravioli in particular), gnocchi, polenta, and pizza. The ravioli is distinctly *Niçois*. It's filled with a mixture of chard, Nice's favorite leafy vegetable, and *daube* (beef stew); or ricotta cheese, or pumpkin and rice, or potato and garlic, or salt cod and herbs . . . You find other dishes in the Comté de Nice that you rarely see elsewhere in Provence—nourishing vegetable tortes; rich chick-pea flour pancakes (*socca*) and *panisses;* vegetables of all kinds stuffed with a mixture of leftover daube or other meat, chard, and herbs; and sweet *torta de blea,* a dessert torte made with chard and raisins.

Even within Provence, gastronomic distinctions are made from one place to another. An Arlesian from the Bouches-du-Rhône would insist that hers is not the cuisine of the Pays d'Apt in the Luberon, and indeed, one would not be likely to find bull meat in Apt, whereas it is a great delicacy of the Camargue. Yet on a Friday the aïoli monstre at the Bistro du Paradou, 10 miles east of Arles, will not differ very much from the one served in the hill town of Viens, 60 miles to the northeast, in the Vaucluse. Bull meat excluded, the Saturday market in Apt is much like the Saturday market in Arles—the same colorful, fragrant produce, the same luscious garlic and herbs, the same endless choice of olives. Likewise along the coast, the Marseillais distinguish their cuisine from that of Toulon, only 40 miles away. Yet in both ports the fish you find on the quais, so fresh they are still moving, is the same. You'll find bouillabaisse in both places too. The Marseillais will insist that his bouillabaisse is not the same as the bouillabaisse from Toulon, and both will eschew the bouillabaisse from Martigues, but the difference may not be so obvious to you. For my part, I've never had a better bouillabaisse than the one prepared at the Restaurant du Bacon in Cap d'Antibes on the Côte d'Azur, Comté de Nice.

What pervades the cuisines of Provence is a "Mediterranean-ness." Dumas hit the nail on the head. Provençal cooking is aromatic. It's based on garlic, olive oil (with the exception of the northern limit of Haute-Provence), onions, herbs (thyme, rosemary, savory, sage, bay laurel, basil, parsley), and the nourishing fruits of its land and sea. Vegetables in particular—summer and winter squash, chard, spinach and other greens, leeks, potatoes (the staple food in Haute-Provence), beans, eggplant, artichokes, tomatoes—transformed into *tians* (gratins), salads, *farcis* (stuffed vegetables), soups, *beignets* (fritters), omelets, and ragouts, define Provençal cooking. Like the other cuisines of the Mediterranean, this is peasant cooking, simple, and, until recent decades, essentially vegetarian, with fish along the coast and meat dishes reserved for Sundays and festivals.

As in Greece and Italy, the gastronomic traditions throughout Provence revolve around the Christian calendar, with the nature of the dishes falling into the category of *maigre* (lean, containing no meat) and *gras* (rich, containing meat). A cycle of sugary desserts begins at Christmas (the famous 13 desserts) and continues through the Carnival season to Lent. These are replaced by fresh fruit (tarts, clafoutis, compotes) in the spring and summer and dried fruit in the fall. Villages all over Provence celebrate their patron saints from spring through the fall equinox with huge feasts—very often aïoli monstre (page 232)—eaten at long tables. The delicious celebrations last for three days in the villages of the Comté de Nice, where they are called *festins* and tables groan with huge round tortes, both sweet and savory, sweet fried ravioli, gnocchi, and polenta, as well as roasted and simmered meat dishes, all washed down with abundant wine.

Provence, more than other parts of France, has absorbed elements of the cuisines of its neighbors, trading partners and immigrants. Saffron and hot peppers no doubt arrived from the eastern Mediterranean via Marseille, the most important shipping center in the western Mediterranean. Nice's taste for sweet and savory combinations also reflects the cuisines of the eastern and southern Mediterranean. Italians made up the largest group of immigrants in southern Provence through World War II, so in addition to the inherent Niçois cuisine we find pasta and pizza all through the region. Couscous and North African cooking are part of the culinary landscape here, not just because of the large number of North African immigrants who have settled in Provençal cities in the past 30 years but also because of the French *pieds noirs,* colonials who returned to France after the Algerian war and brought their beloved Algerian dishes back with them. In the big weekly markets, not just on the coast but in Aix, Apt, Cavaillon, Carpentras, and farther north, there are always North African vendors with tables piled high with hot peppers, lemons, cilantro, couscous, and spices.

Of course Provence is as much a part of the twentieth century as the rest of France, and the dietary habits have changed along with the landscape and everything else. Agricultural workers no longer take portable omelets to the fields, because they can leave the fields at lunchtime in their cars and go home or to a nearby café or bistro to eat. Fast food and supermarkets are as successful here as anywhere else. The Côte d'Azur appears to have as many shopping malls per square mile as southern California. Young people are not likely to think twice about eating meat on a Friday. But the traditions are indelible. A working mother might pop a frozen pizza in the oven one night to feed her family, but when the next family celebration comes along—a baptism, a wedding, a communion—she'll spend all day making a daube, a bouillabaisse, or an aïoli monstre. You still can't get a parking place in Apt on a Saturday, so packed is the market. The same people who buy their potatoes and spring onions at the market will stop at the ATAC Supermarket to buy their mineral water, beer, cleaning supplies, and diapers. I for one think, as I transfer cartons of mineral water from my trolley to the trunk of my car, that it's not so bad having both.

PROVENÇAL LIGHT

Like the other cuisines of the Mediterranean, the cuisines of Provence are inherently healthy. The Provençal diet is based on vegetables, grains, legumes, and fish. People here don't overeat, and nothing goes to waste. Stale bread enriches soups, tops gratins in the form of crumbs or, rubbed with garlic, seasons salads. Yes, there are rich beef daubes. Yes, bacon is commonly used to season dishes. Yes, Provence is famous for its Sisteron lamb. But first by picking and choosing dishes and then by revising traditional recipes slightly to fit my low-fat standards, eliminating certain ingredients (lard and bacon), and reducing olive oil quantities, I've assembled a collection of vibrant, healthy dishes. My purpose is not to provide a complete compendium of Provençal cooking but rather to offer a broad selection of the kind of Provençal dishes that I, and I believe you, like to eat.

There are some famous dishes that you won't find: bourride, for instance, that luxurious Provençal fish soup that is enriched just before serving with aïoli (garlic mayonnaise) and extra egg yolks. But you will find an amazing bouillabaisse (page 166), embellished with a small amount of my relatively-low-fat *rouille* (page 105), and you'll have many other wonderful fish soups to choose from. You won't find *beignets,* the batter-fried vegetables that are so popular in Nice; but you will find a mouth-watering selection of richly flavored vegetable gratins and ragouts. Many of the traditional sweet, often fried Provençal desserts are absent; but luscious fruit tarts, clafoutis, and sorbets stand in for them, and these are just as authentic. You definitely won't find a beef daube, which is a long-cooking beef stew, a traditional Sunday dish. But there's a recipe for a gutsy rabbit daube (page 389), which has a marvelous depth of flavor with much less fat. There are no lamb recipes. I make no excuses; I don't eat red meat. Low-fat cooking and eating begin with choosing the foods that are low-fat to begin with, and the choice in Provence is endless.

On the other hand, you might be surprised to find lots of olives, because they are high in fat. As with so many other foods, however, olives are healthy in moderation. A handful of tiny Niçois olives thrown into a savory chicken stew will add tons of flavor and not enough fat to make them a dangerous addition. And remember, the lipids in olive oil are thought to lower blood cholesterol. The pungent olive paste called *tapenade* may not be a low-fat food, but when you spread it on a crouton you're eating only a small amount of it. And why deprive yourself of something so good if you're not going to eat enough to harm you? The same goes for aïoli, the rich Provençal garlic mayonnaise. I wouldn't think of leaving it out of this collection, but I've modified the recipe so that it's less extravagant; I feel that the harm there might be in the small amount of fat in the mayonnaise is far outweighed by the benefits in the huge selection of vitamin-rich vegetables with which aïoli is usually served. Eggs, too, are an important part of my repertoire. They are a vital food in Provence, and the omelets from the region are simply the best in the world. Naturally, if you have a cholesterol problem, these recipes won't be for you, but you'll have plenty of other dishes to choose from. Deprivation has never been my thing; indeed, Lulu and Lucien Peyraud tell me I must have Marseillais ancestors, because like the Marseillais, I love *la fête*.

HOW TO USE THIS BOOK FOR MAXIMUM LOW-FAT BENEFITS

While all of the recipes in this book are low in fat, they are not austere. I tend to use 1 to 2 tablespoons of olive oil in a given dish for four to six, whereas more extreme diets require less than a tablespoon. Still, the overall fat content and calorie content is low; the nutritional data are comparable to those in my book *Mediterranean Light*. And very few of the fat grams come from saturated fats.

Each recipe is followed by nutritional data calculated by Nutrition Associates. To calculate the number of calories from fat, multiply the number of grams of fat in the dish by 9 (1 gram of fat contains 9 calories). If in a particular recipe more than 30 percent of the calories come from fat, choose dishes for the rest of the meal that have a relatively lower fat content. If, for example, you are making the zucchini gratin with goat cheese on page 352, you will find that, with 2 tablespoons of olive oil, 2 eggs, and 2 ounces of goat cheese, more than 30 percent of the calories come from fat, because the main ingredient in the dish, zucchini, is so low in calories. Choose, then, a low-fat salad and dessert, such as the Provençal wheatberry salad on page 41 and the apricot and strawberry salad on page 411. And remember that all things are relative: a dish can have a high percentage of calories from fat, but if the overall calorie content is very low, then I would not say it is harmful. Count fat grams: If you're having an average 2,000 calories a day, your fat grams should stay under 60 to meet the 30 percent guideline.

LOW-FAT COOKING TECHNIQUES

Most traditional Provençal recipes that involve cooking on top of the stove ask you to sauté vegetables in a *verre,* a glass, of olive oil (equivalent to about two-thirds of a wineglass). Sometimes, as in the case of eggplant, the vegetables are drained afterward on paper towels; still, you've used and will eat a lot of oil. But much less oil is required to soften most vegetables and bring out their flavors. There are three main requirements for top-of-the-stove cooking in a minimum of oil (1 to 2 tablespoons, sometimes less): a heavy-bottomed nonstick pan, low heat, and patience. Patience because low-fat cooking is slower than dramatic throw-it-in-the-hot-oil-and-hear-it-sizzle cooking. Nonstick pans heat up slowly to begin with, and your heat will remain at medium-low for most foods. You must stir often, though not constantly, to make sure the food doesn't stick to the pan. When you're sautéing vegetables, it helps to sprinkle them with a small amount of salt when you add them to the pan. The salt brings out their natural juices, which serve as a fragrant cooking medium. I always keep a jar of coarse, unrefined sea salt next to the stove for this purpose.

As for eggplant, I never use the traditional salting and frying technique. For more than 15 years I've been baking eggplant at high heat before cooking it in dishes like ratatouille (page 312) or gratins. The only olive oil required here is the teaspoon or two for the baking sheet. I cut the eggplant in half lengthwise, score the cut side, and lay the halves cut side down on an oiled baking sheet, which goes into a very hot oven for about 20 minutes. The eggplant releases water and cooks enough so that, even if you then cook it on top of the stove, it won't absorb vast quantities of oil as it cooks.

For fish I simply avoid frying and rely on baking, steaming, poaching, and grilling. I have switched to these techniques in several recipes (for example, fish cooked in raito on page 206 and salt cod in onion, wine, and caper sauce on page 202), where the fish is traditionally fried; the results are delicious and eminently more digestible.

As for chicken, I choose recipes that call for stewing the meat in a fragrant broth or a sauce, and I always remove the skin, where most of the fat is, before I cook it.

For egg dishes, when possible I've given you the choice of substituting egg whites for some of the whole eggs. I don't eliminate the yolks altogether, however, because I feel that some yolk is important for flavor and color, and egg yolk, just like anything else, is all right in moderation.

Always, when developing these recipes, I experimented. How little olive oil could I get away with without sacrificing the quality of the dish? That was always the question; and I found myself to be in the tablespoon as opposed to teaspoon ballpark. For certain dishes I asked, "Will this be good if I do it a completely new way?" For example, I eliminated most of the olive oil from the brandade on page 61 and used more milk. It worked for *brandade*, but none of my ideas worked for *bourride*, so I simply decided not to include that rich fish soup. Desserts were easy once I knew that I'd leave out the famous Provençal nougat (a rich almond taffy) and Niçois *oreillers* (deep-fried ravioli) and concentrate on fruit; after all, southern France *is* a huge fruit basket. And thanks to Greek phyllo pastry, which requires only 2 tablespoons of butter for a crisp, easy, golden crust, fruit tarts have an eminent place on my Provençal table.

VILLAGE SOBRIQUETS
FROM HAUTE-PROVENCE

Anyone who has read the novel or seen the film *Jean de Florette* knows that Provençal peasants do not think very highly of people from the villages closest to their own. Many of the sometimes derisory nicknames used to describe people from nearby villages are gastronomic in nature. Here are some from the Alpes-de-Haute-Provence, the Alpes-Maritimes, and the Vaucluse.

People from
Revest-les-Brousses: *lei manjo-cabro* (goat-eaters)
Mane: *lei manjo-chin* (dog-eaters)
Saint-Michel-l'Observatoire: *lei manjo-sangué* (blood-eaters)
Montjustin: *lei manjo-agasso* (magpie-eaters)
Rougon: *lei manjo-aglan* (acorn-eaters)
Barcelonnette: *lei licho-platèu* (plate-lickers)
Estoublon: *lei manjo-granouio* (frog-eaters)
Colmars: *lei manjo chau-rabo* (kohlrabi-eaters)
Allos: *lei manjo-fége* (liver-eaters)
Lincel: *lei manjo-cougourdo* (pumpkin-eaters)
Forcalquier: *lei manjo-pastissoun* (pasta-eaters)
Banon: *lei manjo-froumage* (cheese-eaters)
Touyet: *lei manjo-afato* (wild plum–eaters)
Peirrevert: *lei manjo-grafièn* (cherry-eaters)
Ascros: *lei manjo-trufo* (potato-eaters)
Nice: *lei cago-blea* (chard-shitters)
Grasse: *lei manjo-fasun* (stuffed cabbage–eaters)
Caseneuve: *lei manjo-pijoun* (pigeon-eaters)

EQUIPMENT

When I was learning about Provençal cooking from chefs, and later testing recipes in my kitchen, I kept reaching for certain pieces of equipment that I realize you might not be accustomed to using. They are simple gadgets people have been using in Provençal kitchens for a long time (electric hand blender excepted), and they really will make a difference in how many dishes taste. Before getting into pots and pans, let me elaborate.

MORTAR AND PESTLE: When garlic is pounded to a paste in a mortar and pestle, the oils are released as in no other way, and you get a very pungent puree, which is essential for aïoli (page 97). Anchoïade (page 45) is another dish best made in a mortar. For one thing, you never make that much at a time; for another, a food processor is too big to achieve the kind of paste you want. *Pistou* is creamier when made in a mortar—but I do usually use a food processor for this condiment. Other dishes traditionally made in a mortar and pestle in Provence are tapenade and brandade, but for these you really can use a food processor. If you can afford one, there's nothing like a big, heavy marble mortar with a wooden pestle. But I've used an olivewood mortar and pestle for years with excellent results. It's important to buy a big enough bowl so that you can mash up garlic or anchovies or spices without things flying all over the place. And the bowl makes a nice serving dish.

FOOD MILL: Long before there were blenders and food processors, there was the food mill. These gadgets, which come with medium, fine, and coarse blades, make cooking certain soups and sauces incredibly easy, because you don't have to peel any of the vegetables (see La Mère Besson's tomato sauce on page 114). The peels will stay in the food mill when you put the mixture through. This tool is absolutely essential if you are going to make bouillabaisse (page 166) or soupe de poissons (page 170), but I also use it every time I make the basic tomato sauce on page 112, which accompanies many of my dishes. Soups put through a food mill have more texture than blended soups.

Hᴀɴᴅ Bʟᴇɴᴅᴇʀ: This gadget has been used by French housewives for decades and is now catching on in America. It's a blender blade on a stick, and it makes pureed soups a cinch. No transferring from the pot to the blender or food processor: you just stick the blender into the soup, turn it on, and move it around. You can control the texture better than you can with a blender or food processor because you're in closer contact with the food. The hand blender is often used in conjunction with a food mill. In bouillabaisse and soupe de poissons (pages 166 and 170), for instance, the fish and vegetables are blended up in the pot before the mixture is put through the coarse blade of a food mill. The same goes for La Mère Besson's tomato sauce (page 114).

Kɪᴛᴄʜᴇɴ Sᴄᴀʟᴇ: I use a kitchen scale for breads, pasta, and pastry. I find it's much easier and more accurate to measure flour in a kitchen scale than in a cup. I never use cup measures for chopped vegetables and fruit for the same reason. I couldn't do without a kitchen scale.

OTHER ELECTRIC GADGETS

Sᴘɪᴄᴇ (ᴏʀ Cᴏꜰꜰᴇᴇ) Mɪʟʟ: I have two coffee mills, one for coffee and one for spices. But spices aren't the only thing I blend up in my mill. It's very useful for making bread crumbs. When bread is very hard, I break it into small pieces and blend it into crumbs in the electric spice mill.

Fᴏᴏᴅ Pʀᴏᴄᴇssᴏʀ: Most of the dishes I make in the food processor were traditionally made in a mortar and pestle, but the food processor does make life easier. It's especially useful for the tapenades (pages 56–60) and brandades (pages 61–68) in this book, as well as for making pasta dough, aïoli, and some purees, such as the apricot puree on page 410.

Eʟᴇᴄᴛʀɪᴄ Mɪxᴇʀ: A heavy-duty electric mixer, such as a Kenwood or KitchenAid, is useful (but not essential) for bread, beating egg whites, and aïoli.

POTS AND PANS

NONSTICK FRYING PANS: Use heavy-bottomed pans. They're easy to find in restaurant equipment stores. You should have a large one (at least 15 inches—37 cm—in diameter) and a smaller one for omelets.

LARGE HEAVY-BOTTOMED SOUP POT OR DUTCH OVEN: For soups, ragouts, and stews. I use a large enameled cast-iron casserole, such as Le Creuset, which heats up slowly, retains the heat well, and lends itself to low-fat cooking.

SAUCEPANS: The 1½- and 2-quart (1½- and 2 l) are convenient sizes. I use enameled cast iron for the reasons already mentioned. But I also have a set of inexpensive lightweight saucepans for steaming vegetables and simmering garlic; they're easier to lift for draining.

STOCKPOT: A large pot for making stocks and cooking pasta. The ones I use are either stainless steel or lightweight enamel. Lightweight pots are especially useful for draining pasta and steaming.

GRATIN OR BAKING DISHES: The earthenware baking dishes used in Provence for gratins are called tians, and so are the gratins baked in them. Your gratin dishes don't have to be earthenware (they are pretty, though); I have both earthenware and enameled cast iron, which are also flameproof, in various sizes. For these recipes you'll need both 2-quart (2 l) and 3-quart (3 l) sizes. You'll also need a baking dish large enough to accommodate a whole fish, but the 3-quart gratin will probably do for this.

LARGE, DEEP, OVENPROOF CASSEROLE: In Provence the casseroles or *poêlons* are round, deep, ovenproof earthenware dishes with a handle on one side. They aren't lidded, but foil, a pizza pan, or a lid from another casserole can stand in. I use mine most often for ratatouille (page 312).

TART PAN: I like the white porcelain pans, 10½ or 12 inches (26 to 30 cm) in diameter. I also have a metal cake pan, about 12 inches (30 cm) in diameter, which I often use for vegetable tortes (see pages 260–64).

PIZZA PANS: I use them for pizzas, but they also make handy stand-ins for lids and baking sheets.

BAKING STONE: For bread and pizza.

UTENSILS AND OTHER NECESSITIES

KITCHEN KNIVES: Mine are stainless steel. I have a large chef's knife about 10 inches (25 cm) long—not the largest by any means, but the most comfortable for me—and several paring knives.

POTATO PEELER: Useful not just for peeling potatoes but for cutting slivers of Parmesan . . . and truffles!

KITCHEN SCISSORS: Essential for snipping herbs. Scissors don't bruise the herbs and are much neater than knives for this task.

MEASURING SPOONS: Have two sets; it makes life easier.

WOODEN SPOONS AND SPATULAS: Long-handled spoons are especially useful.

MEDIUM-SIZE WIRE WHISK

COLANDER

LARGE STRAINER

DEEP-FRY SKIMMER: I use mine all the time, not for deep-frying but for lifting pasta and cooked vegetables out of boiling water.

SKIMMER: For skimming stocks and the simmering cooking water when cooking chicken, fish, and beans. Also very useful for lifting fat out of chilled chicken stock.

CHEESECLOTH: You should never be without a supply in the kitchen, for straining and for holding bouquets garnis that include Parmesan rinds.

STEAMING BASKET: You can also use a steaming pot, which has a perforated top part that sits in the bottom. A couscoussier can double as a steaming pot. A tiered steamer with more than one level is very useful if you are steaming more than one food, as in aïoli monstre (page 232).

ROTARY CHEESE GRATER: A rotary grater is useful not only for grating cheese but also for making bread crumbs from stale bread or zwieback and for grating nuts.

BAKER'S PEEL: A long-handled board used for sliding pizza and bread onto a hot baking stone.

WOODEN CUTTING BOARDS: It helps to have one with a depression around the edge to catch tomato juices.

STAINLESS-STEEL BOWLS

OLIVE PITTER: Essential if you're going to make tapenade. Some garlic presses include olive pitters.

Which leads me to my discussion of . . .

THE GARLIC PRESS: This can be the most annoying of gadgets, and I fully sympathize with all of you who have given it up in favor of chopping and pureeing with a little salt on a cutting board or pounding in a mortar and pestle. However, I am lucky enough to have two garlic presses I like (the rest I've thrown out). One, which my mother found in Italy in the fifties, has a deep cylindrical housing for the garlic clove and a hinged plunger. The holes are plentiful and flat on the surface of the cylinder, and therein lies the key: the garlic, rather than being crushed and for the most part lost in the interstices between the holes, is plunged through the holes. It's like a miniature version of an old-fashioned potato ricer. The cylinder is deep enough, and the plunger leaves no room around the edges for the garlic, so all of it must go through the holes. The other press that works pretty well is a large French model, the one that has the olive pitter on the handle. This isn't cylindrical, but the holes, which are quite large, are still flat on the surface of the housing. It does crush more than my cylindrical one, but it has one advantage: it's large enough so that you can put unpeeled cloves into it. When you squeeze together the two hinged sides, the garlic is crushed and pops through the skin and through the holes. It's easy then to pull the skin out of the housing and clean the garlic press. The disadvantage is that you do lose some of the garlic. You can also use the larger garlic press to press hard-cooked eggs into salads.

HOW TO CLEAN A GARLIC PRESS

You do inevitably have to scrape the inside with your finger. But the garlic will come out in one layer if you first scrub the *outside* of the press with the rough side of a sponge or scouring pad or with a toothbrush. If you really can't bear using your finger to get the rest out of the inside, use a toothbrush. For those useless presses that don't have a flat surface between the holes, you'll have to use a toothbrush to clean it anyway. Another important word of advice: clean the press immediately after using, or at least let it soak in a glass or bowl of water. If the garlic dries, forget cleaning the press right away. If it *does* dry (you've had a really good party and gone straight to bed), soak for several hours in soapy water.

T R U C
A "PINCH" IS A "POINT"

In French recipes the word for "pinch" is point. It means the amount of salt, sugar, garlic, whatever, that you can fit on the point of a knife. This is a much more useful term than pinch: it's easier to measure out. Use this concept and the point of your knife when you see the term pinch in recipes.

T R U C
SUBSTITUTES FOR LIDS

Sometimes the recipe says to cover, and you've used a pot or a pan with no lid. Here are some stand-ins:
· Round pizza pans: I use these when I'm cooking on top of the stove in my large nonstick frying pans. I also use pizza pans in the oven with some of my earthenware casseroles.
· Plates: They fit perfectly over some of my saucepans.
· Aluminum foil: I use foil in the oven, to cover gratin dishes, for example, when I'm baking fish. Heavy-duty aluminum foil is best.

* A truc is a "trick."

CHAPTER 1

SALADS AND STARTERS

The beautiful drive from Bonnieux, a hill town in the Luberon, to Bandol near the coast takes about one-and-a-half to two hours. First you wind your way through the Luberon on a narrow road that cuts right through the rocks and every so often opens out onto beautiful views of lavender fields and mountains. Once you get through the mountains, you either go to Pertuis and pick up the autoroute (a recent development) or continue on to Aix and pick up the autoroute there. Aix-en-Provence, though it seems like such an inland place, is only 20 miles from Marseille. But don't follow the signs for Marseille; take the Toulon cutoff. In about 20 minutes you will come over a rise after you've cut through another spectacular, sun-bleached range of mountains called the *Massif de la Saint Baume*, and you'll see the exit sign for Cassis. Down below you'll get your first glimpse of the shimmering Mediterranean. It will take your breath away.

This is the drive I took the first time I went to Domaine Tempier, a winery in Bandol where I had been invited to lunch early on during my first summer in Provence. There were a number of us that hot, brilliantly sunny day, and Lulu Peyraud, the tiny, beautiful, blue-eyed proprietress, greeted us with a large platter of toasted croutons, some spread with tapenade, others with *brandade de morue*, and a glass of chilled Domaine Tempier rosé. I got an authentic taste of Provence as I bit into each crouton: black olives, capers, garlic, anchovies, and herbs; salt cod, garlic, olive oil. The flavors of tapenade and of brandade became part of my repertoire from that day on.

Dishes like these, along with the other starters and salads in this chapter, are some of the most fundamental, delicious foods of Provence. They are simple, made from basic Provençal ingredients—olives and olive oil, garlic and anchovies, salt cod and tuna. Workers in olive oil mills and farmers traditionally restored them-selves at midmorning with foods like the grilled croutons spread with anchovy paste called *quichets* (page 54) or with croutons spread with tapenade or brandade or simply rubbed with garlic and a cut tomato (page 48).

Many of these dishes are not confined to one part of Provence; you'll find them in the northern part of the region as well as along the coast. That said, the marvelous mixture of salad greens called *mesclun* is typically Niçois, and although it is now popular all over France, you can always count on finding it along the Côte d'Azur. On the other hand, the Provençal wheatberries called *épeautre* that go into the salad on page 41 are a mountain grain, a product of Haute-Provence. Niçois salad, of course, is ubiquitous. But the people who live in the Comté de Nice are emotional about what this salad really is; along the Mediterranean coast it certainly is not the same salad that you will find in Paris cafés or New York restaurants.

Many cooked vegetable salads in Provence, especially Haute-Provence, grow out of a tradition called the *bajano*, or *bajan*. The vegetables (or beans or grains) are cooked in salted water, and the cooking water is eaten as a soup with garlic croutons. The vegetables are then seasoned with a vinaigrette and eaten as a salad. They are the part of the meal called the *bajan*. In Haute-Provence they make a *bajano gras*, where mutton, wheatberries, and vegetables are cooked together, then separated into these various parts: the broth, the meat, and the wheatberries and vegetables seasoned with vinaigrette. I love this concept—nothing goes to waste, and the resulting meal is filling and nourishing. The chick-pea and spinach salad with chick-pea broth on page 35 is a *bajano*.

Other dishes in this chapter, such as the Provençal tabouli on page 32 and the salad with warm goat cheese on page 37, are more recent additions to the region's repertoire. Couscous has installed itself in France during the last 30 years, since the Algerian war. And the goat cheese salad, although it would seem traditional, is a fashion of the last 10 or 20 years. Speaking of fashion, in the last five years or so certain Provençal dishes have become chic in Paris restaurants, and many of these dishes—especially tapenade and brandade—are the leaders in the trend.

Trendy or not, you will love these salads and starters because they are so fresh and vibrant, because, no matter where you are, they'll bring Provençal sunlight into your kitchen.

MELON AND FIGS

SERVES 6

This could as easily be a dessert as the start to a meal. From mid–April through the end of summer the small, juicy Cavaillon melons are always a first-course choice on Provençal restaurant menus. For me this dish (is it a dish? it's nothing more than unembellished, ripe, sweet, sensuous fruit) will always evoke one place, one season, and one time of day: the long white poolside table outside Christine Picasso's house, midsummer, about 2:00 P.M. The sun is beating down, and Christine has put up a huge white umbrella that just about shades all of us. Christine has sliced up three or four Cavaillon melons and arranged them with figs, and sometimes slices of prosciutto, on a big oval blue-and-white ceramic platter made by her father-in-law. As soon as she sets it down on the table, some bees buzz over from the lavender field to join us. It's lunchtime at Cavalier.

2   **ripe cantaloupes, cut into eighths, seeds and rinds removed**

6 to 12   **fresh ripe figs, to taste, whole or cut in half**

        mint sprigs for garnish (optional)

Arrange the fruit on a platter, garnish with mint if desired, and serve. The fruit can be chilled or room temperature.

PER PORTION

Calories	133	Protein	2 G
Fat	.77 G	Carbohydrate	33 G
Sodium	17 MG	Cholesterol	0

Salade Niçoise falls into the same category as many traditional Provençal dishes, such as bouillabaisse (page 166), *artichauts à la barigoule* (page 322), and *la soupe au pistou* (page 134): it's a traditional dish with a score of "traditional" recipes, each one emotionally defended as *"la vraie."* But one thing seems to be consistent: the salad has been bastardized by the introduction of cooked vegetables, namely potatoes and green beans. I decided to do a little survey of great Provençal chefs when I set about writing a salade Niçoise recipe. Roger Vergé, chef/owner of the famous Moulin de Mougins, in the backcountry above Cannes, sent me a delightful letter describing his salade Niçoise for eight people. Here is my translation:

Dear Madam:

I've always thought that people living in the country had the most authentic recipes. What follows, therefore, is the recipe which I've seen prepared by the women of our region and by the fishermen, and which I myself make for my friends:

I cut not-too-ripe tomatoes into quarters, I mince white onions (spring onions), and I cut green peppers, not the thick bell peppers but the thin-fleshed kind, and cucumbers into thick rounds.

I put all of these vegetables together in a large bowl and sprinkle a handful of coarse sea salt over them. Then I toss them together, put a plate on top of them, and let them sit for an hour.

Meanwhile, I cook and peel my hard-cooked eggs, I rinse my anchovy fillets, drain my oil-packed tuna, and assemble my Niçois olives. I chop one or two garlic cloves and a bunch of basil, as well as a few leaves of arugula.

When the hour is up, I drain my vegetables in a large colander and let them sit 10 minutes, so that all of the salty water runs off.

Then I put the vegetables in a bowl with the quartered hard-cooked eggs, the anchovy fillets, the tuna, the olives, basil, garlic, and arugula. Do not salt, but dress generously with olive oil, wine vinegar, and a few turns of the peppermill.

I toss the salad well and serve right away with country bread and well-chilled rosé wine (and I look for a well-shaded summer table).

The salade Niçoise described in *Larousse Gastronomique* "is a typical Mediterranean dish comprised essentially of tomatoes, cucumber, fresh fava beans or small local artichokes [both are pictured in the illustration that accompanies the entry], green peppers, spring onions, hard-boiled eggs, anchovy fillets or tuna, Niçois olives, olive oil, garlic, basil. There should be no cooked vegetables or potatoes."

Notice that neither Vergé nor *Larousse* mentions lettuce. Yet Elizabeth David, in *French Provincial Cooking*, does call for Boston lettuce in one of her four versions of the salad. And Chef Martin of La Mère Besson in Cannes makes a wonderful salade Niçoise that includes a delicious bed of salade mesclun, that typical Provençal mixture of greens. On top of the greens go a mixture of diced celery, red pepper, sometimes fennel, and fresh fava beans in season. Then goes a can of tuna (either water-packed or oil-packed), the usual hard-cooked egg, Niçois olives, and anchovies. Monsieur Martin stirs some pistou into his dressing and adds lots of garlic. This is poured over the salad, which is then tossed.

Jacques Médecin, who was the mayor of Nice for many years until a corruption scandal forced him to flee the country, is also very emotional about salade Niçoise. His book, *La Cuisine du Comté de Nice* (Julliard, 1972), has become a standard text for Niçois cooking. His salad contains lots of young spring vegetables, like purple artichokes and baby fava beans, none of them cooked; cooking vegetables to him is anathema. Here is what he says about *la salada nissarda*, "the (real) Salade Niçoise":

> What crimes have been committed in the name of this pure, fresh salad, which is based on tomatoes, which is made up of nothing but raw vegetables, with the exception of hard-boiled eggs, which is made without vinegar, the tomatoes salted three times and drizzled with olive oil! Sometimes even Niçois eat anchovies and tuna in the same salad; this was never done traditionally, because in the past tuna was extremely expensive, and only utilised for important occasions; most of the time it was replaced by anchovies, which were much more affordable.
>
> I beg of all of those who wish to insure the renown of the cuisine of the area never to incorporate in a salade Niçoise the slightest bit of boiled vegetable or the slightest bit of potato.

Salade Niçoise entered my own kitchen via Julia Child. Hers was a mixture of French potato salad, cooked green beans, Boston lettuce, tomatoes, tuna, anchovies, black olives, hard-cooked eggs, and herbs, all tossed with vinaigrette—and *no mention of garlic or olive oil* (but in the master recipe for the vinaigrette, olive oil is an option)! I might add that my first published salade Niçoise was a vegetarian version—no tuna or anchovies.

In the 1980s it became very popular in American restaurants to serve Niçoise salads with fresh, grilled tuna instead of canned. This is a nice twist. But to me it isn't really salade Niçoise. It's a nice, fresh salad with a beautiful piece of pink grilled tuna on the side. I must admit, as much as I love grilled tuna, in the case of salade Niçoise I like water-packed tuna that I can mash up with the dressing.

So where does that leave *us*? I make salade Niçoise all the time at home. It's one of our favorite main-dish salad meals. And what I make resembles none of the recipes in my now large collection. I love potatoes in the salad, and I love croutons rubbed with garlic (it's one of the main reasons I hang on to my stale bread). Into my very untraditional main-dish salade Niçoise usually go lettuce, a lightly steamed green vegetable of some kind (green beans, broccoli, peas), tomatoes in season (grated carrot if there are no tomatoes to be had), sometimes cucumber, sometimes red or green pepper (sometimes the red pepper is roasted if I have that ingredient in the refrigerator), water-packed tuna, hard-cooked egg (or just the egg white in my low-fat version), lots of herbs, and anchovies. My dressing is a garlicky low-fat yogurt vinaigrette using a small amount of olive oil. It's a hefty meal, and I can never believe that we've cleaned out the bowl, but we do every time.

This marvelous salad doesn't, of course, have to be a meal. Following are two low-fat interpretations, one a main-dish salad, the other a more traditional Provençal starter.

LIGHT SALADE NIÇOISE

SERVES 4 TO 6

This recipe takes ideas from Roger Vergé and from La Mère Besson and tosses them together in a light dressing. The tomatoes should be of good quality but not too ripe.

For the Salad:

4	medium-size tomatoes, cut into wedges
1	regular or European cucumber, peeled if bitter, cut in half lengthwise, seeds removed, diced
1	small green pepper, preferably a sweet thin-skinned variety, diced
1	small red pepper, preferably a sweet thin-skinned variety, diced
3 or 4	scallions, white part and green, chopped
1	tablespoon coarse sea salt
¼ to ½	cup (62 to 125 ml) slivered fresh basil, to taste, or 2 tablespoons low-fat pistou (page 109)
½	pound (225 g) fresh fava beans, if available★
1	small fennel bulb, chopped (optional)
6	ounces (180 g/5 cups) mixed lettuces such as the salade mesclun mixture on page 29, washed and dried
1	6⅛-ounce (173 g) can water-packed tuna, drained
	the whites of 2 hard-cooked large eggs
4 to 8	anchovy fillets, to taste, rinsed
12	black Niçois olives

★ To prepare fresh fava beans, shell the beans, then drop them into a pot of boiling water. After 30 seconds, drain and transfer to a bowl of cold water. Remove the thick outer skin by holding the beans between your thumb and forefinger and squeezing gently. They should pop out of their skins. Set the beans aside in a bowl.

SALADS AND STARTERS

For the Dressing:

1	**tablespoon balsamic vinegar**
2 to 3	**tablespoons red wine vinegar to taste**
3	**garlic cloves, minced or put through a press**
½	**cup (125 ml) plain non-fat yogurt**
2	**tablespoons olive oil**
	freshly ground pepper and salt to taste

Combine the tomatoes, cucumbers, peppers, and scallions in a bowl. Add the coarse salt and toss together gently. Put a plate on the ingredients in the bowl and let sit for 1 hour while you prepare the remaining salad ingredients and the dressing.

For the dressing, mix together the vinegars and garlic. Add the yogurt, olive oil, and pepper and mix together well. If you're using pistou, stir it into the dressing.

Drain the salted vegetables in a colander or a large strainer. Rinse briefly. Allow to sit for 10 minutes. Toss with the fava beans, fennel, and basil.

Place the lettuce in a wide salad bowl. Top with the vegetable/basil mixture. Break up the tuna and scatter it over the top. If you have a garlic press with large holes, press the hard-cooked egg whites through the holes into the mixture. Otherwise sieve the egg whites or finely chop. Top with the anchovies and the olives. Pour on the dressing.

Take the salad to the table, toss thoroughly, and serve.

ADVANCE PREPARATION: All the ingredients and the dressing can be prepared hours before assembling and tossing the salad.

PER PORTION

Calories	150	Protein	13 G
Fat	6 G	Carbohydrate	11 G
Sodium	604 MG	Cholesterol	14 MG

MAIN-DISH SALADE NIÇOISE

SERVES 4 TO 6

This is my very untraditional salade Niçoise. It always makes us very happy. And it always takes me longer to make than I think it's going to; so give yourself plenty of time to prepare all of the vegetables.

For the Vinaigrette:

2 to 3   tablespoons red wine vinegar to taste

2   tablespoons fresh lemon juice

2   garlic cloves, minced or put through a press

1 to 2   teaspoons Dijon mustard to taste

2   tablespoons chopped fresh herbs, such as basil, parsley, sage, tarragon, thyme

salt and freshly ground pepper to taste

3   tablespoons olive oil

½   cup (125 ml) plain non-fat yogurt

For the Salad:

1   pound (450 g/4 medium-size) new potatoes, diced

2   tablespoons dry white or rosé wine

salt and freshly ground pepper to taste

1   6⅛-ounce (173 g) can water-packed tuna

1   small head of Boston lettuce, leaves roughly torn

1   pound (450 g/4 medium-size) tomatoes, quartered, or ½ pound (225 g) carrots, peeled and grated

½   pound (225 g) green beans, broccoli, zucchini, or asparagus, steamed until crisp-tender

1   small cucumber, peeled, seeded, and thinly sliced (optional)

1	green or red bell pepper, thinly sliced (optional)
2	hard-cooked large eggs, yolks removed and whites quartered
2 or 3	anchovy fillets, rinsed and chopped (optional)
½	cup (125 ml) cubed garlic croutons (page 83)
¼ to ½	cup (62 to 125 ml) chopped or slivered fresh herbs such as basil, sage, chervil, tarragon, chives, parsley to taste

For the vinaigrette, combine the vinegar, lemon juice, garlic, mustard, herbs, salt, and pepper. Whisk in the olive oil and yogurt.

Steam or boil the potatoes until tender, about 10 to 15 minutes. Remove from the heat, transfer to a large salad bowl, and toss at once with the wine, salt, and pepper. Add the tuna and toss with 6 tablespoons of the vinaigrette.

Add the remaining vegetables and the egg whites to the bowl. Add the anchovies, garlic croutons, and herbs and toss together with the remaining dressing. Adjust the seasonings and serve.

Note: Other vegetables, such as sliced fresh mushrooms, artichoke hearts, radishes, summer squash, sliced fennel, or peas, can go into this salad.

ADVANCE PREPARATION: The dressing and all of the vegetables can be prepared several hours before serving the salad. The potatoes can be cooked and tossed with the wine, salt, pepper, tuna, and dressing hours ahead of assembling the salad.

PER PORTION

Calories	230	Protein	14 G
Fat	8 G	Carbohydrate	27 G
Sodium	222 MG	Cholesterol	12 MG

THE MAURESQUE

The Niçois have a particular fondness for an aperitif called the mauresque, which is basically a pastis with a little *orgeat* (almond syrup) added to it. I was introduced to the drink by my husband, Bill, who for a time worked in Nice with a printer named Jean-Pierre Bergeret. They worked long hours, but always broke for a long midi-style lunch, which inevitably began with a round of mauresques.

Bill brought this Niçois tradition home to Paris with him, and we in turn brought it back down to our friends in Provence, where we took to drinking mauresques at sunset on hot summer nights. It's a perfect summer aperitif. To make a mauresque, put 3 or 4 ice cubes in a tall glass. Add an ounce (2 tablespoons) of pastis, and 2 teaspoons of almond syrup (orgeat). Fill with water, stir well and serve.

MESCLUN SALAD
Salade Mesclun

SERVES 4

Mesclun is a Provençal blend of salad greens and herbs grown and harvested together when young and tender. What makes it so special is the contrasting flavors of bitter, pungent, and mild ingredients. Traditional Niçois mesclun contains about 9 or 10 ingredients, including red- and green-tipped oak leaf lettuce, arugula, radicchio, romaine lettuce, curly endive (frisée), escarole, chervil, and dandelion greens. I've also seen baby lamb's lettuce and nasturtium petals and/or leaves in the mixture. I think the most important greens to include are the sharp arugula and the delicate chervil, which always delight my palate with their fragrant flavors, as well as some of the bitter lettuces like the endive, radicchio, dandelion greens, and escarole. The contrast of soft and tough textures is also important. The mixture should be tossed with a mild, simple vinaigrette like the one here. For a nice contrast of bitter and sweet, use balsamic vinegar. Mesclun is available in some markets; it's worth looking for and worth the expense.

1	tablespoon vinegar: red wine, sherry, or balsamic
½	teaspoon Dijon mustard
1	small garlic clove, minced or put through a press (optional)
	salt and freshly ground pepper to taste
3 to 4	tablespoons olive oil to taste
6 to 7	ounces (180 to 210 g/4 to 5 cups) mesclun

Mix together the vinegar, mustard, garlic if desired, and salt and pepper. Add the oil and combine well. Just before serving, toss with the mesclun.

ADVANCE PREPARATION: Washed and dried greens will hold for several hours in the refrigerator. Wrap in a clean kitchen towel, then seal in a plastic bag. The vinaigrette will hold for a few hours as well.

PER PORTION

Calories	128	Protein	.67 G
Fat	14 G	Carbohydrate	2 G
Sodium	26 MG	Cholesterol	0

WARM POTATO AND GREEN BEAN SALAD

SERVES 4

I was always set for this satisfying salad during the September I spent at Les Buis, near the village of Gignac, because my neighbor Raymond regularly brought me green beans from his garden, and I always bought lots of my friend Jean-Luc's organically grown potatoes at the Apt market. I love this salad warm, but it's great cold too. You could make a meal of it.

1	pound (450 g/4 medium-size) waxy potatoes, sliced about ½ inch (1.5 cm) thick
1	pound (450 g) green beans, trimmed and broken into 2-inch (5 cm) lengths
2	tablespoons fresh lemon juice
2	tablespoons vinegar: red wine, white wine, champagne, or sherry
2	teaspoons Dijon mustard
1	garlic clove, pounded to a paste or put through a press
	salt and freshly ground pepper to taste
½	cup (125 ml) plain nonfat yogurt
2	tablespoons olive oil

2   **tablespoons chopped fresh herbs such as basil, parsley, chives**

1   **ounce (30 g) Parmesan cheese, shaved into thin slivers, ¼ cup (optional)**

Steam the potatoes until just about tender, about 10 to 15 minutes. Add the green beans and continue to steam for 5 to 10 minutes, until cooked as desired.

Meanwhile, mix together the lemon juice, vinegar, mustard, garlic, salt, pepper, and yogurt. Whisk in the olive oil.

When the vegetables are cooked, remove from the steamer and toss immediately with the dressing and herbs. Add the Parmesan if desired. Serve warm.

ADVANCE PREPARATION: You can cook the potatoes and toss them with half the vinaigrette hours before serving if you are not planning to serve the salad warm. The beans can be steamed hours ahead of time as well, but don't toss with the vinaigrette more than 45 minutes before serving, or they'll lose their bright color.

PER PORTION

Calories	206	Protein	6 G
Fat	7 G	Carbohydrate	31 G
Sodium	112 MG	Cholesterol	.56 MG

PROVENÇAL TABOULI
Taboulé provençal

SERVES 8

Couscous came to Provence from the former North African colonies and is as common throughout France as Mexican food is all over the American Southwest. This lemony salad is called taboulé in Provence, although it's not made with bulgur. If you want it to resemble Middle Eastern tabouli more closely, use the greater amount of parsley.

1½	cups (260 g) couscous
	salt to taste
1	cup (250 ml) fresh lemon juice
½	cup (125 ml) water
1	garlic clove, minced or put through a press
	freshly ground pepper to taste
2 to 3	large bunches (180 g) of flat-leaf parsley (2 to 3 cups leaves, finely chopped, 1 to 1½ cups chopped)
½	cup (125 ml) fresh mint leaves or more to taste, finely chopped
4	scallions, both white and green parts, finely chopped
1	medium-size red bell pepper, diced
1	pound (450 g/4 medium-size) tomatoes, peeled if desired, seeded, and chopped
2	tablespoons olive oil
	inner leaves from a head of romaine lettuce for garnish and to use as scoops
1	fennel bulb, cut into wide strips to use as scoops
1	large red or green bell pepper, cut into wide strips to use as scoops

Place the couscous in a bowl. Combine ¼ to ½ teaspoon salt to taste, the lemon juice, water, and garlic and pour over the couscous. If the couscous isn't covered, add a little more water. Allow the grains to sit and absorb the moisture, rubbing the couscous between your fingers every so often so that they don't clump together. It should be softened (with a slight degree of crunchiness) and fluffy in about 20 minutes. Add more salt if desired and pepper.

Add all the remaining ingredients except the lettuce, fennel, and bell pepper and toss together. Adjust the seasonings, cover, and refrigerate until ready to serve. Serve garnished with the romaine lettuce leaves, fennel strips, and pepper strips.

Note: Other green vegetables, such as steamed peas or green beans, may be added to the salad.

ADVANCE PREPARATION: The salad can be prepared a few hours before serving.

PER PORTION

Calories	201	Protein	6 G
Fat	4 G	Carbohydrate	37 G
Sodium	46 MG	Cholesterol	0

ARUGULA AND PARMESAN SALAD

Salade de roquette et de parmesan

SERVES 6

For the past six years I've accompanied my husband on his March and April business trips to Cannes. I spend my time in the market, working at restaurants, and in Nice. The markets are wonderful at this time of year, because the early spring vegetables are just beginning to arrive. Small farms from the hills sell wild asparagus, new fava beans called *fèvettes*, and arugula tied into luscious bunches. This salad might seem Italian, but it's a Niçois inspiration. I think arugula is wonderful with no olive oil at all, so this ingredient is optional.

½	**pound (225 g/about 5 cups) arugula, stems trimmed**
1½	**ounces (45 g) Parmesan, shaved into thin slivers, about ⅓ cup**
1 to 2	**tablespoons balsamic vinegar to taste**
2	**tablespoons olive oil (optional)**
	freshly ground pepper to taste

Combine the arugula and Parmesan. Toss with the balsamic vinegar, olive oil if desired, and pepper and serve.

ADVANCE PREPARATION: The ingredients can be prepared hours before serving. Toss with the vinegar and oil just before serving.

PER PORTION

Calories	32	Protein	3 G
Fat	2 G	Carbohydrate	.82 G
Sodium	129 MG	Cholesterol	5 MG

—— TRUC ——

Use a potato peeler to shave the Parmesan.

CHICK-PEA AND SPINACH SALAD
WITH A CHICK-PEA BROTH
Li cesa à la vineigreto e la bajano
Les pois chiches en salade et la soupe

SERVES 6

Here is a brilliant, economical way to make a meal. Cook chick-peas, make a warm salad with the peas, and serve the broth with toasted bread and perhaps a few crushed chick-peas as a soup. The dish is a typical *bajano* from the mountainous regions of Provence. Marion Nazet, who has written a beautiful two-volume book called *Misé Lipeto: le Calendrier Gourmand de la Cuisine Provençale d'Hier et d'Aujourd'hui*, has a unique method for cooking chick-peas in the water in which spinach has been blanched. She doesn't add the spinach to the salad, but I do (you could of course use the spinach for another purpose).

4	**quarts (3.75 l) water**
1	**pound (450 g) fresh spinach, stems removed**
1	**pound (450 g/2 cups) dried chick-peas, picked over and soaked overnight in 3 times their volume of water**
1	**bay leaf**
	salt to taste
¼	**cup (62.5 ml) fresh lemon juice**
2	**tablespoons vinegar: red wine, sherry, or white wine**
1	**teaspoon Dijon mustard**
1	**large garlic clove, minced or put through a press**
	freshly ground pepper to taste
½	**cup (125 ml) plain nonfat yogurt**
2	**tablespoons olive oil**
	additional garlic to taste for the soup (optional)
¼	**cup chopped fresh parsley (about 15 g/½ large bunch)**

1	small red onion, chopped, or 4 scallions, both white and green parts, chopped
6	thick slices of slightly stale or toasted country bread, rubbed with garlic
1	ounce (30 g) Gruyère cheese, grated (¼ cup)

Several hours before you wish to cook the chick-peas, bring the water to a rolling boil in a large pot and add the spinach. Boil for 5 minutes and drain, reserving the water. Rinse the spinach with cold water, gently squeeze out the water, coarsely chop the spinach, and set aside. Return 3 quarts (3 l) of the cooking water to the pot and allow to cool.

Drain the soaked chick-peas and add to the spinach water along with the bay leaf. Bring to a boil, reduce the heat, cover, and simmer gently for 1 hour. Add salt to taste and continue to simmer for another 30 minutes to an hour, until the chick-peas are tender.

While the chick-peas are simmering, make the vinaigrette. Mix together the lemon juice, vinegar, mustard, garlic, salt and pepper to taste, and yogurt. Add the olive oil and combine well.

Drain the chick-peas, reserving the water, and return the water to the pot. Taste the broth, add garlic if you wish, adjust the salt, and add pepper. Allow to simmer while you toss the chick-peas in a bowl with the parsley, onion, spinach, and vinaigrette. Cover the salad so it stays warm while you serve the broth.

Distribute the bread among 6 soup bowls and top with the broth. Sprinkle grated cheese over the top and serve the soup, followed by the salad.

ADVANCE PREPARATION: The entire dish can be made hours or even a day ahead of serving, but don't toss the chick-peas and spinach with the vinaigrette until shortly before serving. When you wish to serve, toss the salad in a heavy-bottomed saucepan and reheat gently over medium-low heat.

PER PORTION

Calories	447	Protein	21 G
Fat	12 G	Carbohydrate	67 G
Sodium	292 MG	Cholesterol	6 MG

SALAD WITH WARM GOAT CHEESE
Salade au chèvre chaud

SERVES 4

Surprisingly enough, this salad, which has become such a commonplace through-out France, did not originate in Provence, nor is it a traditional recipe. It is thoroughly modern yet thoroughly Provençal in character, goat cheese being the cheese of this region. There are many kinds, sold at many stages of development. For my salads I prefer cheeses that are fairly fresh but firm enough to withstand heating. A more traditional version of this salad would call for much thicker rounds of goat cheese than I am calling for here. But I don't feel deprived with this lower-fat version. You still get a nice portion of creamy goat cheese to eat with your salad. If you slice the cheese quite thin, you can have two portions per serving.

For the Salad:

4 to 8	**garlic croutons to taste, preferably made with sourdough bread (page 83)**
4	**½-inch-thick (1.5 cm) rounds or 8¼-inch-thick (.75 cm) rounds of fresh but firm goat cheese (about ¼ pound/115 g in all)**
1	**teaspoon fresh thyme leaves or ½ teaspoon dried**
½	**teaspoon chopped fresh rosemary (optional)**
½	**pound (225 g) lettuce, either one kind or a mixture of firm, bitter lettuces such as curly endive (frisée), red-leaf, arugula, and leaf lettuce**
12 to 15	**fresh chervil sprigs if available**
1	**red bell pepper, thinly sliced (optional)**
	radish roses or tiny radishes for garnish

For the Dressing:

2 to 3   **tablespoons red wine vinegar to taste**

1   **tablespoon fresh lemon juice**

1   **teaspoon Dijon mustard or more to taste**

1   **small garlic clove, minced or put through a press (optional)**

¼   **teaspoon crushed dried tarragon or 1 teaspoon chopped fresh**

½   **cup (125 ml) plain nonfat yogurt**

2   **tablespoons olive oil**

salt and freshly ground pepper to taste

Preheat the oven to 425°F (220°C). Place the croutons on a baking sheet and top with the rounds of cheese. Sprinkle with thyme and rosemary if desired.

Make the vinaigrette. Mix together the vinegar, lemon juice, mustard, garlic, and tarragon. Whisk in the yogurt and oil and add salt and pepper.

Shortly before serving the salad, place the cheese-topped croutons in the oven and bake for 6 to 8 minutes or until the cheese is bubbling. Meanwhile, toss the lettuce, chervil, and red pepper, if you're using it, together with the dressing and distribute among salad plates.

Top the salads with the hot cheese croutons, garnish with radishes, and serve at once.

ADVANCE PREPARATION: The croutons can be toasted a day in advance. Store in a sealed plastic container. The lettuce can be washed and thoroughly dried up to a day in advance. Wrap in towels, then seal in plastic bags. The dressing will hold for several hours, in or out of the refrigerator.

PER PORTION

Calories	138	Protein	4 G
Fat	6 G	Carbohydrate	14 G
Sodium	173 G	Cholesterol	.56 MG

SALADS AND STARTERS

I used to call the road where my rented farmhouse at Gignac was located *fromage de chèvre* street because it was marked by a sign for goat cheese. A man up the road from me raised goats and made delicious fresh *tommes* (disks), which we would occasionally buy from him. Often, when I was working inside the house or on the terrace, I would hear the tinkling of bells and look up or come out to greet his herd of curious goats. I loved the sound and the look of them, but their cheese is what I appreciated the most.

The *fromage de chèvre* sign on my road is just one of many dotting Provence. Goat cheese is made by hundreds of small farmers and *fromagiers* throughout the region. It is sold at stalls at every village market, and all the major towns have good *fromageries* selling goat cheeses at various stages of *affinage* (aging). If a town is not large enough for a *fromagerie*, then the butcher will sell the local goat cheeses. They are usually shaped into the round *tommes* (or *tomes*), but sometimes you find pyramid shapes (*pyramides*), hearts (*coeurs*), logs (*buches* and *buchettes*), and squarish *briques*.

The goat cheeses of Provence vary from mild to pungent, depending on how long they have been aged. What they have in common is a marvelous earthy flavor, sometimes almost herbal, which isn't surprising considering all the thyme, savory, and other wild herbs the goats feed on. The harder and older they are, the stronger and saltier. If they are extremely fresh, still sort of wet, and not very firm, they can be somewhat acidic. I look for goat cheeses that are fresh, white, and clean-looking, creamy but firm.

Here are some of the goat cheeses of Provence:

Picodon: These are thin disks weighing 100 grams (3½ ounces) or less. The best come from the mountainous area of northern Provence. Traditionally *Picodons* had to be aged for a month and were strong and hard. Now they can be marketed within 12 days, so there is a range, some mild and creamy, some hard and pungent, even piquant. Very young *Picodons* are sold as *tomme de chèvre;* 8- to 10-day-old *Picodon* is called *tomme fraîche.* When *Picodon* is made in the traditional way and aged for at least a month in glazed earthenware jars, it is sold as *Picodon méthode Dieulefit.* Several disks of the cheese are often wrapped together and sold by weight.

Banon: Provence's most famous cheese, named after the village in the Alpes-de-Haute-Provence where the best *Banons* are made. The cheese was originally made from ewe's milk or goat's milk, but now it can be a mixture of goat's milk and cow's milk. The best is made from goat's milk alone. There are two types: *Banon frais* is young and is not always wrapped in the chestnut leaves we associate with this cheese. Sometimes the young cheeses are shaped into disks; other times they are shaped into log shapes called *buchettes*. *Banon frais* is usually sprinkled with sprigs or leaves of wild savory, called *poivre d'ain* in the region (*pebre d'ai* in Provençal, *sarriette* in French). *Banon vrai* is wrapped in chestnut leaves that have been dipped in eau-de-vie, tied with raffia, and aged for at least three weeks. It's quite creamy and has a very pungent flavor.

Tomme or *tome, tomme de chèvre, tomme fraîche:* Generic words for goat cheese, usually disk-shaped, weighing about 100 to 150 grams (3½ to 5½ ounces). They are firm but creamy and vary in hardness (*demi-sec* to *sec*), depending on how long they have been aged. Sometimes they are ash-coated (*cendrées*), some are white mold–coated, others blue mold–coated.

Pélardon: Another generic word for a number of goat cheeses.

Lou pevre: The cheeses are rolled in grains of coarsely cracked black pepper and have a piquant flavor.

Poivre d'ain or *pebre d'ai*: The cheeses are covered with wild savory.

American Goat Cheeses: We have an excellent selection of goat cheeses in America, and many can be used for the recipes in this book. I use the same criteria in America as I do in France for selecting goat cheese: it should be white, creamy yet firm, and not too salty. The cheeses are usually fresher and less salty than many imported goat cheeses. These are the usual names for American goat cheeses:

Chabis: Young, fresh, mild 5-ounce (145 g) cylindrical cheeses. Marketed at less than one week old.

Pyramide: Cured a little longer than chabis. Ash-coated and sold in 8-ounce pyramid shape.

Log: Aged for approximately 1 week. The 1½-inch-thick (4 cm) logs are either ash-coated or white mold–coated and weigh 8 to 9 ounces (225 to 250 g).

Pepper, herb: 5-ounce disks coated with herbs or pepper.

Crottin: 2½- to 3-ounce (70 to 90 g) disks, aged 2 to 3 weeks. Sharp, pronounced goat flavor and drier texture.

Cabécou: 1-ounce (30 g) disks, cured for 2 to 3 weeks and marinated in olive oil and herbs.

PROVENÇAL WHEATBERRY SALAD
Salade d'épeautre

SERVES 4 TO 6

Wheatberries are often served in Provence with a vinaigrette. This salad is good warm or cold. The dressing is a mustardy, garlicky low-fat yogurt vinaigrette.

For the Salad:

- 1   cup (7 oz/210 g) wheatberries
- 3   cups (750 ml) water
- ½   teaspoon salt
- 1   medium-size red bell pepper, diced
- 1   medium-size green bell pepper, diced
- 1   small red or white onion or 4 scallions, both white part and green, chopped
- 2   medium tomatoes, seeded and diced
- 2   tablespoons drained capers, rinsed (optional)
- ½   cup (125 ml) chopped fresh herbs such as parsley, chives, basil, chervil, tarragon, dill
- 1   head of Boston or romaine lettuce (optional)

For the Dressing:

- 2   tablespoons fresh lemon juice
- 2   tablespoons red wine vinegar or sherry vinegar
- 1   tablespoon Dijon mustard
- 1   large garlic clove, minced or put through a press
    salt and freshly ground pepper to taste
- ½   cup (125 ml) plain nonfat yogurt
- 2   tablespoons olive oil

Combine the wheatberries and water and bring to a boil. Add the salt, cover, reduce the heat, and simmer for 1 hour, until the wheatberries are cooked through (they will remain chewy). Drain and toss with the vegetables, capers, and herbs.

To prepare the dressing, mix together the lemon juice, vinegar, mustard, garlic, salt, pepper, and yogurt. Whisk in the olive oil. Toss with the wheatberries and vegetables. Taste and adjust seasonings.

Line a salad bowl or platter with the lettuce leaves if desired. Top with the salad and serve or chill for 1 hour and serve.

Note: Feel free to add other green vegetables to the salad, such as peas, fava beans, green beans, or broccoli florets.

ADVANCE PREPARATION: All the ingredients for the salad can be prepared up to a day ahead of time. The dressing will hold for several hours. The salad can be tossed an hour before serving (no longer, or the green vegetables will lose their color).

PER PORTION

Calories	196	Protein	7 G
Fat	6 G	Carbohydrate	31 G
Sodium	239 MG	Cholesterol	.37 MG

WARM FOUR-BEAN SALAD
Salade tiède aux quatre haricots

SERVES 4 TO 6 (4 AS A MAIN DISH)

I first ate this salad at a small restaurant called Auberge de Beausset in a tiny hillside village of that name not far from Isle-sur-la-Sorgue. I had a terrible cold that day, but the vibrant flavors came through, even with my blocked sinuses. The contrasting colors and sizes of the dried beans, all speckled with bright green parsley, makes this mixture as beautiful to look at as it is delicious. It's my kind of food, hearty and earthy. Each bean has a distinctive flavor, heightened by the simple, tart, garlicky dressing. Because the beans have different cooking times, you'll have to cook all but the red and white beans in separate pots. Beyond that this is a no-fuss dish.

½ cup (3½ oz/100 g) each dried white beans, dried light green flageolets, dried dark kidney beans, dried favas (giant white beans)

2 quarts (2 l) water for soaking

4 cloves

2 medium-size onions, peeled and cut in half

8 large garlic cloves, 6 slightly crushed and peeled, 2 finely minced or put through a press

3 bay leaves

   salt to taste

3 tablespoons red wine vinegar or sherry vinegar

4 teaspoons olive oil

   freshly ground pepper to taste

½ cup (about 30 g/1 large bunch) finely chopped flat-leaf parsley

   lettuce leaves for serving

Soak each type of bean in its own bowl, in 2 cups (500 ml) water for 6 hours or overnight (the favas will need 12 hours). Drain.

Place the fava beans in one large (at least 2-quart/2 l) saucepan, the flageolets in another, and the white and red beans together in another. Cover the beans with water by 3 inches (7.5 cm). Stick a clove in each onion half and add 2 halves to the pan with the white and red beans and one half to each of the other pans. Add 2 crushed garlic cloves and a bay leaf to each pan and bring to a boil. Cover, reduce the heat, and simmer for 45 minutes.

Add about 1 teaspoon salt, to taste, to each pan. Cover and continue to cook the flageolets for 15 minutes longer. If they are not tender by this time, simmer for 15 minutes more or until tender. The favas should take another 45 minutes and the white and red beans another hour and 15 minutes. This is all variable, depending on the hardness of your water, the age of the beans, and the altitude at which you are cooking (beans take longer to cook at higher altitudes). The beans should be tender but intact, not mushy.

Remove the beans from the heat once they are tender and drain through a strainer set over a bowl. Combine the beans and transfer to a saucepan.

Stir together the vinegar, remaining garlic, olive oil, and ½ cup (125 ml) cooking liquid from the beans (I prefer the broth from the red and white beans). Add salt and pepper and stir into the beans along with the parsley.

Just before serving, heat through until simmering. Serve over lettuce leaves, either on individual plates or on a platter.

ADVANCE PREPARATION: The salad can be prepared hours ahead of serving. Without the parsley this will hold for 3 days in the refrigerator. Add the parsley shortly before serving.

PER PORTION

Calories	282	Protein	17 G
Fat	4 G	Carbohydrate	47 G
Sodium	383 MG	Cholesterol	0

CELERY AND ENDIVES
WITH ANCHOVY PASTE
Céleri et endives à l'anchoïade

SERVES 6

One of the simplest and most popular of Provençal hors d'oeuvres is celery and/or Belgian endive with *anchoïade*, a pungent anchovy paste. The celery and endives are served plain, on a plate, with the *anchoïade* spooned onto the plate or served in a small ramekin. The slightly bitter vegetables make a nice vehicle for the pungent, salty anchovy paste. The amount of *anchoïade* might seem small, but a little goes a long way. Salt-packed anchovies are lower in fat than oil-packed, so use them if possible.

24 anchovy fillets, (1 2-ounce, 60 g, can)
   milk to cover the fillets
4 garlic cloves, minced or put through a press
2 tablespoons olive oil
2 tablespoons red wine vinegar or sherry vinegar
   freshly ground pepper
1 head of celery, trimmed and cut into sticks
6 medium-size or large Belgian endives, trimmed at the stem end and cut lengthwise into quarters

Make the anchovy paste. Soak the anchovies in milk for 20 minutes. Drain and rinse. Pound to a paste along with the garlic, using a mortar and pestle, or a fork. Work in the olive oil and vinegar. The mixture can be slightly coarse, or you can work the sauce until it is smooth, as you wish. Add pepper to taste. You should have about ½ cup (125 ml).

Place the *anchoïade* in a ramekin or an attractive bowl and set on a platter, surrounded by the celery and endives. Or divide up the vegetables and serve on individual plates, placing a generous tablespoonful of the anchovy paste on each plate. Dip the celery sticks and endive leaves into the *anchoïade* or drizzle it over the vegetables.

ADVANCE PREPARATION: The anchovy paste will keep for a few days in the refrigerator. You can cut up the vegetables hours ahead of serving and keep them in a plastic bag or, in the case of the celery, in a bowl of water, in the refrigerator.

PER PORTION

Calories	108	Protein	6 G
Fat	6 G	Carbohydrate	7 G
Sodium	709 MG	Cholesterol	9 MG

LAYERED GRILLED EGGPLANT, PEPPERS, AND ZUCCHINI

SERVES 4 TO 6

When I arrived at Les Buis, a rented house in the Vaucluse, I was happy to find a little barbecue. I was also happy to find beautiful small eggplants and huge red peppers in the market in Apt. Immediately I envisioned a cold terrine of grilled vegetables. The zucchini was an afterthought; my neighbor Raymond brought me a huge one from his garden, and grilling the slices seemed the logical thing to do. I bake the peppers in a hot oven rather than grilling them, because you get more juice that way, and the juice is an important ingredient in the terrine. This wonderful dish is very light.

1½ pounds (675 g/3 large) red bell peppers
salt
1½ pounds (675 g/3 to 4 small) eggplant, sliced lengthwise ¼ to ½ inch (.75 to 1.5 cm) thick
1 pound (450 g/3 medium-size or 1 huge) zucchini, sliced diagonally ¼ to ½ inch (.75 to 1.5 cm) thick
2 to 3 tablespoons olive oil, as needed
1 tablespoon balsamic vinegar

1   **teaspoon Dijon mustard**

2 to 3   **large garlic cloves, to taste, minced or put through a press**

         lots of freshly ground pepper

¼   **cup (60 ml) slivered fresh basil leaves**

Preheat the oven to 400°F (200°C). Place the peppers in a baking dish and bake, turning often, for about 45 minutes, until softened and browned. Remove from the heat, transfer to a bowl, cover tightly, and allow to cool.

Salt the eggplant and zucchini slices and let sit for 20 minutes. Rinse and pat dry.

Meanwhile, prepare a grill. When the coals are ready, brush the eggplant and zucchini slices lightly with olive oil and grill on both sides, basting if necessary with olive oil, until browned and cooked through. Depending on how hot your fire is, this could take anywhere from 3 to 8 minutes per side. Transfer to a bowl or platter as the slices are cooked.

Peel the cooled peppers and remove the seeds and membranes, being careful to retain the juice. Cut or tear the peppers into 2-inch-wide (5 cm) slices.

Mix together the juice from the peppers, balsamic vinegar, mustard, and garlic. Oil a 2-quart (2 l) gratin or soufflé dish.

Starting with eggplant slices, layer the vegetables in the dish, sprinkling each layer with salt, pepper, basil, and a little bit of the vinaigrette. You should have 2 or 3 layers of each vegetable. Try to save some pepper slices for the top layer. Sprinkle with basil, spoon on any remaining dressing, cover tightly, and set aside at room temperature or in the refrigerator until ready to serve.

To serve, cut squares using a sharp or serrated knife, and lift out servings with a spatula.

ADVANCE PREPARATION: This can be made several hours to a day before serving. It looks best if served on the day you make it, but you should definitely give it time to sit and marinate with the garlic and basil.

PER PORTION

Calories	127	Protein	3 G
Fat	7 G	Carbohydrate	16 G
Sodium	34 MG	Cholesterol	0

CROUTONS WITH GARLIC
AND TOMATO
Pain catalan or pain gradaillé

SERVES 4

The word *gradaillé* comes from the Languedocien word *gradalha,* to rub with garlic, which in turn comes from the Languedocien word for garlic clove, *gra d'alh.* In Provence a thick piece of stale bread is rubbed generously with garlic, then drizzled with vinegar and quite a bit of olive oil. Instead of olive oil I've used the juice of a tomato, which makes this more like the Spanish or Catalonian version (which in its traditional form would also contain olive oil). In fact the tomato version of this dish is eaten all over the Mediterranean, so I don't know why the French call it "Catalonian bread." All you need is good, crusty bread, juicy tomatoes, and garlic.

8	**thick slices of country bread, lightly toasted or slightly stale**
1 to 2	**garlic cloves, as needed, cut in half lengthwise**
2	**ripe tomatoes, cut in half**

Rub the bread with the cut garlic, then with the cut half of a tomato, squeezing the tomato a bit so that its juice saturates the bread.

ADVANCE PREPARATION: Eat these as soon as you prepare them.

PER PORTION

Calories	170	Protein	6 G
Fat	2 G	Carbohydrate	33 G
Sodium	351 MG	Cholesterol	0

MINI AÏOLI

Chef Philippin, at the Restaurant du Bacon in Cap d'Antibes, serves a mini aïoli as an *amuse-bouche,* an appetite-whetter served with aperitifs. He serves slivers of vegetables and tiny green beans and cherry tomatoes on a small plate with a little bit of garlic mayonnaise. It's quite charming. I've taken his idea and made it into a first course. It's especially practical if you happen to have leftovers from an aïoli monstre (page 232). You can vary the vegetables.

1	carrot, peeled, steamed until tender (about 20 to 30 minutes), quartered, and cut into thin slivers
1	medium-size waxy potato, steamed or boiled until tender (about 20 to 30 minutes), peeled, quartered, and thinly sliced
1	medium-size beet, peeled, steamed until tender (about 30 minutes), quartered, and cut into small wedges
1	medium-size turnip, peeled, steamed until tender (about 20 minutes), quartered, and cut into small wedges
4	large cauliflower florets, steamed until tender (about 15 minutes), and thinly sliced
24	thin green beans, trimmed and steamed until tender (about 5 to 8 minutes)
¼	pound (115 g) cooked salt cod or other white fish
¼	cup heaped aïoli (60 ml) (page 97)

Arrange the vegetables in an attractive pattern on 4 small plates. Place heaped tablespoons of aïoli in the middle of the plates. Serve as a first course.

ADVANCE PREPARATION: The plates can be made up a couple of hours before serving and held in the refrigerator.

PER PORTION

Calories	200	Protein	10 G
Fat	10 G	Carbohydrate	18 G
Sodium	N/A	Cholesterol	48 MG

OVEN-ROASTED PEPPERS
Poivrons rôtis au four

SERVES 4

Roasting peppers in the oven yields more juice from the peppers than flame-roasting or grilling. The flavor is a little different, sweeter, and without the charcoal-grilled taste. You can use the juice as the marinade, with only minimal oil added. At the restaurant La Mère Besson in Cannes, where I learned this, they don't add any olive oil at all. They just refrigerate the peppers in their juice, and serve them topped with anchovies. Another advantage of this method is that it's neater.

Serve these peppers as a starter or add them to salads, pizza, pasta, and omelets.

4   **medium-size red bell peppers**
    coarse sea salt and freshly ground pepper to taste

Optional:
1   **tablespoon olive oil**
1   **tablespoon red wine vinegar or balsamic vinegar**
    minced or pressed garlic to taste
2   **tablespoons slivered fresh basil or thyme leaves**
8   **anchovy fillets**

Preheat the oven to 400°F (200°C). Place the peppers on a baking sheet or in a baking pan and bake in the hot oven for 30 to 45 minutes, until the peppers are soft and the skin is brown and puffed, turning every 10 minutes.

Remove from the heat and transfer to a bowl. Cover the bowl with a plate and let sit for 30 minutes or longer.

Carefully remove the skins and seeds from the peppers, holding them over the bowl so you don't lose any of the liquid. Cut into wide or thin strips to taste. Toss with salt and pepper.

Add the olive oil, vinegar, and/or garlic if you are using these ingredients, and refrigerate until ready to serve.

Toss with herbs shortly before serving if you wish. Serve topped with the anchovies if desired.

ADVANCE PREPARATION: These will keep for 5 days in the refrigerator. I recommend using the oil if you are keeping them for a few days, because it helps preserve the peppers.

PER PORTION

Calories	20	Protein	.67 G
Fat	.14 G	Carbohydrate	5 G
Sodium	1 MG	Cholesterol	0

TOMATO AND BASIL SALAD
Salade de tomates

SERVES 4

Balsamic vinegar is the solution to bland tomatoes and brings out the sweetness in good tomatoes. I couldn't be without it now. Tomatoes define Provençal summer meals, and this dish is a staple.

2	**pounds (900 g/8 medium-size) tomatoes, cored and cut into wedges★**
1 to 2	**large garlic cloves, to taste, minced or put through a press**
	salt and freshly ground pepper to taste
1 to 2	**tablespoons balsamic vinegar to taste**
¼	**cup (60 ml) slivered fresh basil or 2 tablespoons low-fat pistou (page 109)**

Toss the ingredients together and serve.

★ If the tomatoes have very thick skins, peel them.

ADVANCE PREPARATION: You can make this a few hours ahead, but don't add the basil until shortly before serving.

PER PORTION

Calories	49	Protein	2 G
Fat	.72 G	Carbohydrate	11 G
Sodium	19 MG	Cholesterol	0

BEET SALAD WITH ANCHOVY DRESSING

Ensalado de bledo-rabo is anchoio
Salade de betteraves aux anchois

SERVES 4

Beets are sold already cooked all over France. The best are baked in wood ovens. You can steam or bake the beets for this simple, delicious salad. Since the taste for anchovies varies, I've given a choice between four and eight fillets here.

4	large beets, about 1½ to 2 pounds (675 to 900 g), steamed or baked until tender, peeled, and diced
4 to 8	anchovy fillets, to taste, soaked in milk or water for 15 minutes and rinsed
1	small garlic clove, minced or put through a press
2	tablespoons chopped fresh parsley
2	tablespoons red wine vinegar or sherry vinegar freshly ground pepper to taste
2	tablespoons olive oil
½	cup (125 ml) plain nonfat yogurt

Put the prepared beets in a salad bowl. Mash the anchovy fillets with a fork and add the garlic and parsley. Stir in the vinegar, pepper, olive oil, and yogurt. Toss with the beets and serve.

ADVANCE PREPARATION: This will hold for several hours, in or out of the refrigerator.

VARIATION: Add 1 cup (250 ml) cooked chick-peas or 2 medium-size Belgian endives, sliced.

PER PORTION

Calories	149	Protein	5 G
Fat	8 G	Carbohydrate	16 G
Sodium	338 MG	Cholesterol	4 MG

TOASTED CROUTONS WITH ANCHOVY PASTE
Roustido
Quichets

SERVES 6

Nàutri, li bon Prouvençau
Marinado emé de sau
Esquichan l'anchoio

We others, the good *Provençaux*
We crush the salt-marinated anchovy

FRÉDÉRIC MISTRAL, *LIS ISCLO D'OR*

Called *la roustido dóu moulin* because it used to be a typical midmorning repast (or "*roustido*") enjoyed by olive mill workers, the dish remains an important part of the Provençal repertoire even if the ritual has now been somewhat lost to the mill workers. The name of the dish comes from the Provençal word *quicho,* which means "to press." That's what you do here with anchovies: you season them with vinegar, garlic, and olive oil, spread and press them into slices of bread, and toast the bread.

24	**anchovy fillets, preferably salt-packed, rinsed**
	milk to cover
2	**garlic cloves, peeled (optional)**
2	**tablespoons olive oil**
2	**tablespoons sherry vinegar or red wine vinegar**
	freshly ground pepper to taste
12	**slices of country bread, about ½ inch (1.5 cm) thick**
1	**garlic clove, cut in half lengthwise**

Soak the anchovy fillets in milk to cover for 20 minutes. Drain and rinse. Pat dry.

Crush the anchovies with the peeled garlic—if you're using it—in a mortar

SALADS AND STARTERS

and pestle. Add the olive oil and vinegar and mash until you have a coarse paste. Add pepper.

Preheat the broiler. Rub the bread with the cut garlic and spread on the anchovy paste in an even layer. Place under the broiler for 2 to 3 minutes, until the top is beginning to color, and serve hot.

ADVANCE PREPARATION: The anchovy paste will keep for a few days in the refrigerator. The bread can be rubbed with garlic and spread with the anchovy paste a couple of hours before grilling.

Quicho papa!
Quicho mama!
Quichen tóuti!

PER PORTION

Calories	213	Protein	9 G
Fat	8 G	Carbohydrate	26 G
Sodium	892 MG	Cholesterol	9 MG

TAPENADE
Tapenado

This is not the first time I've published my tapenade recipe, but I can't leave it out of a Provençal cookbook. And much as I'd like to give you a new recipe for this heady olive spread, nothing quite matches this one, which I make time and again to the delight of my guests. Use Nyons olives for this if you can get them.

½	pound (225 g/about 1⅓ cups) imported black Provençal or Greek olives
2	large garlic cloves, minced or put through a press
1½	tablespoons drained capers
4 to 6	anchovy fillets to taste
½ to 1	teaspoon fresh thyme or ¼ to ½ teaspoon dried, to taste
½ to 1	teaspoon chopped fresh rosemary or ¼ to ½ teaspoon crushed dried, to taste
2	tablespoons fresh lemon juice
1	teaspoon Dijon mustard
2	tablespoons olive oil
	lots of freshly ground black pepper
1 to 2	tablespoons cognac (optional)

Pit the olives and puree along with the garlic, capers, anchovies, thyme, and rosemary in a mortar and pestle or a food processor. Add the remaining ingredients and continue to process until you have a smooth paste. Place in a bowl, cover, and refrigerate until ready to use.

Spread on croutons or raw vegetables and serve as an hors d'oeuvre with a Provençal rosé, a dry white wine, or champagne. Or serve with fish (see the recipe on page 220).

ADVANCE PREPARATION: This will hold for a week in the refrigerator. Keep it in a jar or covered container and pour a thin film of olive oil over the surface to keep it from drying out. It can also be frozen.

PER PORTION

Calories	44	Protein	.73 G
Fat	4 G	Carbohydrate	1 G
Sodium	244 MG	Cholesterol	1 MG

TUNA TAPENADE
Tapenade au thon

MAKES ABOUT 1 ¼ CUPS (312 ML), SERVING 6 AS AN ENTREE OR 10 AS AN HORS D'OEUVRE

Provençal tapenade is often made with tuna. Here I've substituted water-packed tuna for half the olives, which makes for a lower-fat tapenade. It's also hearty enough to eat as an entree, with raw vegetables and croutons.

	heaped ½ cup (150 ml/about 115 g/¼ lb) imported black Provençal or Greek olives
2	garlic cloves, minced or put through a press
1½	tablespoons drained capers
4	anchovy fillets (optional)
¼ to ½	teaspoon dried thyme to taste
¼ to ½	teaspoon crushed dried rosemary to taste
2	tablespoons fresh lemon juice
1	teaspoon Dijon mustard
1	tablespoon olive oil
3	tablespoons plain nonfat yogurt
	lots of freshly ground black pepper
1	6⅛-ounce (173 g) can water-packed tuna, drained

Pit the olives and puree along with the garlic, capers, anchovies, thyme, and rosemary in a mortar and pestle or a food processor. Add the remaining ingredients and continue to process until you have a smooth paste. Place in a bowl, cover, and refrigerate until ready to use.

Spread on croutons or raw vegetables and serve as an hors d'oeuvre with a Provençal rosé, a dry white wine, or champagne.

ADVANCE PREPARATION: This will hold for 3 or 4 days in the refrigerator. Keep it in a jar or covered container and pour a thin film of olive oil over the surface to keep it from drying out.

PER PORTION

Calories	26	Protein	3 G
Fat	1 G	Carbohydrate	.78 G
Sodium	105 MG	Cholesterol	3 MG

GREEN OLIVE TAPENADE
Tapenado

MAKES ABOUT 1 ½ CUPS (375 ML), SERVING 12 AS A STARTER

I never liked tapenade made with green olives until I stood in a long line in front of a booth with a sign on it reading *"Les Saveurs du Luberon"* at the Apt market one drizzly Saturday morning and tasted the tapenade made by these artisans. Their tapenade is exciting, with a perfect balance of pungent and herbal flavors. They make three kinds: regular, green olive tapenade with almonds, and green olive tapenade with tuna and basil. They sell at most of the markets in the Luberon—Apt on Saturday mornings, Isle-sur-la-Sorgue on Sundays, and Forcalquier, in the Alpes-de-Haute-Provence, on Mondays. But you don't have to go to France to experience this great taste.

½	**pound (225 g/about 1⅓ cups or 50) imported green Provençal or Greek olives**
2	**large garlic cloves, minced or put through a press**
1½	**tablespoons drained capers**
4 to 6	**anchovy fillets to taste**
½ to 1	**teaspoon fresh thyme leaves or ¼ to ½ teaspoon dried to taste**
½ to 1	**teaspoon chopped fresh rosemary or ¼ to ½ teaspoon dried to taste**
2	**tablespoons fresh lemon juice**
2	**tablespoons olive oil**
	lots of freshly ground black pepper

Pit the olives and puree along with the garlic, capers, anchovies, thyme, and rosemary in a mortar and pestle or a food processor. Add the remaining ingredients and continue to process until you have a smooth paste. Place in a bowl, cover, and refrigerate until ready to use.

Spread on croutons or raw vegetables and serve as an hors d'oeuvre with a Provençal rosé, a dry white wine, or champagne.

GREEN OLIVE TAPENADE WITH ALMONDS: Substitute ¼ cup (625 ml/about 20) blanched almonds for ¼ cup (625 ml) olives and grind along with the olives.

GREEN OLIVE TAPENADE WITH TUNA AND BASIL: Substitute one 6⅛-ounce (173 g) can water-packed tuna for half the olives. Add 2 tablespoons fresh basil leaves. Grind the ingredients together as directed.

ADVANCE PREPARATION: This will hold for a week in the refrigerator. Keep it in a jar or covered container and pour a thin film of olive oil over the surface to keep it from drying out. It can also be frozen.

PER PORTION

Calories	28	Protein	.45 G
Fat	3 G	Carbohydrate	.42 G
Sodium	323 MG	Cholesterol	.55 MG

BRANDADE: SALT COD PUREE
Brandade de morue

MAKES 2 CUPS (500 ML), SERVING 8 AS AN HORS D'OEUVRE OR
4 AS A MAIN DISH

Although in America salt cod is hardly a kitchen staple, it's sensationally good and very much worth seeking out. Brandade is one of the most voluptuous of Provençal dishes. The name comes from the Provençal word *brandar,* which means to stir. It varies from one part of the region to another: in and around Marseille and Toulon the brandade is garlicky, whereas no garlic is added to brandade de morue Nimoise. It's become fashionable in recent years in Paris, usually mixed with mashed potatoes and served as a hot main dish. Traditionally brandade is made by pureeing lightly cooked salt cod with one part hot milk and two parts hot olive oil, and a pound (450 g) of salt cod will usually take about 1 cup (250 ml) of olive oil, sometimes more. So what you have in the end is an unctuous dish that is rather indigestible.

I decided to see what would happen if I substituted milk for all but a couple of tablespoons of the olive oil. I waited until my husband was out of town (not that Bill doesn't love brandade, but too much of a good thing *can* be too much), went out and bought a lot of salt cod, desalted it, and prepared myself to spend a week working on (and eating) brandade. To my delight, my idea worked the first time around! My version is not only light and fluffy but also a milkier white than the heavier brandade. As for the garlic, I wouldn't think of omitting it, but I sauté it a little bit in olive oil before incorporating it into the fish. If you want your brandade to have more garlicky punch, mash the garlic in a mortar and pestle and incorporate it into the salt cod after you've achieved your puree. You can use more garlic than the recipe calls for if you wish.

The two keys to success with this dish are finding a good source of salt cod or making your own (see the recipe on page 195) and not letting the fish boil. Good salt cod should be thick and white. My friend Lulu Peyraud, from the Bandol winery Domaine Tempier, won't buy it unless it still has some of its skin. But I've made delicious brandade with skinned salt cod. If you can find the kind that is salted but not dried, all the better. If you can find only the hard kind, just make sure it's thick and the fish is fairly white. You will need to begin 24 hours ahead of time for soaking salt cod, 48 hours for dried salt cod.

1   pound (450 g) salt cod, either commercial or
    homemade (page 195) (homemade
    recommended)

2   quarts (2 l) water

2   medium-size onions, quartered

5   large garlic cloves or more to taste, 3 cut in half,
    the rest minced or put through a press

2   bay leaves

¾ to 1   cup (185 to 250 ml) low-fat (2%, not skim) milk

2   tablespoons olive oil

    freshly ground pepper to taste

Desalt the fish: Place in a large bowl and cover with water. If convenient, put the bowl in your kitchen sink and keep the water running in a thin stream so that the water in the bowl is constantly renewing itself. If this isn't convenient, change the soaking water several times over 24 hours for salt cod, 48 hours for dried salt cod.

Cut the cod into a few large pieces and place in a heavy-bottomed casserole or stockpot. Add the water, onions, the 3 halved garlic cloves, and the bay leaves. Bring slowly to a simmer over medium-low heat. As soon as the water reaches a simmer and before it comes to a boil—you'll see little bubbles coming up from the bottom of the pot, and the water will be moving without the surface bubbling— cover, turn off the heat, and let sit for 10 minutes. Drain and transfer the fish to a bowl. Allow to cool until you can handle it.

Pick out the bones from the fish and remove the skin. Flake the fish by rubbing it between your fingers or using a fork or wooden spoon. If you use your fingers, it will be easier to verify that you've gotten the bones out. Transfer to a food processor.

Scald the milk in a small saucepan and remove from the heat.

Heat the olive oil over medium-low heat in a heavy-bottomed saucepan and add the remaining garlic. The instant it begins to sizzle, remove from the heat and transfer to the food processor. Turn on the food processor and add the milk in a slow stream until the cod has absorbed all the milk it can. Continue to process until fluffy. Add pepper to taste and more garlic if you wish. You may wish to add salt, but it probably won't be necessary.

If you're serving this as a first course, transfer it to a serving bowl and surround with garlic croutons (page 83). If you're serving it as a main dish, transfer it to an oiled 1½- or 2-quart (1½ or 2 l) gratin dish and heat through in a 425°F (220°C) oven until it begins to brown on the top, about 20 minutes (you can also put it under the broiler for a minute to brown once it's heated through).

A D V A N C E   P R E P A R A T I O N :   Brandade will keep for 3 or 4 days in the refrigerator.

P E R   P O R T I O N

Calories	204	Protein	23 G
Fat	9 G	Carbohydrate	8 G
Sodium	N/A	Cholesterol	53 MG

BRANDADE WITH POTATOES

SERVES 8 AS AN HORS D'OEUVRE, 4 AS A MAIN DISH

This is not considered authentic by French gastronomic authorities like Larousse, but nonetheless it's very common. It makes a milder-tasting, somewhat more comforting brandade.

the salt cod puree from the preceding recipe

½ **pound (225 g/2 medium-size) waxy potatoes, peeled and cooked**

¼ **cup (62 ml) skim milk**

2 **teaspoons olive oil for the hot version**

While you're making the brandade, boil the potatoes in salted water until tender. Mash and stir in the milk.

Stir the potatoes into the brandade. If you use a food processor, use only the pulse action and pulse only a few times, or the potatoes will become gummy. A wooden spoon or pestle works just as well. Adjust seasonings and serve as for the preceding recipe. To serve hot, drizzle on the olive oil before baking.

PER PORTION

Calories	251	Protein	24 G
Fat	9 G	Carbohydrate	18 G
Sodium	N/A	Cholesterol	53 MG

GRILLED RED PEPPER STRIPS
FILLED WITH BRANDADE
Poivrons grillés à la brandade

SERVES 4 AS A MAIN DISH OR 6 AS A STARTER

This idea comes from Le Bistrot du Dôme, which is not in Provence at all but on the rue Delambre just off the boulevard Montparnasse, in Paris. It's a thoroughly modern Provençal idea and makes a wonderful first course or main dish.

1	pound (450 g) salt cod, either commercial or homemade (page 195)
2	quarts (2 l) water
2	medium-size onions, quartered
5	large garlic cloves or more, to taste, 3 cut in half, the rest minced or put through a press
2	bay leaves
¾ to 1	cup (185 to 250 ml) low-fat (2%, not skim) milk
2	tablespoons olive oil
	freshly ground pepper to taste
4	large red bell peppers
2	tablespoons slivered fresh basil leaves
	fresh lemon juice (optional)
	fresh chervil or basil sprigs for garnish
	basic tomato sauce (optional; page 112)

Make the brandade: Desalt the fish. Place in a large bowl and cover with water. If convenient, put the bowl in your kitchen sink and keep the water running in a thin stream so that the water in the bowl is constantly renewing itself. If this isn't convenient, change the soaking water several times over 24 hours for salt cod, 48 hours for dried salt cod.

Cut the cod into a few large pieces and place in a heavy-bottomed casserole or stockpot. Add the water, onions, the 3 halved garlic cloves, and the bay leaves. Bring slowly to a simmer over medium-low heat. As soon as the water reaches a simmer and before it comes to a boil—you'll see little bubbles coming up from the bottom of the pot, and the water will be moving without the surface bubbling—cover, turn off the heat, and let sit for 10 minutes. Drain and transfer the fish to a bowl. Allow to cool until you can handle it.

Pick out the bones from the fish and remove the skin. Flake the fish by rubbing it between your fingers or using a fork or wooden spoon. If you use your fingers, it will be easier to verify that you've gotten the bones out. Transfer to a food processor.

Scald the milk in a small saucepan and remove from the heat.

Heat the olive oil over medium-low heat in a heavy-bottomed saucepan and add the remaining garlic. As soon as it begins to sizzle, remove from the heat and transfer to the food processor. Turn on the food processor and add the milk in a slow stream until the cod has absorbed all the milk it can. Continue to process until fluffy. Add pepper to taste and more garlic if you wish. You may wish to add salt, but it probably won't be necessary. Set aside the brandade while you grill the peppers.

Grill the peppers directly over a flame or under a broiler until uniformly charred. Place in a plastic bag or a large, tightly covered bowl and allow to cool. Remove the charred skin, rinse, and pat dry. Cut the roasted peppers lengthwise into thirds, along the indentations, and remove the seeds and membranes.

Preheat the oven to 400°F (200°C). Oil a baking dish or sheet large enough to accommodate all of the stuffed pepper strips. Spoon about 2 heaped tablespoons of brandade onto the curved bottom end of each grilled pepper strip and gently roll up. Sprinkle lightly with salt and pepper. Transfer to the baking dish.

Heat through for 10 minutes and transfer to plates. Sprinkle on the basil and lemon juice if desired and serve, garnished with sprigs of fresh chervil or basil. If you wish, spread the tomato sauce on the plates and then top with the peppers.

ADVANCE PREPARATION: The brandade can be made a day ahead of time. The stuffed pepper strips will hold for hours, in or out of the refrigerator, before being heated through.

PER PORTION

Calories	223	Protein	23 G
Fat	10 G	Carbohydrate	11 G
Sodium	N/A	Cholesterol	53 MG

SALADS AND STARTERS

TUNA BRANDADE
Brandade de thon

MAKES 1½ CUPS (375 ML), SERVING 6 TO 8 AS A STARTER OR 4
AS A MAIN DISH

This is a brandadelike puree made with tuna instead of salt cod. Although it isn't really authentic, it makes a great spread or filling for little vegetables, and it's incredibly easy to make. Don't use a food processor; the mixture will be too mealy.

2	6⅛-ounce (173 g) cans water-packed tuna, drained
2	tablespoons olive oil
½	cup (125 ml) plain non-fat yogurt
2	large garlic cloves, pureed
1 to 2	tablespoons fresh lemon juice to taste
	salt and freshly ground pepper to taste

Using a fork, flake the tuna until it is quite smooth. Add the olive oil and yogurt and continue to mix together until you have a fairly smooth mixture. Add the garlic and lemon juice, salt if necessary, and pepper.

Serve on croutons or red pepper squares or as a filling for small tomatoes or baby squash.

ADVANCE PREPARATION: This will keep for 3 or 4 days in the refrigerator.

PER PORTION

Calories	92	Protein	12 G
Fat	4 G	Carbohydrate	2 G
Sodium	148 MG	Cholesterol	17 MG

WHITE BEAN "BRANDADE"
Brandade d'haricots

SERVES 8

I once served a white bean pâté at a party, and many of my guests thought it was a fish pâté. So I wasn't startled when I came across this dish in *La Cuisine Provençale de Tradition Populaire,* by René Jouveau. A Marseillaise dish, it's much like the white bean purees you find in the Middle East—not surprising, since Marseille has always been an important trading partner of the eastern Mediterranean countries. In Marseille this puree was traditionally eaten with tuna roe or with anchovies, according to Jouveau. But I'll take it just as it is, on garlic-scented croutons, or with crudités.

½	**pound (225 g/1 heaped cup) dried navy or other small white beans**
1½	**quarts (1.5 l) water**
1	**bay leaf**
	salt to taste
3 to 4	**garlic cloves, to taste, minced or put through a press**
2	**tablespoons olive oil**
2	**tablespoons fresh lemon juice**
2 to 4	**tablespoons low-fat milk (2%, not skim), as needed**

Soak the beans overnight or for at least 6 hours in three times their volume of water (use bottled water if your water is hard). Drain and transfer to a large soup pot or Dutch oven. Add the water and bay leaf and bring to a boil. Reduce the heat, cover, and simmer for 1 hour. Add salt to taste (a teaspoon or more), cover, and continue to simmer for another 30 minutes to an hour, until the beans are tender. Drain, reserving about ½ cup (125 ml) of the cooking liquid.

In a food processor or a mortar and pestle, puree the beans. Add the garlic, olive oil, and lemon juice. Thin out with milk as desired (this will also give the puree a brandadelike appearance). If you want an even smoother mixture, add some of the cooking liquid. Taste and adjust salt.

Serve on garlic croutons or with crudités.

ADVANCE PREPARATION: This will keep for 4 or 5 days in the refrigerator and can be frozen.

PER PORTION

Calories	131	Protein	7 G
Fat	4 G	Carbohydrate	18 G
Sodium	144 MG	Cholesterol	.45 MG

SARDINES MARINATED IN VINEGAR
Sardines en escabeche

SERVES 6

This is one of my favorite sardine dishes. You can keep it on hand in the refrigerator for instant first courses or add the marinated sardines to salads. Sardines are increasingly available at fish markets; if you see them, remember this dish.

- 1 **large onion, thinly sliced**
- 2 **medium-size carrots, thinly sliced**
- 3 **large garlic cloves, sliced**
- 2 **cups (500 ml) water**
- 1 **cup (250 ml) red wine vinegar**
- 10 **peppercorns**
- 10 **coriander seeds**
  salt to taste
- 1 **bay leaf**
- 2 **pounds (900 g) fresh sardines, cleaned and heads removed**
  lettuce leaves for serving

Combine all the ingredients except the sardines and lettuce in a large nonaluminum saucepan and bring to a boil. Reduce the heat, cover, and simmer for 20 minutes. Add the sardines, simmer for another 3 minutes, and turn off the heat.

Remove the sardines from the liquid with a slotted spoon and carefully remove the fillets from the bones. Transfer the fillets to a bowl and pour on the liquid from the pot. Allow to cool and refrigerate.

Serve the sardines cold, over lettuce leaves, with a small amount of the marinade spooned over the top, or toss with salads.

ADVANCE PREPARATION: The sardines will keep for a week in the refrigerator.

PER PORTION

Calories	180	Protein	17 G
Fat	8 G	Carbohydrate	8 G
Sodium	93 MG	Cholesterol	55 MG

CHAPTER 2

A FEW BREADS, SOCCA AND VARIATIONS, AND A SANDWICH

In the famous Marcel Pagnol play, *La Femme du Boulanger* (*The Baker's Wife*), an entire village is mobilized to find the runaway wife of the new village baker, because the baker is so upset that he refuses to bake bread until his Amélie comes home. Neighbors who have been fighting for decades band together; even the priest and the schoolteacher forget about their ideological differences and team up to bring back Amélie. That's how important bread is in Provence.

The Provençal diet is based on grains and vegetables. And grains here means bread. Bread has traditionally been a substantial part of every meal. In the past, workers took bread to the fields or to the olive oil mills where they worked, to serve as a vehicle for their midmorning meal, usually anchovy paste or tapenade, garlic mayonnaise or tomatoes. The evening soup is served over thick garlicky slices. No bread goes to waste. Stale pieces are rubbed with garlic and used to season salads. Bread crumbs top gratins and fill vegetables.

Fougasse is the classic bread of Provence. It has a lyrical shape that matches the spirit of the people here. The ladder is the most typical form, but often these breads are shaped like wheat sheaves (*épis*) or leaves. A classic yeast-raised *fougasse* is a white French bread with a hard crust. But you are just as likely to find this bread filled with olives, anchovies, cracklings, Roquefort cheese, or nuts. My version (page 73) uses part whole-wheat flour.

The *fougasse* shape is used for other, richer breads, such as the *pompe à l'huile* (sweet olive oil bread) and *pompe aux anchois* (olive oil bread with anchovies) on pages 84 and 86. The olive oil bread is a traditional Christmas food, one of the 13 desserts served at the big Christmas Eve dinner called *Le Gros Souper*. I think it makes a terrific breakfast bread as well. The anchovy bread is wonderful served thinly sliced with drinks before dinner.

Provence attracts passionate, health-oriented bakers in the same way that it attracts organic farmers. Since coming here in 1980 I've witnessed an amazing growth in the availability of whole-grain breads. In Apt I have a wide range to choose from: mixed-grain breads, bran breads, whole-wheat sourdoughs, and rye, all sold at the local La Vie Claire, a French natural foods chain, and many at regular bakeries.

I'm also including the Niçois chick-pea flour pancake called *socca* in this chapter, and a chick-pea flour crêpe inspired by *socca*, one of my favorite foods; it's really more of a light meal or starter than a bread, but it fits into this chapter. And where else but a bread chapter would I put the famous Niçois salad sandwich, whose name, *pan bagnat*, means "bathed bread"?

A FEW BREADS, SOCCA AND VARIATIONS...

FOUGASSE WITH WHOLE WHEAT
La fougasso

MAKES 1 LOAF; 20 SLICES

Fougasse—called *fouasse* in other parts of France—in Provence varies in every way imaginable from baker to baker. Some bakeries make a brioche-type fougasse; others make a regular yeast dough. Some shape their fougasse into ladder shapes, others into sheaves of wheat, others into leaflike shapes (which I like best). In Haute-Provence you're bound to find fougasse studded with cracklings or olives; on the Côte d'Azur anchovies are often added to the dough. *Larousse Gastronomique* calls a sweet bread with orange flower water, much like the Pompe à l'Huile on page 84, a fougasse.

The fougasse I like is made with a regular yeasted bread dough. No matter which way I shape the dough, I find that it's best to put it into the oven shortly after shaping the loaf, or the holes or spaces will close up.

2½	**teaspoons (¼-ounce/7 g envelope) active dry yeast**
1½	**cups (37.5 cl) lukewarm water**
1	**tablespoon olive oil**
½	**pound (225 g/1¾ cups) whole-wheat flour**
10 to 12	**ounces (285 to 300 g/2 to 2⅝ cups) unbleached white flour**
2¼	**teaspoons salt**

Dissolve the yeast in the water in a large bowl, or in the bowl of your electric mixer; let sit for 5 minutes. Stir in the olive oil.

Kneading the dough by hand: Mix together the whole-wheat flour, 10 ounces (285 g/2 cups) of the unbleached flour, and the salt. Fold it into the yeast mixture a cup at a time. As soon as the dough holds together, scrape it out onto your kneading surface. Knead, adding unbleached white flour as necessary, for 10 minutes. The dough will be sticky at first but will become very elastic, though it will remain tacky on the surface. Shape into a ball.

Using an electric mixer: Combine the whole-wheat flour and 10 ounces (285 g/ 2 cups) of the unbleached white flour and the salt. Add it all at once to the yeast mixture. Mix together with the paddle, then change to the dough hook. Mix at low speed for 2 minutes, then at medium speed for 8 to 10 minutes. If the dough seems very wet and sticky, sprinkle in up to 2 ounces (60 g/scant ½ cup) unbleached white flour. Scrape out the dough onto a lightly floured surface and knead for a minute or so by hand. Shape into a ball.

Rinse out your bowl, dry, and brush lightly with olive oil. Place the dough in the bowl, seam side up first, then seam side down. Cover with plastic wrap and a kitchen towel and set in a warm place to rise for 1½ hours or until the dough has doubled in size.

Punch down the dough, cover, and let rise for another hour.

Preheat the oven to 425°F (220°C) with a baking stone in it. Turn out the dough onto a lightly floured board, knead for a minute or two, and shape into a ball. Roll or press out into an oval about 12 inches (30 cm) long and 8 inches (20 cm) wide. Now slash the bread. For a leaf shape, make 3 diagonal slashes out from the center of the bread and one at the top, as if the slashes are veins of a leaf. Leave a 2-inch (5 cm) border around the edge of the dough and 1½ inches (4 cm) between the slashes. Gently pull the dough apart at the slashes. Place on a cornmeal-dusted baking peel, cover with a kitchen towel, and let rest for 5 minutes.

Gently slide the dough from the baking peel onto the stove in the preheated oven. Spray the oven with water and bake for 35 minutes, spraying twice during the first 10 minutes. The bread is done when it's brown and crusty and responds to tapping with a hollow sound. Remove from the heat and cool on a rack.

FOUGASSE AU SÉSAME: Add ¼ cup (60 ml) toasted sesame seeds and knead them into the dough just before shaping it. Proceed with the recipe.

FOUGASSE AUX OLIVES: Add 1 cup (115 g/¼ lb) imported black olives. Pit and coarsely chop the olives. Work them into the dough when you punch it down and knead into a ball.

FOUGASSE AUX NOIX: Add 1 cup (115 g/¼ lb) chopped walnuts and work them into the dough as for the olives in the preceding variation.

PAIN À L'AIL: This bread variation makes great, extra-garlicky garlic croutons. Sprinkle 1 tablespoon chopped fresh garlic (3 good-size cloves) over the dough after punching it down and knead for a few minutes to work the garlic evenly into the dough. Shape into a ball or into two baguette shapes. Place in a cloth-lined bowl or basket, a *banneton*, or on a lightly oiled, cornmeal-dusted baking sheet, cover with a damp towel, and let rise 1 hour longer, while you preheat the oven to 400°F (205°C). If the dough has risen on a baking sheet, gently reshape the loaves, since they will have spread out.

Turn the dough out of the *bannetons* onto a baking stone, or place the baking sheet directly on the stone. Spray the loaf and the oven with water and bake for 45 minutes, spraying twice more during the first 15 minutes, until brown and crusty, and it responds to tapping with a hollow sound. Remove from the heat and cool on a rack.

ADVANCE PREPARATION: The bread keeps well for a few days and freezes well. (The garlic in the garlic version will not taste as fresh if stored.)

PER SLICE

Calories	106	Protein	3 G
Fat	1 G	Carbohydrate	21 G
Sodium	248 MG	Cholesterol	0

TRUC

MAKING BREAD CRUMBS OUT OF STALE BREAD

Use a rotary cheese grater or a spice mill to make bread crumbs. Put a slice of bread, either stale or fresh, in the grater and grate as you would a slice of cheese. This is very neat and easy for a small amount of bread crumbs, provided the bread is stale. My friend Christine Picasso uses zwieback for bread crumbs and grates them this way.

If the bread is very hard, break it into small pieces and grind in an electric spice mill.

SAFFRON "BOUILLABAISSE" BREAD

MAKES 1 LOAF; 20 SLICES

Saffron surprises the palate when you bite into this beautiful, crusty yellow bread. The bread is great not only with bouillabaisse but also with other fish and vegetable soups and with salads.

2½	teaspoons (¼-ounce/7 g envelope) active dry yeast
1½	cups (37.5 cl) lukewarm water
1	teaspoon sugar or mild honey
1	tablespoon olive oil
¼	teaspoon powdered saffron or ½ teaspoon saffron threads
2	teaspoons salt
3	ounces (90 g/½ cup) stoneground yellow cornmeal
1 to 1¼	pounds (450 to 565 g/3½ to 4⅜ cups) unbleached white flour, plus up to 2 ounces (60 g/½ cup) for kneading

Dissolve the yeast in the water in a large bowl or in the bowl of your electric mixer and let sit for 10 minutes. Stir in the sugar, oil, and saffron. Mix the salt and cornmeal together.

Kneading the dough by hand: Stir the cornmeal into the yeast mixture and then the flour, a cup at a time, until the dough holds together. Turn it out onto your kneading surface. Place a small amount of flour on your kneading surface, turn out the dough, and knead until smooth and firm, about 10 minutes. The dough will be sticky.

Using an electric mixer: Dissolve the yeast in the water in the bowl of your electric mixer and let sit for 10 minutes. Add the sugar, oil, and saffron. Combine the salt, cornmeal, and all but 1 scant cup (¼ pound/115 g) of the flour and add to the bowl. Mix together with the paddle, then change to the dough hook. Beat at low speed for 2 minutes. Beat at medium speed for 8 minutes. Add the extra flour if the dough seems very sticky. Scrape out of the bowl and knead for a minute by hand on a lightly floured surface. The dough will be sticky.

A FEW BREADS, SOCCA AND VARIATIONS . . .

Form into a ball and place the dough in a lightly oiled bowl, seam side up first, then seam side down. Cover with plastic wrap and allow to rise in a warm place until doubled, about 1½ hours.

Punch down the dough, knead a few times on a floured surface, then shape into either a large round loaf or 2 baguettes or round loaves.

Place the loaf on a lightly oiled cornmeal-dusted baking sheet or a well-oiled bowl or towel-lined *banneton*, cover lightly with a kitchen towel, and let rise for 1 hour or until doubled. Because this is a soft, sticky dough, it will spread out as it rises, so I recommend the oiled bowl or the *banneton* for rising.

Thirty minutes before baking, preheat the oven to 400°F (200°C), preferably with a baking stone in it. If the dough has risen in a bowl or *banneton*, turn it out onto the hot baking stone or onto a lightly oiled cornmeal-dusted baking sheet and slash with a razor blade or a sharp knife. If the dough has risen directly on the baking sheet, reshape gently and slash. Bake for 40 to 50 minutes, spraying the loaf three times with water during the first 10 minutes, until golden brown and the loaf responds to tapping with a hollow sound. Remove from the oven and cool on a rack.

Note: If you want a grainier, heavier loaf, make the same bread with double the amount of cornmeal and subtract the same amount of flour. The bread will have a close crumb. This dough is easier to manipulate and works well as a sausage shape.

ADVANCE PREPARATION: The bread keeps for about 3 days. Cover the cut edge with foil. You can also freeze it.

PER SLICE

Calories	129	Protein	3 G
Fat	1 G	Carbohydrate	25 G
Sodium	221 MG	Cholesterol	0

PAN BAGNAT ROLLS

MAKES 6 LARGE ROLLS

In the south of France, pan bagnat, the Niçois salad sandwich, is almost always made on large, round, hard-crusted white rolls. Bialy rolls work nicely, but I prefer this part-whole-wheat homemade bread.

2½	teaspoons (¼-ounce/7 g envelope) active dry yeast
2	cups (500 ml) lukewarm water
1	tablespoon olive oil
½	pound (225 g/1¾ cups) whole-wheat flour
1	pound (450 g/3½ cups) unbleached white flour, as needed
2¼	teaspoons salt

Dissolve the yeast in the water in a large bowl or in the bowl of your electric mixer and let sit for 5 minutes. Stir in the oil.

Kneading the dough by hand: Mix together the whole-wheat flour, three-fourths of the unbleached flour, and the salt. Fold it into the yeast mixture a cup at a time. As soon as the dough holds together, place ½ cup (2 ounces/60 g) of the remaining flour on your work surface and scrape out the dough. Knead, adding unbleached white flour as necessary, for 10 minutes. The dough will be sticky at first but will become very elastic, though it will remain tacky on the surface. Shape into a ball.

Using an electric mixer: Combine the whole-wheat flour, three-fourths of the unbleached white flour, and the salt, and add all at once to the yeast mixture. Mix together with the paddle, then change to the dough hook. Mix at low speed for 2 minutes, then at medium speed for 8 to 10 minutes. Add more unbleached flour if the dough seems very sticky. Scrape out the dough onto a lightly floured surface and knead for a minute or so by hand. Shape into a ball.

Rinse out your bowl, dry, and brush lightly with olive oil. Place the dough in the bowl, seam side up first, then seam side down. Cover with plastic wrap and a kitchen towel and set in a warm place to rise for 1½ hours or until the dough has doubled in size.

A FEW BREADS, SOCCA AND VARIATIONS . . .

Punch down the dough, cover, and let rise for another hour.

Preheat the oven to 400°F (200°C). Turn out the dough onto a lightly floured board, knead for a minute or two, and shape into a ball. Divide into 6 pieces and shape each piece into a ball. Place on 2 oiled, cornmeal-dusted baking sheets, cover loosely with a damp kitchen towel, and let rise for 20 to 30 minutes, until the rolls spread out and almost double in size.

Bake for 20 to 30 minutes in the middle and top third of the oven, until the crust is hard and brown and the rolls respond to tapping with a hollow sound. Switch the baking sheets halfway through the baking. Remove from the heat and cool on racks.

ADVANCE PREPARATION: The rolls will keep for a couple of days and can be frozen. Since pan bagnat is supposed to be soggy, it doesn't matter if the bread dries out a bit.

PER PORTION

Calories	447	Protein	14 G
Fat	5 G	Carbohydrate	87 G
Sodium	828 MG	Cholesterol	0

PAN BAGNAT
Salade Niçoise Sandwich

SERVES 6

This is the hamburger of the Côte d'Azur, but oh so much better than a hamburger. I've eaten these sandwiches on beaches and in cafés all along the Mediterranean coast. I ate my most recent and memorable pan bagnat (which means "bathed bread" because the bread is drenched with vinaigrette and meant to be soggy) on an extremely hot summer day, at a roadside stand—a small trailer with an awning—across from the beach on the Languedoc highway running from Marseille right down to Barcelona (we were not technically in Provence, but near enough). It was probably 100 degrees, and we had been driving for a few hours and were extremely hungry and hot. I saw a sign that said, *"pan bagnat, boissons fraîches,"* and I got off the road. Two young girls were serving very cold drinks and sandwiches out of their parents' little trailer. They were listening to a Bob Marley tape. I expected them to pull a sandwich from a cooler, but no, I watched the girls cut baguettes in half, douse them with dressing, and strew lettuce, tomatoes, onions, peppers, olives, and tuna down the length. It was one of the best lunches I've ever eaten.

You can be creative with pan bagnats, filling them with leftover vegetables, cucumbers, grated carrots—whatever you have on hand. This version is fairly classic (although I add mustard), except that for our low-fat purposes I've made the olives optional and there's very little olive oil; a traditional pan bagnat drips with it. But ripe tomatoes and vinegar suffice to make a correctly soggy sandwich. It's meant to be a messy, hedonistic affair.

1½	pounds (675 g/6 medium-size) tomatoes, ½ pound (225 g) peeled and finely chopped or blended to a puree in a food processor, the rest sliced
3	tablespoons vinegar: red wine, sherry, balsamic, or a mixture (if your tomatoes aren't ripe, use some balsamic vinegar to add sweetness)
1	tablespoon Dijon mustard or more to taste
3	garlic cloves, minced or put through a press
	salt and freshly ground pepper to taste

2	tablespoons olive oil
2	long baguettes (2 feet/61 cm or a little more) or 6 hard round rolls, cut in half lengthwise
1	small head of Boston lettuce, washed, dried, and torn into smallish pieces
1	6⅛-ounce (173 g) can water-packed tuna, undrained
1	bunch of basil, snipped with scissors, or 2 tablespoons low-fat pistou (page 109)

Optional:

1 to 2	tablespoons drained capers, to taste
1	small cucumber, peeled if waxed, seeded and thinly sliced
½	pound (225 g) thin green beans, steamed and cut into ½-inch (1.5 cm) pieces
½	pound (225 g) carrots, grated
18	imported black olives, pitted and cut in half
12 to 24	anchovy fillets, to taste, rinsed and chopped
1	large green or red bell pepper or 1 small green pepper and 1 small red pepper, cut in half lengthwise and thinly sliced crosswise
1	large red or white onion, thinly sliced

Blend together the chopped or pureed tomatoes with the vinegar, mustard, garlic, salt, pepper, and oil. Lay out the bread halves, cut side up, and spread with a generous spoonful of this mixture. Press it into the bread with the back of your spoon or with a brush. (If the baguettes are too long to work with comfortably, cut them into thirds.)

Toss together the lettuce, tuna with its brine, basil, any of the optional ingredients, and any remaining tomato-vinegar mixture. Add salt and pepper to taste. Distribute evenly among the bottom halves of the bread and press the mixture down into the bread. Top with the sliced tomatoes, peppers, and onions. Place the top halves of the bread over the vegetable/tuna mixture and press down hard. Wrap tightly in foil and weight between 2 cutting boards or plates. Refrigerate for an hour or longer (up to 24 hours, but remove the weight after 1 hour).

Unwrap the sandwiches, cut long baguettes into several wide slices, and serve.

ADVANCE PREPARATION: These are best prepared a few hours ahead of serving so that the bread can become deliciously saturated with all of the garlicky Provençal flavors.

PER PORTION

Calories	270	Protein	15 G
Fat	7 G	Carbohydrate	38 G
Sodium	532 MG	Cholesterol	12 MG

GARLIC CROUTONS
Capouns
Les chapons

They never throw out stale bread in Provence. Slices are rubbed with cut garlic cloves and added to salads and most often served with soup.

I have fond memories of standing around the kitchen at Domaine Tempier in Bandol on harvest evenings toasting bread and rubbing the slices with garlic. The croutons were necessary for many of the big noonday meals, like bouillabaisse, fish soup, or as a vehicle for tapenade or brandade. I loved hanging out and learning to speak French with all of the Peyraud women in the kitchen at night as we sliced baguettes, put them in the oven on a baking sheet, and rubbed the slices with garlic as soon as they were crisp. I watched the same task being done first thing every morning by one of the *commis* at the Restaurant du Bacon, in Cap d'Antibes, where they go through croutons by the hundreds.

You'll find garlic croutons called for again and again in this collection, especially in soup recipes. Sometimes you just don't have much stale bread around the house, so you toast fresh bread to make your own garlic croutons.

Use country bread or baguettes. It can be a few days old and stale. Thinly slice unless otherwise instructed and toast, in a toaster or a 350°F (180°C) oven. Remove from the heat and rub with a cut clove of garlic. Cut large slices into pieces about 2 inches (5 cm) wide.

ADVANCE PREPARATION: Croutons will keep for a day, wrapped in aluminum foil.

PER SLICE

Calories	95	Protein	3 G
Fat	1 G	Carbohydrate	18 G
Sodium	209 MG	Cholesterol	0

ORANGE-SCENTED
CHRISTMAS BREAD
Poumpo à l'oli
Pompe à l'huile

MAKES 1 LARGE OR 2 SMALL LOAVES, SERVING 16

This is one of the traditional 13 Provençal Christmas desserts. But why wait for Christmas? It's a sweet briochelike loaf containing olive oil instead of butter and scented with orange flower water and grated orange zest. I love it with tea, morning or afternoon. Some Provençal cooks shape their pompe à l'huile into rings; others roll them out into flattened circles or rectangles and cut out oval spaces so that the breads look somewhat like fougasses (page 73). The bread has different names in different places. In Apt the briochelike version is called *gibacier à l'huile d'olive.*

1	cup (250 ml) lukewarm water
2½	teaspoons (1¼-ounce/7 g envelope) active dry yeast
¼	cup (50 g) sugar
1¼	pounds (565 g/4⅜ cups) unbleached white or whole-wheat pastry flour or a combination, plus up to 1 ounce (30 g/¼ cup) for kneading
2	large eggs at room temperature
¼	cup (60 ml) olive oil
1	tablespoon orange flower water
2	tablespoons finely chopped or grated orange zest, from 2 oranges
2	teaspoons salt
1	large egg white, lightly beaten

Place the water in a large bowl or the bowl of your electric mixer and add the yeast. Stir to dissolve and add 1 tablespoon of the sugar. Let sit for 5 minutes and stir in 1½ cups (6 ounces/180 g) of the flour. Whisk until the mixture is smooth, cover with plastic wrap, and set in a warm place for 30 minutes or until the mixture is bubbling (it is now a sponge).

Kneading the bread by hand: Beat the remaining sugar, the eggs, olive oil, and orange flower water into the sponge. Stir in the orange zest and the salt. Begin adding the remaining flour, a cup at a time. When the dough holds together, scrape it out onto your kneading surface and begin to knead, adding flour as necessary. The dough will be quite sticky. Knead for 10 minutes or until the dough is stiff and elastic, then form into a ball.

Using an electric mixer: Add the remaining sugar, the eggs, olive oil, orange zest, and salt as directed. Add all the flour and mix briefly using the paddle attachment. Change to the dough hook and knead for 2 minutes at low speed, then 8 minutes at medium speed. Add flour if the dough seems very sticky. Scrape the dough out onto a floured surface to knead briefly with your hands. Shape into a ball.

Rinse out the bowl, dry, and brush lightly with olive oil. Place the dough in it, rounded side down first, then rounded side up. Cover with plastic wrap and a kitchen towel and let rise in a warm spot for 2 hours, until doubled in size.

Punch down the dough and scrape out onto a lightly floured board. For rings, divide the dough into 2 equal pieces and shape into balls. Use a rolling pin to flatten the balls slightly, then make a hole in the center by plunging your thumb in and pulling the dough gently apart with your fingers.

For a flat round or rectangular pompe, shape the dough into a ball, then roll out in a round or rectangular shape about 1 to 1½ inches (2.5 to 3.5 cm) thick. Using a sharp knife, make three or four 2-inch-long (5 cm) slits on each side of the dough and pull the dough apart gently at the cuts.

Place the dough on oiled baking sheets and cover with a damp towel. Set in a warm spot to rise for 45 minutes to an hour. Meanwhile, preheat the oven to 375°F (190°C).

Brush the loaf gently with the beaten egg white and bake for 30 to 35 minutes, until golden brown and the loaf responds to tapping with a hollow thumping sound. Remove from the oven and cool on a rack.

A D V A N C E   P R E P A R A T I O N :   The bread freezes well. Wrap tightly in foil and place in a plastic bag. It will keep for only a day or two before going stale. But use the stale bread for French toast. It's terrific.

PER PORTION

Calories	195	Protein	4 G
Fat	5 G	Carbohydrate	33 G
Sodium	287 MG	Cholesterol	27 MG

OLIVE OIL BREAD WITH ANCHOVIES
Pompe aux anchois

MAKES 1 LOAF; 20 SLICES

This is a rich, briochelike bread with anchovies hidden in the dough. Serve it thinly sliced, as an aperitif or with tomato or vegetable soups.

1	**cup (250 ml) lukewarm water**
2½	**teaspoons (1¼-ounce/7 g envelope) active dry yeast**
	pinch of sugar
1¼	**pounds (565 g/4⅜ cups) unbleached white or whole-wheat pastry flour or a combination, plus up to 1 ounce (30 g/¼ cup) for kneading**
2	**large eggs at room temperature**
¼	**cup (60 ml) olive oil**
2	**teaspoons salt**
16	**anchovy fillets or 1 2-ounce (60 g) can, rinsed thoroughly**
1	**large egg white, lightly beaten**

Place the water in a large bowl or the bowl of your electric mixer and add the yeast and sugar. Stir to dissolve. Let sit for 5 minutes and stir in 1½ cups (6 ounces/180 g) of the flour. Whisk until the mixture is smooth, cover with plastic wrap, and set in a warm place for 30 minutes or until the mixture is bubbling (it is now a sponge).

Kneading the dough by hand: Beat the eggs and olive oil into the sponge. Stir in the salt. Begin adding the remaining flour a cup at a time. When the dough holds together, scrape it out onto your kneading surface and begin to knead, adding flour as necessary. The dough will be quite sticky. Knead for 10 minutes, or until the dough is stiff and elastic, and form into a ball.

Using an electric mixer: Add the eggs, olive oil, and salt as directed. Add all of the flour and mix briefly using the paddle attachment. Change to the dough hook and knead for 2 minutes at low speed, then 8 minutes at medium speed. Add extra flour if the dough seems very sticky. Scrape the dough out onto a floured surface to knead briefly with your hands. Shape into a ball.

A FEW BREADS, SOCCA AND VARIATIONS . . .

Rinse out the bowl, dry, and brush lightly with olive oil. Place the dough in the bowl, rounded side down first, then rounded side up. Cover with plastic wrap and a kitchen towel and let rise in a warm spot for 2 hours, until doubled in size.

Punch down the dough and scrape out onto a lightly floured board. Divide the dough into 2 equal pieces and shape into balls. Using a rolling pin or your hands, roll or press one of the balls into an oval shape about ¾ inch (2 cm) thick. Distribute the anchovy fillets over the top and roll or press out the second ball. Place on top of the first piece of dough and pinch the edges together tightly all the way around. Using a sharp knife, make three or four 2-inch-long (5 cm) slits on each side or in the middle of the dough and pull the dough apart gently at the cuts.

Place the dough on an oiled baking sheet, brush with beaten egg white, and cover with a damp towel. Set in a warm spot to rise for 25 to 30 minutes. Meanwhile, preheat the oven to 400°F (200°C).

Bake for 35 to 45 minutes, until golden brown and the loaf responds to tapping with a hollow thumping sound. Brush again with the egg white halfway through the baking. Remove from the oven and cool on a rack.

ADVANCE PREPARATION: The bread will keep for only a day or two before turning stale, but it freezes well. Wrap tightly in foil and place in a plastic bag.

PER SLICE

Calories	152	Protein	4 G
Fat	4 G	Carbohydrate	23 G
Sodium	347 MG	Cholesterol	23 MG

SOCCA
CHICK-PEA FLOUR PANCAKE

SERVES 4 TO 6

Socca batter is a simple mixture of water, chick-pea flour, salt, and olive oil, and when it's scraped out of its pan it should be slightly crisp on the outside but moist and dense, kind of like smooth polenta, within. It has an earthy, not surprisingly chick-pea flavor. The socca you buy on the streets of Nice is about ¼ inch thick, crumbly, and greasy. Mine is less greasy than traditional socca and creamy in the middle rather than runny. It makes a wonderful starter, side dish, or snack.

This recipe is slightly different from the one in *Mediterranean Light*. Luckily my husband likes this marvelous, earthy dish as much as I do, for I experimented with my socca recipe for several days. I made it in a standard nonstick pizza pan and in a heavy Le Creuset gratin dish. It was thinner and slightly crispier when made in the pizza pan, but trickier to make, because the socca batter splashes when you pour it into the hot pan, so you have to be very careful or you'll have a stove full of burning batter. I'm giving instructions for both here. The key to successful socca, no matter what kind of pan you cook it in, is a very hot oven and a hot baking dish.

> 1   **cup (5 oz/140 g) chick-pea flour (available in specialty stores and some natural food stores)**
>
> 3   **cups (750 ml) water**
>
> ½   **teaspoon salt**
>
> 3   **tablespoons olive oil**

Preheat the oven to 500°F (260°C). Whisk or blend the chick-pea flour, water, and salt together. Put through a strainer and whisk in 2 tablespoons of the olive oil. Let sit for 30 minutes or longer.

Brush a heavy 13- or 14-inch (33 to 35 cm) pizza pan or a 14- by 10-inch (30 by 25 cm) enameled cast-iron gratin dish with the remaining tablespoon of olive oil and heat for 5 to 10 minutes in the oven or until the oil is just short of smoking. The oven and the pan must be very hot.

Remove the pan from the oven. Whisk the batter and, if you're using a pizza pan, pour in half the batter. If you're using the enameled cast-iron gratin, pour in all of the batter (it should be about ¼ inch/⅔ cm thick). Pour very carefully because the batter will splash. Return to the oven and bake for 10 to 20 minutes or until brown on the top. You have to watch the socca, because it may cook faster in the pizza pan. Remove from the heat and serve, scraping the socca out of the pan. Don't worry if it sticks to the bottom, but scrape out as much as you can.

ADVANCE PREPARATION: The batter can be made hours ahead. The socca should be served hot from the pan.

PER PORTION

Calories	146	Protein	5 G
Fat	8 G	Carbohydrate	14 G
Sodium	188 MG	Cholesterol	0

SOCCA CRÊPES
Crêpes socca

MAKES TWELVE 6-INCH (15 CM) CRÊPES, SERVING 6

This idea comes from a restaurant in New York called May We. The crêpes have that wonderful chick-pea socca flavor, but they're lighter than socca, and they can be filled. Try them with ratatouille and goat cheese (page 315), brandade (page 61), or as a bed for the tomato and basil salad on page 52.

2	**large eggs**
⅔	**cup (165 ml) skim milk**
2	**tablespoons olive oil**
½	**cup (2 ounces/60 g) sifted chick-pea flour**
2	**tablespoons sifted unbleached white flour**
	heaped ¼ teaspoon salt

Blend or whisk together the eggs, milk, and oil. Slowly add the flours and the salt. Blend or whisk for 1 minute. If you're using a whisk, put the batter through a strainer. Set aside in a bowl or large glass measuring cup for 30 minutes or longer.

Heat a well-seasoned crêpe pan over medium heat and brush lightly with butter or olive oil. Ladle in about 2 tablespoons batter per crêpe. It should sizzle when it hits the pan. Tilt the pan to distribute the batter evenly and cook on the first side for about 1 minute. Turn the crêpe and brown on the other side for about 30 seconds. Transfer to a plate and continue with the remaining batter, stacking the crêpes as they are done.

Wrap the crêpes in foil and reheat for 15 minutes in a 350°F (180°C) oven before serving.

ADVANCE PREPARATION: You can let the batter sit for several hours before making the crêpes. The crêpes will keep for a couple of days in the refrigerator as long as they are well wrapped, and they freeze well. Stack between pieces of parchment or wax paper and wrap tightly in foil.

PER PORTION

Calories	129	Protein	5 G
Fat	8 G	Carbohydrate	9 G
Sodium	160 MG	Cholesterol	75 MG

A FEW BREADS, SOCCA AND VARIATIONS...

THE BEST FAST FOOD
ON THE CÔTE D'AZUR

I've never been one to recommend greasy fast food, but I cannot resist *socca*, the fragrant and earthy-tasting Niçois chick-pea flour pancake. You can get socca in the markets of Cannes and Monte Carlo, but if I am within a 20-mile radius of Nice, that is where I go to eat it. Nice is where I discovered socca, on a very cold, gray winter day years ago. It couldn't have been more comforting, warming my numb fingers as I walked through the narrow cobbled streets of the Vieille Ville. Since then I have sampled it at several places in Nice; it is sold from stands—windows, really—throughout the Vieille Ville that usually sell pizza and other Niçois specialties as well. Nowhere does it measure up to the socca at René Socca.

René Socca (now owned by a gravelly-voiced leather-jacketed man named Paul) could accurately be called the best fast-food establishment in Provence. It consists of two yellow stucco green-shuttered buildings straddling a tiny pedestrian passage. Throughout the day, but especially at lunchtime, fast-moving queues of hungry people line up at the windows and order their Niçois favorites—pizzas, socca, tortes, farcis à la Niçoise (little stuffed vegetables), vegetable and fish beignets, pan bagnats (the Niçois salad in a bun)—all on display in the cases below the windows. Socca and pizzas never stop emerging from the ovens, which are in full view. The socca is baked in enormous round copper pizzalike pans; as the last portion is served up, fresh batter is poured into the pan, and into the wood-burning oven it goes.

Whether you take your socca to a table on a plate or carry it away in a greaseproof package, you won't get a fork. A sign written on the back of another socca pan and prominently displayed on the yellow stucco wall of the bar informs customers in four languages (Provençal, French, English, and Vietnamese) that "Outside we eat with our fingers." You need lots of napkins, but it's very satisfying to pick away at your savory mound of socca while you sip bone-dry rosé from the region.

CHAPTER 3

SAUCES

Southbound on the French autoroute A6, one of the brown-and-white signs that I like best marks the watershed in France: over a ripple symbolizing water is written LA LIGNE DE PARTAGE DES EAUX. At this point rivers run toward the Mediterranean rather than the English Channel. We are not yet in Provence, but we're getting there.

There should be another sign, south of Lyon, reading LA LIGNE DE PARTAGE DES SAUCES. The sauces used in Provençal cuisines could define the north-south gastronomic divide. Once you get to this region, the sauces are made with olive oil, not butter. They are vibrant and rustic, defined by their ingredients and their aromas. *Pistou* (page 109), for example, is so linked in people's minds with its main ingredient, basil, that the words are often used interchangeably. The word *aïoli* (page 97) is a Provençal conjunction of its two main ingredients, garlic (*aïet*) and olive oil (*òli*). Tomato sauces and concassées are so frequently used that they are considered an *ingredient de base*, a household ingredient that requires no recipe in many Provençal cookbooks. Recipes just instruct the cook to serve the fish, gratin, or whatever with a tomato sauce, or a tomato sauce or puree is called for in the list of ingredients in another dish.

As Dumas noted when he described Provençal cuisine, garlic is present almost everywhere, especially in its sauces. It is often uncooked, pounded, and marvelously pungent. The only sauce in this collection that doesn't include garlic is the olive oil béchamel on page 111.

Provençal sauces are substantial; they have body; they're real foods. The traditional versions of some of these, particularly aïoli and pistou, contain a much greater quantity of olive oil than our light cuisine allows for, and I've altered these sauces to make them fit our standards. As I explain in the aïoli recipe, the mayonnaise is not light, but it's light*er*. I couldn't leave it out of this collection; but I have two alternative garlic sauces (the cooked garlic puree on page 103 and the mashed potato aïoli on page 100) for those of you who want the garlic without the oil.

Unlike classical French cuisine, Provençal cooking does not include a huge repertoire of sauces. They aren't necessary for a cuisine that has so much inherent flavor. But the ones they do have they use so well. All of these sauces—condiments might be a better word—are unforgettable. I hope they become standards for you as they have for me.

L'aïoli grise légèrement, sature le corps de chaleur et baigne l'âme d'enthousiasme. Dans son essence, il concentre la force, l'allégresse du soleil de Provence. Autour d'un aïoli bien embaumé et roux comme un fil d'or, où sont, répondez-moi, les hommes qui ne se reconnaissent point frères?

Aïoli intoxicates slightly, saturates the body with warmth and bathes the soul with enthusiasm. In its essence it concentrates the power and the joy of the Provençal sun. Around an aïoli, pungent and yellow-orange as a thread of gold, tell me where you will not find men who recognize each other as brothers.

AÏOLI (GARLIC MAYONNAISE)

To make a good aïoli, *first of all you must have a good mortar, either made of wood, ceramic or marble, and a good pestle, preferably made of wood; and most of all you need a strong grip.*

C. CHANOT-BULLIER, *VIEILLES RECETTES DE CUISINE PROVENÇALE*

The poet Frédéric Mistral named his Provençal journal *L'Aïoli*. This tawny mayonnaise, incredibly pungent with pounded raw garlic and fragrant with olive oil, is what Provençal cooking is all about. It's an essential ingredient in fish soups and the heart and soul of aïoli monstre (page 232), a huge platter of simply cooked fish and vegetables served with the mayonnaise. It's not for the faint-hearted as far as garlic is concerned (in Provence it is reputed to repel flies) and should probably not be eaten right before a business meeting.

Creating a low-fat aïoli was a challenge. How do you make a mayonnaise that isn't a mayonnaise? It had to be partly mayonnaise, or it wouldn't work in aïoli monstre and as a condiment for soups and fish dishes. What I finally settled for is not really low-fat. But it is lower fat; I call it relatively low-fat aïoli. If I reduced the olive oil more, I'd have to call the sauce something else. I've adapted one of the traditional Provençal methods of incorporating mashed potatoes into the mayonnaise (page 100) so that I don't have to use as much oil. If I want to stretch the mayonnaise, I use fromage blanc, an extremely low-fat fresh pot cheese. But the fromage blanc is optional, for a little aïoli goes a long way.

Lower-fat aïolis are more pungent than the all-mayonnaise versions. I'm not exactly sure why, but it's clear that the mashed garlic reacts differently when suspended in oil than when mixed with fromage blanc, yogurt, or mashed potatoes. For this reason you might want to start out with the smaller amount of garlic, then add more if you wish.

There are three methods for making the mayonnaise here. In the first one the mayonnaise is made in the traditional way, using a mortar and pestle from start to finish, with pounded garlic and salt, egg yolks, mashed potatoes, and olive oil. Once the mayonnaise is achieved (it will be more like a sauce than the kind of thick mayonnaise we're used to, because there is only half the usual quantity of olive oil), you stir in the optional low-fat fromage blanc.

The second version is identical to the first in ingredients, but I've made the potatoes optional. It's my favorite method; the mayonnaise, before adding the fromage blanc, is thick enough to stand a spoon in (one of the Provençal criteria for a successful aïoli), but it's not exhausting to make, since you're using an electric whisk.

In the third version you mash the garlic and potatoes to a paste in a mortar and pestle, then add it to food processor mayonnaise, which you make with a whole egg instead of 2 egg yolks (so obviously this one contains less cholesterol than the first two). The food processor mayonnaise is stiffer than mortar and pestle mayonnaise, but with the fromage blanc the aïoli is still rather creamy. The flavors of the second and third aïolis are slightly less pungent than the mortar and pestle aïoli, because you don't work the garlic as much.

I urge you to try all three methods. I love the physicality of making mayonnaise in a mortar and pestle and watching the slow, miraculous transformation of the egg yolk and olive oil. It's almost like making bread: as you work the olive oil drop by drop into the egg yolk and garlic, the mixture emulsifies and firms up; it becomes mayonnaise. Its texture is not as stiff or gummy as blender or food processor mayonnaise, and it has a beautiful yellow-green color, the color of egg yolk and olive oil.

The recipes that follow are for pungent aïolis. Feel free to reduce the garlic if you wish. Try to find young, fresh garlic for this and always remove the green germ, which is bitter. Also, make sure you have a good source of fresh eggs.

MORTAR AND PESTLE AÏOLI

MAKES 1 TO 1½ CUPS (250 TO 375 ML), DEPENDING ON
WHETHER YOU ADD FROMAGE BLANC

3 to 6	large garlic cloves, to taste, peeled and cut in half
½	teaspoon salt
2	large egg yolks
⅓	cup (85 ml/1 small) sieved mashed potatoes
⅔	cup (165 ml) olive oil
½	cup (125 ml) fromage blanc (page 99) or 6 tablespoons (90 ml) low-fat cottage cheese blended until perfectly smooth with 2 tablespoons plain low-fat yogurt (optional)
1	tablespoon fresh lemon juice (optional)
	freshly ground pepper to taste (optional)

Place the garlic cloves in the bowl of a mortar and pestle with the salt and pound and mash until the mixture is smooth. Add the egg yolks and potatoes and continue to mash together with the garlic until the mixture is uniform.

Begin adding the olive oil, drop by drop, stirring with the pestle and incorporating each drop into the egg yolks. As you add more olive oil, the mixture will thicken. Stir constantly with the pestle. It will take about 20 minutes to stir in all the olive oil. The mixture will be smooth and thick. Now stir in the fromage blanc if desired. Taste and correct salt. Add lemon juice and pepper if desired. Refrigerate until ready to use.

ELECTRIC MIXER AÏOLI: Place the garlic cloves in the bowl of a mortar and pestle with the salt and pound and mash until the mixture is smooth. Mix in the potatoes, if you wish; they're optional in this variation. Place the egg yolks in the bowl of an electric mixer fitted with the balloon whip or eggbeaters. Beat at high speed until smooth. Begin adding olive oil, a few drops at a time, and continue to beat at high speed. When you've added half the olive oil, you can add the rest in a very slow, thin stream or by the tablespoonful. The mayonnaise will be very thick. When all of the oil has been added, mix in the garlic mixture and the fromage blanc at low speed. Taste and correct salt. Add lemon juice and pepper if desired. Refrigerate until ready to use.

FOOD PROCESSOR AÏOLI: Place the garlic cloves in the bowl of a mortar and pestle with the salt and pound and mash until the mixture is smooth. Work in the mashed potatoes. Set aside. Instead of using 2 egg yolks, break 1 egg into the bowl of a food processor fitted with the steel blade and turn it on. With the food processor running, slowly add the olive oil in a very thin stream or drop by drop. When all the olive oil has been added, mix in the mashed garlic and potatoes. Remove the mayonnaise from the food processor and stir in the optional fromage blanc using a wooden spoon, a spatula, or a whisk. When thoroughly blended, taste and adjust the salt. Add lemon juice and pepper if desired. Cover and refrigerate until ready to use.

ADVANCE PREPARATION: Aïoli will keep for 2 or 3 days in the refrigerator but is best at its freshest.

PER TABLESPOON (WITHOUT FROMAGE BLANC)

Calories	95	Protein	.53 G
Fat	10	Carbohydrate	2 G
Sodium	70 MG	Cholesterol	27 MG

—————————— TRUC ——————————

REMOVING THE GREEN STEM
FROM GARLIC

This makes garlic much more digestible. Not all garlic has a green stem inside, but if it does, cut the clove in half lengthwise and lift out the stem. All Provençal recipes instruct cooks to do this if the garlic is not to be cooked.

FROMAGE BLANC

MAKES 1 CUP

Fromage blanc is a fermented milk product. It's thicker and less acidic than yogurt, and is very useful as a substitute for cream, sour cream, or crème fraîche in sauces, toppings, and spreads. In France, fromage blanc is made in high-fat, medium-fat, and nonfat versions. I dream of the day this product will be marketed in the United States, but while we're all waiting, here is a substitute, made by blending 2 parts nonfat cottage cheese with 1 part nonfat yogurt.

⅔ cup nonfat cottage cheese
⅓ cup plain nonfat yogurt

Combine the cottage cheese and yogurt in a food processor fitted with the steel blade and blend until completely smooth. Transfer to a jar or container and store in the refrigerator.

ADVANCE PREPARATION: Check the sell-by dates on the cottage cheese and yogurt; your fromage blanc will last the same amount of time in the refrigerator.

PER 1 TABLESPOON PORTION

Calories	10	Protein	1 G
Fat	0	Carbohydrate	1 G
Sodium	37 MG	Cholesterol	1 MG

MASHED POTATO AÏOLI

MAKES 1½ CUPS (375 ML), SERVING 10

I developed this pungent aïoli for two reasons. First of all, I wanted a garlic sauce that had as little oil as I could get away with; second, I wanted an alternative containing no raw eggs. With this delicious puree there will be an aïoli for everyone. It's easy to make, and I urge you to serve both this and one of the aïolis on the preceding pages if you throw an aïoli party.

2 **large heads of garlic, cloves separated and peeled**
3 **quarts (3 l) water**
1½ **teaspoons salt**
1 **pound (450 g) waxy potatoes, peeled, cooked, mashed, and strained (1¼ cups/312 ml)**
2½ **tablespoons olive oil**
2 to 3 **additional garlic cloves, to taste, peeled and green germ removed**
freshly ground pepper to taste (optional)

Combine the heads of garlic and 1 quart (1 l) of the water in a saucepan and bring to a boil. Pour off the water and add the second quart to the saucepan. Bring to a boil. Pour off the water and add the third quart. Bring to a boil, add 1 teaspoon of the salt, reduce the heat, and simmer for 30 to 40 minutes, covered or uncovered, until the garlic is thoroughly tender and the broth fragrant. Remove from the heat.

Using a slotted spoon or skimmer, transfer the garlic from the broth to a food processor fitted with the steel blade. Blend until thoroughly smooth. Transfer to a large bowl and add the potatoes. Whisk or stir together until the mixture is homogenous and add the olive oil and 2 tablespoons of the reserved garlic broth.

Place the remaining garlic and salt in a mortar and pestle and mash together until you have a smooth paste. Stir into the potato/garlic mixture. Taste and adjust seasoning, adding more garlic, salt, or pepper if desired.

ADVANCE PREPARATION: This will keep for 3 days in the refrigerator, but like all aïolis, the fresher it is, the better.

Calories	34	Protein	.64 G
Fat	1 G	Carbohydrate	5 G
Sodium	71 MG	Cholesterol	0

TRUC

BOILING GARLIC THREE TIMES

When garlic is simmered in several changes of water, the pungency goes out with the first two changes of water. If you're making any dish that calls for a number of cooked garlic cloves, such as the green garlic and parsley puree on page 107, the dish will be sweet and mild if you combine the peeled cloves of garlic with water, bring it to a boil, boil for 1 minute, drain, and repeat the process once more before adding the final quart of water, or more, depending on the recipe, and simmering the garlic until cooked through.

GARLIC AND ITS VOLATILE OILS

The way you prepare garlic will partly determine how strong it is. The more and the harder you pound, the stronger your garlic will be because of volatile oils being released. Here are preparation techniques in ascending order of pungency:

1. Slice
2. Chop
3. Puree with a knife
4. Mash with the side of a knife or a fork
5. Put through a press
6. Mash in a mortar and pestle

TRUC

PUREEING GARLIC WITH A KNIFE

With the help of a little salt, you can reduce garlic to a much finer puree than you would with a garlic press, but the puree won't be as pungent as it is when you use a mortar and pestle. Peel the garlic clove and remove the green germ if necessary. Place on a cutting board and spoon about ⅛ to ¼ teaspoon of salt onto the board next to the garlic clove. Using either a paring knife or a blunt knife, such as a dinner knife, scoop up a little salt and scrape the blade of the knife down the side of the garlic clove, toward the cutting board. You should be scraping and crushing at the same time; the salt will help to break down the garlic. When you've scraped off most of the garlic, mash the remaining bit of clove together with the scraped garlic and the salt.

Another technique is to chop the garlic finely, sprinkle with salt, then mash.

TRUC

TO PREVENT BURNING GARLIC

Always add the garlic to the pan just before you introduce liquid or vegetables that will release liquid as they cook. For instance, if a recipe asks you to sauté onions and garlic, cook the onions first, then add the garlic. Garlic cooks extremely quickly, and once it browns and sticks to the pan the flavor becomes bitter.

COOKED GARLIC PUREE
Purée à l'ail

MAKES ½ CUP (125 ML)

This is an amazing dish: pure garlic, but simmered until it isn't pungent. It still has a strong flavor but is milder than raw or slightly cooked garlic. It is marvelous as an embellishment for fish, chicken, or vegetables, and for those who want a garlic sauce without the oil in a mayonnaise, it can be substituted for aïoli in Aïoli Monstre (page 232), as long as you double or triple the recipe. It's also a great garnish for soups.

3   quarts (3 l) water
2   large heads of garlic, cloves separated and peeled
1   bay leaf
1   teaspoon salt
     additional salt and freshly ground pepper to taste
2   tablespoons skim milk (optional)

Combine 1 quart (1 l) of the water and the garlic in a saucepan and bring to a boil. When the water reaches a rolling boil, drain. Return the garlic cloves to the pot, add another quart (l) of water, bring to a boil, and boil for 5 minutes. Drain and return the garlic cloves to the pot. Now add the last quart (l) of water, the bay leaf, and the salt. Bring to a boil, reduce the heat, cover, and simmer for 30 to 40 minutes, until the garlic is thoroughly soft. Drain. Save the stock for use as a soup base. Discard the bay leaf.

Puree the garlic until perfectly smooth and fluffy in a food processor, a mortar and pestle, or a bowl with a fork. Add salt and pepper and the milk if you wish. Transfer to a ramekin or a serving dish. Serve warm or cold.

ROUILLE MAIGRE (SPICY GARLIC PUREE): This is a
spiced-up version to be used as a low-fat substitute for rouille (page 105) in soups
and stews. You can make this dish with baked garlic (such as the oven-roasted garlic
on page 363) as well as simmered garlic.

1 to 2   **small dried hot peppers, ground, to taste**
¼   **teaspoon saffron threads or powder**
    additional salt and freshly ground pepper to taste
2   **tablespoons skim milk or stock (optional)**
1   **tablespoon olive oil (optional)**

Cook the garlic as directed. Meanwhile, pound 1 to 2 whole cayenne peppers, to
taste, together with ¼ teaspoon saffron threads or powder in a mortar and pestle.
(Or use ⅛ to ¼ teaspoon ground cayenne and skip the pounding.) Puree the garlic
as directed, season, and add the milk (or use stock) and 1 tablespoon olive oil if you
wish. Add the cayenne and saffron and mix together well.

ADVANCE PREPARATION: This will keep for 3 or 4 days in
the refrigerator, but the flavor is best when it's freshly made.

PER TABLESPOON

Calories	23	Protein	1 G
Fat	.08 G	Carbohydrate	5 G
Sodium	70 MG	Cholesterol	0

GARLIC MAYONNAISE WITH CAYENNE AND SAFFRON
La rouio
Sauce rouille à l'ail

MAKES 1 TO 1½ CUPS (250 TO 375 ML), DEPENDING ON
WHETHER YOU ADD FROMAGE BLANC

This spicy mayonnaise, really an aïoli with cayenne to make it hot and saffron to give it color, is always served with bouillabaisse and fish soup in Provence. It's also great with other fish dishes, like the salt cod with garlicky tomato sauce on page 197. Sometimes rouille contains bread or mashed potatoes, and often it is colored with the broth from the soup. I'm using the mashed potatoes here, because I use less oil than is called for in a traditional rouille, and the mashed potatoes give the sauce the necessary body.

2	large, fat garlic cloves, cut in half
½	teaspoon salt, or more to taste
1	small dried hot pepper
¼	teaspoon saffron threads, or more to taste
¼	cup (62 ml/90 g) mashed potatoes
2	large egg yolks for mortar and pestle or 1 whole egg for food processor
⅔	cup (165 ml) olive oil
½	cup (125 ml) fromage blanc (page 99 optional)
	freshly ground pepper to taste (optional)

Pound the garlic, salt, hot pepper, saffron, and potatoes together in a mortar and pestle until smooth.

Using a mortar and pestle: Add the egg yolks and continue to mash together with the garlic until the mixture is uniform. Begin adding the olive oil, drop by drop, stirring with the pestle and incorporating each drop into the egg yolks. As you add more olive oil, the mixture will thicken. Stir constantly with the pestle. It will take about 20 minutes to stir in all the olive oil. The mixture will be smooth and thick. Now stir in the fromage blanc if desired. Taste and correct salt. Add pepper if desired. Refrigerate until ready to use.

Using a food processor: Break the egg into the bowl of a food processor fitted with the steel blade and turn it on. With the food processor running, slowly add the olive oil in a very thin stream or drop by drop. When all the olive oil has been added, mix in the garlic and potato mixture using the pulse action. Remove the mayonnaise from the food processor and stir in the fromage blanc if desired, using a wooden spoon, a spatula, or a whisk. When it has been thoroughly blended, taste and adjust the salt. Add pepper if desired. Cover and refrigerate until ready to use.

ADVANCE PREPARATION: This will keep for 3 or 4 days in the refrigerator, but it's best at its freshest.

PER TABLESPOON

Calories	94	Protein	.47 G
Fat	10 G	Carbohydrate	1 G
Sodium	70 MG	Cholesterol	27 MG

GREEN GARLIC AND PARSLEY PUREE

Purée d'ail nouveau au persil

MAKES ½ CUP (125 ML), SERVING 6 AS AN APPETIZER OR
4 AS A SAUCE WITH FISH

This emerald-green puree is absolutely gorgeous. It's not a traditional Provençal recipe but my own invention, inspired by a spring crop of new garlic. It's amazing how unctuous it is with only a tablespoon of olive oil. Spread it on garlic croutons and serve it as an appetizer or serve it as a garnish for fish.

2	heads of green garlic, cloves separated and peeled
3	quarts (3 l) water
1	teaspoon salt (more to taste)
	leaves from 1 large bunch of flat-leaf parsley (about 1 cup/30 g)
1 to 2	teaspoons fresh lemon juice to taste
	additional salt and freshly ground pepper to taste
1	tablespoon olive oil

Combine the garlic and 1 quart (1 l) of the water in a saucepan and bring to a boil. Boil for 1 minute, drain, return the garlic to the saucepan, and add a second quart (l) of water. Bring to a boil, boil for 1 minute, and drain. Return the garlic to the saucepan, add the last quart (l) of water, bring to a boil, and add the 1 teaspoon salt. Turn the heat down to medium and boil gently, uncovered, for 30 minutes, until the garlic is tender.

Meanwhile, finely chop the parsley in a food processor fitted with the steel blade. Drain the garlic and add to the parsley in the food processor. Turn on the machine and puree with the parsley. Add the lemon juice and salt and pepper to taste and continue to process until the mixture is fairly smooth, scraping it down from the sides of the bowl from time to time. With the machine running, add the olive oil and continue to process for another minute or so, until the mixture has a smooth, even consistency.

Transfer to a ramekin and serve with croutons or serve with fish fillets or a whole baked, grilled, or poached fish.

ADVANCE PREPARATION: This will hold for a couple of hours, in or out of the refrigerator.

PER PORTION

Calories	35	Protein	1 G
Fat	2 G	Carbohydrate	5 G
Sodium	142 MG	Cholesterol	0

PROVENÇAL OLIVE OIL

Most Provençal olive oils are delicate and light, which is why I've always favored them above other Mediterranean olive oils. The ones I've used the most over the years are beautifully aromatic, yet not overassertive. My favorite is the extra virgin olive oil from Domaine de la Gautière in the Drôme, not far from Nyons. This is not to say that full-bodied, gutsy oils are not to be found; the famous virgin oil made by the olive oil cooperative in Maussane-les-Alpilles, near les Baux-de-Provence, is bursting with flavor.

I'm always discovering new olive oils in Provence. The most recent was at Oppède, a tiny village in the Luberon between Cavaillon and Ménerbes. Just outside the village is an olive oil mill where you can buy delicious, fairly light virgin olive oil, olives, soaps, honeys, preserves—the usual fare of the land—and crafts.

The olive oils I've tasted from the Pays Niçois are quite fragrant, but lighter than those from the Maussane area. The ones I know and love are from the Huilerie de la Brague in Opio and from Alziéri in Nice. But virtually any olive oil imported from Provence will be delicious.

LOW-FAT PISTOU

This is a breakthrough recipe, and I don't know why it didn't occur to me earlier. The pistou, or Provençal pesto, which is traditionally stirred into heady vegetable soups in Provence, is often made with the addition of a tomato. One summer evening I was making my pistou for the enormous vegetable soup I'd made that day (see the recipe on page 134). I chopped up all the basil in the food processor, then added a tomato, at which point I realized I'd need to add only a tablespoon or so of oil instead of the usual 6 tablespoons to achieve the right consistency. The tomato provided the liquid. I'm using a small amount of cheese here to keep the fat content low. Double it if you wish, but know that you'll be doubling the fat content as well.

I make as many batches of pistou as I can during the summer to assure lots of easy impromptu dinner parties all winter long. This version is slightly watery when thawed, compared to the traditional high-fat pistou, but it doesn't matter once you've tossed it with pasta or stirred it into a soup.

2	cups (2½ ounces/75 g) tightly packed fresh basil leaves
¼	teaspoon salt (more to taste)
2	large garlic cloves, peeled
1	medium-size tomato (3 to 4 ounces/90 to 115 g), peeled and seeded
1	tablespoon olive oil
1	ounce (30 g) Parmesan cheese,★ grated (¼ cup)
	freshly ground pepper to taste

Place the basil and salt in the bowl of a food processor fitted with the steel blade and turn it on. Drop in the garlic cloves and let the processor run until the basil and garlic are finely chopped.

Turn off the machine, scrape the leaves down from the sides of the bowl, and turn it on again. With the processor running, drop in the tomato and add the olive oil. Puree until smooth.

★ If you're using the pistou for a soup (page 134), simmer a Parmesan rind in the soup with the bouquet garni.

Remove from the food processor and stir in the cheese and pepper. Taste and adjust seasonings. Transfer to a serving bowl or a covered jar and store in the refrigerator until shortly before serving.

ADVANCE PREPARATION: The pistou will keep for several days in the refrigerator and can be frozen for several months. When you're making it for the freezer, don't add the garlic, cheese, or pepper until after thawing.

PER PORTION

Calories	44	Protein	2 G
Fat	3 G	Carbohydrate	4 G
Sodium	127 MG	Cholesterol	2 MG

OLIVE OIL BÉCHAMEL

MAKES 2 CUPS (500 ML)

In Provence the classic French béchamel is made with olive oil. It comes up in this book in certain gratins and with pasta and gnocchi.

- 3 **cups (750 ml) skim milk**
- 2 **tablespoons olive oil**
- 2 **tablespoons unbleached white flour**
  salt and freshly ground pepper to taste
  pinch of freshly grated nutmeg (optional)

Bring the milk to a simmer in a saucepan. Meanwhile, heat the olive oil in a large heavy-bottomed saucepan over medium heat. Add a pinch of flour; if it sizzles, add the rest. If not, heat the oil a little longer and repeat. Whisk together and cook over medium heat, stirring constantly with a wooden spoon, for a couple of minutes. Do not allow the mixture to brown.

Remove the pan from the heat and whisk in the milk all at once. Return the pan to the heat and bring the sauce to a simmer, stirring constantly with a whisk. When the sauce begins to thicken, reduce the heat to low and simmer, stirring often and being careful not to let it stick to the bottom of the pan and burn, for 15 to 20 minutes, until the sauce has a smooth, creamy consistency and no trace of a floury taste. Add the salt, pepper, and nutmeg if desired, then remove from the heat.

ADVANCE PREPARATION: The béchamel can be covered and held in the refrigerator for up to a day. Place a sheet of plastic wrap over the surface of the sauce. A skin may form on the top, but this can be whisked away when you reheat the sauce.

PER TABLESPOON

Calories	17	Protein	.83 G
Fat	.88 G	Carbohydrate	1 G
Sodium	12 MG	Cholesterol	.45 MG

BASIC TOMATO SAUCE

MAKES 2 CUPS (500 ML); SERVING 4 TO 6

Here is one of the great aromas of Provence: tomatoes simmering with garlic. The thick, fragrant sauce is a very simple one, and of course is best made with fresh, sweet, ripe tomatoes, at the height of summer. It's great with pasta, fish, and vegetable gratins.

1	teaspoon olive oil
3	large garlic cloves, minced or put through a press
3	pounds (1.35 kg/12 medium-size) sweet, ripe tomatoes, seeded and quartered (may use canned)
1 or 2	pinches of sugar
	salt to taste
2 to 3	tablespoons slivered fresh basil to taste
	freshly ground pepper to taste (optional)

Heat the oil over medium heat in a large heavy-bottomed nonstick skillet and add the garlic. When it begins to color, add the tomatoes, sugar, and salt. Cook, stirring often, for 20 to 30 minutes, until the tomatoes are cooked down and beginning to stick to the pan. Stir in the basil, simmer for a few more minutes, and remove from the heat.

Put through the medium blade of a food mill. Adjust salt, add pepper if desired, and reheat gently before serving.

Note: If you don't have a food mill, peel, seed, and chop the tomatoes before cooking. After simmering, puree the sauce in a food processor using the steel blade.

ADVANCE PREPARATION: This will keep for a few days in the refrigerator and freezes well.

Calories	81	Protein	3 G
Fat	2 G	Carbohydrate	16 G
Sodium	29 MG	Cholesterol	0

——— TRUC ———

HOW TO BRING OUT SOME FLAVOR IN HOPELESSLY DULL TOMATOES

Tomatoes are rarely as sweet as we want them to be. For cooked tomatoes, add ¼ to ½ teaspoon—or a small lump—of sugar to the pan along with the tomatoes to balance the acid (for gratins, sprinkle the tops of the tomatoes with the sugar). For uncooked tomato sauces and salads, toss with a tablespoon or two of balsamic vinegar.

LA MÈRE BESSON'S TOMATO SAUCE

MAKES 1½ QUARTS (1½ L), SERVING 12 TO 18

I was amazed by the way the chef/owner Monsieur Martin made tomato sauce at the restaurant La Mère Besson in Cannes. He stewed onions, leeks, celery, and whole heads of garlic, unpeeled and cut in half across the middle in lots of oil in a huge pot, then added canned tomatoes and their liquid, tomato puree, salt, pepper, and thyme and let the mixture simmer for quite a long time. Then he blended it in the pot and put it through a food mill. So the peeling of the garlic wasn't necessary, because all the fibers were left behind in the food mill. I've used the same method for this sauce, but using low heat and a heavy-bottomed pot I need only a tablespoon and a half of olive oil. All the vegetables and herbs give this sauce a very earthy quality.

1½ tablespoons olive oil
1   medium-size onion, peeled and coarsely chopped
2   leeks, trimmed, well washed, and thickly sliced
2   celery ribs, including leaves, thickly sliced
1   head of garlic, unpeeled, base trimmed, cut in half crosswise
2   28-ounce (800 g) cans tomatoes with juice, the tomatoes coarsely cut up
3   heaped tablespoons tomato paste
1   teaspoon dried thyme or 2 teaspoons fresh leaves or more to taste
1   teaspoon dried basil or oregano or 1 tablespoon chopped fresh or more to taste
    salt and freshly ground pepper to taste

Heat the olive oil in a large heavy-bottomed lidded casserole over low heat. Add the onion, leeks, celery, and garlic and stir together. Cover and cook slowly for 15 minutes, stirring often, until the vegetables are softened and fragrant but not browned. Add the remaining ingredients, increase the heat to medium, and bring to a simmer. Reduce the heat to low, cover partially, and simmer for 1 hour, stirring from time to time. Remove from the heat and puree in a blender or right in the pot using a hand blender.

Put through the fine or medium blade of a food mill and return to the pot. Taste and adjust seasonings, adding more garlic, salt, pepper, or herbs as desired. Use as a sauce for pasta, meat, or fish.

ADVANCE PREPARATION: This will keep for 5 days in the refrigerator and freezes well.

PER PORTION

Calories	74	Protein	2 G
Fat	2 G	Carbohydrate	13 G
Sodium	273 MG	Cholesterol	0

SPICY TOMATO SAUCE
Sauce piquante aux tomates

Every once in a while they throw a cayenne pepper or two into a tomato sauce in Provence, just as they do in Italy. This is great with pasta, on pizza, with gnocchi or fish.

1	teaspoon olive oil
3	large garlic cloves, minced or put through a press
3	pounds (1.35 kg/12 medium-size) sweet, ripe tomatoes, seeded and quartered (may use canned)
1 or 2	pinches of sugar
2	dried cayenne peppers, crushed in a mortar and pestle, about ⅛ teaspoon
1	teaspoon fresh thyme leaves or ½ teaspoon dried salt and freshly ground pepper to taste
2 to 3	tablespoons slivered fresh basil to taste (optional)

Heat the oil over medium heat in a large heavy-bottomed nonstick skillet and add the garlic. When it begins to color, after about 30 seconds, add the tomatoes, sugar, crushed pepper, thyme, and salt. Cook, stirring often, for 20 to 30 minutes, until the tomatoes are cooked down and beginning to stick to the pan. Stir in the pepper and basil, simmer for a few more minutes, and remove from the heat.

Put through the medium blade of a food mill. Adjust salt, add more cayenne if desired, and reheat gently before serving.

Note: If you don't have a food mill, peel, seed, and chop the tomatoes before cooking. After simmering, puree the sauce in a food processor using the steel blade.

ADVANCE PREPARATION: This will keep for a few days in the refrigerator and freezes well. But keep in mind that freezing will make it even hotter.

Calories	81	Protein	3 G
Fat	2 G	Carbohydrate	16 G
Sodium	28 MG	Cholesterol	0

TRUC

PEELING TOMATOES AND PEACHES

The usual thing is to drop them into a pot of boiling water. I find it's much more efficient to place the tomatoes or peaches in a bowl and bring enough water to cover them to a boil in my electric water kettle. I pour the water over the fruit, wait for a minute or so, then drain and cool in cold water. Peels come off easily.

FRESH TOMATO CONCASSÉE
WITH BASIL
Concassée de tomates

MAKES 3 CUPS (750 ML), SERVING 4 TO 6

This sweet and pungent uncooked tomato sauce makes a great quick sauce for ravioli. It's also great with fish, pasta, and pizza.

2	**pounds (900 g) sweet, ripe tomatoes, peeled, seeded, and finely chopped**
1	**tablespoon olive oil**
2 to 3	**garlic cloves or more to taste, minced or put through a press**
1	**tablespoon balsamic vinegar**
¼	**cup (60 ml) fresh basil leaves, snipped with scissors**
	salt, preferably coarse sea salt, and freshly ground pepper to taste

Combine all the ingredients and stir together well. Adjust salt and pepper. Refrigerate or leave at room temperature.

ADVANCE PREPARATION: This can be made several hours before serving.

PER PORTION

Calories	53	Protein	1 G
Fat	3 G	Carbohydrate	7 G
Sodium	13 MG	Cholesterol	0

RAITO
Red Wine Sauce with Onions, Herbs, Tomatoes, and Olives

MAKES 1 QUART (1 L), SERVING 6 GENEROUSLY

This is a pungent sauce made with lots of onions, red wine, tomatoes, and garlic. Everything is cooked together until the sauce is quite thick, then put through a food mill. Afterward, chopped olives and capers are added, and the sauce is cooked some more until it's permeated with their flavors. The sauce is terrific for fish (you can cook the fish right in the *raito;* see page 206); it can also be served with pasta or polenta, on chicken, or as a topping for croutons. Also try it as a topping for the *panisse* gratin on page 373 or as a salsalike dip.

1	tablespoon olive oil
2	medium-size or large onions, finely chopped
4	large garlic cloves, peeled and crushed
1	bottle full-bodied red wine such as a Côtes du Rhône
2	cloves
2	cups (500 ml) water
1¼	pounds (565 g/5 medium-size) tomatoes, coarsely chopped
1	bay leaf
½	cup (125 ml) chopped mixed fresh herbs such as basil, thyme, rosemary, savory, parsley; or 1 teaspoon dried thyme and 1 teaspoon dried oregano
	salt and freshly ground pepper to taste
⅓	cup (85 ml) black Nyons or Niçois olives (12 Nyons olives), pitted and finely chopped
3	tablespoons drained capers, rinsed and finely chopped
2 to 3	tablespoons chopped fresh parsley to taste

Heat the oil in a large heavy-bottomed casserole over low heat and add the onions. Sauté, stirring often, until the onions begin to brown, about 20 minutes. Add one of the garlic cloves and sauté with the onions, stirring, until it just begins to color, about 1 minute. Add the wine and cloves, raise the heat to medium-high and bring to a boil. Boil for 5 minutes. Add the remaining garlic, the water, tomatoes, bay leaf, herbs, about ½ teaspoon salt, and some pepper, and bring back to a boil. Reduce the heat to low and simmer, uncovered, for about 1½ hours, stirring from time to time. The mixture should be thick, its volume reduced by about half. Most but not all of the liquid will have evaporated. Remove from the heat.

Remove the cloves and bay leaf and discard. Put the sauce through the fine blade of a food mill. Return to the pot and stir in the olives and capers. Heat through over medium heat for about 15 minutes. Taste and adjust salt and pepper. Just before serving, stir in the parsley.

ADVANCE PREPARATION: This sauce will hold for 2 or 3 days in the refrigerator and can be frozen.

PER PORTION

Calories	64	Protein	2 G
Fat	3 G	Carbohydrate	10 G
Sodium	146 MG	Cholesterol	0

ANCHOVY VINAIGRETTE
Pissalat

MAKES A GENEROUS ½ CUP (125 ML)

I knew I was in an authentic Niçois restaurant when, lunching at Lou Basilic in Nice, the waiter asked us if we preferred pissalat or vinaigrette on our salade mesclun. Pissalat, an anchovy-olive oil paste, is a traditional Provençal/Niçois condiment, yet I had never heard it called by its proper name until I went to Lou Basilic. It makes the basis for a wonderful salad dressing.

4   **anchovy fillets, rinsed and soaked in water or milk for 15 minutes if desired**

1   **medium-size or large garlic clove, peeled**

1   **tablespoon drained capers, rinsed**

2   **tablespoons red wine vinegar**

6   **tablespoons (90 ml) olive oil**

    freshly ground pepper to taste

Using a mortar and pestle or a fork, mash the anchovy fillets, garlic, and capers together to a smooth paste. Work in the vinegar and olive oil. Season to taste with pepper. Toss with the salad of your choice.

ADVANCE PREPARATION: This will keep for a week in the refrigerator.

PER TABLESPOON

Calories	95	Protein	.59 G
Fat	10 G	Carbohydrate	.24 G
Sodium	101 MG	Cholesterol	1 MG

LOW-FAT YOGURT VINAIGRETTE

Vinaigrette au yaourt

MAKES 1 CUP (250 ML), SERVING 6

This creamy salad dressing contains no oil at all. You can use it as a substitute dressing for any of the salads in this book.

2	tablespoons fresh lemon juice
1 to 2	tablespoons vinegar to taste: red wine, champagne, cider, sherry, or balsamic
1	small garlic clove, minced or put through a press
	salt and freshly ground pepper to taste
1 to 2	teaspoons Dijon mustard to taste
¾	cup (185 ml) plain low-fat yogurt
2	tablespoons snipped fresh herb leaves such as tarragon, basil, parsley, chives, chervil, dill

Mix together the lemon juice, vinegar, garlic, salt, pepper, and mustard. Whisk in the yogurt. Add the herbs just before tossing with the salad.

ADVANCE PREPARATION: This will hold in the refrigerator for a few hours.

PER PORTION

Calories	7	Protein	.61 G
Fat	.04 G	Carbohydrate	1 G
Sodium	22 MG	Cholesterol	.21 MG

SAUCES

HOT PEPPER AND HERB OIL

MAKES 2 CUPS (500 ML)

P*ili-pili* is a fiery-hot mixture of small dried red peppers and herbs that are usually sold in small sachets in markets and specialty stores all over Provence. I think its presence in the region is due to the North African influence. That said, I tend to use it most often to make a seasoned olive oil, which I use as a condiment for pizzas and pastas. I infuse the spices in olive oil, and keep the oil in an attractive bottle or cruet, which is passed at the table and used sparingly. A little of this hot stuff goes a long way.

1   **tablespoon small dried hot red peppers**

5   **sprigs of fresh thyme, or 1 teaspoon dried thyme**

1   **3-inch sprig of fresh rosemary, or 1 teaspoon crumbled dried rosemary**

2   **cups (500 ml) olive oil**

Place the peppers and herbs in an attractive bottle, cruet, or jar, and pour on the olive oil. Cover and keep in a pantry or cupboard. It will take a few days for the olive oil to take on the heat of the peppers, but it will soon be quite hot. Drizzle sparingly onto pizzas and pasta dishes.

ADVANCE PREPARATION: This oil will keep for months in a cool, dry, dark place.

PER TABLESPOON

Calories	120	Protein	.01 G
Fat	14 G	Carbohydrate	.13 G
Sodium	.07 MG	Cholesterol	0

CHAPTER 4

VEGETABLE SOUPS

La soupo tapo un trau.

Soup plugs up a hole.

The typical Provençal peasant meal can be characterized by one word: soup. The principal dish of the region, this is what people *eat*, at the house or in the fields, cold or hot, thick or thin. And because it symbolizes poverty and frugality, it is what they *don't* eat at special meals, such as Sunday lunch and holiday feasts. The word itself originally referred to the pieces of bread that were moistened with bouillon; it evolved to mean the contents of the pot, bread or no bread.

Most of the Provençal soups that begin or make up the whole of a Provençal meal are *maigre*, without animal fat. They are easily made, fragrant vegetable soups, seasoned with garlic and local herbs. Most of the time they're served over a thick slice of stale bread that has been rubbed with garlic, and olive oil is drizzled over the top. Gruyère or Parmesan and sometimes an egg or two provide further enrichment. Thus these soups are perfect for this book, for the olive oil and cheese can be reduced to a minimum or eliminated. It's the vegetables and herbs, after all, that make these soups so aromatic.

The most simple, unadorned Provençal soup is *aigo boulido*, "boiled garlic" (page 132). It's a known cure for hangovers, weak stomachs, and other ailments, but it is much more than a cure. The mother of all garlic soups, aigo boulido can be enriched with eggs and cheese, filled out with vegetables, potatoes, or pasta, made more or less garlicky.

There is a tradition in Provence of separating the elements of a soup once the vegetables have been cooked. The broth is served over garlic croutons as a first course, and the vegetables are served on the side, sometimes with an egg that has been poached in the broth, and often seasoned with a vinaigrette (see the discussion of *bajano* in the salads chapter, on page 19). In other, richer soups, such as bean soups (pages 151–55) and la soupe au pistou (page 134), all of the elements remain together, and the potage makes a filling meal. I tend to leave everything together and make a meal out of all of these vegetable soups. Sometimes, as in the incredibly sweet fresh pea bouillabaisse on page 140 and spinach bouillabaisse on page 138, an egg is poached in the soup at the last minute. As you eat the soup, the yolk oozes into the broth, and the total effect is incredibly sensuous and nourishing, a marvelous meal in a bowl.

VEGETABLE SOUPS

VEGETABLE STOCKS

These are quick and easy. The vegetable stock is sweet and fragrant, the garlic stock incredibly aromatic though not pungent. I probably use the garlic stock most of all, not only for soups but also as a setting for some of the ravioli on pages 276–78.

VEGETABLE STOCK

MAKES 7 CUPS (1.75 L)

2   quarts (2 l) water

2   large onions, quartered

2   large carrots, coarsely sliced

2   large leeks, well washed and sliced

3   large garlic cloves, peeled

2   celery ribs with leaves, coarsely sliced

    a bouquet garni consisting of a bay leaf, a few sprigs of parsley and a sprig or two of thyme

½   pound (225 g/2 medium-size) potatoes, diced

    salt to taste

1   teaspoon black peppercorns

Combine all the ingredients in a stockpot and bring to a boil. Reduce the heat, cover, and simmer for 1 to 2 hours. Strain and discard the vegetables. This will keep for 4 days in the refrigerator and freezes well.

PER 1 CUP PORTION

Calories	15	Protein	.38 G
Fat	.02 G	Carbohydrate	3 GM
Sodium	6 MG	Cholesterol	0

CHICKEN OR TURKEY STOCK

MAKES 2 ½ QUARTS (2.5 L)

You can make this chicken stock with a fresh uncooked carcass or with the remains of a chicken or turkey you've cooked. Make it in quantity and freeze in 1-quart (1 l) containers. Remember to make it a day before you need it so that you can skim off the fat, which will congeal in the refrigerator.

	a fresh carcass and giblets of 1 chicken or turkey or the carcass of a cooked chicken or turkey
3	**medium-size carrots, sliced**
1	**medium-size onion, quartered**
1	**leek, white part and the tender part of the green, well washed and sliced**
5 or 6	**garlic cloves, to taste, peeled and crushed**
	a bouquet garni made with a bay leaf, 2 fresh thyme sprigs, and 2 parsley sprigs
2	**celery ribs, sliced**
3	**quarts (3 l) water or enough to cover everything by an inch**
½	**teaspoon black peppercorns**
	salt to taste

If you're using a fresh carcass, crack the bones slightly with a hammer. Combine all the ingredients in a soup pot. Bring to a boil and skim off any foam that rises. Reduce the heat, cover, and simmer over very low heat for 2 hours. Strain and remove pieces of chicken from the bones (you can use it for salads or stuffed vegetables). Discard the bones.

Place the stock in a bowl, cover, and refrigerate overnight. The next day, remove the stock from the refrigerator and skim off any fat that has risen to the surface. Use in soups and sauces or as a cooking bouillon for rabbit or chicken (see the recipes on pages 377, 381, 383); or freeze.

ADVANCE PREPARATION: This will keep for about 3 days in the refrigerator and freezes well.

PER 1 CUP PORTION

Calories	39	Protein	.50 G
Fat	2 G	Carbohydrate	5 G
Sodium	4 MG	Cholesterol	0

GARLIC STOCK

MAKES 7 CUPS (1.75 L)

2	quarts (2 l) water
2	heads of garlic, cloves separated and peeled (see note)
	a bouquet garni consisting of a bay leaf, a few sprigs of parsley and a sprig or two of thyme
1 to 2	teaspoons salt to taste
6	black peppercorns
1	tablespoon olive oil (optional)

Combine all the ingredients in a stockpot and bring to a boil. Cover, reduce the heat, and simmer for 1 to 2 hours. Strain and adjust the salt.

Note: To peel all the garlic cloves, hit them with the bottom of a jar or glass or lean on them with the flat side of a knife. The skins will pop off, and it doesn't matter if the garlic cloves are slightly crushed.

ADVANCE PREPARATION: This will keep for 3 or 4 days in the refrigerator and freezes well.

PER PORTION

Calories	14	Protein	.55 G
Fat	.05 G	Carbohydrate	3 G
Sodium	472 MG	Cholesterol	0

L'Oulo canto sus lou fiò:
Oh! la bono aigo-boulido!
Entre li dous grand cafiò
Lando, lando regalido!
Nòsti gènt vènon dina,
Arrena.
Un brout de sàuvi dins l'oulo
Reviscoulo
Lou crestian. . . .

The soup pot sings on the stove:
Oh the good garlic soup!
Between the two big andirons
Burn, joyous flame!
Our people are coming to dine,
Exhausted.
From one sprig of sage in the pot
The Christian
Draws strength. . . .

FROM "LIS ISCLO D'OR" BY FRÉDÉRIC MISTRAL

SIMPLE, MILD GARLIC SOUP
Aigo boulido   Eau bouillie

SERVES 4

L'Aigo boulido sauvo la vido.

Aigo boulido is a lifesaver.

This classic Provençal garlic soup is the chicken soup of the region. As with so many traditional dishes, every Provençal cook has her own way of making it. Most often it's a mild soup, with only two or three crushed garlic cloves added to a quart of salted water. Some cooks add bay leaves, some sage, some both. Sometimes a bit of orange zest is added. I'll give you the simplest recipe first, followed by variations.

2 to 6	**large garlic cloves, to taste, crushed**
1	**quart (1 l) water**
1	**bay leaf**
	pinch of rubbed sage or 1 fresh sage sprig
1 to 2	**teaspoons salt to taste**
	freshly ground pepper
1	**large egg yolk (optional)**
4	**garlic croutons (page 83)**
1	**ounce (30 g) Gruyère cheese, grated (¼ cup) (optional)**

Combine the garlic, water, bay leaf, sage, and salt in a soup pot and bring to a boil. Reduce the heat and simmer for 15 minutes. Taste, adjust salt, and add pepper. Remove from the heat.

Remove the garlic and bay leaf. Beat the egg yolk in a bowl or soup tureen and slowly stir in the broth. Serve over garlic croutons in wide soup bowls with Gruyère sprinkled over the top if desired.

Note: You can omit the egg and cheese. It'll still be *aigo boulido*.

VARIATIONS:

- Don't remove the garlic.
- Simmer peeled but not crushed garlic cloves from 2 heads of garlic in the water for 1 hour with the herbs, then strain and proceed with the recipe.
- Put the garlic through a press; the soup will have a stronger garlic flavor.
- Add a piece of orange zest and 2 cloves.
- Use 2 egg yolks.
- Add 1 tablespoon olive oil to the egg yolk.
- Cook 1 cup (250 ml) broken vermicelli in the simmering soup before adding the broth to the egg yolk.
- Use Parmesan instead of Gruyère.
- Add ½ to 1 pound (225 to 450 g) green vegetables, such as broccoli florets, cut-up green beans, or peas, to the simmering broth for 5 to 10 minutes before serving.
- Add ½ to 1 pound (225 to 450 g) sliced new potatoes to the soup along with the garlic and simmer until the potatoes are tender, 15 to 20 minutes.

ADVANCE PREPARATION: You can simmer the garlic a few hours before serving. Strain, reheat and add the egg etc. shortly before serving.

PER PORTION

Calories	102	Protein	3 G
Fat	1 G	Carbohydrate	20 G
Sodium	1,033 MG	Cholesterol	0

VEGETABLE SOUP WITH PISTOU
La soupe au pistou

SERVES 6 GENEROUSLY

This is one of the classic soups of Provence, a thick vegetable and bean soup, enriched at the last minute with pistou, that all-time favorite paste made with basil, garlic, tomato, olive oil, and Parmesan cheese. The soup itself has many versions, and as in most traditional Provençal dishes, all the people I talked to about this soup say theirs is the authentic one, *la vraie*. When fresh *haricots écossés* (borlotti beans) are in season, there's nothing better. Otherwise dried white beans alone will be just fine. What all the different versions of soupe au pistou have in common is the simple, straightforward method of making the soup. Nothing is sautéed first; all the vegetables go into a huge soup pot and are cooked together until tender and fragrant (this differs from the way I had always made this soup before, and I've changed my method accordingly). Dried beans are cooked separately, then added. The pasta is added shortly before serving and finally the crowning pistou enrichment. In my own version I hold back some of the green beans and zucchini until the last 10 minutes of cooking, because I like to have some bright green vegetables in the soup. And, of course, the pistou I use is my low-fat version.

Although this is a spring/summer soup in Provence (most of the people I've talked to in Provence use only fresh beans and spring vegetables in season), I love to pull a jar of frozen pistou out of my freezer in late fall or winter and bring sunshine into my kitchen by making a rich, warming pot of this potage. It's a very popular meal.

½	**pound (225 g) green beans or half green beans and half yellow wax beans, trimmed and broken into 1-inch (2.5 cm) pieces (2 cups)**
2	**medium-size zucchini, scrubbed and diced**
1	**large or 2 medium-size onions, chopped**
6	**large garlic cloves, minced or put through a press**
1½	**pounds (675 g) fresh borlotti (cranberry) beans (2 heaped cups, shelled) or 2 cups (500 ml) cooked white beans**
2	**large carrots, chopped**

VEGETABLE SOUPS

2 celery ribs, chopped

2 leeks, white part only, well washed and sliced

2 medium-size turnips, peeled and diced

1 pound (450 g/4 medium-size) new potatoes, diced

1 pound (450 g/4 medium-size) tomatoes, peeled, seeded, and chopped

3 quarts (3 l) water

   a bouquet garni made with a bay leaf, a few fresh thyme sprigs, a Parmesan rind if desired, and a parsley sprig

   salt and freshly ground pepper to taste

¼ pound (115 g) macaroni, fusilli, vermicelli, or broken spaghetti

1 recipe low-fat pistou (page 109)

Set aside half the green beans and half the zucchini. Combine the vegetables, the fresh beans if you're using them, the water, bouquet garni, salt, and pepper in a large soup pot and bring to a boil. Reduce the heat, cover, and simmer for 1½ hours. Add the white beans if you're using them. Taste and adjust salt and pepper.

Add the reserved green beans and zucchini and the pasta. Cook for 10 minutes or until the pasta is cooked al dente and the vegetables are tender but still bright green.

Serve in wide soup bowls and top each serving with a tablespoon of pistou, to be stirred into the soup. Pass the remaining pistou at the table. (You can also stir the pistou into the soup, but it's more fun to let people do it themselves, and the flavor of the basil paste will be more intense when stirred directly into the individual servings.)

Note: You can omit the Parmesan from the pistou for an even lower-fat version. Use the Parmesan rind in the bouquet garni to get a cheesy flavor.

ADVANCE PREPARATION: This soup will keep for hours on top of the stove and can be cooked a day or two ahead of time, up to the adding of the reserved green beans, zucchini, and pasta. It makes great leftovers and freezes well, although the pasta will become very soggy. The pistou will keep for a few days in the refrigerator and for months in the freezer.

VARIATIONS: You can add other vegetables, such as fresh peas, yellow squash, or greens, to the soup. You could also double the quantity of pistou.

PER PORTION

Calories	378	Protein	16 G
Fat	5 G	Carbohydrate	71 G
Sodium	248 MG	Cholesterol	3 MG

''ONE-EYED'' BOUILLABAISSE (LEEK, POTATO, AND TOMATO SOUP WITH POACHED EGGS)

Aigo sau d'iou   Bouillabaisse borgne

SERVES 4 GENEROUSLY

I can't figure out why this is called "one-eyed bouillabaisse," but that's the literal translation. The food writer Waverley Root thinks the name is meant to be a put-down because this vegetable soup is far from a rich fish bouillabaisse. And yet it is incredibly nourishing and tasty and makes a wonderful supper with a tossed green salad and a glass of chilled rosé or fruity red wine. In Provence the dish is eaten like a traditional bouillabaisse, with the broth served in a bowl over garlic croutons and the potatoes and eggs eaten separately. But I like it all served together in a wide soup bowl.

1   tablespoon olive oil
2   large leeks, white part only, well washed and sliced
1   large onion, chopped
1   pound (450 g/4 medium-size) tomatoes, peeled, seeded, and chopped
4   large garlic cloves, crushed or put through a press
    salt to taste
6   cups (1.5 l) water

VEGETABLE SOUPS

**a bouquet garni made with 2 bay leaves, a few fresh
thyme and parsley sprigs, and a fennel stalk if available**

1   **strip of orange zest**

1   **pound (450 g/4 medium-size) new or boiling
    potatoes, thinly sliced**

¼   **teaspoon saffron threads**
    freshly ground pepper to taste
    pinch of cayenne pepper (optional)

4   **medium-size eggs**

¼   **cup (about 15 g/½ large bunch) chopped fresh
    parsley**

8   **thick garlic croutons (page 83)**

Heat the oil in a large, heavy-bottomed soup pot or casserole over medium-low heat and add the leeks and onion. Sauté, stirring, until they begin to soften, about 5 minutes, and add the tomatoes, garlic, and salt. Stir together and cook for a minute or two, then add the water, bouquet garni, orange zest, and potatoes and bring to a boil.

Add the saffron, more salt if desired, and pepper. Cover, reduce the heat to medium, and simmer for 15 to 20 minutes or until the potatoes are tender. Add the cayenne if desired, taste, and adjust seasonings.

Turn the soup down to a bare simmer. Carefully break the eggs into the soup. As soon as they are set—after about 4 to 6 minutes—sprinkle on the parsley and serve.

To serve in the traditional Provençal way: Using a slotted spoon, transfer the potatoes and poached eggs to a warm serving platter. Serve the broth over the croutons in wide soup bowls and the potatoes and eggs on side plates.

To serve in one bowl: Place the croutons in wide soup bowls and carefully ladle in the soup and potatoes, with a poached egg in each bowl.

ADVANCE PREPARATION: The soup can be prepared up until the addition of the eggs hours ahead of serving. Reheat and add the eggs just before serving.

PER PORTION

Calories	371	Protein	14 G
Fat	10 G	Carbohydrate	59 G
Sodium	298 MG	Cholesterol	187 MG

SPINACH BOUILLABAISSE
Boui-abaisso d'espinarc   Bouillabaisse d'épinards

SERVES 4 GENEROUSLY

This is a classic Provençal soup and makes a filling and comforting supper. Traditionally the spinach is blanched first, then chopped, then cooked with the onion etc. I think it's a shame to throw out the blanching water, so I use that as the stock.

4	quarts (3.75 l) water
1½	tablespoons salt or to taste
2½	pounds (1.2 kg) fresh spinach, stems removed
1	tablespoon olive oil
1	medium-size onion, chopped, or 2 medium-size leeks, white part only, well washed and chopped
8	large garlic cloves, minced or put through a press
1	pound (450 g/4 medium-size) new or boiling potatoes, sliced
	a bouquet garni made with a bay leaf, a few sprigs of fresh thyme, a fennel stick if available, and a few sprigs of fresh parsley
¼	teaspoon saffron threads
	freshly ground pepper to taste
4	large eggs
1	ounce (30 g) Gruyère cheese, grated (¼ cup) (optional)
4	thick garlic croutons (page 83)

Bring the water to a boil in a large pot and add the salt and spinach. When the water comes back to a boil, count to 20 and drain over a bowl. Press the water out of the spinach with the back of a wooden spoon, and when the spinach is cool enough to handle, chop coarsely. Set aside 6 cups (1.5 l) of the blanching water.

Heat the olive oil in a large heavy-bottomed soup pot or casserole over medium-low heat and add the onion. Cook, stirring, until tender and translucent, about 5 to 8 minutes, and add the garlic and spinach. Stir together for about 30 seconds and add the blanching water, potatoes, and bouquet garni. Bring to a boil, add the saffron, reduce the heat, cover, and simmer for 15 to 20 minutes, until the potatoes are tender but not falling apart. Add pepper, taste, and adjust seasonings.

Turn the soup down to a bare simmer. Carefully break the eggs into the soup. As soon as they are set—after about 4 to 6 minutes—sprinkle on the cheese and serve. Place a crouton in each bowl and carefully ladle in the soup with an egg on top.

ADVANCE PREPARATION: The vegetables can be prepared hours ahead of serving, but the soup should be served right away.

PER PORTION

Calories	367	Protein	18 G
Fat	10 G	Carbohydrate	53 G
Sodium	1,368 MG	Cholesterol	213 MG

BOUILLABAISSE OF FRESH PEAS

Boui-abaisso de pichoun pese   Bouillabaisse de petits-pois

SERVES 4 GENEROUSLY

The great Provençal gastronome J. B. Reboul almost apologizes for including a recipe for this soup in his famous Provençal cookbook, *La Cuisinière Provençale.* "This is not a very distinguished dish," he says, "but it was often eaten in the old days in Provence, and is still quite popular today." Why make excuses? The nourishing soup fills your mouth with the sweet flavor of fresh peas. It makes a perfect spring dish. Only sweet fresh peas will work.

1½	quarts (1.5 l) water
1	tablespoon olive oil
1	medium-size onion, chopped
1½	pounds (675 g/6 medium-size) waxy potatoes, sliced
4	pounds (1.75 kg) fresh peas, shelled, 4 cups
4	large garlic cloves, minced or put through a press
	a bouquet garni made with 1 bay leaf, a few fresh thyme sprigs, a few parsley sprigs, and a fennel stalk if available
¼	teaspoon saffron threads
	salt and freshly ground pepper to taste
4	medium-size eggs
3	tablespoons chopped fresh parsley or a mixture of herbs such as basil, chives, tarragon, mint
4 to 8	thick garlic croutons (page 83)

Bring the water to a boil in a saucepan.

Heat the olive oil in a large heavy-bottomed soup pot or casserole over medium heat and add the onion. Stir until the onion begins to soften, then add the potatoes and peas. Stir together for a minute and add the boiling water, garlic, bouquet garni, saffron, salt, and pepper. Cover and simmer for 20 minutes, until the peas and potatoes are tender and the broth sweet.

Turn the soup down to a bare simmer. Carefully break the eggs into the soup. As soon as they are set—after about 4 to 6 minutes—sprinkle on the herbs and serve. Place 1 or 2 croutons in each bowl and carefully ladle in the soup with an egg on top.

ADVANCE PREPARATION: The vegetables can be prepared hours ahead of serving, but the soup should be served right away.

PER PORTION

Calories	480	Protein	21 G
Fat	10 G	Carbohydrate	77 G
Sodium	289 MG	Cholesterol	187 MG

LITTLE GARDEN SOUP
Ourteto

SERVES 4

On some of the evenings during the fall I spent in Provence, my dinner consisted of the fruits of an afternoon walk in the hills with my neighbor Raymond. "What's this?" I'd ask, pulling up a leaf. "Oh that, that's wild spinach. Or do you mean the dandelion greens, there?" The nettles I could recognize; picking them was an altogether different challenge. You can choose from a number of herbs or greens for this soup, which has the same healing powers, according to Provençal legend, as aigo boulido (page 132). The Provençal word *ourteto* means "little garden."

1	**pound (450 g) spinach, preferably young, tender leaves, stems removed and leaves coarsely chopped (8 cups)**
2	**cups (500 ml/120 g) combined greens such as nettles, sorrel, watercress, dandelion greens, arugula, beet greens, radish greens, parsley, stems removed and leaves coarsely chopped**
1	**bunch of scallions, both white and green parts, thinly sliced**
4	**garlic cloves, or more to taste, minced or put through a press**
1½	**quarts (1.5 l) water**
	salt and freshly ground pepper to taste
4	**thick garlic croutons (page 83)**
1	**tablespoon olive oil**
2	**large eggs, beaten**

Combine the spinach, greens, scallions, garlic, water, salt, and pepper in a large soup pot or Dutch oven and bring to a boil. Reduce the heat, cover, and simmer for 20 to 30 minutes, until you have a sweet, fragrant broth. Taste and adjust seasonings, adding more salt, pepper, or garlic as desired.

Brush the garlic croutons with olive oil and place in wide soup bowls.

Remove the soup from the heat. Beat the eggs in a bowl and stir in a ladleful of the hot soup. Stir this back into the soup. Serve at once over the croutons.

ADVANCE PREPARATION: The greens can be washed and chopped hours ahead of time, but the soup should be made shortly before serving. You can, however, make the broth, turn off the heat, and allow it to sit for about an hour while you have drinks and a first course. Reheat and proceed with the eggs just before serving.

PER PORTION

Calories	202	Protein	10 G
Fat	7 G	Carbohydrate	26 G
Sodium	324 MG	Cholesterol	106 MG

GARLIC SOUP WITH GREENS AND POACHED EGG
Ourteto 2

SERVES 4

In this version of ourteto, a small garden in a bowl, the greens are barely cooked. I ate this soup for a week once, when I had a bad cold. I'd bought a bag of dandelion greens at the market, and every night I'd throw them into my garlic broth. It was a wonderful meal in a bowl. If you want to strain out the garlic cloves you can, but I like to eat them with the soup.

2	quarts (2 l) water
1	head (about 16 cloves) of garlic, cloves mashed slightly and peeled
1	bay leaf
1 or 2	fresh sage or thyme sprigs
1 to 2	teaspoons salt to taste
2	cups (120 g) dandelion or other greens, stems removed
	freshly ground pepper to taste
4	large eggs
4	thick garlic croutons (page 83)
¼	cup (about 15 g/½ large bunch) chopped fresh parsley

Combine the water, garlic, bay leaf, sage, and salt in a large soup pot or Dutch oven and bring to a boil. Reduce the heat, cover, and simmer for 30 to 40 minutes, until the garlic is tender and the broth fragrant. Taste and adjust salt. Remove the herbs and garlic cloves if you wish.

Stir the greens into the soup and add pepper. Carefully break the eggs into the soup and poach. This should take 4 to 6 minutes.

Distribute the croutons among 4 wide soup bowls. Sprinkle the parsley into the soup and serve, carefully ladling a poached egg, with the broth and greens, into each bowl.

ADVANCE PREPARATION: The broth can be prepared hours before serving and removed from the heat. Bring back to a simmer and proceed with the recipe shortly before serving.

PER PORTION

Calories	203	Protein	11 G
Fat	6 G	Carbohydrate	26 G
Sodium	1,120 MG	Cholesterol	213 MG

VEGETABLE AND CILANTRO SOUP

SERVES 4 TO 6

On Saturday mornings at the big market in Apt there are many Arab vendors as well as French. Their tables are piled high with cilantro, peppers, mint, lemons, and couscous. I'm sure this soup is inspired by North African cuisines brought to Provence when the French colonialists—the *pieds noirs*—came back to France in the sixties, after the Algerian war. This is a simple but rich-tasting, pungent soup with a smooth, comforting texture.

1	**pound (450 g) carrots, chopped**
2	**medium-size leeks, white part only, well washed and sliced**
4	**garlic cloves, minced or put through a press**
½	**pound (225 g/2 medium-size) waxy potatoes, peeled and diced**
5	**cups (1.25 l) water**
	salt and freshly ground pepper to taste
2	**bunches of cilantro, stems trimmed**
½ to 1	**cup (125 to 250 ml) low-fat (2%, not skim) milk to taste**
	cilantro leaves for garnish

Combine the carrots, leeks, garlic, potatoes, water, salt, and pepper in a soup pot. Bring to a boil, reduce the heat, cover, and simmer for 1 hour.

Add the cilantro to the soup and blend until fairly smooth in a blender or food processor, or with a hand blender. Return to the pot, add the milk, and heat through. Taste and adjust seasonings. Serve, garnishing each bowl with a few leaves of cilantro.

ADVANCE PREPARATION: The soup can be made hours ahead of serving and reheated gently. It freezes well and will be even more pungent when you thaw it. Blend or whisk vigorously after thawing to restore the soup's texture.

PER PORTION

Calories	109	Protein	4 G
Fat	1 G	Carbohydrate	22 G
Sodium	63 MG	Cholesterol	2 MG

SABINE'S TOMATO SOUP

Soupe aux tomates de Sabine

SERVES 4

My close friend Sabine Boulongne doesn't come from Provence, yet she's always coming up with delicious meals that excite the palate with the flavors of the south of France. She tells me she learned this tomato soup from her Swiss mother, but I wonder if the amazing broth isn't due to her own gift for seasoning and talent for making simple, mouth-watering dishes. "There's only one secret," she says, "good fresh tomatoes and herbs."

3   **pounds (1.35 kg/12 medium-size) tomatoes, quartered**

1   **quart (1 l) water**

½   **cup (125 ml) fresh rosemary leaves**

¼   **cup (62 ml) fresh thyme leaves**

1   **bay leaf**

   salt and freshly ground pepper to taste

Combine all the ingredients in a saucepan and bring to a boil. Reduce the heat, cover, and simmer for 1 hour.

Press the soup through the fine blade of a food mill or through a strainer. Return to the pot, taste, and adjust seasonings. Heat through and serve.

ADVANCE PREPARATION: This will hold for several hours, in or out of the refrigerator. It's also good the day after you make it.

PER PORTION

Calories	74	Protein	3 G
Fat	1 G	Carbohydrate	16 G
Sodium	29 MG	Cholesterol	0

- Add a few cloves of garlic to the mixture, either minced, pressed, or whole. Serve over garlic croutons (page 83).
- Stir in a tablespoon or two of low-fat pistou (page 109) and 2 or 3 tablespoons freshly grated Parmesan or Gruyère cheese just before serving.
- Once you've strained the soup and returned it to the pot, add 1 pound (450 g/4 medium-size) waxy potatoes, sliced, and simmer until cooked through.
- Once you've strained the soup and returned it to the pot, add 1 cup (100 g) fusilli, macaroni, or penne and simmer until cooked through.

TOMATO-RICE SOUP

La soupo de riz à la poumo d'amour
La soupe de riz à la tomate

SERVES 4

Use a chewy round rice, like Italian Arborio (or rice from the Camargue if you can get it), for this comforting soup. Fresh or canned tomatoes will do, so it makes a meal at any time of year. Traditionally this would be served with grated cheese, but I omit the cheese and add a Parmesan rind to the broth as it simmers to give the soup a cheesy flavor.

1	tablespoon olive oil
1	medium-size onion, chopped
1	medium-size carrot, chopped
1	medium-size celery rib, chopped
4	garlic cloves, minced or put through a press
1¼	pounds (565 g/5 medium-size) fresh or canned tomatoes, peeled, seeded, and chopped
	pinch of sugar
	salt and freshly ground pepper to taste
1½	quarts (1.5 l) garlic stock (page 130), chicken stock (page 128), or water
1	bay leaf
2	teaspoons fresh thyme leaves or 1 teaspoon dried
2	teaspoons chopped fresh oregano or 1 teaspoon dried
1	Parmesan rind
½	cup (100 g) rice

Heat the olive oil in a large heavy-bottomed soup pot or Dutch oven over medium-low heat and add the onion, carrot, and celery. Cook, stirring, until the onion begins to soften, about 5 minutes. Add one of the garlic cloves and cook, stirring, for a minute, until the garlic begins to color. Add the tomatoes, remaining garlic, sugar, salt, and pepper. Stir together and simmer over medium heat, stirring often, for 10 minutes, until the tomatoes have cooked down a bit and are beginning to smell fragrant.

Add all the remaining ingredients except the rice and bring to a boil. Reduce the heat, cover, and cook for 30 minutes. Taste and adjust seasonings, adding more salt, herbs, or garlic if you wish. Stir in the rice, cover, simmer for 15 to 20 minutes, until the rice is cooked al dente, and serve.

ADVANCE PREPARATION: This can be made hours ahead of serving and reheated. The rice will no longer be al dente, however, and will have absorbed some of the broth.

PER PORTION

Calories	195	Protein	5 G
Fat	4 G	Carbohydrate	36 G
Sodium	738 MG	Cholesterol	0

PUMPKIN OR WINTER SQUASH SOUP
La Soupe de courge

SERVES 4

Winter squash is made into many different kinds of soup throughout Provence. Some are thickened with potatoes, others with bread. This sweet-tasting, comforting winter soup is thickened with rice.

1	tablespoon olive oil
1	medium-size onion, chopped
2	pounds (900 g) fresh pumpkin or other winter squash such as Hubbard or acorn, peeled and diced (about 6 cups)
2	large garlic cloves, minced or put through a press
1½	quarts (1.5 l) water or chicken, vegetable, or garlic stock (pages 127–30)
1	bay leaf
2	teaspoons fresh thyme leaves or 1 teaspoon dried
½	cup (100 g) short-grain rice
	salt and freshly ground pepper to taste
	pinch of freshly grated nutmeg
¼	cup (about ½ bunch) chopped fresh parsley

Heat the oil in a heavy-bottomed soup pot or Dutch oven over medium-low heat and add the onion. Cook, stirring often, until tender, 5 to 8 minutes. Add the pumpkin and garlic, stir together for about 30 seconds, and add the water, bay leaf, and thyme. Bring to a boil and add the rice, salt, and pepper. Reduce the heat, cover, and simmer for 1 hour, until the squash is tender and the broth fragrant.

Remove the soup from the heat and puree with a hand blender or in a blender or food processor fitted with the steel blade, or put through the medium blade of a food mill. Return to the heat, add the nutmeg, taste, and adjust seasonings. Heat through, sprinkle on the parsley, and serve.

ADVANCE PREPARATION: You can make this soup hours before serving and hold it in or out of the refrigerator. Add the parsley shortly before serving.

PER PORTION

Calories	183	Protein	4 G
Fat	4 G	Carbohydrate	35 G
Sodium	5 MG	Cholesterol	0

PUMPKIN AND WHITE BEAN SOUP
Soupe de courge et haricots

SERVES 6

This is just one of many Provençal white bean soups. It's thinner and lighter than many. In summer tomatoes would replace the pumpkin or winter squash, and basil might replace the sage.

1 **pound (450 g/2 heaped cups) dried white beans, washed, picked over, and soaked in 1 quart (1 l) water for at least 6 hours**

2 **quarts (2 l) water**

1 **onion stuck with 2 cloves**

1 **bay leaf**

salt to taste

1 **tablespoon olive oil**

2 **medium-size leeks, white part only, well washed and minced**

1 **pound (450 g) pumpkin or winter squash, peeled and finely diced**

2	garlic cloves, minced or put through a press
	freshly ground pepper to taste
6 to 10	fresh sage leaves, to taste, cut into thin slivers, plus additional sage leaves, slivered if large, for garnish

Drain the beans and combine with the water, onion, and bay leaf in a large soup pot or Dutch oven. Bring to a boil and skim off any foam that rises. Reduce the heat, cover, and simmer for 1 hour. Add about 2 teaspoons salt or more to taste and continue to simmer.

Heat the olive oil in a saucepan or a nonstick skillet over medium-low heat and add the leeks. Cook, stirring, until the leeks begin to soften, about 5 minutes. Add the pumpkin and garlic and sprinkle with about ¼ teaspoon salt. Continue to cook for about 5 minutes, stirring often, until the pumpkin begins to soften. Ladle in some stock from the beans. Stir together and transfer the mixture back to the bean pot. Cover and simmer for 30 to 60 minutes, until the beans are thoroughly tender, even mushy. Taste, adjust salt, and add pepper.

Remove the bay leaf and the cloves from the onion. Return the onion to mixture. Put the mixture through the fine or medium blade of a food mill and return to the heat. Stir in the slivered sage, heat through gently, stirring, and serve, garnishing each bowl with additional fresh sage.

ADVANCE PREPARATION: The soup will hold for a few days in the refrigerator and freezes well.

PER PORTION

Calories	322	Protein	19 G
Fat	3 G	Carbohydrate	57 G
Sodium	21 MG	Cholesterol	0

VEGETABLE SOUPS

THICK CHICK-PEA SOUP
La soupe aux pois chiches

SERVES 4 TO 6

This is a hearty soup, very easy to make. If you use a hand blender to puree the chick-peas as I usually do, you will have a coarse mixture, thick enough to eat with a fork. If you wish, you can thin it out with more water, but I like it this way. It definitely makes a meal, with a green salad and good crusty bread.

1	**pound (450 g/2 heaped cups) dried chick-peas, picked over and soaked overnight or for at least 6 hours in 1½ quarts (1.5 l) water**
2	**quarts (2 l) water**
1	**large leek, white part only, well washed and chopped**
4 to 5	**garlic cloves, to taste, minced or put through a press**
1	**pound (450 g/4 medium-size) canned or fresh tomatoes, peeled, seeded, and chopped**
	a bouquet garni made with 1 bay leaf, a few fresh thyme sprigs, and a Parmesan rind
	salt and freshly ground pepper to taste
1	**tablespoon olive oil**
¼	**cup (about 15 g/½ large bunch) chopped fresh parsley or sage**
4 to 6	**garlic croutons (page 83)**

Drain the soaked chick-peas and combine with the water in a large soup pot or Dutch oven. Bring to a boil. Skim off any foam that rises. Add the leek, all but one of the garlic cloves, the tomatoes, and the bouquet garni. Reduce the heat, cover, and simmer for 1 hour. Add salt to taste and simmer for another 30 to 60 minutes, until the chick-peas are thoroughly tender. Remove from the heat. Discard the bouquet garni.

Puree the mixture coarsely, using a hand blender or food processor, or put the mixture through the medium blade of a food mill. Return to the pot and heat through, stirring. Add lots of pepper and adjust the salt. Stir in 2 teaspoons of the olive oil, the remaining clove of garlic, and the parsley or sage.

Serve, garnishing each bowl with a few drops of the remaining olive oil and a garlic crouton.

ADVANCE PREPARATION: This will keep well for 2 days in the refrigerator, without the final addition of garlic, oil, and parsley. Add after heating through, just before serving. The soup will be quite thick after refrigeration, so you might want to thin it out.

PER PORTION

Calories	423	Protein	19 G
Fat	8 G	Carbohydrate	71 G
Sodium	356 MG	Cholesterol	0

LENTIL SOUP
Soupe de lentilles

SERVES 6

Provençal lentil soup is a simple puree served with garlic croutons and garnished with parsley. It needs little else. Some of the recipes I've seen call for a ham bone or bacon, but I like the pure taste of lentils (with garlic, of course). The goat cheese makes a delicious garnish.

1	pound (450 g/2 heaped cups) lentils, picked over and washed
1	medium-size onion, chopped
3 to 4	large garlic cloves, to taste, minced or put through a press
2	quarts (2 l) water
1	bay leaf
	salt and freshly ground pepper to taste
2½	ounces (75 g) fresh goat cheese, thinly sliced
6	garlic croutons (page 83)
¼	cup (about 15 g/½ large bunch) chopped fresh parsley

Combine the lentils, onion, 2 garlic cloves, the water, and the bay leaf in a large heavy-bottomed soup pot or Dutch oven and bring to a boil. Reduce the heat and simmer for 30 minutes. Add salt and pepper and continue to simmer for 15 to 30 minutes, until the lentils are thoroughly tender. Remove from the heat, remove the bay leaf, and puree the soup coarsely in a blender or food processor, or in the pot with a hand blender, or put through the medium blade of a food mill. Return to the pot, stir in the remaining garlic, taste, and adjust the seasoning. Heat through.

Distribute the soup among warmed wide soup bowls. Float a slice of goat cheese and a garlic crouton in each bowl, sprinkle with parsley, and serve.

ADVANCE PREPARATION: The soup can be made hours or even a day ahead of serving. It also freezes well. The remaining garlic should be added to the soup shortly before serving.

Calories	398	Protein	27 G
Fat	4 G	Carbohydrate	65 G
Sodium	262 MG	Cholesterol	5 MG

WHEATBERRY SOUP
La soupo d'espeuto   Soupe d'épeautre

SERVES 6

Une vraie soupe provençale

A real Provençal soup

Epeautre, a strain of wheat, has been cultivated for centuries throughout Provence. It's a delicious, sweet-tasting grain, with the same golden-brown color and chewy texture as wheatberries, but the kernels are not quite as round and are a little softer. In Provence it's the main ingredient in thick, hearty soups, and more recently restaurant chefs have been using it in "risotto" (which I call pilaf; see the recipe on page 366).

Soupe d'épeautre is traditionally eaten at the end of the wheat harvest in Provence, around the time of the autumnal equinox. Families that haven't farmed for a generation or two still gather on an autumn Sunday for the soup. There are many versions, some of which combine the grain with beans, all differing from mine in that the grain is cooked with mutton or a ham bone. My soupe d'épeautre is vegetarian, and I must say I prefer it to the Provençal soup, because the subtle perfume of the wheat is not overpowered by stronger-tasting ingredients.

½   **ounce (15 g/½ cup) dried porcini**
2   **cups (500 ml) boiling water**
1   **tablespoon olive oil**
1   **large onion, chopped**

1	pound (450 g/3 to 4 large or 6 to 10 medium or small) carrots, peeled and chopped
1	medium-size turnip, peeled and diced
1	celery rib with leaves, chopped
1	large leek, white part only, well washed and chopped
4	large garlic cloves, minced or put through a press
2	cups (15 oz/420 g) whole wheatberries, rinsed
3	quarts (3 l) water
	a bouquet garni made with a bay leaf, a few fresh thyme sprigs, and a parsley sprig
	salt and freshly ground pepper to taste
1	teaspoon fresh thyme leaves or ½ teaspoon crushed dried, or more to taste
1½	cups (375 ml/1 15–ounce/420 g can) cooked white beans (optional)
⅓	cup (about 20 g/⅔ large bunch) chopped fresh parsley (optional)
2	ounces (60 g) Gruyère cheese, grated (½ cup) (optional)

Place the mushrooms in a bowl and pour on the boiling water. Let sit for 15 to 30 minutes, until softened. Drain through a cheesecloth- or paper towel-lined strainer and reserve the soaking liquid. Rinse the mushrooms thoroughly and squeeze dry over the strainer. Chop coarsely and set aside.

Heat the oil in a large heavy-bottomed soup pot or Dutch oven over medium-low heat. Add the onion, carrots, turnip, celery, and leek and cook, stirring, for 5 to 10 minutes, being careful not to brown, until the onion has softened and the vegetables are fragrant.

Add the garlic, wheatberries, chopped mushrooms, water, mushroom-soaking liquid, and bouquet garni. Bring to a boil and add the salt, pepper, and thyme. Cover and simmer for 1 hour, until the grains are tender and the soup is aromatic. Stir in the beans if you're using them and the parsley and serve, sprinkling each serving with Gruyère cheese if desired.

ADVANCE PREPARATION: This will keep for 3 or 4 days in the refrigerator. You may want to add more water when you reheat the soup, because the grains will continue to absorb the broth.

PER PORTION

Calories	289	Protein	10 G
Fat	5 G	Carbohydrate	56 G
Sodium	54 MG	Cholesterol	0

COLD ZUCCHINI SOUP WITH FRESH MINT
Soupe de courgettes à la menthe

SERVES 4

My friend Sabine Boulongne makes this thick, refreshing soup in the summer. It's incredibly easy to make, and the mint gives zucchini a new dimension.

2 **pounds (900 g) zucchini, thickly sliced**

2 **cups (500 ml) water**

3 **cups (750 ml) plain low-fat yogurt or fromage blanc (page 99)**

1 **teaspoon crushed coriander seeds**

2 **garlic cloves, minced or put through a press (optional)**

¼ **cup (62 ml) slivered mint leaves**

salt and freshly ground pepper to taste

2 **tablespoons fresh lemon juice**

fresh mint sprigs for garnish

Steam the zucchini above the water for 10 to 15 minutes or until thoroughly tender. Blend with the water in a food processor, blender, or hand blender or put through the medium blade of a food mill.

Mix in the yogurt, coriander, garlic if you're using it, and mint. Add salt and pepper. Chill for several hours. Just before serving, stir in the lemon juice. Garnish with mint and serve.

ADVANCE PREPARATION: This must be made several hours before serving. It can be made a day ahead of time, but don't add the mint until a few hours before serving.

PER PORTION

Calories	131	Protein	12 G
Fat	.69 G	Carbohydrate	21 G
Sodium	136 MG	Cholesterol	3 MG

CHAPTER 5

FISH SOUPS

Every Mediterranean country has its fish soup, but none are as famous as the fish
soups of Provence. That is why I've put these soups into their own chapter.
Bouillabaisse, especially, is one of the emblematic dishes of this French region.
Eating this hearty, filling meal is a ritual, and as you can see from the quote, the
people of Provence are very emotional about what constitutes an authentic one.

Not all of the fish soups from Provence are as demanding and time-
consuming or expensive as bouillabaisse and *soupe de poissons* (rich fish soup). The
other soups in this chapter are very light and require no preliminary fish broth or
soupe; the liquid part of the soup is flavored by the aromatics that go into it and by
the fish as it cooks, so preparation is simple. But all of the soups in this chapter make
a meal, even if some, such as mussel soup, salt cod bouillabaisse, and the *soupe de
poissons,* usually appear on the *entrée* (first-course) section of Provençal restaurant
menus. And despite what Dr. A. Magnan from Nice says about the types of fish
required for a *"vraie"* bouillabaisse, you don't have to use the Mediterranean fish
that traditionally go into this soup; indeed, you wouldn't be able to make it
elsewhere without deviating. The most important requirement for any fish dish is
that the fish be utterly fresh. So for the bouillabaisse and the *aigo sau,* a much simpler
fish soup, I've given you lots of suggestions for fish. The character of the soups will
be slightly different, because the texture and flavors of the fish are different; but that
essential Provençal perfume—garlic, herbs, orange peel, saffron, tomatoes—will be
present.

The tradition of eating the elements of fish soups separately, as is also done
with some vegetable soups, often prevails in Provence. Once cooked, the fish and
vegetables (potatoes, usually) will be transferred to a warm platter and moistened
with a small amount of broth. The *soupe* will be served first, usually accompanied by
garlic croutons and *rouille,* a spicy garlic mayonnaise (page 105). Then the fish will
be eaten with the vegetables. I sometimes follow this procedure (see the delicious

FISH SOUPS

mackerel bouillabaisse on page 177), but just as often I eat everything together in one big, filling bowl. Given the fact that we're already breaking all of the Provençal rules by using other-than-Provençal fish, I figure we can eat our fish soups however we please.

FISH STOCK
Fumet de poissons

Fish stock, or fumet, is made by simmering fish bones and heads in water with onions, aromatics, and white wine. If you can't get hold of fish bones or heads, make a mild fish fumet using about ½ pound (225 g) fish fillets. Avoid fatty fish like salmon, bluefish, catfish, and mackerel, because their flavors are too strong. Carcasses of flatfish like sole, flounder, brill, and whiting are the best.

2¼	pounds (1 kg) lean flatfish bones and heads
1	shallot, minced
1	medium-size onion, chopped
2	ounces (60 g) mushrooms, sliced
1	carrot, sliced
1	celery rib, sliced
1	leek, white part only, well washed and sliced
2	garlic cloves, peeled
	a bouquet garni made with a bay leaf, a fresh thyme sprig, and several parsley sprigs
1½	quarts (1.5 l) water
	salt to taste
½	cup (125 ml) dry white wine

Separate the fish heads from the skeletons. Soak the fish bones and heads in a bowl of cold water while you prepare the vegetables. Drain, pat dry, and crush the bones slightly with a rolling pin or place in a plastic bag and break the skeletons up with your hands.

Combine everything but the wine in a large soup pot or saucepan and bring to a simmer over medium heat. Skim off all the foam that rises. Continue to skim until no foam remains, then cover, reduce the heat, and simmer for 15 minutes. Add the wine and simmer, covered, for 15 minutes longer. Remove from the heat. Don't cook any longer, or the fumet will be bitter.

Strain the fumet at once into a bowl through a fine strainer or a strainer lined with cheesecloth, pressing the fish bones against the strainer with the back of a ladle or wooden spoon. Correct the seasoning. Cool and refrigerate until ready to use.

ADVANCE PREPARATION: This can be kept for a day in the refrigerator and can be frozen, but it won't taste as mild once thawed.

PER PORTION

Calories	42	Protein	9 GM
Fat	.14 G	Carbohydrate	4 GM
Sodium	237 MG	Cholesterol	0

La bouillabaisse is not like Canon Law, constant from Lille to Montpellier. La Bouillabaisse is rather like a woman! One person prefers the blond, shapely Rubens, the other prefers the brunette with big dark eyes, the other a thick-haired redhead. Some like a virtuous woman, others prefer her more vulgar—i.e., a bouillabaisse without a Provençal accent, or on the contrary, one full of onions, garlic, thyme, fennel, bay laurel, other spices and saffron. These aromatics often mask the simplicity or the paucity of fish, for did you know that to prepare a real, authentic bouillabaisse you need a number of very ordinary fish?

I will name them: *langouste-rascasse* [spiny lobster] (two species live in the Mediterranean); *le rouget* [red mullet], called the "sea rooster," with its firm, tasty flesh; *la vive* [weever], with its delicate flesh—but be careful of its dangerous spines! the elegant, agile *roucauo* [wrasse], with its blue-back and greenish tints; the curious *Saint-Pierre* [John Dory]; *le congre* [conger eel], eel of the sea; *la baudroie* [monkfish], called the sea-devil, with its enormous head and ugly body; *le loup* [sea bass]; *le merlan* [whiting]; the crabs which you must not disdain and must know how to blend up. Finally we should know that the special flavors of the bouillabaisse come especially from *rascasses* [scorpion fish], beautifully colored *girelles* [rainbow wrasses]—scarlet, turquoise, violet; from *langoustines* [Dublin Bay prawns] . . . and from saffron, the same saffron that goes into so many sauces: elixir of Garus, Irish liqueur of Hacubac, general stimulant and emmenagogue.

I have not enumerated this long list of fish to discourage you from making bouillabaisse or so that you will punish me for not giving you the recipe. I simply wanted to show that there is bouillabaisse and bouillabaisse.

DR. LOUIS CAMOUS, NICE
FROM *LE TRÉSOR DE LA CUISINE DU BASSIN MÉDITER-RANÉEN*

BOUILLABAISSE "DÉGUSTATION"
Lou boui-abaisso

SERVES 6

This is based on the least filling of the two versions of bouillabaisse served at the Restaurant du Bacon in Cap d'Antibes. It is called *Bouillabaisse Dégustation*, or Tasting Bouillabaisse, because fish fillets, rather than whole fish, are served with the rich fish broth and accompaniments. There's less fish, so the dish is lighter (that said, this is a filling meal). It's also easier to serve. Everything else about this version is the same as in the traditional bouillabaisse: the rich fish soup base, *la soupe de poissons,* is made in the same way, and the fish and soup are served with sliced potatoes and croutons topped with a garlicky *rouille.*

Obviously you won't be able to get the same Mediterranean fish that go into Provençal bouillabaisse, but with a selection of at least three kinds of the fresh fish suggested here you'll come up with something quite memorable. I'm listing the fish first in the recipe, even though you don't cook them until the very end. Hopefully you'll be able to find some of these unfilleted, so you can use the heads and bones for the *soupe.* It's this intense fish broth that makes a good bouillabaisse.

Don't be alarmed by the amount of fish here (it's much less than would be served with a traditional Restaurant du Bacon bouillabaisse or even the restaurant's tasting bouillabaisse) and especially the volume of fish heads and bones you'll use for the broth. This soup is so intense because it is made by concentrating so much fresh, flavorful fish into a few quarts of broth. It really helps here to have a hand blender. If you have to blend up the fish and vegetables in a regular blender, you probably won't be able to blend the large fish heads.

Note that the fish fillets are not cooked in the fish soup. Chef Philippin of the Restaurant du Bacon believes that once the soup base is achieved, cooking more fish in it would intensify the flavor too much (it's already pretty intense).

Bouillabaisse takes time. For a quick fish soup, see the recipe for aigo sau on page 173.

Note: I am putting an asterisk next to the fish that I think work best in this dish. All fish should be refrigerated until about 15 minutes before cooking.

For the Fish:

2 **pounds (900 g) monkfish★ or swordfish steaks or a combination, sliced about ¾ inch (2 cm) thick**

1 pound (450 g) fillets of porgy★, snapper★, whiting, sea bass★, or a combination, cut into at least 6 equal pieces

1 pound (450 g) fillets of John Dory★, rockfish★, halibut★, red mullet★, turbot★, or a combination, cut into at least 6 equal pieces

For the "Soupe":

5½ pounds (2.5 kg) fish heads and trimmings (include heads and trimmings from the fish you have had filleted for the bouillabaisse) and small rockfish if available

7 quarts (6.5 l) water

½ cup (125 ml) fresh thyme sprigs and leaves

¾ cup (185 ml) fresh tarragon sprigs and leaves

2 bay leaves

2 parsley sprigs

3 dried fennel stalks or 1 small fresh fennel bulb with stem, coarsely chopped

3 to 4 tablespoons olive oil as needed

3 medium-size onions, coarsely chopped

2 large leeks, white part only, well washed and sliced

3 heads of garlic, trimmed across the bottom and cut in half

1 celery rib, coarsely chopped

1 tablespoon tomato paste

2 large or 3 medium-size tomatoes, chopped

2 dried cayenne peppers

1 tablespoon coarse sea salt, approximately

¾ pound (340 g) small crabs (optional)

1 teaspoon saffron, preferably threads, or more to taste

freshly ground pepper to taste

For the Garnishes:

            salt to taste

¼   **teaspoon saffron threads**

1½   **pounds (675 g) firm boiling or new potatoes, peeled if desired and thinly sliced**

            garlic croutons (page 83)

½ to ¾   **cup (125 to 185 ml) garlic mayonnaise with cayenne and saffron (page 105) or spicy garlic puree (page 103)**

MAKING THE ''SOUPE''

If you've been able to find small rockfish, clean them, wash, and drain. Rinse the fish heads and carcasses. Bring 4 quarts (4 l) of the water to a boil in a pot. Tie together the thyme sprigs, tarragon, bay leaves, parsley, and fennel stalks (if used) into a bundle to make a large bouquet garni.

Heat 3 tablespoons of the olive oil in a very large heavy-bottomed casserole over medium heat and sauté the onions and leeks until tender, about 5 minutes. Add the garlic, celery, and fennel bulb (if used). Cook gently, stirring often, for 7 minutes. Off the heat, stir in the tomato paste; return to the heat and continue to cook, stirring, for another 4 minutes. If the mixture begins to stick to the pan, add a ladleful of the simmering water. Add the tomatoes, the cayenne peppers, fish heads and trimmings and small fish, and bouquet garni (the pot will be crowded). Stir together well with a large, long-handled wooden spoon or paddle over medium heat and add the 4 quarts (4 l) boiling water or enough water to cover the fish and vegetables without overflowing the pot, and about 1 tablespoon coarse sea salt.

At this point, if you're using the crabs, heat the remaining tablespoon of oil over medium-high heat in a large heavy-bottomed skillet and add the crabs. Cook, stirring and shaking the pan, until the crabs turn bright pink, about 5 minutes. Transfer to the soup pot. Bring the water to a second boil, then simmer for 10 minutes. Remove from the heat.

Use a hand blender if you have one and coarsely blend up the solids in the soup pot—heads, shells, and all. If you don't have a hand blender, use your regular blender, using the pulse action (you may have to discard large fish heads). The fish bones are likely to lodge in the blender blades from time to time, so be prepared to spend a while at this.

Now put the soup through the coarse blade of a food mill. Transfer the solid bits remaining in the food mill to a bowl.

Change to the fine blade of your food mill and press the soup through once more. Again, transfer the solid bits to the bowl.

Return the broth to the pot, bring it back to a boil, add the saffron, boil for about 30 seconds, and strain once more through a fine strainer, pressing all the liquid through with the help of the back of a wooden spoon or a pestle.

Return the soup to the pot, taste, and adjust salt, pepper, and saffron. Set aside. You will be reheating this just before serving, but you should never let it come to a boil, or the soup will separate.

FOR THE BOUILLABAISSE

Bring the remaining 3 quarts (3 l) water to a simmer. Place the solids from the strained fish in a strainer or the top part of a steamer pot and pour the water through. Transfer 1 quart (1 l) of this bouillon to a saucepan. Bring to a simmer and add a teaspoon of sea salt and ¼ teaspoon saffron. Add the potatoes and cook until tender but not falling apart. Remove the potatoes and transfer to a warm bowl.

Add salt to taste to the remaining 2 quarts (2 l) broth. Just before serving, bring this broth to a bare simmer, add the fish steaks, and cook for 1 minute. Add the fish fillets and cook for another 2 minutes. The fish should be barely cooked through, because it will continue to cook in the hot *soupe*. Meanwhile, reheat the *soupe,* taking care that you do not let it reach the boiling point. Put the pot on a Flame Tamer to make sure.

Remove the cooked fish from the bouillon using a skimmer and distribute among heated wide soup bowls. Make sure there is some of each kind in each bowl. Top with several potato slices. Ladle in the *soupe* and serve, topping each serving with croutons rubbed with garlic and spread with a little rouille.

ADVANCE PREPARATION: The vegetables for the soup base can be prepared a day ahead of time and kept in the refrigerator. The soup base will hold for several hours, in or out of the refrigerator. The rouille or garlic puree and croutons can be made a day ahead of time.

PER PORTION

Calories	742	Protein	70 G
Fat	30 G	Carbohydrate	55 G
Sodium	1,502 MG	Cholesterol	137 MG

RICH FISH SOUP
La soupe de poissons

SERVES 6

You are likely to find soupe de poissons on every menu on the Côte d'Azur. Don't order it unless you're sure of the quality of the restaurant. There's nothing better than a good one, but a bad one can be downright dangerous. Fish soup is nothing more—or less—than the base used in bouillabaisse. It should be that rich, that good, and that time-consuming to prepare. It's served with croutons, rouille, and grated Gruyère cheese and can be a first course or a meal.

For the Soup:

5½	pounds (2.5 kg) fish heads and trimmings and small rockfish if available
4	quarts (3.75 l) water
½	cup (125 ml) fresh thyme sprigs
¾	cup (185 ml) fresh tarragon sprigs
2	bay leaves
2	parsley sprigs
3	dried fennel stalks or 1 small fresh fennel bulb with stem, coarsely chopped
3 to 4	tablespoons olive oil, as needed
3	medium-size onions, coarsely chopped
2	large leeks, white part only, well washed and sliced
3	heads of garlic, trimmed across the bottom and cut in half
1	celery rib, coarsely chopped
1	tablespoon tomato paste
2	large or 3 medium-size tomatoes, chopped
2	dried cayenne peppers
1	tablespoon coarse sea salt, approximately
¾	pound (340 g) small crabs (optional)

1   teaspoon saffron, preferably threads, or more to
    taste
    freshly ground pepper to taste

For the Garnishes:
    toasted croutons
    cut garlic cloves
½ to ¾   cup (125 to 185 ml) garlic mayonnaise with
         cayenne and saffron (page 105) or spicy garlic
         puree (page 103)
3   ounces (90 g) Gruyère cheese, grated (¾ cup)

If you have been able to find small rockfish, clean, wash, and drain them. Rinse the fish heads and trimmings. Bring the water to a simmer in a pot. Tie together the thyme, tarragon, bay leaves, parsley, and fennel stalks if you're using them—a large bouquet garni.

Heat 3 tablespoons olive oil in a very large heavy-bottomed casserole over medium heat and sauté the onions and leeks until tender, about 5 minutes. Add the garlic, celery, and fennel bulb if you're using it. Cook gently, stirring often, for 7 minutes. Off the heat, stir in the tomato paste; return to the heat and continue to cook, stirring, for another 4 minutes. If the mixture begins to stick to the pan, add a ladleful of the simmering water. Add the tomatoes, cayenne peppers, fish heads and trimmings and small fish, and bouquet garni (the pot will be crowded). Stir together well with a large long-handled wooden spoon or paddle over medium heat and add the boiling water or enough water to cover the fish and vegetables without overflowing the pot, and about 1 tablespoon coarse sea salt.

At this point, if you're using the crabs, heat the remaining tablespoon of oil over medium-high heat in a large heavy-bottomed skillet and add the crabs. Cook, stirring and shaking the pan, until the crabs turn bright pink, about 5 minutes. Transfer to the soup pot. Bring the water to a second boil, then simmer for 10 minutes. Remove from the heat.

Use a hand blender if you have one and coarsely blend up the solids in the soup pot, heads, shells, and all. If you don't have a hand blender, use the pulse action of your regular blender (you may have to discard large fish heads). The fish bones and trimmings are likely to lodge in the blender blades from time to time, so be prepared to spend a while at this. Now put the soup through the coarse blade of a food mill. Discard the solid bits remaining in the food mill.

Change to the fine blade of your food mill and press the soup through once more. Discard the solid bits.

Return the broth to the pot, bring it back to a boil, add the saffron, boil for about 30 seconds, and strain once more through a fine strainer, pressing all the liquid through with the back of a wooden spoon or a pestle.

Return the soup to the pot, taste, and adjust salt, pepper, and saffron. Set aside. You will be reheating this just before serving, but you should never let it come to a boil, or the soup will separate.

Shortly before serving, reheat the soup gently, but do not boil. Serve, passing the croutons, cut cloves of garlic, rouille or spicy garlic puree, and the grated cheese on a platter.

ADVANCE PREPARATION: The vegetables for the soup base can be prepared a day ahead of time and kept in the refrigerator. The soup will hold for several hours, in or out of the refrigerator. The rouille or garlic puree and croutons can be made a day ahead of time.

PER PORTION

Calories	447	Protein	20 G
Fat	30 G	Carbohydrate	35 G
Sodium	1,419 MG	Cholesterol	60 MG

SIMPLE FISH AND GARLIC SOUP
Aigo sau   Eau-sel

SERVES 6

One of my Provençal cookbooks tells me that this is a dish for convalescents and people who have a delicate stomach. The literal translation of the French and Provençal names is "Water-Salt." As opposed to a bouillabaisse or soupe de poissons, this is a very quick fish soup made with white-fleshed fish. It's true that the soup is light and simple, with a delicate broth redolent of potatoes and garlic. We appreciated it during the Christmas season in Provence, on the days between the feasts.

1 to 1½	pounds (450 to 675 g/4 to 6 medium-size) waxy potatoes, sliced about ½ inch (1.5 cm) thick
1	medium-size onion, thinly sliced
2	medium-size tomatoes, peeled and chopped
6 to 8	garlic cloves, to taste, minced or put through a press
1	bouquet garni made with a bay leaf, 2 stalks of fennel if available, a couple of sprigs of fresh thyme, celery leaves from one stick of celery, and a couple of sprigs of parsley
	salt and freshly ground pepper to taste
2	quarts (2 l) water
1½	pounds (675 g) filleted white fish, such as sea bass, porgy or bream, grey mullet, snapper, sole, cod, and whiting, cut into large chunks
6	garlic croutons (page 83)
½	cup (125 ml) garlic mayonnaise with cayenne and saffron (page 105) or spicy garlic puree (page 103)

Combine the potatoes, onion, tomatoes, garlic, bouquet garni, salt, pepper, and water in a large soup pot and bring to a boil. Reduce the heat, cover, and simmer over medium-high heat for 20 minutes or until the potatoes are cooked through.

Add the fish and simmer for another 10 to 15 minutes, until it is cooked through and the broth fragrant. Adjust salt and pepper.

There are two ways to serve this. Traditionally the fish and potatoes are served separately on a plate, and the broth is served in a bowl with croutons topped with rouille. But it's just as good, in my opinion, if you serve the fish and soup together in a wide bowl, topped with the croutons and rouille.

ADVANCE PREPARATION: The soup, up to the adding of the fish, can be made hours before serving and held in or out of the refrigerator.

PER PORTION

Calories	433	Protein	27 G
Fat	17 G	Carbohydrate	43 G
Sodium	394 MG	Cholesterol	82 MG

FISH SOUPS

SALT COD BOUILLABAISSE

Boui-abaisso de merlusso   Bouillabaisse de morue

SERVES 6

In contrast to traditional bouillabaisse, this fragrant fish soup is very quick and easy to make.

1½	pounds (675 g) salt cod, either homemade (page 195) or commercial
2	tablespoons olive oil
2	medium-size onions, chopped
1	tablespoon tomato paste
2	large tomatoes, peeled and chopped
4 to 5	large garlic cloves, minced or put through a press
1 or 2	dried cayenne peppers to taste
2	quarts (2 l) water
	a bouquet garni made with several fresh thyme sprigs, several parsley sprigs, 2 bay leaves, 2 fennel stalks if available, and a wide slice of orange zest
	salt and freshly ground pepper to taste
2	pounds (900 g/8 medium-size) new or boiling potatoes, sliced about ¼ inch (.75 cm) thick
½	teaspoon saffron threads or more to taste
¼	cup (about 15 g/½ large bunch) chopped parsley
3	tablespoons garlic mayonnaise with cayenne and saffron (page 105) or cooked garlic puree (page 103) (optional)
12	thick garlic croutons (page 83)

One or two days before you wish to serve the soup, desalt the cod in a large bowl of cold water for 12 to 24 hours, depending on the saltiness of the fish, changing the water often. Drain and cut into 1-inch pieces.

Heat the olive oil in a large heavy-bottomed soup pot or casserole over medium heat. Add the onions and cook, stirring, until tender but not browned, about 3 to 5 minutes. Add the tomato paste and stir together for a couple of seconds; then add the tomatoes, garlic, and cayenne and stir together for about 30 seconds. Add the water, bouquet garni, salt (go easy on the salt, because the cod is salty), pepper, and potatoes and bring to a boil. Add the saffron, turn down the heat a little, cover, and boil for 10 minutes.

Add the salt cod and continue to simmer for another 10 minutes or until the potatoes are cooked through. Taste and adjust the seasonings. Remove from the heat and stir in the parsley.

If you are using the rouille or garlic puree, spread it on the croutons. Place two croutons in each bowl, ladle in the soup, and serve.

Note: In Provence the broth is ladled into the bowls over the croutons, and the fish and potatoes are served separately, on a warm platter. But I prefer the fish and potatoes to be served with the broth.

ADVANCE PREPARATION: The soup base, before the salt cod is added, will hold for several hours, in or out of the refrigerator.

PER PORTION

Calories	441	Protein	28 G
Fat	12 G	Carbohydrate	56 G
Sodium	N/A	Cholesterol	62 MG

MACKEREL BOUILLABAISSE WITH FRESH PEAS OR ZUCCHINI
Boui-abaisso d'auriou   Bouillabaisse de maquereaux aux petits pois

SERVES 4

Mackerel's rich flesh can have a very strong taste, but I was intrigued by this dish when I read it in a Provençal cookbook. I found that the fish, simmered this way in a fragrant broth, is neither too strong tasting nor too rich. I think it's nice to find small mackerel and serve them whole, after you serve the soup, in the traditional manner of a bouillabaisse.

I first tested this recipe in September in Provence. It was the first dinner party I gave at my rented house near Gignac. Peas weren't in season, and my neighbor had brought me several pounds of zucchini from his garden, so I used sliced zucchini instead. The squash makes a sweet broth that isn't unlike the broth that the peas make, and I recommend both versions. This is a very easy and inexpensive dish to make, because it doesn't require a fish stock. A bonus is that mackerel are omega-rich; the fat content may look high when you review the nutritional values for this recipe, but the omega-rich fat that mackerel contains is the kind reputed to lower cholesterol.

4	**mackerels, about 8 or 9 ounces (225 to 250 g) each, cleaned, heads removed if desired**
1	**large onion, sliced**
2	**large tomatoes, peeled, seeded, and chopped**
5	**large garlic cloves, minced or put through a press**
1	**slice of lemon**
	a bouquet garni made with 1 bay leaf, a fennel sprig, a few fresh thyme sprigs, and a few parsley sprigs
1 to 1½	**tablespoons olive oil as needed**
	salt to taste
1	**strip of orange zest**
2	**quarts (2 l) water**

1   pound (450 g/4 medium-size) potatoes, thinly sliced

     freshly ground pepper to taste

2   pounds (900 g) fresh peas, shelled (2 cups/50 cl) or ½ pound (225 g/2 small) zucchini, sliced ¼ inch thick (2 cups)

     generous pinch of saffron threads

     lemon wedges

3   tablespoons chopped parsley

4   thick garlic croutons (page 83)

Combine the fish, onion, tomatoes, 2 garlic cloves, the lemon, bouquet garni, and 1 tablespoon of the olive oil in a large heavy-bottomed casserole. Marinate for 1 hour.

Remove the fish from the casserole and, if you're not cooking right away, transfer it to a plate and return it to the refrigerator.

Heat the vegetables in the casserole over medium-high heat. Cook, stirring, for 5 to 10 minutes or until the onion has softened and the mixture is fragrant. Add another 1 to 1½ teaspoons of olive oil if the vegetables begin to stick. Remove the lemon slice and add the salt, orange zest, water, and potatoes. Bring to a boil, add the remaining garlic, reduce the heat, cover, and simmer for 20 minutes or until the potatoes are tender.

Add the pepper, peas, and saffron. Cover and continue to simmer for another 10 minutes, until the peas are cooked through and the broth is fragrant. Adjust salt and pepper and remove from the heat.

About 15 minutes before serving, bring the soup to a simmer and add the whole fish. Check after 10 minutes, and if the flesh flakes easily when you pierce it with a fork, gently remove the fish and place on an attractive warm platter (if the fish resists the fork, simmer for another 5 to 10 minutes). Remove some of the potatoes from the broth and garnish the fish. Add some lemon wedges and keep warm in a very low oven or one that has been heated and turned off.

Add the parsley to the soup and serve over the garlic croutons in wide soup bowls. Once your guests have had a bowl of soup, serve the fish in the same wide bowls or on separate plates. Pass lemon wedges and leave the platter in the middle of the table for fish bones.

Note: If you prefer fillets to whole fish, have your fishmonger fillet the mackerel, leaving the skin on. Cook the fillets in the simmering broth as directed for 5 minutes, until opaque.

ADVANCE PREPARATION: The soup can be made right up to the addition of the mackerel hours ahead of serving.

PER PORTION

Calories	602	Protein	36 G
Fat	24 G	Carbohydrate	61 G
Sodium	348 MG	Cholesterol	91 MG

MUSSEL SOUP
Soupo de muscle   Soupe de moules

SERVES 4

I wonder if our word for mussels is a direct derivation from the Provençal word (the French and English words for the homonym *muscle* are the same). This one is a classic Provençal preparation, a wonderful combination of mussels and their broth, aromatics (the usual Mediterranean trio of onions, tomatoes, garlic), vermicelli, and a final sprinkling of Gruyère. All of the Provençal recipes I've ever seen say to cook the vermicelli for 20 minutes, but I think it gets too soggy if cooked that long. So cook it just until al dente, about 7 minutes.

2½   **pounds (1.25 kg) mussels**
3   **tablespoons vinegar**
1   **cup (250 ml) dry white wine**
5   **cups (1.25 l) water**
2   **medium-size onions, chopped**
4   **large garlic cloves, minced or put through a press**
2   **bay leaves**
1   **fennel sprig or stalk**

1	tablespoon olive oil
½	pound (225 g/2 medium-size) fresh or canned tomatoes, peeled, seeded and chopped
	salt to taste
	pinch of cayenne pepper
¼	teaspoon saffron threads
	freshly ground pepper to taste
5	ounces (140 g) broken vermicelli or spaghettini
2	tablespoons chopped parsley
1	ounce (30 g) Gruyère cheese, grated (¼ cup)

A couple of hours before serving, clean the mussels. Brush and rinse the mussels one at a time and discard any that are open or cracked. Place the mussels in a bowl of water in the kitchen sink. Turn the water on low and let a slow stream of water run over the mussels for an hour. Drain the mussels and pick through them again; pull out the beards and place in a bowl of water to which you have added 3 tablespoons vinegar. Let sit for 15 minutes. Drain and rinse several times. You can now refrigerate the mussels for a few hours.

Combine the wine, water, one of the onions, 2 garlic cloves, one of the bay leaves, the fennel, and the mussels in a large pot and bring to a boil. Give the mussels a stir, cover, and cook for 3 to 4 minutes, just until they open, giving them a stir halfway through the cooking. Remove the mussels with a slotted spoon or deep-fry skimmer and transfer to a bowl. Discard any that haven't opened. Strain the cooking liquid into a bowl through several thicknesses of cheesecloth. When the mussels are cool enough to handle, remove them from their shells. If they are still sandy, give them a quick rinse under cold water. Set them aside and discard the shells.

Heat the olive oil in a large heavy-bottomed casserole over medium heat and add the remaining onion. Sauté, stirring, until the onion is tender, about 5 to 8 minutes. Add the remaining garlic cloves, the tomatoes, and a very small amount of salt. Cook, stirring, for a minute or two; then add the cooking liquid from the mussels, the remaining bay leaf, the mussels, and the cayenne. Bring to a boil, add the saffron, taste, and add salt if necessary and pepper.

Add the vermicelli to the boiling soup and cook al dente—until cooked through but firm. Stir in the parsley and serve, topping each serving with a sprinkling of grated Gruyère.

ADVANCE PREPARATION: You can cook the mussels and remove them from their shells hours ahead of making the soup. Keep the shelled mussels in the refrigerator.

PER PORTION

Calories	316	Protein	18 G
Fat	8 G	Carbohydrate	42 G
Sodium	310 MG	Cholesterol	31 MG

CHAPTER 6

FISH AND SHELLFISH

I learned much of what I know about fish cookery in Provence, first from Lulu Peyraud at Domaine Tempier, then from Serge Philippin and the Sordello brothers at the Restaurant du Bacon in Cap d'Antibes. I loved going to buy fish with these people. Lulu would go to the market at Bandol or to the seaside quais in Sanary or Toulon to look at the day's catch before she decided for sure on what she would cook for lunch. Adrien Sordello shopped for his fish at the Cannes market, one of the best markets on the Côte d'Azur. The fish that Adrien Sordello, Lulu Peyraud, and other careful fish buyers choose has been caught early that morning by fishermen who go out well before dawn in small boats and fish until shortly after daybreak, when the fish stop biting. They put the fish in Styrofoam boxes or plastic buckets and bring them to the quais or the markets, where they (or their wives) sometimes set up a small table to display their catch. The fish are often still moving when you buy them. They are glistening and firm, their eyes clear. A surprise catch of one type or another—big, fresh, funny-looking John Dorys or shiny silver bream—will determine that day's menu at the Restaurant du Bacon or at Domaine Tempier. Most often these extremely tasty, fresh fish are simply grilled and served with lemon. They need no further embellishment.

I'll never forget the first time I watched Lulu prepare fish. She was making lunch for the grape pickers and cooked 25 bonito steaks (which she called *pélamide*—I hardly spoke French at the time and kept thinking they were called "palaminos") on a grill outside the kitchen without overcooking a single one. She served the fish with a garlicky tomato-caper sauce and boiled potatoes. What a meal.

But you can make all the dishes in this chapter with fish that doesn't come from the Mediterranean. They even do it, to a certain extent, in Provence! Having just waxed lyrical about the impressive independent fishermen and the wonderful markets I've seen along the Mediterranean coast of France, I must also say that the fish is running out in this beautiful, polluted sea. Some of the fish you get in restaurants along the coast (but not the better ones) don't come from the Mediterranean at all but from the Atlantic. However, with today's methods of refrigerated transportation, a sea bass that hasn't been bought that morning on the nearest quai can still be fresh and good.

Morue—salt cod—and preserved anchovies are the fish that everyone in Provence eats, from the coast to the high Alps. People from the parts of Provence that are not on the sea—the interior and Haute-Provence—used to enjoy river fish from the Rhône and the small rivers that run through the hills and valleys (the Durance, the Loup, the Ouvèze, among others). Now, *hélas,* pollution has taken its toll, and with the exception of farmed trout, fresh fish is not too easy to come by once you leave the coast. There are reliable fishmongers, but you have to seek them out. However, the rose-fleshed farmed trout is quite good; I cook it *en papillote,* with sprigs of rosemary or herbes de Provence and lemon slices (see page 226).

The important thing to consider when making any of these dishes is to shop carefully for the fish. Try to find a good fishmonger—perhaps in the fish department of a supermarket or maybe in a separate shop. Get to know the purveyor, asking questions and seeing what you can learn. I realize that finding whole fish is not the easiest thing, but whole fish are preferable to fillets, even if you are going to have them filleted or sliced, because you can see the eyes. And the eyes are the best sign of freshness. They should not be sunken or clouded over. The quality of the flesh will also tell you how fresh the fish is; it should be firm and resilient to the touch, and the scales should be shiny. Fillets should also be firm and of uniform color. They should glisten. And a fish department or store should *never* smell "fishy."

These recipes are perfect for low-fat eating and make elegant dishes for entertaining. A whole, succulent fish, baked with whole cloves of garlic (page 218), scented with fennel (page 212), or accompanied with tapenade (page 215), is always a hit at a dinner party. Small red mullet wrapped in grape or lettuce leaves and baked or grilled, fish fillets spread with tapenade or tomato coulis and cooked in phyllo dough (pages 215 and 216) make surprising, pleasing main dishes. And tuna steaks with a pungent pistou-enriched tomato concassée (page 209) are a favorite summer dish.

A FRENCH-PROVENÇAL-ENGLISH GLOSSARY OF FISH

FRENCH	PROVENÇAL	ENGLISH
ANCHOIS	**L'ANCHOIO**	**ANCHOVY**

CUISINE: Salted anchovies, packed in coarse salt or olive oil, are used as both a seasoning and a condiment in Provençal cooking. They are mashed into a spread (*anchoïade*) and top pizzas, go into salads, sauces, and vegetable dishes.

FRENCH	PROVENÇAL	ENGLISH
ANGUILLE	**L'ANGUIÉRO**	**EEL**

CUISINE: Rich-fleshed fish cooked in stews, fried, braised, and grilled.

FRENCH	PROVENÇAL	ENGLISH
BARBUE	**LOU ROUN**	**BRILL**

CUISINE: Lean, white-fleshed fish found in European waters. Bake, broil, grill, poach or steam.
STAND-INS*: Turbot, halibut, flounder

FRENCH	PROVENÇAL	ENGLISH
BAUDROIE OR LOTTE	**LOU BÓUDROI OR BÓURDREIL**	**ANGLERFISH OR MONKFISH**

CUISINE: Firm, moderately lean white-fleshed fish. Bake, braise, poach, or steam. Very good in fish soups and bouillabaisse.
STAND-INS: Lobster in some recipes

FRENCH	PROVENÇAL	ENGLISH
BONITE OR PÉLAMIDE	**LOU BONITO OR LA PÉLAMIDO**	**BONITO**

CUISINE: Firm, moderately fatty, light-colored flesh, member of the tuna family. Very good grilled. Can also be baked or panfried.
STAND-INS: Swordfish, tuna

---

* STAND-INS are other fish that can be used in place of the given fish if you can't find the given fish at your fish store. The flavor is never quite the same, but the texture is similar enough that the cooking method will work for the stand-in.

FRENCH	PROVENÇAL	ENGLISH
CAPELAN	**LOU CAPELAN**	**POOR COD**

CUISINE: Lean white-fleshed fish. Bony. Bake, poach, or steam. Good in fish soups.
STAND-INS: Cod, lingcod, scrod

FRENCH	PROVENÇAL	ENGLISH
CARRELET	**LOU ROUN**	**PLAICE**

CUISINE: Flat, lean, delicate white-fleshed fish. Bake, panfry, or steam.
STAND-INS: Flounder, sole

CONGRE	**LOU FIÉLAS**	**CONGER EEL**

CUISINE: Tasty but bony white flesh. Good in soups and braised.
STAND-INS: Monkfish

DAURADE	**L'AURADO**	**GILTHEAD BREAM**

CUISINE: A prized firm white-fleshed fish. Grill or bake.
STAND-INS: Pompano, porgy, snapper, redfish, grouper, mahimahi

DENTÉ	**LOU DÈNTI**	**DENTEX**

CUISINE: A firm, lean white-fleshed fish in the bream family. Grill or bake.
STAND-INS: Swordfish, snapper, pompano, grouper, mahimahi

GALINETTE	**LA GALINETO OR LOU PERLON**	**TUB GURNARD**

CUISINE: Firm, lean white-fleshed fish. Bake, braise, poach. Good in fish soups.
STAND-INS: Gurnard, snapper, redfish, cod, orange roughy

GOBIE	**LOU GOBÍ**	**GOBY**

CUISINE: Small-fry fish. Used in *fritures*.
STAND-INS: Sprats, whitebait

FRENCH	PROVENÇAL	ENGLISH

GRONDIN · **LOU GOURNAU** · **GURNARD**

CUISINE: Firm, lean white-fleshed fish. Bake, braise, poach. Good in fish soups.

STAND-INS: Snapper, redfish, grouper, cod, orange roughy

LIMANDE · **LA LIMANDO** · **LEMON SOLE**

CUISINE: Flat, lean, delicate white-fleshed fish. Bake, panfry, or steam.

STAND-INS: Sole, flounder

LOUP, BAR · **LOU LOUP OR LOUBINO** · **SEA BASS**

CUISINE: A prized moderately lean, tender white-fleshed fish. Grill, bake, steam. Good in fish soups.

STAND-INS: Grouper, other bass

MAQUEREAU · **L'AURIOU** · **MACKEREL**

CUISINE: Fatty, rich-fleshed, strong-tasting fish. Grill, bake, or poach. Makes a good soup on its own (page 177).

STAND-INS: Mullet, bluefish, tuna, shark

MERLU OR COLIN · · **HAKE**

CUISINE: Tasty lean white-fleshed fish. Grill, bake, poach, or steam. Good in fish soups.

STAND-INS: Cod, lingcod, petrale sole

MERLAN · **LOU MARLUS** · **WHITING, SILVER HAKE, PACIFIC HAKE**

CUISINE: Delicate, lean white-fleshed fish. Bake, poach, panfry, grill. Good in fish soups.

STAND-INS: Hake, cod, snapper

FRENCH	PROVENÇAL	ENGLISH
MÉROU	**L'ANFOUNSOU**	**GROUPER**

CUISINE: Lean, delicate white-fleshed fish. Bake, grill, or poach. Good in fish soups.
STAND-INS: Sea bass, cod, snapper, halibut, cod, orange roughy

| **MUGE OR MULET** | **LOU MUJOU** | **MULLET** |

CUISINE: Versatile reddish, fairly fatty-fleshed fish. Grill, bake, or poach. Used in many fish soups and couscous.
STAND-INS: Mackerel, bluefish

| **NOUNAT, NONAT** | **NOUNAT** | **TRANSPARENT GOBY** |

CUISINE: Small-fry fish. Used in *fritures, beignets,* and omelets.
STAND-INS: Whitebait, smelts

| **PAGEAU OR PAGEOT** | **LOU PAGÉU** | **PANDORA (BREAM)** |

CUISINE: Firm, lean white-fleshed member of the bream family. Grill or bake.
STAND-INS: Porgy, snapper, pompano, mahimahi

| **PAGRE** | **LOU PAGRE** | **SEA BREAM OR PORGY** |

CUISINE: Firm, lean, white-fleshed member of the bream family. Grill or bake.
STAND-INS: Pompano, snapper, grouper

| **PERCHE OR SERRAN** | **LA PERCO** | **PERCH OR COMBER** |

CUISINE: Lean, bony white-fleshed fish. Fry or use in fish soups.
STAND-INS: Grouper, snapper, cod, orange roughy

FRENCH	PROVENÇAL	ENGLISH
		SARDINE AND ANCHOVY
POUTINE	**LA POUTINO**	**ALEVINS**

CUISINE: Available mid-February to mid-March. The tiny larval fish are made into delicious omelets and soups.

RAIE	**LA CLAVELADO**	**SKATE OR RAY**

CUISINE: Lean, sweet-tasting, pinkish white-fleshed fish. Braise, poach, or bake.
STAND-INS: Flounder, sole

	LA RASCASSO,	**SCORPION FISH**
RASCASSE,	**LOU CAPOUN,**	**OR OCEAN**
CHAPON	**OR L'ESCÔRPI**	**PERCH**

CUISINE: Firm, lean white-fleshed fish prized for bouillabaisse. Can also be baked or steamed.
STAND-INS: Grouper, porgy, snapper, rockfish, redfish

ROUQUIER	**LOU ROUCAU**	**WRASSE**

CUISINE: Lean, white-fleshed fish used mainly in fish soup.
STAND-INS: Damselfish, parrotfish, hake, grouper

		RED MULLET,
ROUGET	**LOU ROGET**	**GOATFISH**

CUISINE: Delicate, lean white-fleshed fish with distinctive flavor. Best grilled or baked. Fillets often panfried.
STAND-INS: Sole

SAINT-PIERRE	**LOU SAN PIARÉ**	**JOHN DORY**

CUISINE: Firm, lean white-fleshed fish. Excellent grilled or baked.
STAND-INS: Snapper, grouper, redfish

FISH AND SHELLFISH

FRENCH	PROVENÇAL	ENGLISH
SARD	**LOU SAR**	**BREAM FAMILY**

CUISINE: Firm, lean white-fleshed member of the bream family. Grill or bake.

STAND-INS: Porgy, pompano, snapper, grouper, redfish, mahimahi

SARDINE	**LA SARDINO**	**SARDINE**

CUISINE: Small rich-fleshed, strong-tasting fish. Grill, bake, or prepare *en escabeche* (page 69).

STAND-INS: Small mackerel, small herring

SOLE	**LA SOLO**	**SOLE**

CUISINE: Flat, lean, delicate white-fleshed fish. Bake, panfry, broil, grill, or steam.

STAND-INS: Flounder, lemon sole

THON	**LO TOUN**	**TUNA**

CUISINE: Rich red-fleshed fish. Grill, bake, or panfry.

STAND-INS: Bonito, swordfish, shark

	LOU TURBOT	
	OR LOU ROUN-	
TURBOT	**CLAVELA**	**TURBOT**

CUISINE: Flat, lean white-fleshed fish with rich flavor. Poach, grill, bake, braise.

STAND-INS: Plaice, flounder

VIVE	**L'ARAGNO**	**WEEVER**

CUISINE: Firm, lean white-fleshed fish used in bouillabaisse. The spines are venomous.

STAND-INS: Hake, grouper

FRENCH	PROVENÇAL	ENGLISH

CRUSTACEANS AND MOLLUSKS

CALMAR OR ENCORNET	**LA TAUTÉNO**	**SQUID**

CUISINE: Fried, stewed, braised, stuffed.

CIGALE	**LOU CHÀMBRI**	**FLAT LOBSTER**
CRABE	**LA FAVOUIO**	**SHORE CRAB**

CUISINE: Used mainly in soups.

CRABE VELU OR ERIPHIE	**LOU FIOU PELAN VO COURENTIHO**	**CRAB**

CUISINE: Prized crab, poached and used in soups.

CREVETTE	**LOU CARAMBO VO CAMBARO**	**SHRIMP**

CUISINE: Boil, poach, add to soups, grill, stew.

MOULE	**LOU MUSCLE**	**MUSSEL**

CUISINE: Steam open in wine; cook with tomatoes, garlic, onions.

COQUE, CLOVISSE, PALOURDE	**LOU CLAUVISSO**	**CLAMS (DIFFERENT SPECIES)**

CUISINE: Steam open in wine; cook with tomatoes, garlic, onions.

FISH AND SHELLFISH

FRENCH	PROVENÇAL	ENGLISH
HOMARD	**LA LIGOMBAU**	**LOBSTER**

CUISINE: Boil, poach, grill, bake.

FRENCH	PROVENÇAL	ENGLISH
LANGOUSTE	**LA LINGOUSTO**	**SPINY LOBSTER**

CUISINE: Poach, add to soups, grill.

FRENCH	PROVENÇAL	ENGLISH
LANGOUSTINE		**DUBLIN BAY PRAWN**

CUISINE: Poach, add to soups, grill, stew.

FRENCH	PROVENÇAL	ENGLISH
POULPE	**LOU POURPRE**	**OCTOPUS**

CUISINE: Stew in wine or tomato sauce.

FRENCH	PROVENÇAL	ENGLISH
SEICHE	**LA SÙPI**	**CUTTLEFISH**

CUISINE: Stew, braise, or stuff.

FRENCH	PROVENÇAL	ENGLISH
SUPION	**LOU SÙPION**	**SMALL CUTTLEFISH**

CUISINE: Stew, braise, or stuff.

MISCELLANEOUS

FRENCH	PROVENÇAL	ENGLISH
POUTARGUE	**LA POUTARGO**	**MULLET ROE**

CUISINE: Sliced and served with lemon juice and olive oil or made into a paste and spread on bread.

FRENCH	PROVENÇAL	ENGLISH
MORUE	**LOU MERLUSSO**	**SALT COD**

CUISINE: Desalted, poached, baked, added to soups, blended into brandade (page 61).

COURT BOUILLON

MAKES 7 CUPS (1.75 L)

Court bouillon is used to poach fish, to cook shellfish, and sometimes to cook chicken. It's a light vegetable broth, to which you can add wine, lemon juice, or vinegar for a more acidic medium.

4	**cloves**
1	**medium-size onion, quartered**
2	**quarts (2 l) water**
2	**medium-size carrots, minced**
2	**leeks, well washed and sliced**
1	**celery rib, minced**
1	**fresh thyme sprig**
1	**small bay leaf**
2	**parsley sprigs**
1	**tablespoon salt or to taste**
1	**cup (250 ml) good-quality wine vinegar or sherry vinegar, or 1½ cups (375 ml) dry white wine, or juice of 2 lemons (optional)**
6	**black peppercorns**

Stick a clove into each onion quarter. Combine all the ingredients except the peppercorns in a large soup pot or Dutch oven and bring to a boil. Reduce the heat, cover, and simmer for 45 minutes. Add the peppercorns and simmer for another 10 minutes. Remove from the heat and strain through a cheesecloth-lined strainer.

ADVANCE PREPARATION: This can be made a day ahead and can be frozen.

COOKING A FISH IN COURT BOUILLON

Allow the court bouillon to cool. If you are cooking a large fish, wrap it in a clean kitchen towel or cheesecloth to facilitate lifting from the court bouillon. Place the fish in a poacher or a large casserole and pour in the court bouillon. If it doesn't cover the fish, cover the fish with a clean kitchen towel or with celery leaves, but don't dilute the court bouillon with more water. Bring slowly to a simmer and simmer for 10 minutes per inch (2.5 cm) of thickness of the fish, measured at the thickest part. If you're serving the fish hot, lift from the bouillon and transfer to a platter. If you're serving it cold, reduce the cooking by 5 minutes and allow the fish to cool in the broth. Transfer to a platter and remove the skin.

Strain the court bouillon, which is now a fish stock, refrigerate, and serve within a day or two as the base for a soup or sauce.

Note: You can make a simple court bouillon with water, garlic cloves, onions, thyme, and bay leaf, which will be fine for cooking strong fish such as salt cod.

PER PORTION

Calories	9	Protein	.22 G
Fat	.03 G	Carbohydrate	2 G
Sodium	947 MG	Cholesterol	0

HOMEMADE SALT COD

MAKES 1 POUND (500 G)

This is such an obvious answer to the "How do I find salt cod?" question. Why didn't I think of it sooner? I had the idea of salting my own cod from the chef at the Restaurant du Bacon in Cap d'Antibes. The only requirement here is exceptionally fresh cod. With your own salt cod, your brandade (page 61) will always be a hit.

> 1   **pound (450 g) very fresh cod fillets**
> ½   **cup (¼ lb/115 g) coarse sea salt, plus more as needed**

Remove as many of the bones from the fillets as you can. Sprinkle some of the salt over the bottom of a baking dish large enough to accommodate the cod fillets in a single layer. Lay the fillets on top and cover with the rest of the salt. Cover and refrigerate for 12 hours.

Pour off the water that has accumulated in the baking dish. Sprinkle on more salt if the salt has dissolved, cover, and refrigerate for another 12 hours.

Desalt the fish for 12 to 24 hours, as you would for brandade.

Note: You can desalt and cook the salt cod after 12 hours, but the texture will be more like fresh cod than traditional salt cod (you may prefer this).

ADVANCE PREPARATION: The salt cod keeps for a week in the refrigerator. Continue to pour off water that accumulates in the pan each day and to sprinkle the fish with more salt. Cover with plastic wrap. It's best, though, used as soon after salting as possible.

PER 1 POUND

Calories	372	Protein	81 G
Fat	3 G	Carbohydrate	0
Sodium	N/A	Cholesterol	195 MG

SALT COD

For several years many of us cookbook writers have been trying to talk our American readers into appreciating salt cod. I'm not sure it's worked. But before you skip over the next six recipes, let me tell you the good news: you can make your own salt cod, and it won't be hard and leathery! The recipe is on page 195.

I think one of the problems with salt cod in America is the quality of the available product. Sometimes what you find is rock-hard, like the Provençal stockfish; or it's packed in plastic and smells unappetizing when you open it. When I buy salt cod in France, I look for thick white flexible slabs covered with coarse salt and sold in loose pieces (not packaged). If you can't find this product, then make your own. As you'll see when you try the previous recipe, there's nothing tricky about salting your own cod. All you need is very fresh fish, good coarse sea salt, and fore-thought (you have to salt it for a day or two, then desalt it). Then you can make all of the recipes and discover what this low-fat, high-protein, versatile cured fish is all about.

As Colman Andrews points out when he writes about salt cod in *Catalan Cuisine* (Atheneum, 1988), "salt cod is . . . the ham of the sea—animal flesh cured at the time of its slaughter to last, and add flavor to dishes, all year round." Its firm, satiny texture is different from that of fresh fish, and its flavor is more complex than that of regular cod. A dish based on salt cod is almost meaty. And it will not be too salty if you desalt the fish properly (page 62).

SALT COD WITH GARLICKY TOMATO SAUCE

Merlusso i poumo d'amour   Morue aux tomates

SERVES 4 TO 6

This dish is called Morue à la Provençale at one of my favorite Paris restaurants, Le Caméléon. But it's only one of the many ways they use salt cod in Provence. My version is quite garlicky, with lots of basil added at the end. Serve it with aïoli (page 97) or cooked or spicy garlic puree (pages 103–4) for a filling, gutsy meal.

1	**pound (450 g) salt cod, homemade (page 195) or commercial, desalted and cooked in water with bay leaf, onion, and garlic as for brandade (page 61)**
1	**tablespoon olive oil**
1	**large onion, chopped**
4 to 6	**large garlic cloves, to taste, minced or put through a press**
3	**pounds (1.35 kg) fresh tomatoes or 2 28-ounce (800 g) cans, peeled and chopped (about 4 cups/1 l)**
	pinch of sugar
1	**bay leaf**
1	**teaspoon fresh thyme leaves or ½ teaspoon dried**
	salt to taste
¼	**cup (62 ml) chopped fresh basil**
	pinch of cayenne pepper
	freshly ground pepper to taste
¼	**cup (about 15 g/½ large bunch) chopped parsley**
1	**pound (450 g) small new potatoes, boiled or steamed until tender**
1	**cup (25 ml) aïoli or either cooked or spicy garlic puree (optional)**

Drain the cooked salt cod and, when cool enough to handle, remove any skin and bones and break it up into small pieces. You should have about 3 cups (75 cl) of fish. Set aside.

Heat the olive oil in a large heavy-bottomed saucepan or casserole over medium-low heat and add the onion. Sauté, stirring, until the onion is tender, about 5 to 8 minutes. Add one of the garlic cloves and stir for about 30 seconds. Stir in the tomatoes, remaining garlic, sugar, bay leaf, thyme, and some salt; bring to a simmer. Cover and simmer for 15 minutes. Uncover, add the basil and cayenne, and cook for another 15 to 25 minutes, stirring often, until thick. Add pepper, taste, and adjust salt and garlic. Don't oversalt, because the fish is salty.

Stir the fish into the tomato sauce and heat through. Transfer to a warm platter or individual plates, sprinkle on the parsley, surround with potatoes, and serve, passing the aïoli or garlic puree at the table.

Note: You could serve this dish with rice instead of potatoes. Cook the rice with a pinch of saffron added to the water.

ADVANCE PREPARATION: The tomato sauce can be made up to a day ahead of time and held in the refrigerator.

PER PORTION

Calories	210	Protein	17 G
Fat	4 G	Carbohydrate	28 G
Sodium	N/A	Cholesterol	33 MG

SOCCA CRÊPES FILLED WITH BRANDADE

Crêpes à la brandade avec concassée de tomates

SERVES 4

Brandade is so versatile. It can be eaten on its own, spread on croutons, or spooned into vegetables. Here brandade with potatoes is folded into socca crêpes and sauced with a tangy tomato concassée. In winter you can serve the crêpes with the basic tomato sauce on page 112 instead of the concassée. The dish is lovely for dinner parties.

1	recipe brandade with potatoes (page 64)
8	socca crêpes (page 90)
1	tablespoon olive oil
2	pounds (900 g) sweet, ripe tomatoes, peeled, seeded, and finely chopped
2 to 3	garlic cloves, or more to taste, minced or put through a press
1	tablespoon balsamic vinegar
¼	cup (60 ml) fresh basil leaves, snipped with scissors
	salt and freshly ground pepper to taste

Preheat the oven to 375°F (190°C). Oil a baking dish large enough to accommodate all of the filled crêpes in a single layer. Spoon about ¼ heaped cup (4 heaped tablespoons) of the brandade onto one half of each crêpe and gently fold the crêpe over. Transfer to the baking dish. Drizzle on 1½ teaspoons of olive oil and cover with foil.

Combine the tomatoes, garlic, vinegar, basil, and remaining olive oil. Add salt and pepper.

Heat the crêpes for 20 to 30 minutes in the preheated oven and serve with the concassée on the side.

ADVANCE PREPARATION: The crêpes will hold for several weeks in the freezer or for a few days in the refrigerator. The brandade will hold for

a couple of days in the refrigerator but is best freshly made. You can assemble the crêpes several hours before baking and hold in the refrigerator. The tomato concassée can be made several hours before serving. I like to serve it at room temperature, but you can also serve it chilled.

PER PORTION

Calories	472	Protein	32 G
Fat	22 G	Carbohydrate	39 G
Sodium	N/A	Cholesterol	128 MG

BRANDADE AND SPINACH GRATIN
Tian de brandade aux épinards

SERVES 4

Brandade, stretched with mashed potatoes, has become a popular contemporary bistro dish. In this version the brandade is embellished with spinach. The fragrant, comforting gratin is incredibly easy to throw together once you've made the brandade.

- **1 pound (450 g/4 medium-size) waxy potatoes, boiled or steamed until tender and peeled**
- **½ cup (125 ml) low-fat (2%, not skim) milk**
- **1 recipe brandade (page 61)**
- **¾ pound (340 g) spinach, stemmed and washed, or 1 10-ounce package frozen, thawed**
- **salt and freshly ground pepper to taste**
- **2 teaspoons olive oil**

Mash the cooked potatoes and work in the milk. Using the pulse action of the food processor or a wooden spoon, combine with the brandade.

Preheat the oven to 425°F (220°C). Oil a 2-quart (2 l) gratin. If you're using fresh spinach, blanch it in a large pot of boiling water or wilt it in a large nonstick

FISH AND SHELLFISH

skillet in the water left on its leaves after washing (this will take a couple of minutes at most once the water on the leaves begins to bubble). Transfer to a bowl of cold water, then drain and squeeze out the moisture. Chop fine. You should have about 1 cup of chopped cooked spinach. If you're using thawed frozen spinach, squeeze out the moisture and chop if not chopped already.

Stir half the spinach into the brandade. Layer half the brandade/spinach mixture in the gratin dish. Scatter the remaining spinach over the brandade and sprinkle with salt and pepper. Top with the remaining brandade. Drizzle on the olive oil.

Bake for 20 minutes, until the top begins to brown. Serve hot.

ADVANCE PREPARATION: The brandade can be made a day ahead of time. The dish can be assembled and held in the refrigerator for a day before baking.

PER PORTION

Calories	335	Protein	28 G
Fat	12 G	Carbohydrate	30 G
Sodium	N/A	Cholesterol	56 MG

SALT COD IN AN ONION, WINE, AND CAPER SAUCE

Morue en capilotade

SERVES 6

Capilotade is a Provençal sauce made with onions, wine, vinegar, capers, and sometimes tomatoes. There are many versions; sometimes white wine is called for, sometimes red, sometimes vermouth. It is usually thickened with flour, but in some versions tomato paste or chopped tomatoes alone are called for. I've taken all of these variations into consideration here. You can make this dish with fish other than salt cod. The sauce is also used with chicken (page 379).

1½ **pounds (675 g) dried salt cod, homemade (page 195) or commercial, desalted (page 62), or fresh cod or snapper fillets**

a bouquet garni made with a bay leaf, a few fresh thyme sprigs, a few parsley sprigs, and a wide slice of orange zest

1 **tablespoon tomato paste**

½ **cup (125 ml) dry red wine**

2 **tablespoons olive oil**

2 **large onions, chopped**

2 **large garlic cloves, minced or put through a press**

2 **teaspoons unbleached white flour**

1 **tablespoon red wine vinegar**

¼ **cup (60 ml) drained capers, rinsed**

salt and freshly ground pepper to taste

3 **tablespoons chopped parsley**

Place the fish in a deep lidded flameproof casserole or pan and cover with water. Add the bouquet garni. Gradually bring to a simmer, but don't allow the water to boil. As soon as the water begins to tremble, cover, turn off the heat, and let sit for 10 minutes. Remove the fish from the water and transfer to a platter. Reserve 1½ cups (375 ml) of the stock and stir in the tomato paste and wine: set aside.

Heat the oil in a large heavy-bottomed skillet over medium-low heat and add the onions. Cook, stirring, until they soften, about 5 minutes. Add the garlic and continue to cook, stirring, until the garlic begins to color, ½ to 1 minute. Stir in the flour and vinegar and cook, stirring, for about 1 minute, until the mixture just begins to brown and stick to the pan.

Add the wine mixture to the onions along with the capers, salt, and pepper. Cook, uncovered, for 5 to 10 minutes, stirring often, until the sauce thickens slightly.

Stir the fish back into the mixture, heat through, sprinkle with parsley, and serve.

ADVANCE PREPARATION: This can be made hours ahead of serving and can also be held overnight in the refrigerator. Reheat in a 350°F (180°C) oven for 10 to 15 minutes or stir over medium-low heat in a flameproof casserole.

PER PORTION

Calories	184	Protein	21 G
Fat	5 G	Carbohydrate	9 G
Sodium	N/A	Cholesterol	49 MG

SPINACH AND SALT COD GRATIN
Tian de morue aux épinards

SERVES 4

When I eat fish in a restaurant, I always order spinach on the side if it's available. I don't know why fish and spinach make such a great combination; maybe it's the inherent freshness and vitality in each ingredient. This is a simple, homey dish, and I love it. Try it with regular cod if you don't like salt cod.

1	pound (450 g) salt cod, homemade (page 195) or commercial, or fresh cod fillets
4	garlic cloves, minced or put through a press
1	bay leaf
1	medium or large onion, quartered
3	pounds (1.35 kg) spinach, stems removed
	salt and freshly ground pepper to taste
1	cup (250 ml/½ recipe) olive oil béchamel (page 111)
2	tablespoons fine whole-wheat or white bread crumbs
1	tablespoon olive oil

Desalt the salt cod. Place in a large bowl and cover with water. If convenient, put the bowl in your kitchen sink and keep the water running in a thin stream so that the water in the bowl is constantly renewing itself. Otherwise, change the soaking water several times over 24 hours for salt cod, 48 hours for dried salt cod.

Cut the cod into a few large pieces and place in a heavy-bottomed casserole or stockpot. Add water to cover, 2 garlic cloves, the bay leaf, and the onion. Slowly bring to a simmer over medium-low heat. As soon as the water reaches a simmer and before it comes to the boil—you'll see little bubbles coming up from the bottom of the pot and the water will be moving without the surface bubbling—cover, turn off the heat, and let sit for 10 minutes. Drain and transfer the fish to a bowl. Allow to cool until you can handle it.

If you're using fresh cod, simply poach as directed or steam for 5 minutes. The fish should break apart easily but not be quite cooked through.

Pick out the bones from the fish and remove the skin. Flake the fish by rubbing it between your fingers or using a fork or wooden spoon. If you use your fingers, it will be easier to verify that you've gotten the bones out.

Preheat the oven to 425°F (220°C). Oil a 2-quart (2 l) gratin dish. Either blanch the spinach in a large pot of salted boiling water or wilt in a large heavy-bottomed nonstick skillet over high heat in the water left on the leaves after washing. Wilting should take no more than 2 minutes once the water begins to boil. Remove from the heat, refresh in a bowl of cold water, and transfer to a colander. When cool enough to handle, squeeze out excess water, chop, and toss with the remaining garlic, the salt, pepper, and béchamel.

Layer half the spinach in the gratin dish and top with the fish. Cover with the remaining spinach. Sprinkle on the bread crumbs and drizzle on the olive oil. Bake for 20 minutes, until the gratin is sizzling and the top is beginning to brown. Serve hot.

ADVANCE PREPARATION: Each element—the spinach, the salt cod, the béchamel—can be prepared a day ahead of assembling and baking the gratin.

PER PORTION

Calories	266	Protein	31 G
Fat	10 G	Carbohydrate	17 G
Sodium	N/A	Cholesterol	51 MG

FISH COOKED IN RAITO

SERVES 6

I like to use firm white-fleshed fish like lingcod, redfish, or snapper for this dish. Their mild flavor contrasts beautifully with the pungent raito.

olive oil for the baking dish
1   **recipe raito (page 119)**
1   **pound (450 g) fish fillets, such as snapper, redfish, lingcod, or cod**
    salt and freshly ground pepper to taste

Preheat the oven to 450°F (230°C). Oil a baking dish large enough to accommodate all the fish in one layer lightly with olive oil. Spoon a ladleful of the raito into the dish. Rinse the fish fillets and pat dry. Lay them side by side in the baking dish and sprinkle with salt and freshly ground pepper to taste. Spoon more sauce over them, using up about two-thirds of the sauce. Cover tightly with foil.

Bake for 10 to 15 minutes or 10 minutes per inch (2.5 cm) of thickness of the fillets, measured at the thickest point, until the fish flakes easily with a fork at the thickest part. Meanwhile, reheat the remaining raito in a saucepan on top of the stove.

Remove the fish from the oven and serve at once, topping with the additional sauce.

Leftovers: Flake the leftover fish and mix with leftover sauce. Toss with cooked pasta.

ADVANCE PREPARATION: The sauce will hold for 2 or 3 days in the refrigerator. The fish with the sauce in the baking dish can be assembled hours before baking. Allow it to come to room temperature before baking.

PER PORTION

Calories	168	Protein	18 G
Fat	5 G	Carbohydrate	13 G
Sodium	243 MG	Cholesterol	28 MG

SMOKED HADDOCK AND POTATO PUREE
Brandade de haddock

SERVES 4 TO 6 AS A MAIN DISH, 8 AS AN HORS D'OEUVRE

The idea for a brandade made from smoked haddock instead of salt cod comes not from Provence but from a Paris bistro called L'Echanson. This dish has a smokier, milder flavor than traditional brandade, and it's a bit easier to make. Although you probably wouldn't find the dish in Provence, you might have an easier time finding smoked haddock than salt cod elsewhere. I add lots of garlic to give it the big Provençal taste.

1	**pound (450 g) smoked haddock**
3½	**cups (875 ml) low-fat (2%, not skim) milk**
2	**bay leaves**
1	**onion, quartered**
5 to 6	**large garlic cloves, 2 cut in half, the rest minced or put through a press**
1	**pound (450 g/4 medium-size) new or boiling potatoes, peeled**
1	**tablespoon olive oil, plus 1½ teaspoons for the hot version**
	salt and freshly ground pepper to taste

Two hours before you wish to make the dish, place the haddock in a bowl or baking dish and pour in 1 cup (25 cl) of the milk and enough water to cover. Soak for 2 hours and drain.

Place the haddock in a heavy-bottomed saucepan and add another cup (25 cl) of milk and enough water to cover. Add the bay leaves, onion, and the 2 cut garlic cloves. Slowly bring to a simmer, cover, and simmer for 8 minutes. Remove from the heat, drain the fish, and allow to cool.

Meanwhile, boil the potatoes in salted water for about 30 minutes until completely tender, drain, and mash with ½ cup (125 ml) of the milk.

When the fish is cool enough to handle, remove the skin and bones and flake with your fingers, a fork, or a wooden spoon.

Scald the remaining cup (250 ml) of milk and remove from the heat.

Heat 1 tablespoon of the olive oil in a large heavy-bottomed saucepan or skillet and add 3 minced garlic cloves. As soon as the garlic begins to sizzle, stir in the haddock and stir and mash until the fish has absorbed all of the oil. Remove from the heat and transfer to a food processor.

Using the pulse action so that you don't puree the fish too finely, mix in the scalded milk a little at a time, pulsing with each addition. Stir in the potatoes (you can use the food processor, but pulse only a few times so that they don't turn gummy). Transfer to a bowl and add salt, pepper, and more garlic to taste.

If you're serving this as a first course, transfer it to a serving bowl and surround with garlic croutons (page 83). If you're serving it as a main dish, transfer it to an oiled 1½- or 2-quart (1.5 or 2 l) gratin dish, drizzle the remaining 1½ teaspoons olive oil over the top, and heat through in a preheated 425°F (220°C) oven until it begins to brown on the top, about 20 minutes.

Note: You can also place the dish briefly under the broiler to brown the top after you've heated it through.

Leftovers: Use as a filling for ravioli (see the salt cod and herb ravioli on page 276).

ADVANCE PREPARATION: This will keep for 3 to 4 days in the refrigerator but is best the day it's made.

PER PORTION

Calories	247	Protein	23 G
Fat	8 G	Carbohydrate	19 G
Sodium	615 MG	Cholesterol	63 MG

GRILLED TUNA WITH TOMATO CONCASSÉE AND PISTOU

SERVES 6

A dinner guest once said to me: "This is wonderful, and I hate tuna!" It's a great, easy summer dish. The tuna steaks are seared on a grill so that they remain pink in the middle and served with a heady uncooked tomato sauce heightened with low-fat pistou.

2½	pounds (1.25 kg/10 medium-size) tomatoes, peeled, seeded, and finely chopped
2	large garlic cloves, minced or put through a press
1 to 2	tablespoons balsamic vinegar to taste
	coarse sea salt to taste
3	tablespoons low-fat pistou (page 109)
1½	tablespoons olive oil
6	tuna steaks, about ¾ inch (2 cm) thick and ¼ pound (115 g) each without the bone
	salt and freshly ground pepper to taste
	fresh basil sprigs for garnish

Mix together the tomatoes, garlic, vinegar, salt, pistou, and 1 tablespoon of the olive oil and set aside.

Heat a grill and brush the fish steaks with a small amount of olive oil; sprinkle on a little salt and pepper. Cook over high heat or hot coals for 1 minute on each side and transfer to a platter or individual plates.

Serve with the sauce spooned partially on top of the fish and partially on the side. Garnish with basil.

ADVANCE PREPARATION: The sauce will hold for a day in the refrigerator.

PER PORTION

Calories	254	Protein	29 G
Fat	11 G	Carbohydrate	10 G
Sodium	124 MG	Cholesterol	44 MG

TUNA STEAK BAKED IN A BED OF LETTUCE

Toun a la chastrouso   Thon à la chartreuse

SERVES 4

I've always been intrigued by this dish, which I've seen in many cookbooks but never on a menu. I would say it's the meatiest fish dish I've ever tasted. The thick tuna steak should be pink in the middle, so measure it before you determine the cooking time. I love the tangy taste that the sorrel gives this dish, but it's delicious without it as well. The lettuce moistens the tuna as it cooks, so the fish remains succulent. The cooked lettuce has a fresh, herbal flavor; you can serve it with the fish or discard it.

2½ cups (625 ml) water

2 tablespoons red wine vinegar

1 2-inch-thick (5 cm) slice of tuna, about 1½ pounds (675 g)

4 anchovy fillets, rinsed and chopped (optional)

1 tablespoon olive oil

2 medium-size onions, thinly sliced

4 large garlic cloves, minced or put through a press

1 pound (450 g/ 4 medium-size) tomatoes, peeled, seeded, and coarsely chopped

salt and freshly ground pepper to taste

3	heads of Boston lettuce, tough outer leaves discarded
1	lemon, sliced
1	cup (1½ ounces/45 g) fresh sorrel, cut into chiffonade (optional)
¾	cup (185 ml) dry white wine

Combine 2 cups (500 ml) of the water with the vinegar. Place the tuna in a bowl and pour on the vinegared water. Let soak for 1 hour while you prepare the remaining ingredients. Drain and pat dry. If you are using the anchovies, pierce the tuna in several places with a sharp knife and slide pieces of anchovy into the pierces.

Preheat the oven to 425°F (220°C). Heat the oil in a large heavy-bottomed nonstick pan or casserole over medium-low heat. Add the onions and sauté, stirring, until they begin to soften, about 5 minutes. Add the garlic, tomatoes, salt, and pepper and continue to cook, stirring, for another 5 minutes. Transfer to a bowl.

Turn up the heat and sear the tuna for 30 seconds on each side. Remove from the heat and sprinkle with salt and pepper.

Lightly oil a lidded large ovenproof casserole. Layer half the lettuce on the bottom of the casserole and top with half the onion-tomato mixture and half the lemon slices. Lay the tuna on top and sprinkle the sorrel, if you're using it, over the tuna. Top with the remaining onion-tomato mixture and lemon slices and layer the remaining lettuce on top. The lettuce will fill the casserole, but it will cook down quite a bit, so don't worry about the quantity.

Pour in the remaining ½ cup (125 ml) water and the wine. Cover tightly and bake for 30 minutes—20 minutes if the fish is 1½ or 1¾ inches (4 to 4.5 cm) thick rather than 2 inches (5 cm). It should remain pink in the middle.

To serve, remove the top leaves of lettuce and transfer the tuna to a warm serving platter. Spoon the juice in the pan, along with the onions and tomato, over the tuna. I usually discard the lettuce, but serve it if you wish. Either slice the fish as if it were a sirloin steak or cut it into thick wedges. Serve, passing additional liquid from the baking dish in a gravy boat.

ADVANCE PREPARATION: The dish can be prepared up to the point of filling the casserole (before the ½ cup/12.5 cl water is added) and held several hours in the refrigerator before being baked. Allow it to come to room temperature before baking.

PER PORTION

Calories	383	Protein	44 G
Fat	14 G	Carbohydrate	23 G
Sodium	97 MG	Cholesterol	65 MG

GRILLED OR BAKED SEA BASS WITH FENNEL
Loup grillé ou rôti au fenouil

SERVES 4

This is a classic coastal dish, from Marseille to Menton on the Italian border. It's one of the simplest and finest fish dishes and always has a prominent, expensive place on a good seaside menu. Usually the fish is grilled, with fennel branches in the fire and under and inside the fish. But if you don't have a grill or you want to make this dish in winter, it's just as good baked. In fact, it may be better baked, because the flavors are more concentrated and the fish has less chance to dry out. My fishmonger in Paris just brushes the fish with olive oil and spreads the fennel stalks over the top. I add fennel seeds. Fennel branches are sold in gourmet groceries and herb shops. If you can't get them, you can obtain a similar effect by adding pastis or anisette to the baking dish.

salt and freshly ground pepper to taste

1 **2- to 2½-pound (900 g to 1.25 kg) sea bass, cleaned**

1 **tablespoon olive oil**

2 **teaspoons lightly crushed fennel seeds**

1 **bunch of dried fennel stalks, about 2 ounces (60 g), or ¼ cup (62 ml) pastis or anisette liqueur**

lemon wedges for garnish

FISH AND SHELLFISH

Salt and pepper the fish and rub with olive oil. Place the fennel seeds and one or two stalks in the cavity.

To grill the fish: Prepare a grill. Place some of the fennel stalks on top of the coals when they're just about ready. Place the remaining fennel stalks underneath the fish, either in a hinged grilling rack or directly on top of the grill. Grill the fish for about 12 minutes on each side (4 minutes for each ½ inch/1.5 cm of thickness), until the flesh is opaque and comes away from the bone easily. Transfer to a flameproof platter.

If you're using the pastis: Place the pastis in a pan, heat slightly, and light. Pour the flaming pastis over the fish. As soon as it goes out, serve the fish, with lemon wedges.

To bake the fish: Preheat the oven to 425°F (220°C). Oil a baking dish large enough to accommodate the fish with olive oil. Place the fish in the baking dish and cover with the fennel stalks. If you're using the pastis, add to the baking dish. Cover tightly with lightly oiled foil. Bake 20 to 30 minutes (4 to 5 minutes for each ½ inch/1.5 cm of thickness), until the flesh is opaque and comes away from the bone easily. Serve hot, with lemon wedges.

ADVANCE PREPARATION: The fish can be prepared, with the fennel, several hours before cooking.

PER PORTION

Calories	130	Protein	19 G
Fat	6 G	Carbohydrate	.50 G
Sodium	69 MG	Cholesterol	41 MG

PASTIS

Anise-flavored drinks are popular throughout the Mediterranean—Greece has its ouzo and Turkey its raki—but nowhere are they such a part of the cultural and gastronomic landscape as in Provence. Here pastis is the aperitif par excellence. The milky-yellow drinks are what you expect to see people drinking in cafes, at any time of day, and indeed, even if you don't think pastis is your cup of tea, you might find yourself developing a taste for it after a few days wandering about the region. The drink, which comes to you in a glass, with a pitcher of icewater for diluting (when you pour in the water the pastis turns from clear to milky), is wonderfully refreshing (but very high in alcohol). You can keep stretching it by topping it up with water, so that it becomes a very long drink.

Pastis means *mélange,* or mixture, in Provençal; it is made by macerating a mixture of star anise, which came to Marseille from China, and local herbs and plants in alcohol. In the past, families made their pastis at home, and jealously guarded their recipes (some still do). The mixtures of herbs and the maceration times are the variables. Most pastis in France—200 million bottles a year—is industrial stuff, with very little nuance and a lot of licorice. But lately a few artisanal *pastis gastronomiques* have been springing up, created by passionate drinkers of the aperitif. These are worth seeking out in wine stores.

The Provençal love of anise goes beyond the local bar, where the flavor is strong. In the kitchen it's a subtle perfume, derived from dried fennel sticks and fennel seeds, as well as the occasional splash of pastis. Fish is grilled over a bunch of dried fennel sticks (see the recipe on page 212); dried fennel sticks are part of many bouquet garnis, especially when it comes to fish soups. Chicken is marinated in pastis and stewed (page 377). Pastry, cookies, and festive breads are spiced with fennel seeds.

In the United States dried fennel sticks are not so easy to come by (though fennel grows wild all over California; it would be easy to pick and dry your own). But fennel seeds are easily found in supermarkets and pastis is easy to find in liquor stores. A little goes a long way, but a tablespoon or two will work for perfuming, say, a fish that a Provençal cook would grill over fennel stalks.

FISH COOKED IN PHYLLO
WITH TAPENADE
Filets de poisson en bric à la tapenade

SERVES 4

Provence has a large population of *pieds noirs,* former colonials in North Africa who returned to France after the Algerian war in the 1960s. The presence of these French, plus the North African immigrants, has lent its character to Provençal cuisine. I ate this dish at the house of Mamine, a friend's surrogate grandmother, who lives in the hills above Cannes. Mamine lived in Algeria for many years and, like so many colonial French, picked up many North African cooking ideas there. Cooking fish in *feuilles de bric,* the North African equivalent of phyllo dough, is one such idea. This is nice with a tomato gratin or sauce (pages 346 and 112–18) on the side but also stands alone.

4   ¼-pound (115 g) fillets of snapper, whiting, sole, redfish, or cod

    salt and freshly ground pepper to taste

¼   cup (62 ml) tapenade (page 56)

2   sheets of phyllo dough (available at Greek markets and gourmet shops)

1   tablespoon olive oil

Preheat the oven to 425°F (220°C). Oil a baking sheet or dish large enough to accommodate the fish in one layer. Rinse the fish fillets and pat dry. Sprinkle with salt and pepper and spread a tablespoon of tapenade along the surface of each one.

Cut the sheets of phyllo dough in half crosswise. Place a piece of phyllo dough with a narrower edge facing you on a work surface. Brush lightly with olive oil. Lay a fish fillet across it, about 3 inches (8 cm) down from the top. Fold the sides of the strip of phyllo in over the ends of the fish fillet, then fold the top over the fish. Now roll up the phyllo dough. Brush with olive oil and place on the baking sheet or dish. Continue with the remaining fillets.

Bake for 10 to 15 minutes, until the phyllo is crisp and brown at the edges. Remove from the heat and serve.

ADVANCE PREPARATION: The tapenade can be prepared days ahead and refrigerated. You must bake the fish right after you wrap it, however, or the phyllo will become soggy.

PER PORTION

Calories	215	Protein	25 G
Fat	10 G	Carbohydrate	6 G
Sodium	363 MG	Cholesterol	43 MG

FISH FILLETS BAKED IN PHYLLO WITH TOMATO CONCASSÉE
Filets de poisson en bric à la concassée de tomates

SERVES 8 AS A STARTER, 4 AS A MAIN DISH

This is based on one of my favorite *amuse-bouches,* or hors d'oeuvres, that Chef Sordello serves at Le Restaurant du Bacon in Cap d'Antibes. He takes 2 minuscule red mullet (*rouget*) fillets, sandwiches a garlicky tomato concassée with lots of basil between them, wraps them in a small piece of *feuille de bric,* a very thin North African pastry that resembles phyllo dough (it's slightly thicker), and quickly bakes this at very high heat. It's served with a little bit of tomato concassée on the side. I've taken his idea and enlarged it a little so the packages are a bit easier to handle. Sole makes a nice substitute for the red mullet. Sweet fresh tomatoes and fresh basil are essential; see the note for a winter substitute.

 2 pounds (900 g) tomatoes, peeled, seeded, and finely chopped

2 to 3 garlic cloves, or more to taste, minced or put through a press

 1 tablespoon balsamic vinegar

 ¼ cup (60 ml) fresh basil leaves, snipped with scissors

 salt, preferably coarse sea salt, and freshly ground pepper to taste

2 **tablespoons olive oil**

2 **sheets of phyllo dough (available at Greek
  markets and gourmet shops), cut in half**

1 **pound (450 g) red mullet fillets or sole fillets cut
  in half so they are 3 to 4 inches (8 to 10 cm) long**

Preheat the oven to 450°F (230°C). Lightly oil a baking dish large enough to accommodate all the packages in one layer.

Mix together the tomatoes, garlic, balsamic vinegar, basil, salt, and pepper. Add 1 teaspoon of the olive oil. Set aside.

Keeping the rest of the phyllo dough covered with a slightly damp kitchen towel, place one piece of phyllo with a narrower edge facing you on a work surface. Brush it very lightly with olive oil. Place a piece of fish 2 inches (5 cm) from the top edge. Spoon a thin layer of tomato coulis on top of the fish and top with another piece of fish.

Fold the sides of the phyllo over the fish, then fold the top edge up over the fish. Roll up the fish in the dough and brush lightly with olive oil. Set on the baking sheet and continue with the remaining fillets. Hold back at least a third of the concassée to serve alongside the baked packages.

Bake for 10 minutes, until the phyllo is browned, and serve hot, garnished with more tomato concassée.

Note: If you can't get good fresh tomatoes, make the basic tomato sauce on page 112 with canned tomatoes. Season with dried basil and include the balsamic vinegar.

ADVANCE PREPARATION: The tomato concassée can be prepared hours ahead of serving this, but the fish should be baked and served as soon as it is wrapped, or the phyllo will get wet and tear.

PER PORTION

Calories	140	Protein	12 GM
Fat	7 G	Carbohydrate	8 G
Sodium	69 MG	Cholesterol	28 MG

WHOLE ROAST FISH WITH GARLIC
Poisson rôti à l'ail

SERVES 6

This is the fish version of the famous chicken with garlic on page 383. Fish has a more delicate flavor than chicken, so it requires less garlic. Bream or porgy, red snapper, and sea bass all work well.

	salt and freshly ground pepper to taste
1	**whole red snapper, bream, porgy, or sea bass, about 3 pounds (1.35 kg) or a little more, cleaned and scaled**
1	**tablespoon olive oil**
2	**heads of garlic, about 20 to 30 cloves, peeled and lightly crushed**
2	**quarts (2 l) water**
2 or 3	**fresh rosemary sprigs to taste**
4	**medium-size tomatoes, sliced (optional)**
1	**bay leaf**
	lemon wedges for garnish

Preheat the oven to 425°F (220°C). Oil a baking dish large enough to accommodate the fish. Salt and pepper the fish and rub with olive oil.

Combine the garlic and 3 cups (750 ml) water in a large saucepan. Bring to a boil and drain off the water. Return the garlic to the saucepan, add another 3 cups (750 ml) water, bring to a boil, and drain. Return the garlic to the saucepan, add the remaining 2 cups (500 ml) water, bring to a boil, add ½ to 1 teaspoon salt, to taste, and simmer for 20 minutes. Drain and reserve ¼ cup (62 ml) of the cooking water.

Fill the cavity of the fish with the rosemary sprigs and simmered garlic cloves. Surround with any garlic that won't fit into the cavity and with the tomato slices if you're using them. Place the bay leaf on top of the fish and pour in the reserved garlic broth. Cover tightly with foil or a lid.

Bake for 30 minutes (or 5 minutes for each ½ inch/1.5 cm of thickness of the fish). The fish should come away from the bone easily when pierced with a fork.

Serve from the baking dish or transfer the fish to a serving platter. Remove the garlic cloves from the cavity.

Serve the fish with the garlic cloves, tomato slices, and lemon wedges on the side.

Leftovers: Remove all the fish from the bone. Toss with the garlic cloves with pasta or with salad.

ADVANCE PREPARATION: The garlic can be simmered and the fish prepared for baking hours ahead. Refrigerate until 30 minutes before baking.

PER PORTION

Calories	165	Protein	25 G
Fat	5 G	Carbohydrate	4 G
Sodium	78 MG	Cholesterol	44 MG

WHOLE FISH WITH TAPENADE
Poisson à la tapenade

SERVES 4

Tapenade makes a wonderful garnish for baked, grilled, or poached fish. It's especially welcome with blander fish, like whiting, but doesn't have to be confined to these. You can also serve tapenade with grilled or baked tuna or swordfish steaks. In summer, poach the fish and serve the dish cold.

	salt and freshly ground pepper to taste
1	**large whole fish, 2 to 2½ pounds (900 g to 1.25 kg), or 4 8-ounce (225 g) fish such as whiting, snapper, porgy, sea bass, or red mullet, cleaned and scaled for baking or poaching, scales left on for grilling**
	juice of 1 lemon
1	**tablespoon olive oil for baking or grilling or 1 quart (1 l) court bouillon (page 194) for poaching**
⅓	**cup (85 ml) tapenade (page 56)**
2	**large or 4 small fresh rosemary sprigs**
	Boston lettuce leaves, blanched,★ for baking (optional)
2	**tablespoons dry white or rosé wine for baking**
	lemon wedges for garnish

Salt and pepper the fish and squeeze on the lemon juice. To grill or bake, rub with the olive oil. For a large fish, place 2 teaspoons tapenade and 2 rosemary sprigs in the stomach cavity. For small fish, place ½ teaspoon tapenade and 1 rosemary sprig in the cavity of each fish.

Preheat the oven to 425°F (220°C) or prepare a grill or court bouillon. To bake the fish, oil a baking dish large enough to accommodate the fish. Wrap the fish

★ Lettuce leaves help fish retain moisture and remind me a bit of the grape leaves often wrapped around fish in Provence. Pour boiling water over the lettuce leaves, drain, rinse with cold water, and gently squeeze dry.

in blanched lettuce leaves if desired. Place the fish in the baking dish, add the wine, and cover tightly with foil that has been lightly oiled on the underside.

Grill the fish 4 minutes per ½ inch (1.5 cm) of thickness at the thickest point. Bake for 5 minutes per ½ inch (1.5 cm) of thickness at the thickest point. To poach, bring the court bouillon to a bare simmer, add the fish, and poach for 5 minutes per ½ inch (1.5 cm) of thickness at the thickest point. Remove from the court bouillon or the grill and transfer to a platter (you can serve baked fish directly from the dish).

Serve the fish, passing the remaining tapenade in a bowl and garnishing each plate with lemon wedges.

ADVANCE PREPARATION: The tapenade will hold for several days in the refrigerator. The court bouillon can be prepared hours ahead of poaching. The fish can be prepared hours before cooking and held in the refrigerator. Remove from the refrigerator 30 minutes before cooking. The poached fish can also be served cold.

PER PORTION

Calories	182	Protein	25 G
Fat	8 G	Carbohydrate	2 G
Sodium	239 MG	Cholesterol	44 MG

RED MULLET WITH TOMATOES AND OLIVES
Rougets à la niçoise

SERVES 6

The small red mullet from the Mediterranean called *rougets* are among the most popular fish along the Côte d'Azur. This recipe is a classic. If you can't find red mullet, try the luscious, gutsy sauce with other fish, such as whiting or snapper. A summer dish, it requires sweet ripe tomatoes.

6	**medium-size (8 to 10 ounce/225 to 285 g) or 12 small (5 to 6 ounce/140 to 180 g) red mullet, cleaned and scaled**
	salt and freshly ground pepper to taste
1	**tablespoon olive oil**
1	**medium-size onion, chopped**
3 to 4	**large garlic cloves, to taste, minced or put through a press**
3	**pounds (1.35 kg/12 medium-size) tomatoes, seeded and quartered**
1 or 2	**pinches of sugar**
2 to 3	**tablespoons slivered fresh basil to taste**
18	**Niçois olives**

Rinse the fish and pat dry. Preheat the oven to 425°F (220°C). Oil a gratin dish large enough to accommodate the fish in one layer and lay the fish in the dish. Salt and pepper lightly.

Heat the oil in a large heavy-bottomed nonstick skillet over medium-low heat and add the onion. Cook, stirring, until it begins to soften, about 5 minutes. Add the garlic and cook until it begins to color, about 30 seconds. Add the tomatoes, sugar, and salt to taste. Turn the heat to medium and cook, stirring often, for 20 to 30 minutes, until the tomatoes are cooked down and beginning to stick to the pan. Stir in the basil, simmer for a few more minutes, and remove from the heat.

Put the sauce through the medium blade of a food mill. Stir in the olives,

222

FISH AND SHELLFISH

adjust the salt, add pepper, and pour the sauce over and around the fish in the gratin dish. Cover the dish tightly with foil.

Bake for 15 to 25 minutes, until the fish flakes easily when pierced with a fork. Serve with steamed potatoes, rice, or pasta on the side.

ADVANCE PREPARATION: The sauce can be made a day or two ahead of time. The dish can be assembled hours before baking and held in the refrigerator. Remove from the refrigerator 30 minutes before cooking.

PER PORTION

Calories	250	Protein	29 G
Fat	9 G	Carbohydrate	14 G
Sodium	207 MG	Cholesterol	66 MG

SARDINE AND SPINACH GRATIN

Gratin de sardines aux épinards

SERVES 4

The earth and the sea come together here as they do so often in Provençal cooking. Although fresh sardines aren't that easy to come by, every once in a while you do find them, and if you do, this is one of the most uniquely Provençal of dishes. The sardines are boned (this is easy) and filled with blanched spinach and surrounded by more spinach in a gratin. You can use spinach only or a combination of spinach and other herbs and greens.

12	large fresh sardines
2	pounds (900 g) spinach or a combination of spinach and other greens, such as chard, mustard greens, dandelion greens, beet greens, stems removed
2	tablespoons olive oil
1	medium-size onion, finely chopped
2	garlic cloves, minced or put through a press
½	cup (30 g/1 large bunch) chopped parsley
1	teaspoon fresh thyme leaves or ½ teaspoon dried
1	tablespoon unbleached white flour
⅓	cup (85 ml) skim milk
	salt and freshly ground pepper to taste
	pinch of freshly grated nutmeg
2	tablespoons fresh or dry, coarse or fine bread crumbs

Prepare the sardines. Snap off the head of the sardine and pull away most of the innards with it. Tear off the center back fin from the tail end toward the head, pulling off the little bones attached to it. Run your thumb along the belly, scooping out the remaining intestines, and open out the sardine so that it's flat. Gently loosen the spine ribs from the flesh and pull away toward the tail. Rinse and pat dry. Open them out flat and set aside on a paper towel.

Preheat the oven to 425°F (220°C). Oil a 2-quart (2 l) gratin dish.

Either blanch the spinach and greens in a large pot of salted boiling water or wilt in a large heavy-bottomed nonstick skillet over high heat in the water left on the leaves after washing. This should take no more than 2 minutes once the water begins to boil. Remove from the heat, refresh in a bowl of cold water, and transfer to a colander. When cool enough to handle, squeeze out excess water and chop.

Heat 1 tablespoon of the oil in a large heavy-bottomed nonstick skillet over medium-low heat and add the onion. Cook, stirring, for 5 minutes or until tender. Add the garlic, stir together for about 30 seconds, and stir in the spinach, herbs, and flour. Stir together for about 30 seconds, then add the milk, salt, pepper, and nutmeg. Stir together for a minute or two, until the mixture is fairly dry. Remove from the heat, taste, and adjust seasonings.

Spread a thin layer of the spinach mixture over the bottom of the gratin dish. Fill each sardine with a small amount of the spinach mixture, close the two sides together, and roll up from head to tail. Place on top of the spinach and cover with the remaining spinach. Sprinkle on the bread crumbs and drizzle on the remaining olive oil.

Bake for 10 to 15 minutes, until the sardines are cooked through and the dish is sizzling. Serve hot.

ADVANCE PREPARATION: The dish can be assembled hours before cooking. The spinach or spinach and greens can be prepared a day ahead of time.

PER PORTION

Calories	293	Protein	22 G
Fat	17 G	Carbohydrate	15 G
Sodium	252 MG	Cholesterol	53 MG

TROUT BAKED IN FOIL WITH ROSEMARY AND LEMON
Truite saumonée en papillote

SERVES 4

Trout has always been an important river fish in Provence. Now that the rivers are largely polluted, the trout is farmed, and it can be quite good. These rose-fleshed fish, fragrant with rosemary and lemon, make one of the easiest, most satisfying meals I can think of. I love the color of the salmon trout, but if you can't find it, regular trout is also delicious. In Provence I often sprinkle *herbes de Provence* over the inside of the fish. It's good either way.

- **4   teaspoons olive oil**
- **8   large fresh rosemary sprigs**
- **4   salmon trout or regular freshwater trout, about ½ pound (225 g) each, cleaned**
- **salt and freshly ground pepper to taste**
- **4   lemons, 2 cut into thin rounds, 2 cut into wedges for garnish**

Preheat the oven to 425°F (220°C). Cut 4 sheets of heavy-duty foil about 12 inches (30 cm) square. Spoon a teaspoon of olive oil onto the dull side of each one and brush it evenly over the foil.

Place a sprig of rosemary in the cavity of each fish and salt and pepper generously. Lay each trout on a piece of foil and top with a few rounds of lemon and another sprig of rosemary. Fold the foil loosely over the fish and crimp the edges together tightly. Place the packets on a baking sheet or in a baking dish and bake for 20 minutes, until the fish flakes easily when pierced with a fork. Remove from the heat.

Slit the packets across the top and serve the fish in the foil. Guests should transfer their fish to their plates and pour the juices in the foil over the fish. Have a dish on the table for the foil. Pass extra lemon wedges.

ADVANCE PREPARATION: The foil envelopes can be assembled hours before you cook the fish. Refrigerate if holding for more than an hour, but allow the fish to come to room temperature before baking.

PER PORTION

Calories	217	Protein	30 G
Fat	9 G	Carbohydrate	6 G
Sodium	40 MG	Cholesterol	80 MG

HERBES DE PROVENCE

Herbes de Provence are just that: the herbs that grow in this rocky, arid countryside. They are gathered, dried, and sold all over France in various combinations, all labeled *herbes de Provence.* The jar I have now consists of savory, rosemary, thyme, oregano, basil, and marjoram, "in varying proportions." One herb missing from my mixture is fennel seed, which is sometimes included, sometimes not. The label states that "the herbs of the backcountry come together to perfume your grilled meats and tomato sauces." That's not the only thing. I love to sprinkle these herbs inside trout and cook the fish *en papillote,* as well as sprinkle them over pizzas and tomato gratins. It's easy to make up your own mixture of *herbes de Provence* by combining the herbs mentioned in whatever proportions you prefer.

SQUID AND RED WINE RAGOUT

Touteno en dobo
Calmars en daube

SERVES 4 TO 6

In southern Provence they often make this dish with octopus, but I prefer the more delicate *calmars,* small squid. They become extremely tender when cooked in the wine. As usual, I dispense with the bacon that would go into the traditional Provençal version of this dish.

2½	**pounds (1.25 kg) squid, cleaned and cut into 1-inch (2.5 cm) pieces**
2	**tablespoons olive oil**
2	**medium-size onions, chopped**
4	**garlic cloves, minced or put through a press**
4	**medium-size or large tomatoes, seeded and chopped**
	salt to taste
¼	**cup (60 ml) cognac**
2	**teaspoons unbleached white flour**
2	**cups (500 ml) dry, fruity red wine, such as a Côtes du Rhône**
1	**dried hot chili or a pinch of cayenne pepper**
	freshly ground pepper to taste
1	**large egg yolk**
	chopped fresh parsley for garnish

Rinse the squid and pat dry with paper towels.

Heat 1 tablespoon of the oil in a heavy-bottomed casserole over medium heat and add the onions. Sauté for 5 minutes, until tender, and add the garlic. Sauté for another 3 to 5 minutes, until the onion is golden. Add the tomatoes, sprinkle with salt, and sauté, stirring, for 5 minutes, until the tomatoes have cooked down slightly. Transfer to a bowl and wipe out the pan with a paper towel.

Heat the remaining oil in the same casserole over medium heat and sauté the squid pieces until they begin to color (the edges will brown, and the surface will turn pinkish), about 5 to 10 minutes. Add the cognac, heat for a minute, and light it with a match to flame. When the flames die down, add the flour, wine, tomato mixture, hot pepper, and a pinch of salt. Stir together well. Add enough water to cover by 1 inch (2.5 cm). Bring to a simmer, cover, and simmer for 45 minutes or until the squid is tender, stirring from time to time. Taste and add more garlic if desired and salt and pepper to taste.

Just before serving, remove a ladleful of the broth and mix in the egg yolk. Stir back into the stew, being very careful not to let the mixture boil.

Sprinkle with parsley and serve hot over rice or with steamed potatoes or fresh pasta on the side.

ADVANCE PREPARATION: The entire ragout, up to the final addition of the egg yolk, can be made a day in advance and held overnight in the refrigerator.

PER PORTION

Calories	237	Protein	25 G
Fat	8 G	Carbohydrate	16 G
Sodium	80 MG	Cholesterol	379 MG

MUSSELS WITH TOMATOES
AND GARLIC

Moules à la provençale

SERVES 4

This is one of my favorite ways to eat mussels. It's easy to make, although it takes a while to clean all the mussels. I like to drink a chilled rosé from Bandol with this.

4½	**pounds (2 kg) mussels**
3	**tablespoons red or white wine vinegar**
1	**tablespoon olive oil**
2	**medium-size onions, chopped**
6	**garlic cloves, minced or put through a press**
1	**dried cayenne pepper**
3	**pounds (1.35 kg) tomatoes, peeled and chopped, or 2 28-ounce (800 g) cans, drained and chopped**
	salt to taste
1	**cup (250 ml) dry white wine**
1	**bay leaf**
¼	**teaspoon saffron threads**
	freshly ground pepper to taste
½	**cup (30 g/ 1 large bunch) chopped parsley or a mixture of parsley and basil**

A couple of hours before serving, clean the mussels. Brush and rinse the mussels one at a time and discard any that are open or cracked. Place the mussels in a bowl of water in the kitchen sink. Let a slow stream of cold water run over the mussels for an hour. Drain the mussels and pick through them again; pull out the beards and place the mussels in a bowl of water to which you have added the vinegar. Let sit for 15 minutes. Drain and rinse several times. You can now refrigerate the mussels for a few hours.

    Heat the olive oil over medium heat in a large heavy-bottomed casserole and add one of the onions. Sauté, stirring, until the onion is tender, about 5 to 8 minutes, and add 4 of the garlic cloves and the cayenne pepper. Sauté for a minute

FISH AND SHELLFISH

or so and add the tomatoes and a very small amount of salt (you will be adding the mussel broth later, and it will be salty). Cook, uncovered, stirring often, for 15 minutes, until the tomatoes are cooked down and fragrant. Turn off the heat or turn the heat very low while you cook the mussels.

Combine the wine, the remaining onion and garlic, the bay leaf, and the mussels in a large pot and bring to a boil. Give the mussels a stir, cover, and cook for 3 to 4 minutes, just until the mussels open. You can do this in batches if you don't have a big enough pot to accommodate all the mussels. After 3 minutes, give the mussels a stir or shake the pan vigorously. Remove the mussels with a slotted spoon or deep-fry skimmer and transfer them to a bowl. Discard any mussels that haven't opened and cover the bowl tightly with foil. Strain the cooking liquid through several thicknesses of cheesecloth.

Add the strained liquid from the mussels to the tomato sauce, bring to a simmer, and add the saffron. Taste and adjust salt. Add pepper to taste, simmer for a minute, and add the parsley. Distribute the mussels among 6 warmed wide soup bowls and spoon on the tomato sauce. Serve at once, with crusty bread.

Note: You can reheat the mussels by stirring them into the tomato sauce, but this might be somewhat unwieldy.

ADVANCE PREPARATION: You can clean the mussels and make the tomato sauce several hours before serving.

PER PORTION

Calories	307	Protein	22 G
Fat	8 G	Carbohydrate	30 G
Sodium	463 MG	Cholesterol	42 MG

AÏOLI MONSTRE
Huge Salt Cod and Vegetable Platter with Garlic Mayonnaise

SERVES 10

C'est, par excellence, le plat national des Provençaux.

RENÉ JOUVEAU, *LA CUISINE PROVENÇALE DE TRADITION POPULAIRE*

This is not a "fish dish." It's not a "vegetable dish." It's a feast.

Aïoli monstre, or *le grand aïoli,* is one of those great Provençal traditions that grew out of the Christian rituals of deprivation, only to become one of the great feast dishes of the region. Traditionally it is eaten on Fridays and before Christmas and Easter, when religious custom calls for lean, meatless meals (*repas maigres*). And what better garnish could there be for boiled salt cod and vegetables than a pungent garlic mayonnaise? I have had blissful aïoli meals celebrating the end of the grape harvest at Domaine Tempier in Bandol, at village festivals in the Vaucluse, at Friday lunch at Le Bistro du Paradou in a small village near Arles, and at La Mère Besson in Cannes. When I worked in the kitchen at La Mère Besson, the Friday meal was the busiest of the week. The kitchen staff would cook all the vegetables and lay them out in a big wooden frame divided by slats into several spaces, a different colorful vegetable in each space. As the orders came in, the vegetables would be submerged in simmering water to reheat for about half a minute, then placed on a platter with the poached salt cod and hard-cooked eggs. It was wonderful to behold these beautiful vegetables, all cooked and ready to go in their designated spaces. At Le Bistro du Paradou, which serves one of the best aïolis I've eaten—probably because of the great olive oil from Maussane-les-Alpilles just up the road—they are very generous with snails. Not being a snail enthusiast myself, I'm leaving them out of this recipe. You can add them if you want.

I think I had the most fun with aïoli monstre when I gave a Friday night aïoli dinner party to try out my different aïoli recipes on six close friends. There were seven of us and enough food for an army. I served traditional aïoli mayonnaise, my relatively low-fat version (page 97), and the mashed potato aïoli on page 100. All

FISH AND SHELLFISH

of the aïolis were appreciated, with the highest marks going to the relatively low-fat version.

You can pick and choose with the vegetables. If you can't find all of the vegetables listed here, substitute others or leave them out. Or add more to the list. You will certainly have enough to eat. Traditionally, hard-cooked eggs are served with aïoli, but I just don't think they're necessary. Add them if you wish. And you can substitute steamed or poached fresh cod (or other white fish) for salt cod. In France an aïoli monstre would call for twice as much garlic mayonnaise, but I think 1½ cups (375 ml) for 10 people, or 2 heaped tablespoons per person, is plenty.

Because you have so many vegetables to prepare and cook here, I recommend you cook everything in advance, then reheat just before serving in simmering water. It will help to have a tiered steamer so that you can cook several vegetables at once. And have a number of platters for the fish and vegetables.

Aïoli monstre is meant to be a meal in itself. It requires no first course or salad and only fresh fruit (which can be served as a soufflé, such as the pear and apple soufflé on page 429, or a sorbet) for dessert. It's a feast to enjoy on a Friday or Saturday night or on a Sunday afternoon, with time set aside afterward for a nap; the garlic mayonnaise is reputed to be a soporific.

2	**pounds (900 g) salt cod, homemade (page 195) or commercial, or fresh cod, snapper, or whiting fillets**
2	**quarts (2 l) water**
2	**garlic cloves, peeled**
1	**bay leaf**
½	**teaspoon salt**
8	**medium-size leeks, white part only, well washed and cut in half lengthwise**
12	**medium-size carrots, peeled, trimmed, and cut in half lengthwise**
12	**medium-size potatoes, cut in half**
1	**small or medium-size head of cauliflower, broken into florets**
¾	**pound (340 g) green beans, trimmed**
3	**large or 6 medium-size beets, peeled and quartered**

6	medium-size turnips, peeled and quartered
4	small fennel bulbs, trimmed and quartered
4 or 5	medium-size zucchini, ends trimmed, cut in half lengthwise and then crosswise
5	artichokes, cut in half lengthwise, rubbed with lemon juice, chokes removed, and leaves trimmed
½	pound (225 g) dried chick-peas, soaked overnight, cooked, and left in their cooking water (see note)
1½	cups (375 ml) aïoli (page 97) or mashed potato aïoli (page 100) or both

Note: To cook chick-peas, soak overnight in 1 quart of water. Drain and combine with 1½ quarts of water in a saucepan. Bring to a boil over high heat. Reduce the heat to low, cover, and simmer 1 hour. Add 2 teaspoons salt and continue to simmer ½ to 1 hour, until tender.

Desalt the cod according to the directions on page 62. Cut into 10 pieces.

Combine the water, garlic cloves, bay leaf, salt, and leeks and bring to a boil. If you have a tiered steamer or a large steaming pot, use the bottom part to cook the leeks and steam the carrots in the basket above the leeks. Reduce the heat to medium if you're steaming the carrots, to low if not; cover and cook the leeks (and steam the carrots) for 30 minutes or until the vegetables are quite tender. Remove the leeks from the simmering water with a slotted spoon or deep-fry skimmer and the carrots from the steaming rack and transfer both to a platter.

Transfer the fish—dried or fresh—to the simmering leek-cooking water and immediately turn off the heat and cover the pot (if the fish isn't covered with water, add enough to cover, bring to a simmer, and turn off the heat). Let sit, covered, for 10 minutes. Fresh fish should flake easily with a fork. Dried cod should be cooked through, should fall apart easily, and should be slippery. If you don't think it's cooked, let sit for another 2 minutes. Remove from the water with a slotted spoon, transfer to a bowl, and spoon a small amount of the water over the fish to keep it warm. Discard the remaining cooking water.

Steam all of the other vegetables until tender. The potatoes should take about 20 to 30 minutes, the cauliflower about 15 minutes, the green beans 5 to 8 minutes, the beets 30 minutes or longer, the turnips 20 minutes, the fennel 20 to 30 minutes, the zucchini 15 minutes, and the artichokes about 40 minutes (you can cook these for a longer or shorter time, depending on your taste; I like the vegetables fairly well cooked for an aïoli). If you are cooking the vegetables in a tiered steamer, cook the artichokes last and separately, because their steam will be bitter.

Shortly before serving, reheat the chick-peas in their cooking water and bring a large pot of water to a boil. Plunge each vegetable into the water for 30 seconds, remove with a strainer or deep-fry skimmer, and arrange on a platter (everything can also be served at room temperature if you wish). The fish does not have to be hot, but you can reheat it, for about 5 seconds, in the same way. Drain the chick-peas and transfer to a bowl.

Pass the fish, vegetables, and chick-peas. Pass the aïolis separately in serving bowls or the bowls from mortars and pestles.

ADVANCE PREPARATION: Everything can be prepared hours or even a day ahead of time and held in the refrigerator. Reheat the fish and vegetables in simmering water as directed.

PER PORTION

Calories	749	Protein	34 G
Fat	26 G	Carbohydrate	100 G
Sodium	4,373 MG	Cholesterol	103 MG

CHAPTER 7

EGGS AND
SAVORY TORTES

Provençal omelets are unlike any others. If you are unprepared for them, as so many of the film people who crowd into the most Provençal of restaurants, La Mère Besson in Cannes, must be, you'll be in for a surprise: a *truccha* at La Mère Besson is not just a Swiss chard or spinach omelet; it also contains large chunks of uncooked garlic. Hollywood producers have found this dismaying (maybe it's difficult to make a big movie deal if you're distracted by garlic breath); I love it.

The recipes in this chapter are among my favorites in the Provençal repertoire. Omelets are important dishes that are eaten widely in the region; they make marvelous vehicles for its delicious herbs, cheeses, and vegetables. The layered vegetable omelet called *crespeou* (page 251)—thin, colorful omelets, one on top of the other in alternating hues—is one of the most beautiful dishes I've ever seen. If you have the time, it's a sure way to impress guests at a dinner party, and it's gorgeous on a buffet.

Most of these dishes are portable. They were the foods that agricultural workers used to take with them to the fields for their lunch. Omelets are usually flat, like Spanish tortillas. They are simple and quickly made, many of them as good cold as hot.

Vegetable tortes are also portable, though they require a bit more time to put together. These are hearty, savory foods, beautiful to look at, delicious hot or cold. They make great picnic fare and school lunches. The most common ones in Provence are a savory *tourta dé bléa*, filled with Swiss chard, onions, and rice; and *tourte aux courgettes*, filled with the same zucchini and rice mixture that goes into the *tian* on page 354; and in the fall and winter, *tourte de courge*, a pumpkin and rice torte. Although the tortes are usually double-crusted, I've eaten *tourtes* in Nice that had only a bottom crust, like a quiche. In one *traiteur* in Nice I counted five different kinds: cheese; eggplant and tomato; zucchini; tomato; and rice, chard and ham. The quality of the crusts varies from place to place in the south of France. Sometimes it is a butter-based or oil-based short crust; other times it's yeasted. I use a light, nutty-tasting yeasted olive oil crust.

Eggs may be high-cholesterol foods, but they are a high-quality source of protein, and they have a definite place, in moderation, in my regimen. I wouldn't eat an omelet every night, but every so often nothing can beat these. They are cooked in a minimum of oil, and you can substitute egg whites for some of the yolks in most of these recipes.

For individual omelets, use a heavy-bottomed 8-inch nonstick pan. For large omelets use a heavy-bottomed 12-inch nonstick pan.

EGGS AND SAVORY TORTES

FLAT ONION OMELET
La meissouneiro
Omelette moissonnière

SERVES 6

The *moisson* is the harvest, and this is one of the typical lunches that Provençal farm workers would carry in their sacks when they went off for a long day in the fields— before the advent of cars and fast food. The sweeter the onions you use, the better.

2 or 3	**cloves**
1	**pound (450 g/2 large or 3 medium-size) white onions, peeled**
2	**tablespoons red wine vinegar**
2	**tablespoons olive oil**
9	**large eggs or 6 eggs and 7 egg whites**
3	**tablespoons skim milk**
	salt and freshly ground pepper to taste

Stick a clove into each onion and soak for a half a day in water to which you have added the vinegar. Drain, pat dry, and mince.★

Heat 1 tablespoon of the oil in a large heavy-bottomed nonstick skillet over medium-low heat and add the onions. Sauté, stirring often, for 10 minutes, until slightly colored but not browned. Remove from the heat.

Beat the eggs in a bowl. Add the milk, salt, and pepper. Stir in the onions. Wipe out the surface of the pan with paper towels.

Heat the remaining olive oil in the pan over medium-high heat. Drizzle in a bit of egg; if it sizzles, pour in the egg and onion mixture. (If not, heat for a little longer.) Tilt and swirl the pan to coat the bottom evenly and gently lift the edges of the eggs to let egg run underneath. Shake the pan gently, turn the heat to low, cover, and cook for 10 minutes, until just about set. Meanwhile, preheat the broiler.

Finish the omelet under the broiler about 3 inches from the heat, for 1 to 3 minutes, until the top is set and just beginning to brown. Remove from the heat, cut into wedges, and serve. Or allow to cool and serve cold.

★ This step is optional. You will have a good omelet if you don't do it, but the onions will be noticeably less pungent if you do.

ADVANCE PREPARATION: This will keep for a day in the refrigerator.

PER PORTION

Calories	182	Protein	10 G
Fat	12 G	Carbohydrate	8 G
Sodium	101 MG	Cholesterol	319 MG

―――― TRUC ――――

REDUCING THE PUNGENCY OF ONIONS

In Provence certain recipes for oniony dishes call for sticking a clove in the peeled onion and soaking it for half a day in vinegared water. Onions treated this way are extremely sweet when cooked and, at least in my experience, seem to be more digestible. Uncooked onions treated this way are much milder.

One way to prevent tears while chopping onions: Run cold water while you are chopping onions and chop near the sink. It often works!

RICOTTA AND HERB OMELET
Omelette à la brousse

SERVES 4

This is one of the most delicious dishes made with *brousse*, the ricottalike cheese made throughout Provence from sheep's milk. If you can get semihard ricotta or ricotta salata that can be cut into squares, I recommend it, because it's a little easier to scatter over the omelet as it's cooking. But it's not too difficult to place the softer ricotta/chive mixture over the eggs by the spoonful. You can make individual omelets or one big one.

½ **pound (225 g/heaped ½ cup) low-fat ricotta or ricotta salata at room temperature**

   freshly ground pepper to taste

8 **large eggs or 4 eggs and 8 egg whites at room temperature**

3 **tablespoons skim milk**

   salt to taste

1 **tablespoon olive oil**

¼ **cup (62 ml) snipped fresh chives or slivered fresh basil leaves or a combination**

Depending on the consistency of the ricotta, either cut it into small dice or soften it with the back of a wooden spoon. Toss with or stir in pepper.

Beat the eggs and milk together. Add salt and pepper.

Heat the olive oil in a large nonstick skillet over medium-high heat. Drizzle in a bit of egg; if it sizzles, add the eggs and tilt the pan to cover it evenly. (If not, heat for a little longer.) Shake and tilt the pan gently with one hand while you gently lift the edges of the eggs and let them run underneath for about 2 minutes (30 to 60 seconds if you're making individual omelets).

Place the cheese down the middle of the omelet. Sprinkle on the herbs. Turn the omelet and let cook for a minute or two (30 to 60 seconds for individual omelets), then slide it out of the pan. Serve at once.

ADVANCE PREPARATION: This is a quick, last-minute dish.

Calories	254 (231)	Protein	21 (23) G
Fat	17 (14) G	Carbohydrate	4 (4) G
Sodium	202 (265) MG	Cholesterol	435 (276) MG

Note: Amounts in parentheses relate to the use of 4 eggs and 8 egg whites.

TRUCCHA
Flat Swiss Chard Omelet
à la Niçoise

SERVES 2

My favorite restaurant in Cannes, La Mère Besson, specializes in Niçois cuisine. This garlicky Swiss chard omelet and salade mesclun are my favorite dishes on the menu. La Mère Besson is not afraid to add whole chunks of garlic, but the garlic is always very fresh. Look for young, fresh garlic for this and remove the green stems from the center of the cloves. Obviously I've taken liberties with the traditional recipe, substituting egg whites for some of the whole eggs. Unlike some of the other omelets in this chapter, this is supposed to be a bit runny on the top.

1 **pound (450 g) Swiss chard**
4 **large young, tender garlic cloves, coarsely chopped**
2 **large eggs**
4 **large egg whites**
  salt and freshly ground pepper to taste
1 **tablespoon olive oil**

Tear off the leaves from the Swiss chard and set aside the stems for another purpose (such as the gratin on page 342). Wash thoroughly and wilt over high heat in the liquid that remains on the leaves in a dry frying pan; this will take from 1 to 3 minutes. Remove from the heat, squeeze dry, and chop coarsely.

For each omelet, beat together 1 whole egg and 2 egg whites and mix in a couple of handfuls of chopped chard, 2 garlic cloves, and salt and pepper.

EGGS AND SAVORY TORTES

Heat ½ tablespoon of olive oil in a nonstick omelet pan and add the egg mixture. Cook, shaking the pan and lifting the sides of the omelet and tilting slightly so that egg can run underneath. When the omelet is just about set on the top, slide onto a plate and serve. If you want it cooked solid all the way through, you can flip it over or run it under a broiler for 30 seconds, about 3 inches from the heat. But it's best slightly runny. You can keep this warm in a low oven while you make the second one or serve it at once. Repeat with the remaining ingredients.

ADVANCE PREPARATION: You can prepare and wilt the chard hours ahead of cooking the omelet.

PER PORTION

Calories	219	Protein	18 G
Fat	12 G	Carbohydrate	12 G
Sodium	619 MG	Cholesterol	213 MG

FLAT SORREL OMELET
Omelette à l'oseille

SERVES 4

These flat, tasty omelets are much like the truccha on page 242. Sorrel gives them a very sharp flavor. Like the truccha, they should be slightly runny on the top, but if you wish, you can turn the omelet or run it under a broiler.

½   **pound (225 g/5 cups) fresh sorrel**

8   **large young, tender garlic cloves, coarsely chopped**

8   **large eggs or 4 eggs and 8 egg whites**

     salt and freshly ground pepper to taste

2   **tablespoons olive oil**

Wash the sorrel and heat through over high heat in a dry skillet just until it wilts in the water left on its leaves after washing. This should take about 1 to 3 minutes. The color will change from bright green to olive. Remove from the heat and chop coarsely.

For each omelet, beat together 2 eggs or 1 egg and 2 egg whites and mix in a couple of tablespoons of chopped sorrel, 2 garlic cloves, and salt and pepper.

Heat 1½ teaspoons of olive oil in a nonstick omelet pan and add the egg mixture. Cook, shaking the pan, lifting the sides of the omelet, and tilting them slightly so that egg can run underneath. When the omelet is just about set on the top, slide onto a plate and serve. If you want it cooked solid all the way through, you can flip it over or run under a broiler for 30 seconds, about 3 inches from the heat. But it's best if it's slightly runny. You can keep this warm in a low oven while you make the remaining omelets or serve it at once. Repeat with the remaining ingredients.

ADVANCE PREPARATION: The sorrel can be prepared hours or even a day ahead of time and refrigerated until 30 minutes before making the omelets.

PER PORTION

Calories	236 (195)	Protein	14 (15) G
Fat	17 (11) G	Carbohydrate	7 (7) G
Sodium	130 (177) MG	Cholesterol	425 (212) MG

Note: Amounts in parentheses relate to the use of 4 eggs and 8 egg whites.

FLAT TOMATO OMELET
Omelette aux pommes d'amour

SERVES 4

One of the most delicious recurring moments in Marcel Pagnol's *La Gloire de Mon Père* is when Marcel, his father, and his uncle eat their tomato omelets at lunchtime when they're out hunting. They're always enormously hungry by this time. They stop under a tree, and the omelets, which mother and aunt have packed in their rucksacks early in the morning, along with a lamb chop destined for an outdoor fire, some bread, and goat cheese, are a welcome first course. Father and uncle follow their noontime repast with a nap, but not the young Marcel, who runs around setting and checking his traps after the noonday meal.

Most of the recipes I see in Provençal texts for tomato omelets are for rolled omelets, but Marcel Pagnol's mother's version must have been flat and portable. I hope he would have appreciated my version almost as much as Madame Pagnol's. The color alone is scrumptious. Only sweet, ripe tomatoes will do here.

1½	tablespoons olive oil
4	large garlic cloves, minced or put through a press
3	pounds (1.35 kg/12 medium-size) sweet, ripe tomatoes, peeled, seeded, and chopped
1 or 2	pinches of sugar
	salt and freshly ground pepper to taste
6	large eggs or 4 eggs and 5 egg whites
3	tablespoons slivered fresh basil or chopped parsley or more to taste

Heat 1 teaspoon of the oil in a large heavy-bottomed nonstick skillet over medium heat and add half the garlic. When it begins to color, after about 30 seconds to a minute, add the tomatoes, remaining garlic, sugar, and salt. Cook, stirring often, for about 20 minutes, until the tomatoes are cooked down and beginning to stick to the pan and their juice has evaporated. Add pepper and remove from the heat. Rinse the pan and wipe dry.

Beat the eggs in a large bowl. Stir in the tomato sauce and basil. Add salt and pepper if desired.

Heat the remaining olive oil in the nonstick skillet over medium-high heat. Drizzle in a bit of egg; if it sizzles, pour in the egg mixture. (If not, heat a little longer.) Tilt and swirl the pan to coat the bottom evenly and gently lift the edges of the eggs to let some of the egg run underneath. Shake the pan gently, turn the heat to low, cover, and cook for 8 to 10 minutes, until just about set. You can leave the top slightly runny or preheat the broiler to set the top.

Finish the omelet under the broiler, about 3 inches from the heat, for 2 to 3 minutes if desired, until the top is set and just beginning to brown. Remove from the heat, cut into wedges, and serve. Or allow to cool and serve cold.

ADVANCE PREPARATION: I'm sure Marcel Pagnol's mother and aunt made the omelets the night before their husbands left to go hunting, for they left at dawn. This will keep for a day in the refrigerator and is great cold or at room temperature.

PER PORTION

Calories	230 (214)	Protein	12 (14) G
Fat	14 (11) G	Carbohydrate	17 (17) G
Sodium	123 (160) MG	Cholesterol	318 (212) MG

Note: Amounts in parentheses relate to the use of 4 eggs and 5 egg whites.

FLAT TOMATO OMELET 2, WITH UNCOOKED TOMATOES
Omelette aux pommes d'amour 2

SERVES 6

The uncooked tomatoes are very refreshing in this juicy omelet. It's like eating salad and main course at the same time. This omelet is good if you serve it slightly runny, *baveuse*, on the top, but it's also fine to run it under the broiler to cook it through. You can make one large omelet or six individual ones. Use the sweetest tomatoes you can find.

1½	pounds (675 g/6 medium-size) sweet, ripe tomatoes, sliced crosswise about ½ inch (1.5 cm) thick
2	large garlic cloves, minced or put through a press
	salt and freshly ground pepper to taste
2 to 3	tablespoons slivered fresh basil to taste
9	large eggs or 6 eggs and 7 egg whites
3	tablespoons skim milk
1½	tablespoons olive oil

Gently toss together the tomatoes, garlic, salt, pepper, and basil.

Beat the eggs in a large bowl. Add the milk, salt, and pepper.

Heat the olive oil in a large nonstick skillet over medium-high heat. Drizzle in a bit of egg; if it sizzles, pour in the eggs. (If not, heat it a little longer.) Tilt and swirl the pan to coat the bottom evenly and gently lift the edges of the eggs to let some of the egg run underneath. Shake the pan gently and turn the heat to low. Distribute the tomatoes in an even layer over the eggs, scraping out all of the juice, garlic, and seasoning from the bowl. Cover and cook for 10 minutes, until just about set. Meanwhile, if you want the omelet to be cooked through, preheat the broiler.

If you wish, finish the omelet under the broiler, about 3 inches from the heat, for 2 to 3 minutes, until the top is set and just beginning to brown. Remove from the heat, slide onto a platter, cut into wedges, and serve. Or allow to cool and serve cold.

ADVANCE PREPARATION: This will keep for a day in the refrigerator and is great cold or at room temperature.

PER PORTION

Calories	169 (151)	Protein	11 (12) G
Fat	11 (9) G	Carbohydrate	7 (7) G
Sodium	108 (140) MG	Cholesterol	319 (213) MG

Note: Amounts in parentheses relate to the use of 6 eggs and 7 egg whites.

OMELET WITH HORN OF PLENTY MUSHROOMS
Omelette aux trompettes de la mort

SERVES 4

You can make this exquisite omelet rolled or flat. But no matter what, mix the mushrooms into the beaten eggs so that they're distributed throughout and not just down the middle. What a perfect supper this makes.

> 4 **large eggs**
>
> 8 **large egg whites**
>
> 1 **recipe sautéed horn of plenty mushrooms (page 329)**
>
> 4 **large young, tender garlic cloves, coarsely chopped (optional)**
>
> ½ **cup (1 large bunch) chopped parsley**
>
> **salt and freshly ground pepper**
>
> 4 **teaspoons olive oil**

For each omelet, beat together 1 whole egg and 2 egg whites and mix in a quarter (scant ½ cup) of the sautéed mushrooms. Add a clove of garlic if you wish and a couple of tablespoons of parsley. Season with salt and pepper.

EGGS AND SAVORY TORTES

Heat 1 teaspoon of olive oil in a nonstick omelet pan over medium-high heat and add the egg mixture. Cook, shaking the pan and lifting the sides of the omelet and tilting them slightly so that egg can run underneath. When the omelet is just about set on the top, slide it onto a plate and serve, or fold over, cook for another 30 seconds, and slide out onto a plate. If you want it cooked solid all the way through you can flip it over or run it under a preheated broiler for 30 seconds, about 3 inches from the heat. But it's best slightly runny. You can keep the omelets warm in a low oven while you make the rest or serve at once. Repeat with the remaining ingredients.

ADVANCE PREPARATION: You can prepare the mush-rooms a day or two ahead of making the omelet and hold in the refrigerator.

PER PORTION

Calories	204	Protein	16 G
Fat	12 G	Carbohydrate	8 G
Sodium	271 MG	Cholesterol	213 MG

SAGE AND GARLIC OMELET

Omelette à la sauge et à l'ail

Sage grows all over Provence. To my delight, my neighbor Raymond had planted it next to the house I rented, so I treated myself to sage dinners all the time during the months I spent at Les Buis.

4	large eggs or 2 large eggs and 4 large egg whites
¼	cup (62 ml) fresh sage leaves, cut into slivers
4	large young, tender garlic cloves, coarsely chopped or put through a press
	salt and freshly ground pepper to taste
1	tablespoon olive oil

For each omelet, beat together 2 eggs or 1 whole egg and 2 egg whites and mix in a couple of tablespoonsful of the sage, 2 garlic cloves, and salt and pepper.

Heat ½ teaspoon of olive oil in a nonstick omelet pan over medium-high heat and add the egg mixture. Cook, shaking the pan and lifting the sides of the omelet and tilting them slightly so that egg can run underneath. When the omelet is just about set on the top, slide it onto a plate and serve. Or fold it over, cook for another 30 seconds, and slide it out onto a plate. If you want it cooked solid all the way through, you can flip it over or run it under a broiler for 30 seconds, about 3 inches from the heat. But it's best slightly runny. You can keep this warm in a low oven while you make the second one or serve it at once. Repeat with the remaining ingredients.

ADVANCE PREPARATION: This is a last-minute meal.

PER PORTION

Calories	223 (183)	Protein	13 (14) G
Fat	17 (12) G	Carbohydrate	4 (4) G
Sodium	127 (174) MG	Cholesterol	425 (213) MG

Note: Amounts in parentheses relate to the use of 2 eggs and 4 egg whites.

LAYERED VEGETABLE OMELET
Le crespeou

SERVES 12 AS A STARTER, 8 AS A MAIN DISH

One of the prettiest of Provençal dishes, le crespeou combines the colors and flavors of Provence in a series of thin, flat omelets set one on top of the other. It's served cold and makes a beautiful first course. This is a time-consuming dish—but is so worth the effort. It takes at least a couple of hours—and you can make some or all of the fillings the day before you make the crespeou. Use as many different types of omelet as you wish. This spectacular one has seven layers, but you could make it with three or four as well or up to ten.

1   **medium-size eggplant (about ¾ pound/340 g), cut in half lengthwise and scored down to the skin but not through it**

¼   **cup (60 ml) olive oil, plus ½ teaspoon**

4   **large garlic cloves, minced or put through a press**

1   **pound (450 g/4 medium-size) tomatoes, peeled, seeded, and chopped**

    pinch of sugar

    salt and freshly ground pepper to taste

2   **tablespoons slivered fresh basil**

2   **medium-size red bell peppers**

2   **medium-size or 1 large white onion, chopped**

1   **teaspoon fresh thyme leaves or ½ teaspoon dried**

½   **pound (225 g) spinach, stems removed, or ¾ cup (185 ml) thawed frozen chopped spinach**

1   **cup (60 g/2 large bunches) chopped fresh parsley**

14   **large eggs**

2   **tablespoons tapenade, homemade (page 56) or commercial**

    basic tomato sauce (page 112) for serving or garnish (optional)

Prepare the vegetables, one by one:

For the eggplant: Preheat the oven to 475°F (245°C). Put the eggplant cut side down on a lightly oiled baking dish and bake for 20 to 30 minutes, until tender. Remove from the heat and, when cool enough to handle, scoop out the flesh and either dice, if possible, or mash to a puree. You should have about 1 cup (60 g).

For the tomatoes: Heat 1 teaspoon of the olive oil in a heavy-bottomed nonstick skillet over medium heat and add 2 of the garlic cloves. As soon as they begin to color, after about 30 seconds, add the tomatoes, sugar, salt, and pepper. Cook over medium heat, stirring often, for 20 minutes or until the juice has evaporated and the tomatoes are cooked down and fragrant. Stir in the basil. Remove from the heat and allow to cool.

For the peppers: Roast the red peppers over a gas burner or under a preheated broiler until uniformly charred. Place in a plastic bag until cool enough to handle. Remove the charred skin, rinse and pat dry, and cut into small dice. Toss with salt and pepper.

For the onions: Heat 2 teaspoons of the olive oil in the skillet you cooked the tomatoes in over medium-low heat, and add the onions and a little salt. Cook, stirring, until tender, about 5 to 8 minutes. Stir in the thyme. Remove from the heat.

For the spinach: Wilt in the water left on its leaves after washing in the nonstick skillet over high heat (1 to 3 minutes). Remove from the heat, allow to cool, squeeze dry, and chop. Add salt and pepper.

Combine the parsley, remaining garlic, and 2 of the eggs. Add salt and pepper.
Combine the tapenade with 2 of the eggs. Mix together well.

Now you're ready to make the omelets. Have an attractive round serving dish ready. Decide the order in which you want your omelets to be stacked. Here is the way I choose to combine this selection:

1. Spinach
2. Eggplant
3. Tomato
4. Onion
5. Tapenade
6. Red peppers
7. Parsley

Heat 1½ teaspoons olive oil in a 7- or 8-inch (18 to 20 cm) nonstick omelet pan over medium-high heat and cook the omelets one by one. Beat 2 eggs in a bowl and stir in the filling. Season to taste with salt and pepper. Drizzle a small amount of egg into the pan; if it sizzles, pour in the egg mixture. (If not, heat a little longer.) Swirl the pan and lift the edges of the omelet with a spatula so the egg can run underneath; then cover, reduce the heat to low, and let cook for 5 minutes or until the omelet is just about set on the top. Slide out onto the platter. Continue in this fashion, having decided how you want the colors to appear in the layers. Slide each omelet onto the previously cooked omelet. When your omelet layer-cake is complete, put a plate on top to weight it slightly so that it will stay together when cut. Allow to cool, cover, and chill.

Serve cold, cut into wedges. Garnish with the tomato sauce if you wish (it is fine without; I found, when I was testing this and we ate the dish for 3 days in a row, that the sauce made a nice variation).

Other Filling Suggestions:
4   artichoke bottoms, steamed and pureed

1   cup (250 ml) other fresh herbs, such as basil, mint, chervil, chives

1   cup (250 ml) steamed chopped asparagus

2   green bell peppers, roasted and chopped

ADVANCE PREPARATION: This can be made a day or two ahead of serving, and all of the vegetable fillings can be made a day or two ahead of filling the omelet.

PER PORTION (AS A STARTER)

Calories	171	Protein	9 G
Fat	11 G	Carbohydrate	9 G
Sodium	114 MG	Cholesterol	248 MG

November 15

Today I was initiated into truffling. It was an unsuccessful outing, but I still learned a lot. My friend Andrew Corpe invited me to come along with him and Mr. Pinna, who owns the pasta shop in Apt and is an amateur truffler, and Biscuit, Mr. Pinna's truffle dog. Andrew, who is an architect, has a client whose land was once a truffle farm. It's off the beautiful D36, south of Bonnieux. The rugged land is covered with small truffle oaks, which look very much like Texas live oaks, with green leaves. I learned that if there is a clearing of a fairly wide circumference around the oak trees (and a certain small pine, too), almost as if there had been a fire (the French call this phenomenon a *brûlé*) there are bound to be truffles, because the truffles are preventing anything from growing. Biscuit got excited a few times, and Monsieur Pinna would give him a biscuit and say, "*Cherche, Biscuit, cherche!*" Mr. Pinna dug with a screwdriver and took up handfuls of earth and sniffed (a marvelous technique), while Biscuit scratched at the earth, but no truffles. He says it's a bit early; and it's been raining for weeks here, which rots the truffles. Plus, the neighbors had been there before we had and had plundered the place.

Although most serious trufflers use a dog, the *paysans* and Andrew and the organic farmer Jean-Luc Danneyrolle rely on a red fly that loves truffles. If they see a red fly come up from the ground below a truffle oak, they will begin digging with their hands or their pocket knife or a screwdriver, and they are practically assured of finding a treasure. That's how I got my Christmas present from Andrew—a 100-grammer that fed us luxuriously through the holidays.

DUMAS ON TRUFFLES

Here we have come to the gastronome's holy of holies . . . , to the word which gourmands throughout the ages have never pronounced without lifting their hands to their hats; to the "tuber cibarium," to the lycoperdon gulosorum, to the truffle. . . .

You have interrogated the truffle itself, and the truffle has replied to you: "Eat me and adore God." . . .

"Libyan," exclaimed Juvenal, "unyoke your cattle, keep your harvests, but send us your truffles."

SCRAMBLED EGGS WITH TRUFFLES
Brouillade aux truffes

SERVES 4

I am not writing this recipe to annoy you. I know it's not easy to come by fragrant, aromatic fresh truffles, and this is the only kind to use here. Maybe you decide to splurge when you spy truffles in your favorite gourmet store. Or say you're in Provence in December or January and somebody brings you a big truffle. The entire house fills with the aroma. Quickly, you put it in a jar with eggs in the refrigerator, covering it tightly so none of the elusive aroma can get away before you get to eat it. You want to make something wonderful, and you need a recipe. Here it is. Nothing simpler.

I love truffle omelets, and I adore Christine Picasso's amazing truffle soufflés. But I think the best way to let the sensual flavor of truffles nestle into your taste buds is with these creamy (no cream, no butter) scrambled eggs. Take your time; cook the scrambled eggs slowly in a double boiler, and when they're just about set, but creamy just the same, sit down and eat. If you've never experienced fresh truffles, the flavor will be imprinted in your taste memory forever.

1	medium–size fresh truffle, about 1½ to 2 ounces (45 to 60 g)
8	large eggs or 4 large eggs and 8 egg whites salt and freshly ground pepper to taste
3	tablespoons skim milk
1	tablespoon olive oil

Keep your truffles with your eggs in a lidded jar or bowl until shortly before you make the scrambled eggs. Let the eggs come to room temperature before you begin. Brush the dirt off the surface of the truffle with a clean toothbrush. If a lot of dirt still clings to the knobbly surface, run the truffle very briefly under water, then wipe it immediately with a kitchen towel or paper towel. Cut the truffle in half. Either grate half the truffle using a rotary cheese grater or chop it finely, using a vegetable peeler knife to shave off fine slices, then chopping the slices. Cut the other half into very fine slivers, first shaving off slices with the vegetable peeler, then cutting the thin slices into long slivers. Set aside.

Beat the eggs, salt, pepper, and milk together. Stir in the grated part of the truffle.

Warm the olive oil in the top part of a double boiler over low heat. Don't heat it; just warm it. Stir in the slivered half of the truffle, stir for 30 seconds, then remove from the heat. The truffle should not cook; it should just be heated through in the oil. Stir the oil and truffle into the beaten egg, then return the beaten egg to the top part of the double boiler. Use a rubber spatula to get every last bit of the egg mixture into the pan.

Place the top of the double boiler over simmering water and stir, slowly and constantly, to scramble the eggs. This should take 10 to 12 minutes, maybe a little longer (see note). At first very little will happen; then you'll feel the eggs beginning to cook on the surface of the pan. Continue to stir the egg from the surface of the pan into the middle of the egg mixture. When the mixture is like very thick sauce—some of the egg has scrambled, but much of the mixture is still creamy yet cooked—remove from the heat and distribute among 4 warm plates. Serve at once.

Note: If you make this dish using the eggs and egg whites, it will cook faster, in 5 to 8 minutes, and won't be as creamy. It will still taste delicious, however.

ADVANCE PREPARATION: You could prepare the truffles an hour or so before scrambling the eggs, but the longer they are with the eggs in a jar, the more aromatic the eggs will be.

PER PORTION

Calories	186 (145)	Protein	13 (14) G
Fat	13 (8) G	Carbohydrate	2 (2) G
Sodium	132 (179) MG	Cholesterol	425 (213) MG

Note: Amounts in parentheses relate to the use of 4 eggs and 8 egg whites.

Vegetable tortes are not what most people associate with the city of Cannes. But Cannes is where I first bit into a vegetable torte. I bought it in one of the many wonderful charcuteries near the market. It was a *tourte aux courgettes*, a hearty, double-crusted wedge filled with a savory mixture of rice and zucchini cooked in olive oil, with only enough cheese and egg to hold the mixture together. Fresh herbs, onions, and garlic added lots of flavor. I bought a second wedge, this time with a spinach filling, for the long drive home the next day and found to my delight that this was not only delicious but also a convenient picnic food, as good cold as it was hot.

The French gastronome Carême notes that the torte had gone out of fashion by the end of the seventeenth century. In his "Treatise on Hot Entrées," he says, "Tortes are no longer fancy enough to appear on our opulent tables, for the simple reason that their form is too vulgar; the bourgeois class even looks upon them with disdain, and will only eat hot pâtés and vol-au-vents, whereas in the past, important people were happy to begin their home-cooked meal with a modest torte."

Well, I'm happy to say that people are buying them and eating them still in Provence and that most are filled with vegetables, all kinds—spinach, chard, zucchini, pumpkin, leek. The recipes that follow are my low-fat versions, made in a much lighter crust than you'll ever find in Provence.

YEASTED OLIVE OIL PASTRY

This is the crust I use for all of my Provençal vegetable tortes. Nowadays the quiches, tortes, and even pissaladières you find in Provence are often made with puff pastry or a very heavy oil-based pastry. I prefer this breadier version, which has a minimum of olive oil. It's very easy to work with.

1	teaspoon active dry yeast
5	tablespoons lukewarm water
1	large egg at room temperature
3	tablespoons olive oil
¼	pound (115 g/1 scant cup) whole-wheat pastry flour
¼	pound (115 g/1 scant cup) unbleached white flour
½ to ¾	teaspoon salt to taste

Dissolve the yeast in the water and let sit for 5 to 10 minutes. Beat in the egg and the olive oil. Combine the flours and salt and stir in (this can be done in an electric mixer; combine the ingredients using the paddle, then switch to the kneading hook). Work the dough until it comes together in a coherent mass, knead for a few minutes, and shape the dough into a ball. Place in a lightly oiled bowl, cover with plastic wrap, and let rise in a warm spot for 2 hours or a little longer. It will not rise too much, but it will expand and soften.

When the pastry has risen and softened, punch it down gently and divide into 2 pieces for a torte, one piece just slightly smaller than the other. Shape into balls, cover with plastic wrap, and let rest for 10 minutes. Butter or oil a 10- to 12-inch (25 or 30 cm) tart pan or springform pan and roll out the dough to fit the dish. Roll it very thin, about ⅛ inch (1.5 cm) thick and line the dish. Cover loosely with a kitchen towel and let rest for 20 to 30 minutes. Don't roll out the top piece of dough until you have filled the torte.

Fill with the filling of your choice. Roll out the top piece of dough and place over the filling. Seal the edges. Bake at 400°F (200°C), following specific recipe instructions for timing.

ADVANCE PREPARATION: The dough can be assembled hours before making the torte. Wrap in plastic and keep in the refrigerator. It can also be frozen.

PER CRUST

Calories	1,282	Protein	35 G
Fat	53 G	Carbohydrate	171 G
Sodium	1,457 MG	Cholesterol	213 MG

PUMPKIN TORTE
Tourte au potiron

Pumpkin and other winter squashes make a marvelous savory torte with a beguilingly sweet filling. Sage adds the magical *je ne sais quoi*. The filling can be prepared while the dough is rising.

1	yeasted olive oil torte crust (page 259)
2 to 2¼	pounds (900 g to 1 kg) pumpkin or other winter squash, peeled, seeded, and diced
1	tablespoon olive oil
1	large onion, chopped
2	garlic cloves, minced or put through a press
2	tablespoons chopped fresh sage or 1 tablespoon dried
½	cup (100 g) rice, either Italian Arborio or short-grain brown rice, cooked
2	tablespoons chopped parsley
	salt and freshly ground pepper to taste
2	ounces (60 g) Gruyère cheese, grated (½ cup)
2	large eggs, beaten

EGGS AND SAVORY TORTES

Steam the pumpkin or squash for 15 minutes, until tender. Transfer it to a strainer and let drain for 15 minutes. Place in a bowl and mash with a fork or puree in a food processor. You should have just about 2 cups (500 ml) of puree.

Preheat the oven to 400°F (200°C). Heat the olive oil over medium-low heat in a nonstick skillet and add the onion. Cook, stirring until the onion begins to soften, about 3 minutes, and add the garlic. Continue to cook, stirring often, until the onion is tender, about 3 to 5 minutes. Stir in the squash, sage, rice, parsley, salt, and pepper. Transfer to a bowl and stir in the cheese and eggs. Adjust seasonings and turn into the crust. Roll out the top crust and cover. Pinch the bottom and top edges together and cut 4 small slits in the top crust with a sharp knife to allow steam to escape during baking.

Bake for 35 to 45 minutes, until golden brown. Allow to rest for 10 minutes or longer before serving. This can also be served cold.

ADVANCE PREPARATION: The filling will keep for a day or two in the refrigerator. The torte can be served cold as well as hot. It makes a nice picnic dish.

PER PORTION

Calories	292	Protein	10 G
Fat	12 G	Carbohydrate	37 G
Sodium	224 MG	Cholesterol	87 MG

SPINACH, CHARD, OR MIXED GREENS TORTE

Tourte aux épinards ou aux blettes

SERVES 6 TO 8

Tortes make a great vehicle for dark leafy greens. Use one kind only, like spinach or chard, or a mixture, including lots of herbs. The filling can be prepared while the dough is rising.

2 to 2¼	pounds (900 g to 1 kg) spinach or Swiss chard or a mixture of spinach and other greens such as kale, collard greens, beet greens, arugula, or Swiss chard, stems removed
1	tablespoon olive oil
1	large onion, chopped
2 to 4	garlic cloves, to taste, minced or put through a press
2	bunches of flat-leaf parsley, chopped (about 1 cup)
½	cup (100 g) Italian Arborio or short-grain brown rice, cooked
2	tablespoons chopped fresh rosemary or 1 tablespoon crushed dried
1 to 2	teaspoons fresh thyme leaves or ½ to 1 teaspoon dried thyme to taste
	salt and freshly ground pepper to taste
2	ounces (60 g) Gruyère cheese, grated (½ cup)
2	tablespoons freshly grated Parmesan cheese
2	large eggs, beaten
1	yeasted olive oil torte crust (page 259)

Wash the greens in several changes of water. Heat a large nonstick skillet over high heat and add the wet greens. Cook, stirring, until they wilt in the water left on their leaves, 3 to 5 minutes. Remove from the heat and transfer to a colander. Allow to cool, then squeeze dry in a clean kitchen towel. Chop coarsely and set aside.

EGGS AND SAVORY TORTES

Preheat the oven to 400°F (200°C). Heat the olive oil in a large nonstick skillet over medium–low heat and add the onion. Cook, stirring, until the onion begins to soften, about 3 minutes. Add the garlic. Continue to cook, stirring often, until the onion is tender, about 3 to 5 minutes. Stir in the greens, parsley, rice, herbs, salt, and pepper. Transfer to a bowl and stir in the cheeses and eggs. Adjust seasonings and turn into the crust. Roll out the top crust and cover. Pinch the bottom and top edges together and cut 4 small slits in the top crust with a sharp knife to allow steam to escape during baking.

Bake for 35 to 45 minutes, until golden brown. Allow to rest for at least 10 minutes before serving. This can also be served cold.

ADVANCE PREPARATION: The filling will keep for a day or two in the refrigerator. The torte can be served cold as well as hot. It makes a nice picnic dish.

PER PORTION

Calories	310	Protein	13 G
Fat	13 G	Carbohydrate	38 G
Sodium	323 MG	Cholesterol	89 MG

SWISS CHARD AND ZUCCHINI TORTE
Tourte de blettes et de courgettes

SERVES 6 TO 8

Some of the vegetable tortes you find in Nice are more like what we would call tarts or quiches, single-crusted pastries with a custardy vegetable filling. This pretty example is particularly scrumptious. I have a fond memory of eating a similar one on a sunny day in March in Vieux Nice while my husband tucked into an enormous pan bagnat (page 80).

2	**pounds (900 g/about 10 large or 18 smaller stalks) Swiss chard, about 4 cups (1 l) leaves**
1	**tablespoon olive oil**
1	**medium-size onion, chopped**
2	**medium-size zucchini (¾ pound/340 g), scrubbed and chopped**
2	**large garlic cloves, minced or put through a press**
¾	**teaspoon salt**
1	**teaspoon fresh thyme leaves or ½ teaspoon dried freshly ground pepper to taste**
1	**recipe yeasted olive oil pastry (page 259)**
3	**large eggs, beaten**
2	**ounces (60 g) Gruyère cheese, grated (½ cup)**
½	**cup (125 ml) skim milk**

Tear the leaves from the chard stalks, wash, and drop briefly in a large pot of salted boiling water or wilt over high heat for about 5 minutes in a dry large nonstick pan in the water left on the leaves after washing. Rinse with cold water, squeeze dry, and chop. You should have about 1 cup (250 ml) chopped cooked leaves. Set aside. (Refrigerate the stalks and use at a later date for the chard stalk gratin on page 342.)

Heat the oil in a large nonstick skillet over medium-low heat and add the onion. Cook, stirring, until the onion begins to soften, about 5 minutes. Add the zucchini, garlic, and about ¼ teaspoon salt. Continue to cook, stirring often, for another 10 minutes, until the zucchini is tender but still bright green. Stir in the chopped chard leaves, thyme, and pepper and remove from the heat. Taste and adjust salt.

Preheat the oven to 350°F (180°C). Roll out two-thirds of the pastry (freeze the rest) and line a lightly oiled 10½- or 12-inch (27 to 30 cm) tart pan. Brush the piecrust with a bit of the beaten egg and bake for 5 minutes.

Mix the remaining beaten eggs with the cheese and milk. Stir in the vegetable mixture and combine well. Turn into the piecrust and spread it around evenly.

Bake for 35 to 45 minutes, until just beginning to brown on the top and a knife inserted in the center comes out clean. Serve hot or at room temperature.

Leftovers: Cut into small squares or diamond shapes and serve as hors d'oeuvres.

ADVANCE PREPARATION: This tart keeps for a few days in the refrigerator. However, the bottom crust will lose its crispness after a while. The filling can be prepared hours before assembling the tart. Hold in the refrigerator, but allow to come to room temperature before baking.

PER PORTION

Calories	278	Protein	12 G
Fat	13 G	Carbohydrate	30 G
Sodium	668 MG	Cholesterol	114 MG

CHAPTER 8

PASTA, PIZZA, AND GNOCCHI

Imagine waking up from a deep sleep and finding yourself in the old part of a Mediterranean city on a winding cobblestone street filled with food shops. They're all well stocked with dried and fresh pasta, gnocchi, sauces, and several kinds of ravioli and tortellini. Every so often there's a hole-in-the-wall pizza shop with a wood-burning oven inside and a list of about 10 pizzas. You may think you're in Italy, but all of the signs are in French—you're in Nice.

Pasta, gnocchi (considered pasta in the region), and pizza are ubiquitous in Provence, and nowhere is this more evident than in Nice. The Niçois love their pasta as much as their Italian neighbors do. They are especially fond of ravioli. Yet the ravioli you find here is distinctly Provençal, with ingredients and flavors all its own. The most traditional, known simply as *ravioli à la Niçoise* (*raïola* in the Niçois dialect) developed as a vehicle to stretch leftover *daube de boeuf* into a second meal. The meat from the rich beef stew is chopped and mixed with Swiss chard, herbs and Gruyère or Parmesan cheese for the filling, then the dish is sauced with the remaining daube. It has become so popular that today people will sometimes make a daube just as a first step in making ravioli.

But daube isn't a requirement. The people of the region will tell you that any meat can be used in traditional Niçois ravioli—beef, veal, pork, ham, rabbit, chicken, chicken livers, even lamb's brains—*les bons restes* (leftovers) of any kind. For my meat fillings I stick to the foods I eat: chicken and rabbit, finely chopped and mixed with Swiss chard, onions, garlic, and Provençal herbs.

But ravioli with vegetable and cheese fillings far outnumbers the daube-filled ravioli. In Nice ricotta is used, sometimes mixed with spinach or herbs, sometimes plain. All over the rest of Provence—and ravioli is an important food throughout the region, its name changing from one place to another (*ravioles, cussonets, oreilles d'âne, rayolles*)—you find similar ravioli filled with *brousse*, the Provençal equivalent of ricotta cheese. Other traditional vegetable fillings include herbs and spinach and/ or chard, on their own or with wild mushrooms, or just wild mushrooms; pumpkin and rice or potatoes; potato and garlic; potato and anchovy, cabbage, wild herbs, walnuts, leeks. The ravioli can be tossed with either olive oil and cheese, a meat broth, or a tomato sauce. In the northern part of Provence and in the Côte d'Azur backcountry, miniature cheese- and herb- or chard-filled ravioli are sold in big sheets. They are served in soups and tossed with tomato sauce or with olive oil and herbs.

Today imaginative cooks throughout Provence are making extraordinary ravioli. Vincent Miraglio, at his Bistro de Vincent Miraglio in Cagnes-sur-Mer, makes large ravioli filled with minced ratatouille, sauced with a combination of a garlicky, basil-scented tomato concassée and the drained liquid from the ratatouille (page 312). Serge Philippin at Le Restaurant du Bacon in Cap d'Antibes fills his moist, pliable, saffron-hued dough with a creamy puree of salt cod and herbs and sauces it with a tomato-basil concassée (page 118).

In addition to all the different fillings and names, the shapes of filled pasta vary from village to village in Haute-Provence. Sometimes they're shaped in rings, half-moons (*chaussons*), bishop's hats, or gendarme's hats; some ravioli are hand-shaped like tortellini, others cut with a glass or a square or round mold or with a roller or a knife. And some ravioli are fried rather than boiled.

But ravioli is labor-intensive, and in most villages of Haute-Provence it's reserved for grand occasions. Pasta and gnocchi, on the other hand, are foods for every day, and today dried pasta is a welcome ingredient. However, homemade pasta and gnocchi traditions do still exist, and here again ingredients and shapes vary throughout Provence. Water, flour, and salt are the basic ingredients; eggs and oil are optional. Green pasta is made with spinach or chard as is green gnocchi, which also includes potatoes. The pasta can be rolled out and cut into strips or other shapes. Or it can be rolled into sausagelike strips and cut into gnocchilike pieces, which in turn might be shaped with the tip of the finger or a fork. If you travel to isolated villages, especially in the mountains, you might find a confusing number of names. Even on the Côte d'Azur, how would you know that *merda de can* are green gnocchi?

PIZZA

I don't think I've ever been in a Provençal town or village that didn't have a pizzeria—or at least a pizza truck. These large vans are fitted out with counters and cooling racks, with ovens built into them and paneled windows that open on the sides. Their owners travel from market to market and are always a welcome sight and a fragrant draw after a few hours of shopping.

Provençal pizzas are thin-crusted; the tomato sauce is spread on in a thin layer, topped with olives and anchovies, mozzarella and ham, eggplant or mushrooms or peppers, tuna—the food of the region.

The signature pizza of Provence is *pissaladière*, an onion pizza topped with anchovies, capers, and olives. By onion pizza I don't mean a few rings scattered over tomato sauce. A couple of pounds of onions are slowly cooked down to a sweet paste, seasoned with crushed capers, spread on a crust, topped with anchovies and small black olives, and baked in a hot oven.

These gnocchilike pastas, made from flour, water, salt, sometimes eggs, and oil, are shaped over the finger, with ridges on one side. The number of folds varies from village to village, and according to Provençal folklore, a woman's talents as a cook are determined by the number of folds in her *crousets*. The more folds she can make, the better a wife she will be. In the village of Guillaume in the Haute-Var, legend has it that if a man asked for a woman's hand and she intended to say yes, she would make him *cruis*, and if her answer was no she would make him macaroni.

RAVIOLI: BASIC RECIPE

MAKES ENOUGH DOUGH FOR 6 GENEROUS SERVINGS OF RAVIOLI

My ravioli-making life changed forever after a morning watching Serge Philippin make his salt cod ravioli *amuse-bouches* at Le Restaurant du Bacon in Cap d'Antibes. Serge makes a saffron-hued dough that is fairly moist and as soft and pliable as chamois, which is what it looks like draped over a large cutting board. He has the advantage of a large restaurant pasta roller, so that the sheets of dough really are sheets as opposed to my strips. Using Serge's technique, ravioli making, although still time-consuming, has become a real pleasure, free of some of my old ravioli anxieties (about dough sticking or filling escaping).

Both this dough and Serge's technique are certainly different from any Italian recipe I've ever seen. The pasta is slightly moist, and it doesn't require much kneading or resting once it's mixed up. It has a smooth, soft texture and is very pliable. Once the ravioli is filled and cut, it goes directly into a freezer on a dusted board and stays there until it's cooked. Therein lies the solution to the biggest problem I'd always had with ravioli: it would always stick to the board or baking sheet. Flash-freezing on rice flour-, cornmeal-, or semolina-dusted boards is the answer. Get a few pieces of plywood cut to the size of your freezer. Once the ravioli are frozen, you can transfer them to a plastic bag.

The saffron-tinted water adds a beautiful yellow hue and a touch of Provence to the dough.

For Whole-Egg Pasta Dough:

2   **tablespoons water**

⅛   **teaspoon powdered saffron**

3   **scant cups (14 ounces/400 g) unbleached white flour**

½   **teaspoon salt**

3   **large eggs**

For Egg-White-Only Pasta Dough:

1   **tablespoon water**

⅛   **teaspoon powdered saffron**

3¼   **cups (15 ounces/420 g) unbleached white flour or more as needed**

½   **teaspoon salt**

6   **large egg whites**

    rice flour, cornmeal, or semolina as needed

1   **tablespoon salt for the cooking water**

1   **teaspoon olive oil for the cooking water**

Combine the water and saffron in a small bowl and stir to dissolve the saffron. Sift together the flour and salt and place in a mound on a large work surface or in a large bowl. Make a depression in the center of the mound and break the eggs into this well or pour in the egg whites. Add the water-saffron mixture. Using a fork, gently beat the eggs and water together. When they are lightly beaten, begin brushing flour in from the top of the "walls" of the well and incorporating it into the eggs with your fork. Use your free hand to keep the walls of the well intact while you brush in flour a little at a time. Don't worry if the egg breaks through the sides of the well; just push the mixture back into the middle, incorporating flour as you do. As soon as it becomes impossible to incorporate flour into the mixture with your fork, brush in the remaining flour and incorporate as much as you can with your hands. Now brush away any hard bits of egg and flour that haven't been amalgamated and gather the mixture into a ball. It will be slightly sticky and soft.

Using the food processor: Combine the water and saffron and mix together. Put the flour and salt in the bowl of your food processor and mix together by turning on the machine for a few seconds. With the machine off, add the eggs or egg whites and the water-saffron mixture. Now turn on the machine; in just a few seconds (or maybe 30), the dough should come together on the blades. If it doesn't, add a teaspoon of water with the machine running.

Knead the pasta dough for 5 minutes, using the rice flour, cornmeal, or semolina to dust your kneading surface so that the pasta doesn't stick (if pasta made with egg whites only seems very sticky, add flour by the tablespoon to your work surface). Divide the dough into 6 pieces. Wrap the dough you aren't working with in plastic or cover it with a damp towel while you roll out and fill each piece.

For the ravioli: Working with one portion at a time, roll out the pasta into long, wide strips, 3 to 4 inches (8 to 10 cm) wide. Roll it as thin as you can without tearing it: this is setting number 4 on my Atlas pasta roller. Dust the pasta and the cutting board regularly with rice flour, fine cornmeal, or semolina. Cut the long strip of dough crosswise into 2 equal pieces. Lay one strip on the dusted cutting board and dot with teaspoons of the filling, leaving about ¾ inch (2 cm) between spoonfuls. You should be able to get two rows down the length of the strip, 8 to 12 portions in all, depending on the length of the strip. If the pasta becomes dry, lightly spray with water. Gently stretch the second strip and lay it over the bottom strip. Press the two halves together firmly between the mounds and along the edges. Using a ridged pasta cutter, which crimps the edges as you cut, cut the ravioli in the middle of the spaces between the mounds and roll the cutter down the outside edges. Transfer to another dusted board. Roll out and fill the remaining pieces of pasta and transfer on dusted boards to the freezer. Keep the ravioli on wooden boards in the freezer, uncovered, until you are ready to cook and serve. Or once the ravioli is thoroughly frozen, transfer to plastic bags and return to the freezer.

Final cooking and serving★: Bring a large pot of water to a rolling boil. Add about a tablespoon of salt and a teaspoon of olive oil, and reduce to a gentle boil. Carefully transfer the ravioli to the gently boiling water. Cook for about 4 minutes once the water returns to a simmer. Turn the ravioli over once during the cooking so that they cook on both sides. Remove from the water with a slotted spoon or deep-fry skimmer and transfer to a heated serving dish or to warm plates or bowls. Serve as directed in the recipe.

Note: You can also make large ravioli, using twice the amount of filling for each one. This goes a little faster.

★ Some recipes instruct you to cook the ravioli in stock.

PER PORTION (WHOLE EGG)

Calories	278	Protein	10 G
Fat	3 G	Carbohydrate	51 G
Sodium	215 MG	Cholesterol	106 MG

PER PORTION (USING EGG WHITES ONLY)

Calories	275	Protein	11 G
Fat	.69 G	Carbohydrate	54 G
Sodium	238 MG	Cholesterol	0

TRUC

To get every bit of that ⅛ teaspoon of expensive saffron into the dough, instead of dissolving it in all of the water, dissolve it in part of the water and add to the eggs. Then rinse the bowl with the remaining water to get out any saffron left on the sides of the bowl.

POWDERED SAFFRON VS. SAFFRON THREADS

Saffron threads are usually preferable to powdered saffron, because the threads are generally more fragrant, and the product more reliable. Powdered saffron often turns out to be an adulterated powder with lots of color but very little real aroma. But every once in a while a recipe like the one for basic ravioli will call for powdered saffron, because it dissolves so easily in liquid. The powder is usually sold in tiny little canisters, each one containing about ⅛ teaspoon, which constitutes a *dose*—the pinch you would add to a soup or a sauce at the last minute. To be sure you're getting your money's worth when you buy powdered saffron, buy it from a reliable merchant. Then it should be the real stuff.

RAVIOLI WITH RATATOUILLE FILLING

SERVES 6

These wonderfully heady ravioli are inspired by a dish I ate at Le Bistro de Vincent Miraglio, in Cagnes-sur-Mer. Large or small ravioli are filled with minced-up ratatouille and sauced with a combination of a garlicky, basil-scented tomato concassée and the drained liquid from the ratatouille.

1	recipe ratatouille (page 312)
1½	tablespoons olive oil
1	medium-size zucchini, finely minced
	salt to taste
4	large garlic cloves, minced or put through a press
1½	pounds (675 g/6 medium-size) tomatoes, peeled, seeded, and minced
	basic ravioli dough or wonton skins (page 270)
3	ounces (90 g) Parmesan cheese, grated (¾ cup)
1	bunch of basil, about ½ cup (125 ml) leaves, snipped with scissors

Place the prepared ratatouille in a colander over a bowl. Let drain for several hours or overnight. Remove half the ratatouille and refrigerate for another use. Chop the remaining ratatouille fairly fine, but don't puree it. Reserve the liquid.

Heat ½ tablespoon olive oil in a heavy-bottomed skillet or saucepan over medium heat and add the minced zucchini, a pinch of salt, and one of the garlic cloves. Sauté, stirring, until the zucchini is bright green and tender, about 5 minutes. Remove from the heat and stir into the finely chopped ratatouille. This adds color and texture to the filling.

Heat the remaining olive oil in a heavy-bottomed saucepan over medium-low heat and add another garlic clove. As soon as it begins to color, after a minute or so, add the tomatoes, the remaining garlic, and a little salt. Sauté, stirring often, until the tomatoes have melted into a puree, 5 to 10 minutes. Add the drained liquid from the ratatouille. Bring to a boil and boil for 3 minutes or until slightly reduced. Turn off the heat, taste, and adjust seasonings. Set aside.

Using the rolled pasta dough or wonton skins, make the ravioli, each containing a teaspoon of ratatouille and a pinch of Parmesan. Keep the ravioli on wooden boards in the freezer until you're ready to cook and serve.

PASTA, PIZZA, AND GNOCCHI

Final cooking and serving: Have 6 wide soup bowls warmed and ready. Bring a large pot of water to a rolling boil. Add about a tablespoon of salt and reduce to a gentle boil. Bring the tomato-ratatouille liquid mixture back to a simmer in the saucepan. Add the basil.

Carefully transfer the ravioli to the gently boiling water. Cook for about 4 minutes once the water returns to a simmer. Turn the ravioli over once during the cooking so that they cook on both sides. Meanwhile, ladle some of the sauce into each bowl.

Using a slotted spoon or deep-fry skimmer, transfer 8 or 9 ravioli into each soup bowl, making sure to drain off the cooking water as you lift the ravioli from the water. Spoon the remaining sauce over the ravioli, sprinkle with Parmesan, and serve.

ADVANCE PREPARATION: Like all ravioli, these can be frozen for weeks. The ratatouille can be made up to 3 days before the ravioli are filled.

PER PORTION

Calories	575	Protein	23 G
Fat	17 G	Carbohydrate	86 G
Sodium	533 MG	Cholesterol	117 MG

TRUC
USING WONTON SKINS FOR RAVIOLI

This ingenious time-saving idea comes from Deborah Madison's *The Savory Way* (Bantam Books, 1990). I would hate for you not to make these delicious Provençal ravioli dishes because of time constraints. So here's an option for the pasta. For any of the given ravioli fillings on pages 274–85, use fresh wonton skins, found in the produce section of most supermarkets (near the tofu) instead of homemade pasta. You will need 60 to 70 wonton skins for 2 cups (500 ml) of filling. To fill, set a wonton skin on your work surface and top with 2 to 3 teaspoons of the filling. Brush the edges of the wonton with water, place a second wonton over the filling, and gently stretch to cover the filling. Press the edges together and trim with a ravioli crimper to seal. Place on a dusted board as in the basic ravioli recipe on page 270 and freeze and cook as directed.

SALT COD AND HERB RAVIOLI

Ravioli à la morue

SERVES 6

I learned this ravioli from Chef Serge Philippin at Le Restaurant du Bacon in Cap d'Antibes. His version consisted of equal parts of salt cod and cream, into which he introduced lots of chopped garlic and herbs. *Evidemment* the Bacon gets the freshest cod you can find, so fresh that Serge doesn't even cook it after desalting. I'm a little too nervous about the cod we get to do that, and because I'm not using crème fraîche in my recipe, it works best if I make it with the herbs and garlic into a brandade.

½	cup (125 ml) coarse sea salt
1	pound (450 g) very fresh cod fillets
2	quarts (2 l) water
2	medium-size onions, quartered
5 to 6	large garlic cloves or more to taste, 3 cut in half, the rest minced or put through a press
2	bay leaves
1	cup (250 ml) low-fat (2%, not skim) milk
½	pound (225 g/2 medium-size) waxy potatoes, peeled, cooked, and mashed
	freshly ground pepper to taste
¼	cup (60 ml) sage leaves, finely chopped
1	tablespoon fresh thyme leaves or 1½ teaspoons dried
1	tablespoon chopped fresh rosemary or 1½ teaspoons crushed dried
½	cup (30 g/1 large bunch) chopped parsley
	basic ravioli dough or wonton skins (page 270)
	fish stock (page 163), garlic stock (page 130), 2 tablespoons olive oil tossed with 2 tablespoons minced fresh basil, or basic tomato sauce (page 112) for serving

Sprinkle some of the salt over the bottom of a baking dish large enough to accommodate the cod fillets in a single layer. Lay the fillets on top and cover with the rest of the salt. Cover and refrigerate for 12 hours.

Pour off the water that has accumulated in the baking dish. Desalt the fish. Place in a large bowl and cover with water. If convenient, put the bowl in your kitchen sink and keep the water running in a thin stream so that the water in the bowl is constantly renewing itself. Otherwise, change the soaking water several times over 24 hours.

Cut the cod into a few large pieces and place in a heavy-bottomed casserole or stockpot. Add the water, onions, the halved garlic cloves, and the bay leaves. Slowly bring to a simmer over medium-low heat. As soon as the water reaches a simmer and before it comes to a boil—you'll see little bubbles coming up from the bottom of the pot and the water will be moving without the surface bubbling—cover, turn off the heat, and let sit for 10 minutes. Drain and transfer the fish to a bowl. Allow to cool until you can handle it.

Pick out the bones from the fish and flake by rubbing it between your fingers or using a fork or wooden spoon. If you use your fingers, it will be easier to verify that you've gotten the bones out. Place in a food processor fitted with the steel blade.

Scald the milk in a small saucepan and remove from the heat. Turn on the food processor and slowly add the milk to the cod until no more can be absorbed by the fish (this may be after ⅔ or ¾ cup/165 to 185 ml). Process the mixture until fluffy. Mix the remaining milk with the mashed potatoes. Add the mashed potatoes to the processor and pulse a few times to incorporate them into the fish. Add pepper to taste and stir in the herbs and remaining garlic. You may wish to add salt, but it probably won't be necessary.

Roll out, fill, and cook the ravioli according to the directions on page 272. If serving with fish or garlic stock, cook the ravioli directly in the stock.

Note: The brandade de morue on page 61 or the haddock brandade on page 207, without the addition of herbs, would make a terrific filling for ravioli.

ADVANCE PREPARATION: The filling can be made a day before you make the ravioli, and the ravioli freezes well.

PER PORTION

Calories	448	Protein	33 G
Fat	5 G	Carbohydrate	69 G
Sodium	N/A	Cholesterol	142 MG

PUMPKIN RAVIOLI

SERVES 6 TO 8

This is reminiscent of traditional northern Italian pumpkin ravioli and tortellini. Pumpkin, mixed with either rice or potatoes, is also a typical Provençal ravioli filling.

2 pounds (900 g) pumpkin, seeds and membranes removed, cut into chunks

½ pound (225 g/2 medium-size) potatoes, peeled, cooked, and mashed, ¾ cup, or ¾ cup (185 ml) cooked rice

2 teaspoons olive oil

1 leek, white part only, well washed and chopped (¾ cup)

1 large garlic clove, minced or put through a press

2 teaspoons dried sage or 2 tablespoons chopped fresh

¼ teaspoon freshly grated nutmeg or more to taste

3 ounces (90 g) Parmesan cheese, grated (¾ cup)

salt and freshly ground pepper to taste

basic ravioli dough or wonton skins (page 270)

2 cups (500 ml) chicken or garlic stock (page 128 or 130)

2 tablespoons additional slivered sage or 2 tablespoons chopped fresh parsley for garnish

Preheat the oven to 400°F (200°C). Place the pumpkin in a lightly oiled casserole or baking dish, cover, and bake for 1 hour or until tender. Remove from the oven, allow to cool, and cut away the rinds. (If you wish, you may steam the squash instead of baking it; steam for 30 to 40 minutes, until tender.) Place in a colander or a strainer and let sit for 1 hour so that some of the juice drains out of the pumpkin. Puree the pumpkin in a food processor fitted with the steel blade, or through a food mill. You should have 2 cups.

Stir together the pumpkin and potatoes or rice.

Heat the olive oil in a heavy-bottomed nonstick skillet over medium-low heat and add the leek. Cook, stirring, until tender, about 5 minutes. Add the garlic and cook for another minute, until the garlic begins to color. Remove from the heat and stir into the pumpkin mixture along with the sage, nutmeg, ½ cup (60 g) of the Parmesan, salt, and pepper.

Roll out, fill, and cook the ravioli following the directions on page 272.

To serve, heat the stock and distribute it among warmed wide soup bowls. Transfer the cooked ravioli to the soup bowls. Sprinkle with the additional sage and the remaining Parmesan and serve.

ADVANCE PREPARATION: Like all ravioli, these can be made weeks ahead of time and frozen. The filling will keep for a couple of days in the refrigerator.

PER PORTION

Calories	325	Protein	13 G
Fat	7 G	Carbohydrate	52 G
Sodium	338 MG	Cholesterol	87 MG

PUMPKIN RAVIOLI IN GARLIC BROTH WITH PARSLEY AND SAGE

SERVES 4

This heady garlic broth, with lots of sage and parsley added just before serving, is a scrumptious setting for the preceding recipe for pumpkin ravioli. When I make ravioli I always freeze it, and when I get down to the end of the batch I turn it into this marvelous dinner.

2	heads of garlic, cloves separated and peeled, plus 2 additional cloves, peeled
2½	quarts (2.5 l) water
1	bay leaf
2	fresh thyme sprigs
2	teaspoons salt or to taste
	freshly ground pepper to taste
24	pumpkin ravioli (preceding recipe)
1	tablespoon slivered fresh sage leaves
2	tablespoons chopped parsley
2	tablespoons freshly grated Parmesan cheese

Combine the 2 heads of garlic, water, bay leaf, thyme, and salt in a soup pot or Dutch oven and bring to a boil. Reduce the heat, cover, and simmer for 1 hour. Strain and discard the bay leaf and thyme sprigs (mash up the garlic and use for another purpose; see cooked garlic puree, page 103). Return the broth to the pot, taste, and adjust the salt. Add pepper.

Shortly before you are ready to eat, bring the broth back to a slow simmer. Squeeze the 2 remaining garlic cloves into the simmering stock. Carefully transfer the pumpkin ravioli from the freezer to the broth and add the herbs. When the liquid comes back to a boil, simmer for 6 to 8 minutes or until the ravioli is cooked al dente.

Ladle the ravioli and broth into warmed wide soup bowls. Sprinkle the Parmesan over the top and serve.

ADVANCE PREPARATION: The ravioli will keep in the freezer for several months. The broth will hold, in or out of the refrigerator, for several hours.

PER PORTION

Calories	272	Protein	12 G
Fat	6 G	Carbohydrate	44 G
Sodium	1,388 MG	Cholesterol	60 MG

RICOTTA AND HERB RAVIOLI
Ravioli à la brousse

SERVES 6

In Provence there is a ricottalike sheep's milk cheese called *brousse* that is used in several wonderful ravioli fillings. In some the *brousse* is mixed with spinach or chard and herbs; in others just with Parmesan. Monsieur Pinna, who has a fabulous Italian *épicerie* and bistro in Apt, makes a large sweet *brousse* ravioli, which is an intriguing dessert. This particular version of mine is made with ricotta and herbs, without the spinach or chard. It's one of my favorite ravioli recipes.

1　pound (450 g/2 cups) low-fat ricotta cheese

2　ounces (60 g) Parmesan cheese, grated (½ cup)

2　garlic cloves, minced or put through a press

2　cups (500 ml), tightly packed mixed fresh herbs such as basil, parsley, dill, chives, tarragon, thyme, rosemary, chopped (1 cup/250 ml/chopped)

2　large eggs, beaten
　　salt and freshly ground pepper to taste

1　recipe basic ravioli dough or wonton skins (page 270)
　　basic tomato sauce (page 112)

1　ounce (30 g) additional Parmesan, grated (¼ cup) for sprinkling (optional)

Combine the ricotta, ½ cup (125 ml) Parmesan, garlic, herbs, eggs, salt, and pepper.

Roll out, fill, and cook the ravioli as directed on page 272. Serve with basic tomato sauce. Sprinkle on additional Parmesan if desired.

Note: A delicious variation can be made with goat cheese. Substitute 4 to 8 ounces (115 to 225 g) fresh goat cheese for 4 to 8 ounces (115 to 225 g) of ricotta.

ADVANCE PREPARATION: These can be made weeks ahead of time and frozen. The filling will keep for a day in the refrigerator.

PER PORTION

Calories	499	Protein	29 G
Fat	14 G	Carbohydrate	67 G
Sodium	512 MG	Cholesterol	197 MG

CHICKEN AND CHARD RAVIOLI

SERVES 6

Although traditional Niçois ravioli have a veal and pork or beef daube filling, other meats are perfectly acceptable. They are usually combined with Swiss chard and herbs, just as the chicken is in this delicious savory filling. These ravioli are very light; friends have commented that they have an Asian character, but they're pure Provence.

1	**pound (450 g) boneless, skinless chicken breasts**
2	**onions, 1 sliced, 1 chopped**
1	**bay leaf**
1	**quart (1 l) water**
	salt to taste
½	**pound (225 g/5 cups tightly packed) Swiss chard leaves or fresh spinach, or a 10–ounce (285 g) package frozen spinach, thawed**
¼	**cup (62 ml) sage leaves, chopped**
2	**teaspoons fresh thyme leaves or 1 teaspoon crushed dried**
1 to 2	**teaspoons chopped fresh rosemary to taste**
1	**tablespoon olive oil**
4	**large garlic cloves, minced or put through a press**
3	**medium-size tomatoes, peeled, seeded, and pureed, or ¾ cup (185 ml) basic tomato sauce (page 112)**
1	**large egg, beaten**
	freshly ground pepper to taste
	basic ravioli dough or wonton skins (page 270)
2	**cups chicken stock (page 128) or basic tomato sauce (page 112) for serving**

Combine the chicken breasts, sliced onion, bay leaf, water, and ¼ teaspoon salt in a heavy-bottomed saucepan. Bring to a simmer and simmer for 10 to 15 minutes, until the chicken is cooked through. Remove the chicken from the broth, reserving the broth, cut the chicken into pieces, then chop finely in a food processor fitted with the steel blade.

Blanch the chard in a large pot of boiling water or heat a large heavy-bottomed nonstick skillet over high heat and add the chard. Wilt it in the water left on its leaves after washing and continue to stir over medium-high heat until much of the water in the pan has evaporated, about 3 minutes. Remove from the heat, rinse with cold water, and when cool enough to handle squeeze dry in a towel. Chop fine. (If you're using frozen spinach, thaw and squeeze dry in a towel.) Mix together with the chicken and herbs.

Heat the oil in a nonstick skillet over medium-low heat. Add the chopped onion and sauté until just about tender, about 3 minutes. Add the garlic, cook for another minute, and stir it into the chicken mixture. Add the tomato puree, ½ cup (125 ml) reserved chicken broth, the egg, salt and a generous amount of pepper.

Roll out, fill, and cook the ravioli as directed on page 272. Serve in warmed wide bowls in chicken stock (page 128, or use up the stock you reserved in this recipe) or on plates with basic tomato sauce.

ADVANCE PREPARATION: Like all ravioli, this will keep in the freezer for several months.

PER PORTION

Calories	461	Protein	31 G
Fat	8 G	Carbohydrate	64 G
Sodium	365 MG	Cholesterol	186 MG

POTATO-GARLIC RAVIOLI
Raviolis aux pommes de terre et à l'ail

SERVES 6

This creamy, heady filling is my own variation on a Provençal potato ravioli that typically combines potatoes and onions. I prefer this combination. The garlic loses its bite as it simmers, then melds in the most luscious way with the potatoes, milk, and Parmesan.

1	head of garlic, cloves separated and peeled
2	quarts (2 l) water
	salt to taste
1	bay leaf
2	pounds (900 g) waxy potatoes, peeled
½ to ¾	cup (125 to 185 ml) low-fat (2%, not skim) milk, as needed
2	ounces (60 g) Parmesan cheese, grated (½ cup)
2	teaspoons fresh thyme leaves or 1 teaspoon crushed dried
	lots of freshly ground pepper
	basic ravioli dough or wonton skins (page 270)
	basic tomato sauce (page 112)
1	ounce (30 g) Parmesan cheese, grated (¼ cup) for sprinkling

Combine the garlic and 1 quart (1 l) of the water in a saucepan and bring to a boil. Drain and combine the garlic and the second quart (1 l) of water in the saucepan and bring to a boil. Add the salt and bay leaf, reduce the heat, and simmer for 40 minutes or until the garlic is thoroughly tender. Drain, reserving some of the broth. Puree the garlic until very smooth in a food processor fitted with the steel blade.

Meanwhile, steam or boil the potatoes in salted water until tender, about 30 minutes. Drain and return to the saucepan. Warm the milk in another saucepan. Mash the potatoes with a potato masher and add the milk gradually until the mixture is moistened to your taste. Work in the pureed garlic, ½ cup (125 ml) Parmesan, and thyme. Add salt and pepper.

Fill and cook the ravioli as instructed on page 272. Serve with basic tomato sauce and a sprinkling of Parmesan.

GARLIC, POTATO, AND ANCHOVY RAVIOLI

Add 4 to 6 anchovy fillets, chopped, to the filling. Proceed as directed.

ADVANCE PREPARATION: The filling will hold for a couple of days in the refrigerator. Like all ravioli, these freeze well.

PER PORTION

Calories	524	Protein	21 G
Fat	9 G	Carbohydrate	90 G
Sodium	486 MG	Cholesterol	118 MG

PASTA WITH RICOTTA CHEESE, TOMATO SAUCE, AND PARMESAN
Les pâtes à la brousse

SERVES 4

If you are lucky enough to be making this dish in Provence, you can make it with *la brousse*, or *broussa*, a fresh unsalted cheese that is much like ricotta but is made from goat's or sheep's milk. I learned about *pâtes à la brousse* from Mamine (Mamine is a generic endearment for "grandmother"; this particular Mamine is a close friend of a friend; so far I've not met one of her grandchildren, but everyone seems to call her Mamine). Born in the Alpes-Maritimes, Mamine is now in her seventies. She has lived in Nice, Algeria, and Morocco and now lives in the backcountry near Grasse. This is a dish she grew up eating. She says it's best to use a ridged pasta noodle, like pappardelle or narrow lasagne noodles (penne works too), because the ridges catch the cheese. The version below calls for ricotta cheese, which has the same effect, if not quite the same flavor, as *brousse*. You can also use a Bolognese-type sauce for this dish, but I like my meatless version.

2	cups (500 ml) La Mère Besson's tomato sauce (page 114)
1	tablespoon salt
10	ounces (285 g) pappardelle, penne, or other ridged pasta
6	ounces (180 g/¾ cup) low-fat ricotta cheese
1	ounce (30 g) Parmesan cheese, grated (¼ cup)
2 or 3	tablespoons chopped fresh herbs such as parsley, basil, thyme, sage, rosemary to taste

Have the tomato sauce simmering in a saucepan. Bring a large pot of water to a boil; add the salt and the pasta. Have the ricotta in a warm heavy-bottomed serving dish or bowl. Ladle in a half-ladle of boiling water (about ¼ cup/625 ml) and mix with the ricotta. Drain the pasta when it is *al dente* and toss with the ricotta, the hot tomato sauce, the Parmesan, and the herbs. Serve at once.

ADVANCE PREPARATION: The tomato sauce will hold for 5 days in the refrigerator.

PER PORTION

Calories	429	Protein	21 G
Fat	10 G	Carbohydrate	65 G
Sodium	715 MG	Cholesterol	80 MG

PAPPARDELLE WITH ASPARAGUS, FAVA BEANS, AND RICOTTA
Pappardelle à la brousse et aux asperges et fèves

SERVES 4

This simple springtime pasta is dressed up with low-fat ricotta, made creamy simply by mixing the ricotta with a ladleful of cooking water from the pasta. Pappardelle is a good choice of noodle because the ridges catch the ricotta.

3	**pounds (1.35 kg) fresh fava beans**
¼	**pound (115 g/½ cup) low-fat ricotta**
1 to 2	**large garlic cloves, to taste, put through a press or pureed**
1	**tablespoon salt**
10	**ounces (285 g) pappardelle**
1	**pound (450 g) fresh asparagus, trimmed and cut into 1-inch (2.5 cm) lengths**
¼	**cup (about 15 g/½ large bunch) flat-leaf parsley**
1	**ounce (30 g) Parmesan cheese, grated (¼ cup)**
	freshly ground pepper to taste

PASTA, PIZZA, AND GNOCCHI

Shell the fava beans (see "truc" that follows).

Place the ricotta in a heavy-bottomed serving dish. Add the garlic.

Bring a large pot of water to a boil; add the salt and the pappardelle. Cook until just about *al dente,* about 8 minutes, and add the asparagus. Mix a ladleful of the boiling cooking water (about ½ cup/125 ml) with the ricotta and garlic in the serving dish so that the ricotta takes on a creamy consistency. When the pasta is cooked through but still firm to the bite (after the asparagus has cooked a couple of minutes with it), add the fava beans to the boiling water, stir together, and drain.

Toss immediately with the ricotta and garlic, parsley, and Parmesan. Grind in some pepper and serve at once.

ADVANCE PREPARATION: The fava beans can be prepared a day ahead of time. The asparagus can be prepared several hours ahead of time.

PER PORTION

Calories	394	Protein	21 G
Fat	7 G	Carbohydrate	62 G
Sodium	412 MG	Cholesterol	77 MG

TRUC

SHELLING FAVA BEANS

To shell fava beans, remove them from the furry pods and place in a bowl. Pour on boiling water, let sit for 30 seconds, drain, and rinse with cold water. The beans will now pop easily out of their shells. Young favas are extremely small, so you might wonder if it's worth the bother for the small volume you get. But when you taste these sweet morsels, I think you'll agree that it is.

PAPPARDELLE WITH TOMATO SAUCE, RICOTTA, AND SHREDDED RABBIT

SERVES 4

This is a dish made with leftover rabbit cooked in tomato sauce, enriched with additional sauce and ricotta.

2	**cups (500 ml/10 oz) shredded rabbit**
2	**cups (500 ml) La Mère Besson's tomato sauce (page 114)**
¼	**pound (115 g/½ cup) low-fat ricotta**
1	**tablespoon salt**
½	**pound (225 g) pappardelle**
1	**ounce (30 g) Parmesan cheese, grated (¼ cup)**
2	**tablespoons fresh sage leaves, slivered**
	freshly ground pepper to taste

Combine the shredded rabbit and tomato sauce in a saucepan and bring to a simmer.

Meanwhile, bring a large pot of water to a boil. Have the ricotta in a bowl.

When the water comes to a boil, add the salt and pasta. Add a small ladleful (about ½ cup/125 ml) of the water to the ricotta and mix together well so that the ricotta has a creamy consistency.

Cook the pasta *al dente*, about 8 to 10 minutes, drain, and toss at once with the tomato–rabbit mixture, ricotta, Parmesan, sage, and pepper. Serve at once.

ADVANCE PREPARATION: The rabbit can be cooked 2 or 3 days ahead of time, and the sauce will keep for 5 days in the refrigerator.

PER PORTION

Calories	467	Protein	33 G
Fat	13G	Carbohydrate	55 G
Sodium	672 MG	Cholesterol	110 MG

PASTA WITH TOMATO SAUCE
AND WILD MUSHROOMS
Les pâtes aux tomates et aux champignons sauvages

SERVES 4

This easy, fragrant sauce was another wonderful result of my quest for wild mushrooms in the wooded Provençal hills. It's wonderful with *trompettes de la mort*, horn of plenty mushrooms. You can use cultivated mushrooms if you can't find wild ones.

2	pounds (900 g/8 medium-size) tomatoes, quartered
½	cup (125 ml) water
1	tablespoon tomato paste
	coarse sea salt to taste
	a large handful of fresh thyme leaves or 1 teaspoon dried, plus 1 to 2 teaspoons fresh or ½ to 1 teaspoon dried
1	pound (450 g/6 cups) horn of plenty or other wild mushrooms, such as shiitake, cèpes, or oyster mushrooms, cleaned (page 329) and sliced if large
2	teaspoons olive oil
2 to 4	large garlic cloves, to taste, minced or put through a press
	freshly ground pepper to taste
2	tablespoons chopped parsley
1	tablespoon salt
10	ounces (285 g) fettuccine or pappardelle
2	ounces (60 g) Parmesan cheese, grated (½ cup)

Combine the tomatoes, water, tomato paste, ½ to 1 teaspoon sea salt, and the handful thyme in a saucepan and bring to a boil. Reduce the heat, cover, and simmer for 45 minutes. Remove from the heat and put through the fine blade of a food mill or press through a strainer. Taste and adjust seasonings. Return to the saucepan.

Combine the mushrooms and 2 large pinches of sea salt in a large heavy-bottomed nonstick skillet and heat over medium-high heat until they begin to release water, about 1 minute. Cook, shaking the pan or stirring with a wooden spoon, for 5 minutes, until most of the liquid has evaporated. Add the olive oil, 2 of the garlic cloves, and the 2 teaspoons thyme and continue to cook, stirring, for another 2 to 3 minutes, until the garlic is fragrant and beginning to color. Add the pepper and parsley and remove from the heat. Stir into the tomatoes. Taste and add more garlic if you wish. Keep the sauce warm while you cook the pasta.

Bring a large pot of water to a boil; add the tablespoon of salt and the pasta. Cook al dente, 7 to 10 minutes, drain, and toss with the sauce and the Parmesan. Serve at once.

Note: You can also prepare the tomato sauce by peeling and seeding the tomatoes first, cooking them as directed, and pureeing in a food processor fitted with the steel blade.

ADVANCE PREPARATION: The sauce will keep for 2 or 3 days in the refrigerator.

PER PORTION

Calories	431	Protein	20 G
Fat	10 G	Carbohydrate	69 G
Sodium	821 MG	Cholesterol	77 MG

SPAGHETTI WITH CLAMS
Les spaghettis aux coques

SERVES 4

My friend Claude O'Byrne comes from Marseille, and her family has a wonderful old house in a nearby seaside town, formerly an important naval base, called La Ciotat. One cold December day, Claude and her friend Luc invited us down for lunch. We drove through the Luberon and picked up the highway at Aix, and in no time we were in sight of the shimmering Mediterranean. Claude and Luc met us at a harborside bar, and after a pastis we went off to the big family house, which was right across the road from the beach. Our friends set about cleaning two huge bags of clams, and in no time they produced a wonderful meal. *"Les Italiens, ils font la meilleure cuisine,"* said Luc as he served up huge portions of garlicky spaghetti tossed with the clams and their cooking liquid and—amazingly—no oil at all. Yet the clams were local, the garlic was local, the parsley was local. I'm sure all along the Mediterranean coast of France people have been making this dish for as long as their Italian neighbors have. I've added the very Provençal touch of saffron to the dish Luc made for us.

2 to 2½	pounds (900 g to 1.25 kg) littleneck or butter clams
2	tablespoons vinegar (any kind) or coarse salt
2	cups (500 ml) dry white wine, such as a sauvignon or muscadet
8	large garlic cloves, minced or put through a press
	freshly ground pepper to taste
⅛	teaspoon powdered saffron or ¼ teaspoon threads
1	tablespoon salt
¾	pound (340 g) spaghetti or tagliolini
½	cup (30 g/1 large bunch) chopped fresh parsley

An hour or more before you wish to serve this, clean the clams. Brush and rinse the clams one at a time and discard any that are open or cracked. Place them in a bowl of water in the kitchen sink. Turn the water on low and let a slow stream of cold water run over the clams for 20 minutes. Drain the clams and pick through them again; place in a bowl of water to which you have added the vinegar or salt. Let sit for 15 minutes or longer. Drain and rinse several times. You can now refrigerate the clams for a few hours.

Combine the wine, half the garlic, and the clams in a large pot and bring to a boil. Give the clams a stir, cover, and cook for 3 to 4 minutes, just until they open, giving them a stir halfway through the cooking. Remove the clams with a slotted spoon or deep-fry skimmer and transfer to a bowl. Discard any that haven't opened. Strain the cooking liquid into a bowl through several thicknesses of cheesecloth. When the clams are cool enough to handle, remove them from their shells. If they are still sandy, give them a quick rinse in a bowl of cold water. Set aside.

Transfer the liquid from the clams to a saucepan and heat to a simmer. Add the remaining garlic, the pepper, and the saffron. Taste and adjust salt (the liquid released by the clams is quite salty). Stir in the clams. Keep hot but below the simmer.

Meanwhile, bring a large pot of water to a boil; add a tablespoon of salt and the pasta. Cook *al dente*, 8 to 10 minutes, drain, and toss at once with the clams in their liquid and the parsley. Serve at once, in warmed wide bowls, pouring any liquid remaining in the bowl or pot in which you tossed the pasta over each serving.

ADVANCE PREPARATION: The dish can be prepared up to adding the clams to the broth hours before cooking the pasta. Hold the broth with the clams off the heat.

PER PORTION

Calories	363	Protein	17 G
Fat	1 G	Carbohydrate	69 G
Sodium	328 MG	Cholesterol	13 MG

PASTA, PIZZA, AND GNOCCHI

SPAGHETTI WITH TOMATO AND CLAM SAUCE

Les spaghettis aux tomates et aux coques

SERVES 4

This is a gutsy tomatoey variation of the preceding recipe. In summer, use fresh tomatoes and basil; in winter, canned tomatoes and thyme.

2 to 2½	**pounds (900 g to 1.25 kg) littleneck or butter clams**
2	**tablespoons vinegar (any kind) or coarse salt**
1	**cup (250 ml) dry white wine, such as a sauvignon or muscadet**
8	**large garlic cloves, minced or put through a press**
2	**teaspoons olive oil**
1	**medium-size onion, chopped**
1½	**pounds (675 g/6 medium-size/1 28-ounce can, drained) tomatoes, peeled, seeded, and chopped**
	salt to taste
2	**tablespoons chopped fresh basil or 1 teaspoon fresh thyme leaves or ½ teaspoon crushed dried thyme**
	freshly ground pepper to taste
⅛	**teaspoon powdered saffron or ¼ teaspoon threads (optional)**
¾	**pound (340 g) spaghetti or tagliolini**
½	**cup (30 g/1 large bunch) chopped parsley**

An hour or more before you wish to serve this, clean the clams. Brush and rinse the clams one at a time and discard any that are open or cracked. Place them in a bowl of water in the kitchen sink. Turn the water on low and let a slow stream of cold water run over the clams for 20 minutes. Drain the clams and pick through them again; place in a bowl of water to which you have added the vinegar or salt.

Let sit for 15 minutes or longer. Drain and rinse several times. You can now refrigerate the clams for a few hours.

Combine the wine, half the garlic, and the clams in a large pot and bring to a boil. Give the clams a stir, cover, and cook for 3 to 4 minutes, just until they open, giving them a stir halfway through the cooking. Remove the clams with a slotted spoon or deep-fry skimmer and transfer to a bowl. Discard any that haven't opened. Strain the cooking liquid into a bowl through several thicknesses of cheesecloth. When the clams are cool enough to handle, remove them from their shells. If they are still sandy, give them a quick rinse in a bowl of cold water. Set aside.

Heat the olive oil in a medium-size heavy-bottomed saucepan or a large nonstick skillet over medium-low heat and add the onion. Sauté, stirring, until tender, 3 to 5 minutes. Add the remaining garlic and stir for about 30 seconds, until it begins to color. Add the tomatoes, a generous pinch of salt, and the basil. Cook, stirring often, over medium-low heat, for 10 to 15 minutes, until the tomatoes have cooked down somewhat. Add the liquid from the clams and stir together. Bring to a simmer, taste, and add salt if necessary, pepper, and the saffron if you're using it. Stir in the clams and turn down the heat to low. The sauce should stay hot, but the clams shouldn't cook.

Meanwhile, bring a large pot of water to a boil; add a tablespoon of salt and the pasta. Cook al dente, 8 to 10 minutes, drain, and toss at once with the tomato/clam sauce and the parsley. Serve at once, in warmed wide bowls, pouring any sauce remaining in the bowl or pot in which you tossed the pasta over each serving.

ADVANCE PREPARATION: The dish can be prepared through completion of the sauce hours before cooking the pasta, but turn off the heat under the sauce.

PER PORTION

Calories	431	Protein	18 G
Fat	5 G	Carbohydrate	79 G
Sodium	341 MG	Cholesterol	13 MG

NIÇOIS-STYLE GREEN GNOCCHI
OR PAPPARDELLE
Niochi à la niçarda
Gnocchi à la Niçarde

SERVES 6

This recipe is based on a recipe for green Niçois gnocchi, made from a delicious mix of fresh greens, flour, and eggs. I have made it several times as gnocchi and have found that, as delicious as the flavor is, the little dumplings are rather heavy. Throughout Provence the same dough will be gnocchi in some villages and pasta in others—it's a question of tradition—so I decided to try this dough as pasta. It's a bit soft for rolling narrow noodles on a pasta machine but perfect for cutting wide pappardellelike noodles, and absolutely delicious. I'm giving you instructions for both here. Both the gnocchi and the noodles have an amazing garden-fresh flavor.

¼   **pound (115 g) spinach, stems removed and leaves finely chopped**

¼   **pound (115 g) Swiss chard leaves, finely chopped**

¼   **pound (115 g) bitter lettuce or other greens such as watercress, parsley, green chicory, curly endive, or dandelion greens, finely chopped**

3½   **teaspoons salt**

2   **large eggs, beaten**

1   **tablespoon olive oil**

1   **ounce (30 g) Parmesan, grated (¼ cup)**

1¼   **pounds (565 g/4 cups) unbleached white flour, plus additional flour for kneading**

6 to 8   **tablespoons (90 to 125 ml) water as needed**

      La Mère Besson's tomato sauce (page 114), basic tomato sauce (page 112), or 1 tablespoon olive oil and 2 to 4 tablespoons freshly grated Parmesan cheese for serving

Combine the greens in a bowl and toss with 1 teaspoon of the salt. Let sit for 30 minutes. Wrap in a clean kitchen towel and squeeze out all the moisture (do this over a bowl; you might want to save the water for soup stock). You should have about 1 cup (250 ml) of chopped greens.

Place the greens in the bowl of a food processor fitted with the steel blade and add ½ teaspoon salt, the eggs, olive oil, and Parmesan. Mix together. Add the flour and turn on the machine. Add water as needed until the mixture comes together on the blades of the food processor. The dough should be soft but not too sticky. Remove from the food processor and knead on a lightly floured board for a minute or two. Wrap in plastic wrap and allow to rest for 30 minutes or longer.

For gnocchi: Dust your hands with a little flour and divide the dough into 8 pieces. On a lightly floured board, roll each piece into a long strand about ¾ inch (2 cm) in diameter. Cut into ½-inch-thick (1.5 cm) disks. If you wish, press the disks against the tines of a fork to create ridges. Set aside on a lightly floured board.

Bring a large pot of water to a boil. Add the remaining salt and a drop of oil; then add the gnocchi in batches. Cook the gnocchi for about 10 minutes after the dumplings come to the surface of the boiling water. Remove from the water with a slotted spoon and place in a lightly oiled casserole. When all of the gnocchi are cooked, cover with tomato sauce or toss with the olive oil and Parmesan and reheat for about 15 to 20 minutes in a preheated 350°F (180°C) oven.

For pasta: Cut the dough into 8 pieces and roll out each piece into a thin, wide strip with a pasta roller. Dust often with flour or semolina. The dough will be quite soft. Allow the strips to sit for 10 minutes on a flour-dusted board. Then cut with a ravioli crimper or a knife into long, 1-inch-wide (2.5 cm) strips. Allow the pasta to dry for 30 minutes before cooking (or dry completely and store in a jar). Bring a large pot of water to a boil, add salt and oil and then the pasta. Cook for 1 to 2 minutes, until al dente, drain, and toss at once with tomato sauce or oil and Parmesan and serve.

ADVANCE PREPARATION: The uncooked gnocchi can be held in the refrigerator for a day in a covered bowl or on a cutting board, covered with a kitchen towel. They can also be frozen. Transfer directly from the freezer to the boiling water and boil for an extra 3 to 5 minutes. The pasta can be dried or frozen.

PER PORTION

Calories	482	Protein	17 G
Fat	8 G	Carbohydrate	86 G
Sodium	889 MG	Cholesterol	74 MG

NIÇOIS POTATO GNOCCHI WITH
SPICY TOMATO SAUCE

Gnocchis niçois aux pommes de terre

The potato gnocchi in Nice are practically identical to their Italian counterparts. This dish is based on one I sampled at a restaurant called Le Restaurant de Sienne in Vieux Nice.

For the Gnocchi:

2	pounds (900 g/8 medium-size) mealy potatoes, such as baking potatoes
2	large egg yolks
2	tablespoons olive oil
½	teaspoon freshly grated nutmeg
1	teaspoon salt or more to taste
	freshly ground pepper to taste
½	pound (225 g/1¾ cups) unbleached white flour, approximately, as needed

For the Sauce:

1	teaspoon olive oil
3	large garlic cloves, minced or put through a press
3	pounds (1.35 kg) tomatoes (12 medium-size), seeded and quartered
1 or 2	pinches of sugar
2	dried cayenne peppers or to taste, crushed in a mortar and pestle (about ⅛ teaspoon)
1	teaspoon fresh thyme leaves or ½ teaspoon dried
	salt to taste
2 to 3	tablespoons slivered fresh basil to taste (optional)
	freshly ground pepper to taste

1   tablespoon vegetable or olive oil for the gnocchi
     pot

3   ounces (90 g) low-fat mozzarella, cut into small
     cubes

Make the gnocchi: Boil or steam the potatoes for 30 minutes, until thoroughly tender. Remove from the heat and remove their skins. Transfer to a bowl and mash with a potato masher or a fork or put through the medium blade of a food mill. Work in the egg yolks, olive oil, nutmeg, salt, and pepper.

Stir in 1½ cups (180 g) of the flour, ½ cup (60 g) at a time. Place a few tablespoons of flour on your work surface and turn out the dough. Knead gently for 3 to 5 minutes. The dough should be supple and smooth. Add a bit of flour if it's too sticky.

Flour your hands and work surface. Divide the dough into 8 pieces. Roll out each piece into a sausage shape about ½ inch (1.5 cm) thick. Using a sharp knife, cut ½-inch (1.5 cm) pieces and press each piece gently against the inside curve of a fork. Keep flouring your hands so the dough doesn't stick. Cover the gnocchi with a clean kitchen towel and set aside, in the refrigerator if you will not be cooking them within the hour, while you make the sauce.

Make the tomato sauce: (You can also make it before you begin the gnocchi.) Heat the olive oil in a large heavy-bottomed nonstick skillet over medium heat and add the garlic. When it begins to color, add the tomatoes, sugar, crushed cayenne, thyme, and salt. Cook, stirring often, for 20 to 30 minutes, until the tomatoes are cooked down and beginning to stick to the pan. Stir in the basil, simmer for a few more minutes, and remove from the heat. Put through the medium blade of a food mill. Adjust salt and add pepper if desired.

Lightly oil a 2- or 3-quart (2 or 3 l) gratin dish. Preheat the oven to 400°F (200°C). To cook the gnocchi, bring a large pot of water to a boil. Add two teaspoons salt and a tablespoon of oil to the pot and cook the gnocchi in batches. They will sink to the bottom of the pot, then float up to the surface. Remove from the pot with a slotted spoon no more than 1 minute after they float to the top. Drain very briefly on kitchen towels, then transfer to the gratin dish. Gently stir in the tomato sauce and the mozzarella.

Heat through in the oven for 20 minutes, until the sauce is beginning to sizzle and the cheese is beginning to melt.

Note: Gnocchi are also delicious with low-fat pistou (page 109).

ADVANCE PREPARATION: Although I find that gnocchi dough becomes stickier and hard to handle the longer it sits, both the gnocchi

PASTA, PIZZA, AND GNOCCHI

dough and the sauce can be made up a day before cooking the gnocchi and held in the refrigerator. If you do mix up the dough a day ahead of time, don't wrap it in plastic, or it will be quite sticky the next day. Place it in a bowl and cover with a kitchen towel. You will almost certainly have to add more flour in any case on the next day, when you shape the gnocchi. You can shape the gnocchi and hold it on a board, covered with a towel, overnight. Make sure the board has been well dusted with semolina or cornmeal so that the gnocchi won't stick. The cooked gnocchi with the tomato sauce can be assembled and held for a few hours, in or out of the refrigerator.

PER PORTION

Calories	388	Protein	13 GM
Fat	12 G	Carbohydrate	60 G
Sodium	516 MG	Cholesterol	76 MG

PIZZA CRUST

MAKES ENOUGH FOR 3 MEDIUM-SIZE (10-INCH) OR
2 14- OR 15-INCH (35 TO 38 CM) PIZZAS

This is my favorite pizza crust to date. It's crunchy and crusty because of the semolina. The dough is very easy to handle and can be baked either in pizza pans or directly on a hot baking stone.

1	teaspoon active dry yeast
1½	cups (375 ml) lukewarm water
¼	pound (115 g/½ cup) fine semolina
¼	pound (115 g/1 scant cup) whole-wheat flour
2	teaspoons salt
¾	pound (340 g/2⅝ cups) unbleached white flour, plus 2 ounces (60 g/½ cup), as needed for kneading

Dissolve the yeast in the lukewarm water in a large bowl or in the bowl of your electric mixer and let sit for 5 minutes, until the yeast begins to bubble slightly. Stir in the semolina.

Kneading the bread by hand: Mix together the whole-wheat flour and salt and stir into the yeast mixture. Fold in the unbleached white flour, ½ cup at a time, until the dough can be scraped out of the bowl in one piece. Add ½ cup of unbleached flour to your kneading surface and knead, adding unbleached white flour as needed for 10 minutes. The dough will be sticky at first but will become very elastic.

Using an electric mixer: Combine the whole-wheat flour, salt, and the unbleached white flour and add all at once to the bowl. Mix together with the paddle, then change to the dough hook. Mix at low speed for 2 minutes, then at medium speed for 8 to 10 minutes. If the dough seems very wet and sticky, sprinkle in up to the 2 ounces (60 g/½ cup) flour for kneading. Scrape out the dough onto a lightly floured surface and knead for a minute or so by hand. Shape into a ball.

Rinse out your bowl, dry, and brush lightly with olive oil. Place the dough in the bowl, rounded side down first, then rounded side up. Cover with plastic wrap and a kitchen towel and set in a warm place to rise for 2½ hours or until the dough has doubled in size.

PASTA, PIZZA, AND GNOCCHI

Preheat the oven, with a baking stone or baking tiles in it, to 500°F (260°C). Punch down the dough and divide it into 2 or 3 pieces. Cover with plastic or a damp towel the pieces you aren't working with and roll out each piece. Line 2 lightly oiled 14- or 15-inch (35 to 38 cm) pizza pans or roll the dough into 3 smaller round shapes that will bake directly on a stone. The dough should be rolled no thicker than ¼ inch (.75 cm).

If you are baking the pizzas directly on a stone, transfer the dough to a baking peel that has been lightly dusted with semolina or cornmeal. Top with the garnishes of your choice and either gently slide from the peel onto the hot baking stone or place pans on top of the baking stone. Bake for 15 minutes. Serve hot.

ADVANCE PREPARATION: The dough can be frozen, before or after being rolled out. If you have rolled out the dough, do not thaw, but top and bake directly.

PER 14-INCH CRUST

Calories	1,185	Protein	36 G
Fat	10 G	Carbohydrate	235 G
Sodium	2,209 MG	Cholesterol	0

PISSALADIÈRE
Provençal Onion Tart

SERVES 6

This is the ultimate Provençal pizza. I say pizza, but in fact you often find this dish in a regular pastry, either butter based or olive oil based (naturally olive oil is the traditional ingredient, but French pastries found their way into Provence a long time ago). I still prefer it in a yeasted crust, and so, apparently, does *Larousse Gastronomique*, which gives a similar recipe. The name derives from the Provençal/Niçois word *pissalat* or *pissala*, a paste made of anchovies and olive oil seasoned with cloves, thyme, and bay leaf. Traditionally the tart was brushed with this condiment before being baked. *Pissalat* is not very current in Niçois cooking anymore (although I was recently served an anchovy salad dressing called *pissalat* in a Niçois restaurant); now pissaladière is garnished with anchovy fillets instead. Traditionally Niçois olives are used as well for garnish, but for our low-fat purposes I'm leaving them out. According to *Larousse*, a good pissaladière should have a layer of onions half as thick as the crust if you're using bread dough, the same thickness for piecrust. If you don't like anchovies, decorate the top with crust. The trick to a delicious pissaladière is cooking the onions slowly for a long enough time—45 minutes to an hour—to draw out their sweetness.

½	**recipe pizza crust (page 302)**
2	**tablespoons olive oil**
2	**pounds (900 g) white or yellow onions, finely chopped**
	salt to taste
3	**large garlic cloves, minced or put through a press**
½	**bay leaf**
1 to 2	**teaspoons fresh thyme leaves or ½ to 1 teaspoon dried to taste**
	freshly ground pepper to taste
1	**tablespoon drained capers, rinsed and pureed in a mortar and pestle**
12	**anchovy fillets, soaked in water or milk for 15 minutes**

Make the pizza dough, and prepare the onions while it rises. Heat the oil in a large heavy-bottomed nonstick skillet over medium-low heat and add the onions and a little salt. When they begin to sizzle, give them a stir and add the garlic, bay leaf, thyme, and pepper. Turn down the heat to low, cover, and cook slowly for 45 minutes to an hour, stirring often. The onions should melt down almost to a puree. If they begin to stick, add water a few tablespoons at a time. Stir in the capers, taste, and adjust seasonings.

Preheat the oven to 475°F (245°C). Roll out the dough about ¼ to ½ inch (.75 to 1.5 cm) thick and line an oiled 14-inch (35 cm) round or rectangular pizza pan or baking sheet. Pinch a generous lip around the edge. Spread the onions over the dough in an even layer.

Cut the anchovy fillets in half and distribute them over the dough, making X's with every two pieces.

If you're not using anchovies, reserve a quarter of the dough. After topping with the onions, roll out the remaining dough and cut into strips. Make a lattice decoration on top of the dough.

Bake for 15 to 20 minutes, until the edges are brown and the onions beginning to brown. Remove from the heat. Serve hot or cold.

ADVANCE PREPARATION: The filling can be made a day ahead of time and held in the refrigerator. The dough can be frozen, either before or after rolling it out. If you have rolled it out, top with the onions before thawing and put directly into the preheated oven.

PER PORTION

Calories	315	Protein	10 G
Fat	7 G	Carbohydrate	53 G
Sodium	703 MG	Cholesterol	4 MG

PIZZA WITH TOMATO AND PISTOU TOPPING

MAKES 2 LARGE (14- OR 15-INCH) OR 3 MEDIUM-SIZE
(10-INCH) PIZZAS, SERVING 6

This pizza is a transformation of one of my favorite tomato salads.

1	recipe pizza crust (page 302)
1	tablespoon olive oil
1½	ounces (45 g) Parmesan cheese, grated, 6 tablespoons
2	pounds (900 g/8 medium-size) tomatoes, sliced
2	large garlic cloves, minced or put through a press
	salt and freshly ground pepper to taste
1	tablespoon balsamic vinegar
2	tablespoons low-fat pistou (page 109)

Roll out the pizza dough as directed and preheat the oven to 500°F (260°C). Brush with the olive oil. Sprinkle on the Parmesan.

Toss together the tomatoes, garlic, salt, pepper, vinegar, and pistou. Arrange on the pizza dough.

Bake for 15 minutes or until the crust is browned and the tomatoes are bubbling. Serve hot or at room temperature.

ADVANCE PREPARATION: The dough and the tomato mixture can be assembled hours before making the pizza.

PER PORTION

Calories	491	Protein	17 G
Fat	9 G	Carbohydrate	87 G
Sodium	906 MG	Cholesterol	6 MG

PIZZA WITH TOMATOES, PEPPERS, AND ONIONS

MAKES 2 LARGE (14- OR 15-INCH) OR 3 MEDIUM-SIZE
(10-INCH) PIZZAS, SERVING 6 TO 8

This is an easy, relaxed pizza. Nothing has to be cooked. Just scatter the ingredients over the oil-doused dough, put it in the oven for 15 minutes, and enjoy. The cheese baked underneath the tomatoes prevents the dough from getting soggy.

1	recipe pizza crust (page 302)
2	tablespoons olive oil
1½	ounces (45 g) Parmesan cheese, grated (6 tablespoons)
8	large garlic cloves, thinly sliced
2	pounds (900 g/8 medium-size) tomatoes, sliced
	salt and freshly ground pepper to taste
2	small or medium-size red bell peppers, sliced into thin rings
1	medium-size onion, sliced into rings
1	tablespoon *herbes de Provence* (page 227)
	hot red pepper flakes (optional)
	hot pepper and herb olive oil (optional; page 123)

Roll out the pizza dough as directed and preheat the oven to 500°F (260°C). Brush with half the olive oil and sprinkle on the cheese and garlic slices. Arrange the tomato slices on top and sprinkle with salt and pepper. Place the pepper slices and onion rings over and among the tomatoes and sprinkle on the herbs. Drizzle on the remaining olive oil.

Bake for 15 minutes or until the crust is browned on the outside and the tomatoes are bubbling. Serve hot, passing hot pepper flakes and/or hot pepper and herb olive oil for people to drizzle on their slices.

A D V A N C E   P R E P A R A T I O N :   The dough can be made and the toppings prepared hours before assembling and baking the pizzas.

PER PORTION

Calories	260	Protein	8 G
Fat	5 G	Carbohydrate	46 G
Sodium	433 MG	Cholesterol	2 MG

CHAPTER 9

VEGETABLES, GRAINS, AND BEANS

Here is the backbone of Provençal cooking. It's no surprise that this chapter has more recipes than any other chapter in the collection—even after so many vegetable omelets, salads, soups, and tortes. Most of the dishes are gratins, called *tians* in Provence after the dishes in which they are baked, and gutsy, garlicky simmered vegetable ragouts, adapted to my low-fat cuisine by reducing olive oil and in some cases omitting bacon.

Every season of the year brings different vegetables to the markets of Provence and new inspiration. French *commerçants* always write the origin of the produce they are selling on the chalkboard with the price, and when the produce comes from the region they simply write *pays,* "country." That single word always makes me want to buy. In summer and early fall I can't get enough of the juicy local tomatoes, shiny black eggplants, beautiful young zucchini with the flowers still on, fresh borlotti beans in their pods. As fall proceeds, the colors of the market go from red to orange, and winter squash of all sizes and shapes takes center stage. Chard is another fall vegetable, sold in huge bunches of about 10 thick stalks; it also comes back in more tender bunches in the spring.

Fall is also when the wild mushrooms arrive, and so do the mushroom hunters, who take to the woods in droves on the weekends, their wicker baskets slung over an arm. When the season is good—if it has rained—there is hardly a meal without wild mushrooms, or a conversation without mention of them. One rainy fall I rented a house on a beautiful farm near the village of Gignac, about four miles northwest of Viens. I was lucky enough to have a neighbor named Raymond Noe, who took me *"aux champignons"* on several occasions. He would walk me through the woods around his farm for hours, spotting every wild mushroom in sight, and I would feast on our booty for days afterward. The dishes I cooked are all here.

Spring is an exciting time in the markets here. The first new vegetables to arrive are baby fava beans, called *fèvettes*, and young, green asparagus, followed by tiny sweet peas and green beans. Farmers come from the nearby hills to local markets with their bunches of arugula and first spring lettuces. They also bring wild greens and tiny shoots of wild asparagus (called *asperges sauvages* or *boublon*), which they have collected in the hills. The small purple artichokes, such an emblematic vegetable in Provence, are available year-round but are particularly tender at this time of year, and the young shoots of Swiss chard have less rib and more leaf than at other times of the year. The spring crop of spinach is especially sugary.

Potatoes are a very important year-round vegetable in Provence. They began to replace wheat and other grains as a dietary staple in the early nineteenth century and have gained steady ground since then, as they find their way into soups and

VEGETABLES, GRAINS, AND BEANS

ragouts, fricassees and purees, gratins and beignets. There seem to be almost as many Provençal names for the vegetable—*tartifle, tartifla, trufo, pomo de terro, tartifya, tantifula, trufa, trufle*—as there are villages in Haute-Provence.

That last word brings to mind Provence's most sought-after mushroom: the black truffle, called the *rabasse* in the region. I have one truffle recipe in this book, the scrambled eggs with truffles on page 256. I would have included more, for nothing can perfume a potato ragout or a risotto better than a truffle. But why include recipes for an ingredient that is so hard to come by? Canned truffles aren't worth the money you pay for them. You will have to come to Provence in the winter for these. It would be worth the trip.

Because potatoes have replaced grains as a household staple in Provence, I have not come across too many grain dishes. The exception is *épeautre*, a delicious wheatberry that is traditionally cooked in soups (page 156) or eaten with vinaigrette (page 41) and has recently become fashionable in French restaurants, so that you see different variations of *risotto d'épeautre* on restaurant menus (and on page 366). The Camargue is France's rice-growing region, producing a round-grained risotto-inspiring rice called riz de Camargue that is much like Italian Arborio rice, though slightly smaller-grained and a little less chewy.

Polenta is eaten in the Comté de Nice, but what is eaten even more than cornmeal is chick-pea flour. Just as ubiquitous as socca, the chick-pea flour pancake, in Nice is the *panisse*, a polentalike mixture of chick-pea flour cooked in water with olive oil and salt, then molded on or between saucers. *Panisses* are what remain of the *bouillies* or *soupo de bastoun*—flour-and-water soups that are so thick they have to be stirred with a long stick—that used to be such an important part of the Provençal diet, particularly in Haute-Provence. The small thick disks are sold in all of the Côte d'Azur shops that sell pasta. Cookbooks specify cutting them into French-fry-like pieces to be fried in olive oil, but a pasta vendor in Nice told me that there they split the *panisses* crosswise, sprinkle them with cheese, and grill them in the oven. This is so delicious I've taken the idea and made a wonderful gratin of *panisses* (page 373). No matter how you prepare *panisses*, they have a delicious flavor.

Finally, dried beans have as important a place in the cuisines of Provence as they do in other Mediterranean cuisines. Chick-peas and lentils, usually made into soups (pages 153–55), are probably the most widespread legumes, but white beans, red beans, and dried favas are a close second. The latter are more often used in ragouts and gratins than chick-peas and lentils.

Of all the chapters in this book, this was the hardest one for me to finish. If only I could keep myself away from the markets! Some of the dishes here are side dishes, but others can be the centerpiece for a delicious vegetarian meal.

RATATOUILLE
Ratatouia

SERVES 6

Every time I write a cookbook, I include a recipe for ratatouille, and every time, the recipe changes. Ratatouille is a dish that you can keep improving on; each time I use a new technique I'm convinced that I've come up with the best ratatouille yet. That's certainly the case here: all of the vegetables are sautéed briefly, then baked together for 1½ hours in an earthenware dish in a low oven. The mixture cooks very slowly, and as the vegetables gradually soften or "melt," they give forth a marvelous, fragrant broth, which is reduced to a heady syrup at the end and mixed back into the vegetables. Ratatouille cooked this way requires very little oil.

Amazingly enough, this dish, whose name derives from the French word *touiller*, meaning to stir or mix together, did not always have positive connnotations. According to *Larousse Gastronomique*, it was once known as a "not very appetizing stew." Luckily all that has changed now, and in France it is popular as both side dish and a starter. I like it either cold or hot and always try to make it a day or two before I'm going to serve it, because the flavors develop overnight. Ratatouille also makes a great filling for ravioli, crêpes, and omelets and can be mixed with eggs and Parmesan or Gruyère and baked in a crust for a terrific tart.

2	pounds (900 g/3 to 4 small or 2 large) **eggplant**
2	tablespoons plus 1 teaspoon **olive oil**
2	large **onions**, sliced
6	large **garlic cloves**, 4 sliced or minced, 2 put through a press or pureed
1	large **red bell pepper**, cut into slices about 1 inch thick by 2 inches long (2.5 by 5 cm)
1	large **green bell pepper**, cut into slices about 1 inch thick by 2 inches long (2.5 by 5 cm)
	coarse sea salt to taste
1½	pounds (675 g/3 medium-size) **zucchini**, cut in half lengthwise and sliced about ½ inch (1.5 cm) thick

4	large or 6 medium-size tomatoes, peeled, seeded, and coarsely chopped
1	tablespoon tomato paste
1	bay leaf
2	teaspoons fresh thyme leaves or 1 teaspoon crushed dried
1	teaspoon crushed dried oregano or 2 teaspoons chopped fresh
½	teaspoon crushed coriander seeds
	freshly ground pepper to taste
4 to 6	tablespoons (60 to 90 ml) fresh basil leaves, cut into slivers, or 3 tablespoons low-fat pistou (page 109)

Preheat the oven to 475°F (245°C). Cut the eggplants in half lengthwise, then score them lengthwise down the cut side, being careful not to cut through the skin. Brush a baking sheet with about ½ teaspoon olive oil and place the eggplant on it cut side down. Bake for 15 to 20 minutes, until the skins begin to shrivel. Remove from the heat and allow to cool. When cool enough to handle, cut into ½- to 1-inch (1.5 to 2.5 cm) dice, to taste. If you wish, you can peel the eggplant before dicing. Meanwhile, prepare the remaining vegetables.

Turn the oven down to 350°F (180°C). Brush a lidded earthenware casserole with ½ teaspoon olive oil.

Heat 1 tablespoon of the olive oil in a heavy-bottomed nonstick skillet over medium heat and add the onions. Cook, stirring, until they begin to soften, about 5 minutes. Add 2 of the sliced or minced garlic cloves and cook, stirring, for another 4 or 5 minutes. Transfer the vegetables to the casserole.

Heat the remaining tablespoon of olive oil and add the peppers. After a couple of minutes, add about ½ teaspoon coarse sea salt and continue to cook, stirring, until the peppers begin to soften. Add the zucchini and 2 more sliced or chopped garlic cloves and continue to cook together with the peppers for 5 minutes or until the zucchini begins to look a little translucent. Transfer to the casserole with the onions. Add the diced eggplant and half the tomatoes to the casserole along with the tomato paste, bay leaf, thyme, oregano, coriander, and about a teaspoon of coarse salt. Toss everything together, cover, and place in the oven.

Bake the ratatouille for 1½ hours. After the first half hour, give the stew a good stir. After 1 hour, add the remaining tomatoes and the pressed or pureed garlic and adjust the salt. Add pepper and bake for the last 30 minutes. Stir in the basil, cover, and return to the oven. Turn off the heat and leave the ratatouille in the oven for another hour.

Place a colander over a bowl and drain the juices off the ratatouille. Transfer the juices to a saucepan and bring to a boil. Reduce by half. Return the ratatouille to the earthenware dish and stir in the juices. Taste and adjust seasonings. Serve hot or cold.

ADVANCE PREPARATION: Ratatouille is best made a day ahead of time and will keep for 4 or 5 days in the refrigerator. It can be frozen.

PER PORTION

Calories	169	Protein	5 G
Fat	6 G	Carbohydrate	28 G
Sodium	43 MG	Cholesterol	0

TRUC

A LOW-FAT METHOD FOR COOKING EGGPLANT

Eggplant can absorb enormous quantities of oil, and most traditional recipes include unhealthy amounts. Instead, use this simple method. Preheat the oven to 450 to 475°F (230 to 245°C). Brush a baking sheet, preferably nonstick, with olive oil. Cut eggplants in half lengthwise. Score the cut side, right down to but not through the skin. Lay the eggplant halves cut side down on the baking sheet and bake for about 20 minutes, until the skin of the eggplant is beginning to shrivel. Remove from the heat and allow to cool. Prepare and cook the eggplant as directed in the recipe. The eggplant will have cooked partially and released water; it no longer has a spongelike texture that drinks up olive oil, and it won't be bitter.

SOCCA CRÊPES WITH RATATOUILLE AND GOAT CHEESE
Socca crêpes à la ratatouille

SERVES 6

This dish is on the menu at a restaurant in New York called May We. It's a perfect combination of Provençal tastes, and I don't know why nobody in France has thought of it. It makes a marvelous vegetarian main dish. Serve it with the potato and saffron gratin on page 337 for an incredibly colorful plate.

12	socca crêpes (page 90)
1	recipe ratatouille (preceding recipe)
3	ounces (90 g) goat cheese, cut into 12 thin slices
	fresh basil or chervil leaves for garnish

Preheat the oven to 375°F (190°C). Lightly oil a 3-quart (3 l) gratin dish. Place a crêpe in the dish and place a generous spoonful of ratatouille on one half of the crêpe. Top with a thin slice of goat cheese. Fold the crepe over and push to one end of the dish. Continue to fill the remaining crêpes.

Cover the dish with foil and bake for 20 to 30 minutes, until the cheese is softened and the crêpes and filling are warm. If any ratatouille remains, heat it during this time on top of the stove.

Serve 2 crêpes to a plate, with more ratatouille on the side and a generous fresh herb garnish.

ADVANCE PREPARATION: The crêpes will keep in the refrigerator for a couple of days and freeze well. The ratatouille can be made a day or two ahead of time and is in fact better if made a day ahead of time. The dish can be assembled an hour or two before serving.

PER PORTION

Calories	355	Protein	13 G
Fat	19 G	Carbohydrate	37 G
Sodium	277 MG	Cholesterol	86 MG

EGGPLANT AND TOMATO GRATIN
Gratin d'aubergines et de tomates

SERVES 6

This heady gratin has everything I love about eggplant Parmesan, minus the fat. Although I think of it as a summer dish, inspired by the luscious piles of dark purple eggplants and red ripe tomatoes I see in Provençal markets at that time of year, you could make the gratin with canned tomatoes in winter.

3	**pounds (1.35 kg/3 large or 5 to 6 medium-size) eggplant, cut in half lengthwise**
4	**teaspoons olive oil**
3	**large garlic cloves, minced or put through a press**
3	**pounds (1.35 kg/12 medium-size) tomatoes, seeded and quartered**
1 or 2	**pinches of sugar**
	salt to taste
2 to 3	**tablespoons slivered fresh basil to taste**
	freshly ground pepper to taste
1	**ounce (30 g) Parmesan cheese, grated (¼ cup)**
2	**tablespoons fresh or dry, coarse or fine bread crumbs**

Preheat the oven to 475°F (245°C). Cut the eggplants in half lengthwise, score them down the middle, to the skin but not through it, and place cut side down on oiled baking sheets. Bake for 25 to 30 minutes, until thoroughly tender. Remove from the heat and allow to cool. Carefully peel away the skins or scoop the eggplant out from the skins, and cut in ¼-inch-thick (.75 cm) lengthwise slices. Turn the oven down to 425°F (220°C).

While the eggplants bake, heat 1 teaspoon of the oil in a large, heavy-bottomed nonstick skillet over medium heat and add the garlic. When it begins to color, after about 30 seconds to a minute, add the tomatoes, sugar, and salt. Cook, stirring often, for 20 to 30 minutes, until the tomatoes are cooked down and beginning to stick to the pan. Stir in the basil, simmer for a few more minutes, and remove from the heat.

Put the tomatoes through the medium blade of a food mill. Adjust salt and add pepper.

Oil a 3-quart (3 l) gratin dish. Spoon a small amount of tomato sauce over the bottom and top with one-third of the eggplant. Spoon one-third of the remaining tomato sauce over the eggplant. Make 2 more layers, sprinkle on the cheese, and bread crumbs, and drizzle on the olive oil.

Bake for 30 minutes in the hot oven, until the top browns and the mixture is sizzling. Remove from the heat and serve hot or warm.

ADVANCE PREPARATION: This will keep for a couple of days in the refrigerator before baking.

PER PORTION

Calories	161	Protein	6 G
Fat	5 G	Carbohydrate	27 G
Sodium	123 MG	Cholesterol	3 MG

EGGPLANT AND TOMATO RAGOUT
Bohémienne

SERVES 4 TO 6

Much like a ratatouille, the *bohémienne* is a slightly simpler dish, made with onions, garlic, tomato, and eggplant. It's cooked a long time so that the result is almost a confit, heady and wonderful. You can serve this hot or cold, gratinéed or not. Use leftovers as a topping for pasta or pizza. In Provence anchovies are often added at the end of cooking (see note), but I prefer the pure vegetable flavors.

2	**pounds (900 g/2 large or 3 medium-size) eggplant**
2	**tablespoons olive oil**
2	**medium-size onions, thinly sliced**
3 to 4	**large garlic cloves, to taste, minced or put through a press**
2	**pounds (900 g/8 medium-size) fresh or canned tomatoes, peeled, seeded, and chopped**
1	**teaspoon fresh thyme leaves or ½ teaspoon dried**
	salt and freshly ground pepper to taste
2	**tablespoons chopped fresh basil (omit if fresh is unavailable)**
1	**ounce (30 g) Gruyère cheese, grated (¼ cup) (optional)**

Preheat the oven to 475°F (245°C). Cut the eggplants in half lengthwise, score down to the skin but not through it, and place cut side down on oiled baking sheets. Bake for 20 minutes, until the skins shrivel and the eggplant is tender. Remove from the heat and, when cool enough to handle, peel and cut into small dice.

Heat the olive oil in a large heavy-bottomed skillet over medium-low heat and add the onions. Cook, stirring, until tender, about 5 to 8 minutes. Add the garlic, stir, and cook for about a minute, until the garlic begins to color. Add the tomatoes, eggplant, thyme, salt, and pepper and stir. Turn the heat to low, cover, and cook, stirring often, for 45 minutes to an hour, until the mixture has cooked down to a thick puree. Taste and adjust seasonings. Stir in the basil. Serve hot or cold.

If you wish to make this into a gratin, transfer to a lightly oiled gratin dish and sprinkle on the cheese if you're using it. Bake in a 425°F oven for 15 to 20 minutes, until the cheese melts and the mixture is bubbling.

Note: For the optional anchovy addition, mash together 4 anchovy fillets, soaked in water or milk for 15 minutes or longer and drained, and 2 tablespoons skim milk while the vegetable mixture is cooking. Stir into the eggplant mixture when it is done and mix together well. Taste and adjust seasonings.

ADVANCE PREPARATION: This is best made a day ahead of time, but don't make the gratin until you serve the dish. It will keep for 3 or 4 days in the refrigerator.

PER PORTION

Calories	127	Protein	3 G
Fat	5 G	Carbohydrate	20 G
Sodium	20 MG	Cholesterol	0

―――― T R U C ――――

USE LEMON JUICE TO PREVENT DISCOLORING
WHEN WORKING WITH ARTICHOKES, APPLES,
PEARS, QUINCES

Squeeze the juice of ½ lemon into a bowl of cold water.

When you're preparing artichokes and quinces, rub the cut edges continuously with the cut side of the other half of the lemon and place the prepared artichokes in the bowl of lemon water until ready to cook. Apples and pears don't need to be rubbed, but place them in the lemon water as you prepare the fruit.

EGGPLANT FLAN WITH
TOMATO COULIS

Papeton d'aubergines

SERVES 4 AS A MAIN DISH, 6 AS A STARTER OR SIDE DISH

Legend has it that this was a favorite dish with the popes when they moved their headquarters to Avignon in the fourteenth century. Light and creamy with no cream, it makes a beautiful, elegant first course or main dish. Try to find very dark eggplant; the darker they are, the riper.

3	pounds (1.35 kg) eggplant, preferably the long kind
1½	tablespoons olive oil
3	shallots or 1 medium-size onion, chopped
5	large garlic cloves or more to taste, minced or put through a press
	salt and freshly ground pepper to taste
	generous pinch of crushed dried thyme
4	large eggs
3	pounds (1.35 kg) tomatoes, quartered
	pinch of sugar
2	tablespoons slivered fresh basil or 1 teaspoon fresh thyme leaves or ½ teaspoon dried thyme
	whole basil leaves for garnish

Preheat the oven to 475°F (245°C). Cut the eggplants in half lengthwise, score down to the skin but not through it, and place cut side down on oiled baking sheets. Bake for 30 minutes, until thoroughly tender. Remove from the heat and, when cool enough to handle, scrape the pulp from the skins. Turn the oven down to 350°F (180°C). Generously oil a soufflé dish or charlotte mold.

Heat 1 tablespoon of the olive oil in a large heavy-bottomed skillet over medium-low heat and add the shallots. Cook, stirring, until they soften, 3 to 5 minutes, and add 2 garlic cloves. Cook, stirring, for about 30 seconds. Stir in the eggplant, add a generous amount of salt, some pepper, and the thyme, and cook, stirring, for 3 minutes or until the mixture begins to stick to the pan. Remove from the heat.

Put the eggplant mixture through the medium blade of a food mill or puree in a food processor fitted with the steel blade. Add another garlic clove and the eggs and adjust the salt and pepper. Transfer to the oiled soufflé dish and place in a pan of hot water (a bain-marie). Bake for 40 to 50 minutes, until set.

Meanwhile, make the tomato coulis. Heat the remaining olive oil in a nonstick skillet over medium heat and add the remaining garlic. Cook, stirring, until the garlic begins to soften, about 30 seconds. Add the tomatoes, sugar, and salt to taste. Cook, uncovered, over medium heat for 20 to 30 minutes, until the mixture is thick and beginning to stick to the pan. Remove from the heat and put through the medium blade of a food mill. Add the basil and pepper to taste, adjust the salt, and heat through.

Either unmold the eggplant flan or serve from the dish. If you unmold it, top with the coulis and decorate with fresh basil leaves. To serve directly from the mold, place a spoonful of tomato coulis on the plate, top with the eggplant flan, and spoon a little more tomato coulis on top. Garnish with basil leaves. You can also allow the flan and coulis to cool and serve cold.

ADVANCE PREPARATION: The coulis can be made a day or two ahead of time and kept in the refrigerator. If you are serving the eggplant flan cold, you can make it a day ahead of time.

PER PORTION

Calories	194	Protein	8 G
Fat	9 G	Carbohydrate	25 G
Sodium	71 MG	Cholesterol	142 MG

TRUC

SALTING VEGETABLES SO THEY COOK IN THEIR OWN LIQUID

When you're cooking vegetables on top of the stove in very little oil, salt the vegetables to your taste when you add them to the pan. The salt will draw out their natural fragrant juices so that the vegetables won't require more oil to lubricate them in the pan.

PROVENÇAL ARTICHOKE RAGOUT WITH TOMATOES, PEPPERS, AND GARLIC
Artichauts à la barigoule

SERVES 6

I keep looking for and trying new *artichauts à la barigoule* recipes, but I still can't find one I like as much as my friend Christine Picasso's. I've included it in other collections, but it's such a definitive Provençal recipe that I couldn't leave it out of this book. Definitive, I say, yet every single Provençal person I have met has a different version. The last one I heard, described by a Marseillaise friend, sounded exactly like the artichoke and potato ragout on page 324 of this collection, yet my friend called her dish *artichauts à la barigoule*. J. B. Reboul, author of the best-known Provençal cookbook in France (*La Cuisinière Provençale*, now in its twenty-fifth edition), simmers his artichokes in wine with onions and carrots. *Larousse Gastronomique* describes *artichauts à la barigoule* as a dish in which the artichokes are stuffed and braised. Me, I'll stick to the garlicky, tomatoey version I learned to make long ago in Provence. It's the combination of garlic and peppers with the artichokes, all cooked together in the long-simmering tomato and wine sauce, that makes this so good.

2	lemons, cut in half
18	small purple artichokes or 6 globe artichokes
1	tablespoon olive oil
2	medium-size white onions, chopped
1	head of garlic, cloves separated, crushed slightly, and peeled
2	medium-size red bell peppers
	salt to taste
2	pounds (900 g/8 medium-size) fresh or canned tomatoes, peeled, seeded, and chopped
	freshly ground pepper to taste
1	teaspoon fresh thyme leaves or ½ teaspoon dried
1	bay leaf

VEGETABLES, GRAINS, AND BEANS

1 cup (250 ml) dry white or rosé wine

2 cups (500 ml) simmering water as needed

¼ cup (about 15 g/½ large bunch) chopped parsley

Fill a bowl with water and add the juice of one of the lemons. Trim the stems off the artichokes and cut off the tops with a sharp knife. Trim off the spiny tips of the outer leaves with scissors and rub the cut parts with the remaining lemon. Cut small artichokes in half, large artichokes into quarters, and gently scoop out the spiny chokes. Rub the cut sides with lemon and place in the bowl of water as you go along.

Heat the oil in a large heavy-bottomed nonstick skillet or casserole over medium-low heat and add the onions. Cook, stirring, until tender, about 5 minutes. Add the garlic, peppers, and a little salt and stir together for about 5 minutes, until the garlic begins to color and the peppers begin to soften. Add the tomatoes, more salt if desired, and pepper. Cook, stirring often, for about 10 minutes, until the tomatoes have cooked down a bit and are fragrant.

Drain the artichokes and add to the pot along with the thyme, bay leaf, and wine. Bring to a simmer, add 1 cup (250 ml) simmering water, cover, and simmer for 30 minutes. Check the mixture and add another cup of simmering water if the liquid has evaporated. Continue to simmer, covered, for another 15 to 30 minutes, until the artichokes are tender and the leaves come away easily. Stir in the parsley, taste, and adjust seasonings. Serve hot or cold.

ADVANCE PREPARATION: This will hold for a day or two in the refrigerator.

PER PORTION

Calories	153	Protein	7 G
Fat	3 G	Carbohydrate	30 G
Sodium	161 MG	Cholesterol	0

ARTICHOKE AND POTATO RAGOUT
Artichauts et pommes de terres en ragoût

SERVES 6

This wonderful, lemony, warming, long-simmering dish is substantial enough to eat as a main course. You can use the small purple artichokes that you see all over Provence or big California artichokes cut into quarters. They work just as well, absorbing the succulent broth in the most delicious way.

6	**large or 12 small purple artichokes (18 if very small)**
	juice of 2 lemons (½ cup/125 ml)
1	**tablespoon olive oil**
2	**medium-size or large onions, sliced**
4 to 5	**large garlic cloves, to taste, minced or put through a press**
	about 1 quart (1 l) water or chicken, vegetable, or garlic stock (pages 127–30) or more as needed
1	**bay leaf**
	salt and freshly ground pepper to taste
2	**pounds (900 g) new potatoes, quartered or cut into large dice**
1	**teaspoon fresh thyme leaves or ½ teaspoon dried**
¼	**cup (30 g/about ½ bunch) chopped parsley**

Cut away the top leaves of the artichokes and break off the bottom leaves. Trim the bottoms and rub with the cut side of a lemon. Cut small artichokes in half, large artichokes into quarters, and remove the spiny fibers with a sharp knife. Rub the cut edges with a cut lemon and set aside.

Heat the olive oil in a lidded large heavy-bottomed saucepan or casserole over medium-low heat and add the onions. Sauté, stirring, until tender, about 8 minutes. Add half the garlic and cook, stirring, until the garlic begins to color, about 1 minute. Add the artichokes, the juice of ½ lemon, water or stock to cover, the bay leaf, salt, and pepper. Bring to a simmer, cover, and simmer over low heat for 30 minutes.

Add the potatoes, remaining garlic, remaining lemon juice, thyme, and parsley. Make sure the liquid covers everything (add as needed), cover, and simmer for another 30 minutes or until the potatoes are tender. Adjust the seasonings and serve.

A D V A N C E   P R E P A R A T I O N :   This can be made several hours before serving and reheated.

P E R   P O R T I O N

Calories	250	Protein	9 G
Fat	3 G	Carbohydrate	52 G
Sodium	167 MG	Cholesterol	0

M U S H R O O M I N G   W I T H   R A Y M O N D   N O E

October
Les Buis, Gignac

In French the phrase for going mushroom hunting is *aller aux champignons*, which means "to go to the mushrooms." The mushrooms are there, waiting. Finding them, hunting for them, is hardly implied.

I could see the logic in this attitude when my neighbor Raymond took me for my first mushrooming walk in the hills. It was a gray, cool, damp day, perfect for mushrooms. He said that it would be another couple of days before the ones engendered by the big storm two weeks earlier would come out (it takes fifteen days, he said). But there were certainly enough for us. We didn't find any girolles or cèpes, but we found kilos of what he calls *pinens* (a Provençal word for *lactaire* mushrooms, which grow under pine trees; when they're red, they're called *sanguins*; in California I've seen similar mushrooms called Lobster Mushrooms). They're big mushrooms with a top that varies in color from orange to greenish brown. The underside and stem, however, are a yellow-orange. They grow under oaks and pines, so we made our way through the brush to the spots Raymond knew. He used to take his sheep over to this area every day for twenty-five years (now he's retired), so he knows this country like the back of his hand. We went down into a valley and up the opposite hill, stopping at a ruin that used to belong to a Belgian, who tried to make a fortune raising dogs and failed.

We went back into the woods and found more mushrooms—he'd spot them, and I'd bend over and pick them. There was another kind that looks a little like a morel, but more like a sponge (I've seen similar mushrooms called Bear's Heads in California farmers' markets) and we found lots of those, but the worms had found most of them first. We walked and walked and walked, through plum and cherry orchards, past apple trees and blackberries, always back into the woods for the mushrooms. He spoke a lot about how people were robbed all the time here, and kind of scared me, so that every time we heard his dogs barking I was sure somebody had stolen my car. I got a glimpse into a dark rustic mentality that grips people here. I'm told that the suicide rate is high in Provence.

On the way home I asked Raymond how he prepared the mushrooms. He said he soaked them overnight, changing the water often, then cooked them "à la poêle" and ate them with meat ("But you don't eat meat," he said, laughing), or else he puts them up. I thought soaking them overnight was a bit excessive, so I soaked them for about 4 hours, changing the water often and putting a bit of vinegar in the last two soaks. Then I let them dry out a bit in a towel-lined colander overnight (except for the ones I cooked with red wine, garlic, and herbs for dinner). I feasted on ragouts, omelets, and gratins all week.

The mushroom hunting continued. On another day I went out with my friends Andrew and Jean-Luc, to hunt for trompettes de la mort, horn of plenty mushrooms, which are incredibly delicious. Jean-Luc, an organic gardener who grows, among other crops, old varieties of vegetables, especially a lot of New World foods—many varieties of squash, chilies and tomatoes—has a secret spot for them, and we found a lot, which became wonderful omelets, ragouts, and pasta toppings.

I went out again with Raymond, and this time we found girolles, which he spotted just breaking through the ground. They were the real treasure. I just baked them in the oven with a little olive oil and garlic and herbs, along with my tomato gratin.

OVEN-ROASTED GIROLLES
Girolles au four

SERVES 4

To my mind, girolles are the prize among wild mushrooms. Golden, smallish, firm-textured, they have a pronounced flavor and require very little work. I found girolles that had just broken the surface of the wet earth one Saturday afternoon in October, when I was on one of my weekly mushroom walks with my neighbor Raymond. He could see the little tops pushing through the leaves; I would have walked right by.

1	**pound (450 g) girolles, morels, or chanterelles, trimmed and cleaned**
1 or 2	**garlic cloves, to taste, minced**
	coarse sea salt and freshly ground pepper to taste
1	**tablespoon chopped parsley**
2	**teaspoons olive oil**

Preheat the oven to 400°F (200°C). Lightly oil a baking or gratin dish large enough to accommodate the mushrooms in a single layer.

Place the mushrooms in the baking dish and toss with the remaining ingredients. Bake for 20 to 30 minutes, until the mushrooms are tender and beginning to color. Serve hot.

ADVANCE PREPARATION: The mushrooms and other ingredients can be prepared hours before baking and held at room temperature. Add the olive oil just before baking.

PER PORTION

Calories	62	Protein	2 G
Fat	4 G	Carbohydrate	6 G
Sodium	8 MG	Cholesterol	0

CLEANING WILD MUSHROOMS

Purists tell you to brush wild mushrooms and to avoid washing them in water. But let's face it: wild mushrooms are full of dirt; eating improperly cleaned mushrooms is as awful as eating sandy lettuce or sandy mussels. This is the technique I use for "meaty" mushrooms like cèpes or lactaires if they're very sandy and mixed in with bits of leaves and twigs. (For more delicate mushrooms like horn of plenty or clean-looking wild mushrooms—the ones I haven't picked but have bought at the market—I simply cut away the stems, rinse them several times in a bowl of cold water, and gently squeeze dry.)

First cut away the stems (the sandiest part). Fill a large bowl, or the bowl of your salad spinner, with water and add the mushrooms. Swish them around vigorously and lift from the water. Drain the water and repeat. Drain and rinse the bowl and mushrooms again, fill the bowl with water again, and this time add a couple of tablespoons of vinegar (just in case there are worms in your mushrooms; this will kill them or draw them out). Add the mushrooms to the water, swish around, and let sit for 5 to 10 minutes or even a couple of hours. If you leave them for a couple of hours, change the water halfway through and add more vinegar. Drain the mushrooms, wipe dry with paper towels, and let sit to dry further in a towel-lined colander for a few hours or overnight.

SAUTÉED HORN OF PLENTY MUSHROOMS
Trompettes de la mort poêlées

MAKES 2 CUPS (500 ML), SERVING 3 TO 4

Trompettes de la mort, also called (more optimistically) horn of plenty or black chanterelles, are small brownish black wild mushrooms. They're one of the most subtly flavored mushrooms and demand very little to bring out their best qualities. I was lucky enough to be in Provence during a very fruitful season and gathered kilos of these to experiment with. It was the month of October, and for days and days it rained. The wild mushrooms were my compensation. Use this recipe as a basis for omelets, quiches, and pasta or just eat the mushrooms as they are, as a side dish.

1	pound (450 g/6 cups) horn of plenty mushrooms, stems trimmed
1	tablespoon red wine vinegar
2	large pinches of coarse sea salt
2	teaspoons olive oil
3 to 4	garlic cloves, to taste, minced or put through a press
2	teaspoons fresh thyme leaves or 1 teaspoon dried freshly ground pepper to taste
2	tablespoons chopped parsley (optional)

Soak the mushrooms in cold water with about 1 teaspoon of the vinegar for 15 minutes, changing the water and vinegar 3 times. Rinse thoroughly and shake the mushrooms in a kitchen towel. (It's difficult to get all the sand out, but a little sand won't hurt you.)

Combine the mushrooms and sea salt in a large heavy-bottomed nonstick skillet and heat over medium-high heat until they begin to release water, about 1 minute. Cook, shaking the pan or stirring with a wooden spoon, for 5 minutes, until most of the liquid has evaporated. Add the olive oil, garlic, and thyme and continue to cook, stirring, for another 2 to 3 minutes, until the garlic is fragrant and beginning to color. Add the pepper and the parsley if desired, and remove from the heat.

ADVANCE PREPARATION: The cooked mushrooms will keep for a couple of days in the refrigerator.

PER PORTION

Calories	53	Protein	3 G
Fat	3 G	Carbohydrate	6 G
Sodium	96 MG	Cholesterol	0

TRUC

COOKED MUSHROOMS WITH A MINIMUM OF OIL

Mushrooms release so much water when they cook that you can put them in the pan with no oil, just a little salt to draw out the liquid. Cook over medium heat, stirring or shaking the pan, and in a few minutes they will release their water. If you are eventually adding garlic, you can add it at this point; or add a teaspoon or two of olive oil and the garlic after the liquid has evaporated.

SAUTÉED WILD MUSHROOMS
Champignons sauvages à la poêle

SERVES 4 GENEROUSLY

This is my basic recipe for savory skillet mushrooms. Serve them as a side dish with meat or fish, accompany them with grains, or use the mushrooms to top pasta or fill omelets.

2	pounds (900 g) wild mushrooms such as cèpes, girolles, morels, or oyster mushrooms, stems trimmed
	salt to taste
¾	cup (185 ml) dry, fruity red wine, such as a Côtes du Luberon
2	teaspoons fresh thyme leaves or 1 teaspoon dried
2	teaspoons chopped fresh rosemary leaves or 1 teaspoon crushed dried
2	tablespoons olive oil
2 to 4	large garlic cloves, to taste, minced or put through a press
	freshly ground pepper to taste
3	tablespoons chopped parsley

Unless the mushrooms are very sandy and mixed with leaves (which they often are if you pick them yourself), rinse them several times with cold water and gently squeeze or pat dry. If they are quite sandy, clean the mushrooms by soaking them in a large bowl of cold water for a couple of hours, changing the soaking water 4 times. Add 1 tablespoon of vinegar to the water during the last 2 soaks. Drain the mushrooms and wipe dry with paper towels or kitchen towels or place in a large colander in a cool place for several hours or overnight.

Cut the mushrooms into quarters or thick slices if large and place in a large nonstick skillet. Sprinkle with salt and heat over medium-high heat until they begin to release liquid. Cook, stirring, for 5 minutes or until the mushrooms are beginning to stick to the pan. Then add the red wine, thyme, and rosemary. Turn the heat down to medium and cook, stirring, for 5 to 10 minutes or until the wine is just about gone. Add the olive oil, garlic, and pepper. Cook, stirring, until the garlic begins to color, about 5 minutes. Stir in the parsley and remove from the heat. Adjust the seasonings and serve, either as a main dish or as a side dish with meat, fish, or scrambled eggs or tossed with pasta.

ADVANCE PREPARATION: This can be cooked several hours before serving and reheated in the pan over medium heat.

PER PORTION

Calories	156	Protein	5 G
Fat	8 G	Carbohydrate	13 G
Sodium	13 MG	Cholesterol	0

POTATO AND WILD
MUSHROOM GRATIN
Tian de pommes de terres et de Champignons sauvages

SERVES 6

I wish it were realistic for me to instruct you to go out and find a pound of fresh mushrooms in the woods of the Vaucluse, then go and buy organic potatoes from Jean-Luc Dannyrolle at the Apt market and dried cèpes at the Apt butcher. Luckily you don't need to be in Provence to make this. If you can't find fresh wild mushrooms, omit them and use the dried cèpes (porcini) only, which are easy to find in gourmet stores.

1   ounce (30 g/1 cup) dried cèpes (porcini)

1   quart (1 l) boiling water

4   large garlic cloves, minced or put through a press, plus 1 garlic clove, cut in half lengthwise

1   pound (450 g) fresh wild mushrooms, if available, cleaned of grit (page 328) and sliced about ½ inch (1.5 cm) thick if large

    salt to taste

5   teaspoons olive oil

2   teaspoons fresh thyme leaves or 1 teaspoon dried

2   tablespoons red wine, such as a Côtes-du-Rhône

    freshly ground pepper to taste

3   pounds (1.35 kg) waxy potatoes, scrubbed and sliced ½ inch (1.5 cm) thick

1   ounce (30 g) Gruyère or Parmesan cheese, grated (¼ cup)

Place the dried mushrooms in a bowl and pour on the boiling water. Let sit for 20 to 30 minutes or until the mushrooms are softened. Drain through a cheesecloth-lined strainer over a bowl and squeeze the mushrooms over the strainer. Rinse thoroughly to remove the grit, squeeze dry, and chop coarsely. Reserve the soaking liquid.

Preheat the oven to 400°F (200°C). Rub the inside of a 3-quart (3 l) gratin dish with the cut clove of garlic.

Combine the fresh wild mushrooms and salt in a large heavy-bottomed nonstick skillet and heat over medium-high heat until they begin to release water, about 1 minute. Cook, shaking the pan or stirring with a wooden spoon, for 5 minutes, until most of the liquid has evaporated. (If fresh wild mushrooms are unavailable, omit this step altogether.)

Add 1 tablespoon of the olive oil (or heat the olive oil in a nonstick skillet if you don't have fresh wild mushrooms), the chopped dried mushrooms, the remaining garlic, and the thyme and continue to cook, stirring, for another 2 to 3 minutes, until the garlic is fragrant and beginning to color. Add the red wine and pepper and cook for a minute, stirring, until the wine has been absorbed. Remove from the heat and toss with the sliced potatoes. Add more pepper if desired.

Arrange the potatoes and mushrooms in an even layer in the prepared dish. Measure out 3½ cups (875 ml) of the mushroom-soaking liquid and season with 1 teaspoon salt or more or less to taste. Pour it over the potatoes. Bake for about 1½ to 2 hours, until the potatoes are tender and the top is crusty. Every 20 minutes, stir the potatoes from the bottom up to the top. When the top is beginning to color, after about an hour and 15 minutes, sprinkle the cheese and remaining olive oil over the top. Continue to bake until the top is browned, 15 to 30 minutes.

ADVANCE PREPARATION: The gratin can be assembled hours before baking. The mushrooms can be prepared a day or two ahead of time and held in the refrigerator.

PER PORTION

Calories	274	Protein	8 G
Fat	6 G	Carbohydrate	49 G
Sodium	406 MG	Cholesterol	5 MG

VEGETABLES, GRAINS, AND BEANS

PROVENÇAL POTATO GRATIN
Tian de pommes de terre à la Provençale

SERVES 6

Another wonderful potato dish from Provence. Naturally the things that make this potato gratin Provençal are the tomatoes, onions, and garlic. The gratin smells wonderful as it bakes and tastes even better.

3 to 4	**large garlic cloves, to taste, minced or put through a press**
¼	**cup (60 ml) chopped fresh herbs, such as parsley, basil, sage, rosemary, oregano**
1½	**pounds (675 g/6 medium-size) tomatoes, sliced**
2	**pounds (900 g/8 medium-size) waxy potatoes, scrubbed and sliced ¼ inch (.75 cm) thick**
2	**medium-size onions, thinly sliced**
2	**medium-size red bell peppers, thinly sliced**
	salt and freshly ground pepper to taste
2	**teaspoons fresh thyme leaves or 1 teaspoon dried**
1	**cup (250 ml) garlic, vegetable, or chicken stock (pages 127–30)**
1	**bay leaf**
1	**tablespoon olive oil**
1	**ounce (30 g) Gruyère cheese, grated (¼ cup) (optional)**

Preheat the oven to 400°F (200°C). Rub a 3-quart (3 l) gratin dish with a cut clove of garlic (before you mince the 3 to 4 cloves) and brush lightly with olive oil. Gently toss a third of the garlic and a third of the fresh herbs with the tomatoes, a third with the potatoes, and a third with the onions and bell peppers.

Layer half of the tomatoes in the gratin dish. Top with half the onions and bell peppers, then half the potatoes. Sprinkle each layer generously with salt, pepper, and thyme. Repeat the layers. Pour the stock over the gratin and stick the bay leaf in the middle. Drizzle the olive oil over the top.

Bake for 1½ hours or until the potatoes are tender and the top is beginning to brown. Add the cheese to the top of the gratin during the last 20 minutes. Remove the bay leaf and serve hot.

A D V A N C E   P R E P A R A T I O N :   The gratin can be assembled hours before serving. It can be baked a few hours ahead of serving, up to the adding of the cheese, and finished with the cheese shortly before serving.

P E R   P O R T I O N

Calories	202	Protein	5 G
Fat	3 G	Carbohydrate	41 G
Sodium	104 MG	Cholesterol	0

POTATO AND SAFFRON GRATIN

Tian de pommes de terre au safran

SERVES 6

The color alone would make anyone want to feast on this dish. I was introduced to a version of this by my friend Lulu Peyraud, proprietress of Domaine Tempier in Bandol. (Lulu usually includes fish livers in her gratin, the livers of the fish she is serving as a main dish; but we don't have much to do with fish livers in the United States.) She told me that this dish reminded her of the "bouillabaisses" she used to make during the war, when it was difficult to get fish (or much of anything else). She would make a broth with lots of garlic, onions, potatoes, and fennel stalks and call it a bouillabaisse because it would be seasoned with saffron at the end as the fish soup is. You can use either garlic, vegetable, or chicken stock for this gratin. Just make sure you have plenty of fragrant saffron threads. Serve it as a side dish with fish or as part of a vegetarian meal.

5   cups (1.25 l) garlic, vegetable, or chicken stock
    (pages 127–30)
1   head of garlic, cloves separated, slightly
    crushed, and peeled (unless you're using garlic
    broth), plus 1 clove, peeled and cut in half
    lengthwise
1   teaspoon saffron threads
    salt to taste
3   pounds (1.35 kg) waxy potatoes, such as Yukon
    gold or new potatoes, scrubbed and sliced ¼ to
    ½ inch (.75 to 1.5 cm) thick
    a few pinches of coarse salt
    freshly ground pepper to taste

Combine the stock and cloves from the head of garlic in a saucepan and bring to a boil. Reduce the heat, cover, and simmer for 1 hour, until you have a fragrant broth. Strain the broth and return it to the saucepan. Bring to a boil, add the saffron, simmer for a couple more minutes, and remove from the heat. Taste and add salt.

Preheat the oven to 400°F (200°C). Rub a 3-quart (3 l) gratin dish with the cut clove of garlic and slice what remains of the cooked garlic into the broth.

Toss together the potatoes, coarse salt, and pepper. Place in the gratin dish and smooth out the top. Pour in the broth, making sure none of the saffron threads remain in the pot. Bake for 1 to 1½ hours, stirring the potatoes every 20 minutes or so, until most of the broth is absorbed and the top is beginning to brown.

ADVANCE PREPARATION: The broth can be prepared up to the adding of the saffron hours or even a day before making the gratin.

PER PORTION

Calories	208	Protein	5 G
Fat	.51 G	Carbohydrate	46 G
Sodium	444 MG	Cholesterol	0

ROAST POTATOES FILLED WITH SLIVERED BAY LEAVES

Pommes de terres rôties au laurier

SERVES 4

This brilliant idea comes from Roger Vergé, who takes Provençal cuisine to new heights. Slivers of bay leaves are wedged into potatoes, and as the potatoes bake they take on a wonderful herbal aroma and flavor. It's a delicious side dish.

8   medium-size (1 kg/2¼ pounds) waxy potatoes

12   bay leaves, as fresh as you can get them, cut into thin strips

     salt and freshly ground pepper to taste

1   cup (250 ml) vegetable, garlic, or chicken stock (pages 127–30)

1   tablespoon olive oil

Preheat the oven to 425°F (220°C). Oil a smallish gratin dish, large enough to accommodate the potatoes but small enough so that they are close together.

Lay the potatoes down and make several incisions in each one, about ¼ inch (.75 cm) apart, starting at the top and going down to within about ¼ inch (.75 cm) of the bottom of the potato. Place a sliver of bay leaf in each slice. Sprinkle with salt and pepper and place in the baking dish. Pour on the stock and drizzle the olive oil over the potatoes.

Bake for 50 to 60 minutes, basting the potatoes every 10 minutes with a brush or baster, until the potatoes are tender and the stock is just about evaporated. Serve from the baking dish.

ADVANCE PREPARATION: You can prepare the potatoes up to 2 hours before baking. The potatoes can also be baked ahead of time and reheated in a covered baking dish.

PER PORTION

Calories	259	Protein	5 G
Fat	5 G	Carbohydrate	49 G
Sodium	22 MG	Cholesterol	0

POTATOES WITH SAGE
Pommes de terre à la sauge

SERVES 4

Sage, widely used in Provençal cooking, is one of my favorite herbs. I grow it throughout the year on a tiny balcony in Paris, and it grows all around my rented house in Provence. The fresh herb is a perfect match for potatoes. If you can find little new potatoes (the French *rattes* are my favorite) for this recipe, by all means use them.

1   **pound (450 g) new potatoes, preferably small ones, scrubbed and quartered if large**

1   **tablespoon olive oil**

2   **tablespoons slivered fresh sage leaves**

    salt and freshly ground pepper to taste

1   **garlic clove, minced or put through a press (optional)**

Steam the potatoes for 15 minutes or until tender. Toss with the remaining ingredients in a warm serving dish and serve.

ADVANCE PREPARATION: This can be made a few hours before serving and reheated in a heavy-bottomed skillet.

PER PORTION

Calories	122	Protein	2 G
Fat	4 G	Carbohydrate	21 G
Sodium	9 MG	Cholesterol	0

MASHED POTATOES AND GREEN GARLIC
Purée de pommes de terre à l'ail nouveau

SERVES 4

Regular mashed potatoes will never seem the same after you've tasted this dish. The sweetness of the simmered new garlic (page 361) melts into the potatoes. Who needs butter? I leave the skin on the potatoes, but if you wish, you can peel them. If you can find pink new potatoes that are pinkish on the inside, the dish will have a lovely hue.

  2 heads of green garlic, cloves separated and peeled
  3 quarts (3 l) water or more as needed
  2 pounds (900 g) new potatoes, preferably the pink-skinned variety, scrubbed
  1 bay leaf
  2 teaspoons salt, plus more to taste for the puree
  ½ cup (125 ml) skim milk
  2 teaspoons olive oil
     freshly ground pepper to taste

Combine the garlic and 1 quart (1 l) of the water in a saucepan and bring to a boil. Boil for 1 minute, drain, return the garlic to the saucepan, and add a second quart (l) of water. Bring to a boil, boil for 1 minute, and drain. Return the garlic to the saucepan and add the potatoes, bay leaf, and last quart (l) of water. Add more water to cover the potatoes if necessary. Bring to a boil and add 2 teaspoons of salt. Boil, partially covered, for 30 to 40 minutes, until the potatoes are tender. Drain and remove the bay leaf.

Return the potatoes and garlic to the saucepan and mash with a potato masher, a fork, or the back of a wooden spoon. Add the milk and olive oil and continue to mash until the mixture is fairly smooth. Add salt and pepper to taste and serve or heat through and serve.

ADVANCE PREPARATION: This can be prepared a few hours before serving and gently reheated, either on top of the stove or in the oven.

You will probably have to add a small amount of extra water or milk, because the mixture will dry out. You can also retain some of the cooking water for moistening.

PER PORTION

Calories	251	Protein	7 G
Fat	3 G	Carbohydrate	50 G
Sodium	588 MG	Cholesterol	.61 MG

CHARD STALK GRATIN
Gratin de côtes de blettes

SERVES 4 AS A SIDE DISH

Leave it to the French (those from Provence in particular) to find a wonderful dish for everything. How often have I bought Swiss chard and thrown away the stalks? I always felt vaguely ripped off until I learned how good a gratin made with the stalks can be. You can also make this dish with both the leaves and the stalks of chard. I like it in its simplest form, with the cooked chard stalks sprinkled with Parmesan, drizzled with olive oil, and baked in a hot oven until the top is beginning to brown. But you can also make a richer, more substantial dish by tossing the cooked stalks (and leaves, if you're using them), with the olive oil béchamel on page 111.

2   quarts (2 l) garlic or vegetable stock (pages 127 and 130)

     approximately 1¼ pounds (565 g) chard stalks, from 2 to 2¼ pounds (900 g to 1 kg) chard, strings removed, cut crosswise into ½-inch-thick (1.5 cm) slices

     freshly ground pepper to taste

1   recipe olive oil béchamel (optional)

3   tablespoons freshly grated Parmesan cheese

1   tablespoon olive oil

Preheat the oven to 450°F (230°C). Oil a 3-quart (3 l) gratin dish. Bring the stock to a boil in a large saucepan and add the sliced chard stalks. Turn the heat to medium and boil gently for 5 to 7 minutes, until the chard stalks are just cooked through. Meanwhile, oil a gratin dish.

Transfer the chard stalks to the gratin dish with a slotted spoon or deep-fry skimmer. Toss with freshly ground pepper and béchamel if you're using it. Sprinkle with the Parmesan and drizzle on the olive oil.

Bake for 15 minutes, until the top begins to brown. Serve hot.

To use the chard leaves as well: Wash the chard leaves and cook them briefly in a large pot of salted boiling water, or wilt in a large nonstick skillet over high heat for about 2 minutes in the liquid that remains on their leaves. Remove from the heat and squeeze dry. Chop coarsely and toss with the sliced stalks.

ADVANCE PREPARATION: The dish can be assembled hours or even a day before baking and held in the refrigerator.

PER PORTION

Calories	110	Protein	4 G
Fat	6 G	Carbohydrate	11 G
Sodium	1,153 MG	Cholesterol	4 MG

WINTER SQUASH GRATIN
WITH BÉCHAMEL
Tian de courge

SERVES 6

Beautiful orange winter squashes hit the Provençal markets in September. They're made up into delicious tortes (page 260), gratins, and soups. This is just one of many Provençal squash gratin recipes.

3	pounds (675 g) pumpkin or other winter squash, such as butternut or acorn squash
2	tablespoons chopped fresh sage or 1½ teaspoons dried
	salt and freshly ground pepper to taste
1	recipe olive oil béchamel (page 111)
¼ to ½	teaspoon freshly grated nutmeg to taste
2	ounces (60 g) Gruyère cheese, grated (½ cup)
2	tablespoons fresh or dry, coarse or fine whole-wheat bread crumbs
2	teaspoons olive oil

Peel the squash and remove the seeds and membranes. Cut into ¼-inch-thick (.75 cm) slices. Steam for 10 minutes, until tender. Remove from the heat and transfer to a bowl. Toss with the sage, salt, and pepper.

While the squash is steaming, make the béchamel. Season with salt, pepper, and nutmeg. Stir in the cheese.

Preheat the oven to 375°F (190°C). Butter or oil a 2- or 3-quart (2 or 3 l) gratin dish.

Pour the béchamel into the bowl with the pumpkin and gently toss the mixture together. Turn it into the gratin dish. Sprinkle the bread crumbs over the top and drizzle on the olive oil.

Bake for 40 minutes or until the top is beginning to brown and the mixture is bubbling. Remove from the heat and serve hot.

VEGETABLES, GRAINS, AND BEANS

ADVANCE PREPARATION: The gratin can be assembled hours before baking. Hold in the refrigerator if you are assembling this more than a couple of hours ahead of time.

PER PORTION

Calories	195	Protein	9 G
Fat	10 G	Carbohydrate	19 G
Sodium	108 MG	Cholesterol	15 MG

WINTER SQUASH GRATIN 2
Tian de courge 2

SERVES 6

Based on a Richard Olney recipe from *Simple French Food*, this is a simple and luxurious gratin. The time-consuming part is cutting the squash into small cubes. If you wish, you can chop it in a food processor.

3 **pounds (1.35 kg) pumpkin or other winter squash, peeled, seeds removed, cut into very small dice, 8 to 9 cups**

6 to 8 **large garlic cloves, to taste, minced or put through a press**

¼ **cup (1 oz/30 g) unbleached white flour**

¾ **cup (45 g/1½ large bunches) chopped parsley**

salt and freshly ground pepper to taste

2 **tablespoons olive oil**

Preheat the oven to 350°F (180°C). Oil a 3- or 4-quart (3 or 4 l) gratin dish. Combine the pumpkin, garlic, flour, and parsley in a bowl and toss, sprinkling with salt and pepper. The squash should be coated evenly with garlic, flour, parsley, and the seasonings.

Place the squash in the gratin dish and drizzle the oil over the top. Bake for

1½ to 2 hours, stirring every half hour, until the top is quite brown and the squash thoroughly softened. Serve hot.

ADVANCE PREPARATION: This can be assembled hours ahead of baking.

PER PORTION

Calories	116	Protein	3 G
Fat	5 G	Carbohydrate	16 G
Sodium	5 MG	Cholesterol	0

TOMATO GRATIN À LA PROVENÇALE
Gratin de tomates

SERVES 4

This simple dish is downright exciting if you have sweet, ripe tomatoes to work with. If your tomatoes are a little dull, sprinkle them with a pinch of sugar.

2   **pounds (900 g/8 medium-size) tomatoes, cut in half crosswise**

 salt and freshly ground pepper to taste

1   **teaspoon sugar (if needed)**

4   **garlic cloves, minced**

1   **cup (60 g/2 large bunches) flat-leaf parsley leaves, minced (½ cup)**

½   **cup (70 g) fine bread crumbs (fresh or dry)**

2   **tablespoons olive oil**

Preheat the oven to 400°F (200°C). Lightly oil a gratin dish large enough to accommodate the tomatoes.

Gently squeeze the seeds out of the tomatoes and place them cut side up in the gratin dish. Lightly salt and pepper and sprinkle with a little sugar if they aren't

VEGETABLES, GRAINS, AND BEANS

ripe and sweet. Mix together the garlic, parsley, and bread crumbs. Top the tomatoes with this mixture. Drizzle on the oil.

Bake for 20 to 30 minutes, until the bread crumb mixture browns. Serve hot or at room temperature.

ADVANCE PREPARATION: The tomatoes can be prepared and topped with the bread crumb mixture hours before baking. Cover and hold at room temperature or in the refrigerator.

PER PORTION

Calories	138	Protein	2 G
Fat	9 G	Carbohydrate	14 G
Sodium	53 MG	Cholesterol	.22 MG

STOVETOP SLOW-COOKED TOMATOES À LA PROVENÇALE
Tomates à la Provençale

SERVES 6

In this traditional Provençal dish, tomatoes are cooked very slowly on top of the stove, until they shrivel down into incredibly sensuous mouthfuls. I'd had a version of this dish in Bandol, at Domaine Tempier, cooked slowly in the oven. Then I came across this recipe in Andrée Maureau's excellent *Recettes en Provence* (Edisud, 1991). I think it's a little easier to keep an eye on the tomatoes with this version, and if there are only one or two for dinner, you can make the tomatoes in a little pan. All you need is time and patience. It's worth it. As the tomatoes cook, their skin caramelizes. The finished tomatoes don't make the most beautiful dish I've ever seen, but they're incredibly delicious.

12 **medium-size or 18 small tomatoes**

2 **tablespoons olive oil**

 salt and freshly ground pepper to taste

½ **teaspoon sugar, approximately**

6 **garlic cloves, minced**

½ **cup (30 g/1 large bunch) minced flat-leaf parsley**

 water as needed

Cut the tomatoes in half crosswise and gently squeeze out their seeds. Heat the oil in a large nonstick skillet over medium-low heat and add the tomatoes, cut side down. Cover and cook for 15 minutes.

Remove the pan from the heat and gently turn the tomatoes so the cut side is up. Sprinkle with salt, pepper, a tiny bit of sugar, the garlic, and the parsley. Turn the heat as low as it will go and return the pan to the stove. Cover and cook for 1 to 1½ hours, checking every 10 minutes or so to make sure the tomatoes aren't sticking and burning. If they are, gently slide a spatula between the tomatoes and the pan to loosen them, add a tablespoon of water, and return to the heat. Continue with this procedure throughout the cooking. You can put the pan on a Flame Tamer to control the heat. By the end of cooking the tomatoes will be shriveled up, bite size, and the skins will have caramelized.

Serve hot or at room temperature. If the skins are tough, just scoop out the pulp when you eat them.

ADVANCE PREPARATION: This can be made a day ahead of time and reheated gently. The tomatoes can also be frozen.

PER PORTION

Calories	91	Protein	2 G
Fat	5 G	Carbohydrate	11 G
Sodium	21 MG	Cholesterol	0

STUFFED TOMATO GRATIN
Tomates farcies bonne femme

SERVES 6

This is a more elaborate tomato gratin than the one on page 346, another favorite Provençal summer/fall dish that's good hot or cold.

12	**medium-size tomatoes**
	salt and freshly ground pepper to taste
1	**teaspoon sugar (if needed)**
2	**thick slices of stale French bread**
	skim milk to cover the bread
1	**pound (450 g) spinach or Swiss chard leaves, spinach stems removed**
1	**tablespoon olive oil**
1	**large onion, chopped**
6	**large garlic cloves, minced or put through a press**
1	**bunch of flat-leaf parsley, chopped, about (½ cup/30 g)**
1 to 2	**teaspoons fresh thyme leaves or ½ to 1 teaspoon dried to taste**
2	**large eggs, beaten**

Cut a slice from the top of the tomatoes about ½ inch (1.5 cm) down from the stem end and gently squeeze out the seeds. Using a small sharp knife or a spoon, scoop out the pulp, chop, and set aside. Salt and pepper the tomato shells lightly and sprinkle with a little sugar if the tomatoes aren't ripe and sweet.

Preheat the oven to 425°F (220°C). Lightly oil a gratin dish large enough to accommodate the tomatoes in one layer.

Soak the bread in milk to cover while you prepare the rest of the filling.

Wilt the spinach or chard in a large heavy-bottomed nonstick skillet in the water left on its leaves; this will take a couple of minutes once the water begins to boil. Remove from the heat and, when cool enough to handle, squeeze dry in a towel and chop finely. Set aside.

Heat the oil in the same skillet over medium-low heat and add the onion. Sauté, stirring, until tender, about 5 minutes. Add the garlic and sauté, stirring, for about 30 seconds. Add the chopped tomato pulp and some salt and pepper. Cook, stirring, for 5 to 10 minutes, until the tomato pulp has cooked down and the mixture is aromatic. Stir in the spinach, parsley, and thyme. Stir together for a minute or two, remove from the heat, and transfer to a bowl.

Remove the bread from the milk, squeeze out the milk, and stir the bread into the spinach and tomato mixture. Add the eggs and adjust the seasonings.

Fill the tomatoes with the stuffing and place in the oiled baking dish. Bake for 20 to 30 minutes, until browned. Serve hot or at room temperature.

ADVANCE PREPARATION: The filling can be prepared and the tomatoes stuffed hours ahead of baking.

PER PORTION

Calories	157	Protein	7 G
Fat	6 G	Carbohydrate	22 G
Sodium	147 MG	Cholesterol	71 MG

ZUCCHINI GRATIN WITH GOAT CHEESE
Tian de courgettes au chèvre

SERVES 4

A traditional Provençal gratin would contain Gruyère, but goat cheese is even more Provençal than Gruyère, and it goes beautifully with the subtle zucchini.

2	**pounds (900 g) zucchini, coarsely grated or thinly sliced**
	salt
2	**tablespoons olive oil**
	freshly ground pepper to taste
2	**garlic cloves, minced or put through a press**
¼	**cup (about 15 g/½ large bunch) chopped parsley**
2 to 4	**tablespoons slivered fresh basil to taste (omit if fresh is not available)**
2	**medium-size eggs, beaten**
2	**ounces (60 g) fresh goat cheese crumbled (about ½ cup)**
2	**tablespoons fresh or dry bread crumbs**

Preheat the oven to 400°F (200°C). Oil a 2-quart (2 l) gratin. Salt the zucchini and let sit in a colander for 15 to 30 minutes. Rinse and gently squeeze out the moisture.

Heat 1 tablespoon of the oil in a large heavy-bottomed nonstick skillet over medium heat and add the zucchini, salt, and pepper. Cook, stirring, for 10 minutes, until the zucchini is beginning to cook through. Add the garlic and continue to sauté, stirring, for another 5 minutes, until the zucchini is fragrant but still bright green. Stir in the parsley and basil and remove from the heat.

Beat together the eggs and goat cheese. Stir in the zucchini. Adjust the seasonings and transfer to the gratin dish. Sprinkle on the bread crumbs and drizzle on the remaining olive oil.

VEGETABLES, GRAINS, AND BEANS

Bake for 20 to 30 minutes, until the top is browned and the mixture is sizzling. Serve hot or at room temperature.

ADVANCE PREPARATION: The gratin can be assembled hours before baking. It can be baked a few hours before serving and reheated in a medium 350°F (180°C) oven for 15 minutes or in a 400°F (200°C) oven for 5 to 10 minutes.

PER PORTION

Calories	182	Protein	8 G
Fat	13 G	Carbohydrate	9 G
Sodium	96 MG	Cholesterol	100 MG

ZUCCHINI AND RICE GRATIN
Tian de courgettes

SERVES 6 TO 8

This is one of several Provençal zucchini *tians*, and it's one of my favorite dishes. I've published it before, but I couldn't leave it out of this collection, because it's a signature dish of the region. Serve it warm or cold—I prefer it cold—as a starter, main dish, or part of a selection of Provençal hors d'oeuvres.

2	tablespoons olive oil
1	medium-size onion, minced
2	pounds (900 g/6 medium-size) zucchini, finely chopped
2	garlic cloves, minced or put through a press
	salt and freshly ground pepper to taste
2	large eggs
2	ounces (60 g) Gruyère cheese, grated (½ cup)
½	cup (30 g/1 large bunch) chopped parsley
½	cup (100 g) Arborio or short-grain rice from the Camargue, cooked
1	teaspoon fresh thyme leaves or ½ teaspoon dried
2	tablespoons fresh or dry bread crumbs

Preheat the oven to 375°F (190°C). Brush a loaf pan or a 1½ quart (1.5 l) gratin dish lightly with olive oil.

Heat 1 tablespoon of the oil in a large heavy-bottomed nonstick skillet over medium-low heat and add the onion. Cook, stirring, until tender, about 5 minutes. Add the zucchini, garlic, salt, and pepper and cook, stirring often, for 10 minutes, until the zucchini is tender but still bright green. Remove from the heat and allow to cool slightly.

Beat the eggs in a bowl. Stir in the zucchini and onions, the cheese, parsley, rice, and thyme. Stir together, taste, and add more salt and pepper if desired. Transfer to the baking dish. Sprinkle the bread crumbs over the top and drizzle on the remaining oil.

Bake for 45 to 60 minutes (it will take longer in a loaf pan), until firm and browned on the top. Remove from the heat and cool on a rack. Serve warm or cold.

Note: You could transform this into a torte by baking it in the torte crust on page 259. Follow directions for the pumpkin torte on page 260.

To serve: If you've used a loaf pan, slice the gratin. If you are serving it as part of a selection of hors d'oeuvres, you might want to cut the slices in half.

ADVANCE PREPARATION: This can be made a day ahead of time and held in the refrigerator, tightly wrapped.

PER PORTION

Calories	156	Protein	6 G
Fat	8 G	Carbohydrate	16 G
Sodium	49 MG	Cholesterol	61 MG

STUFFED ZUCCHINI FLOWERS
Fleurs de courgettes farcies

SERVES 4 TO 6

This is one of the great delicacies of Provençal cuisine. Fillings vary from cook to cook; I think the light, subtle ones like this are the best. Include fresh mint—at least 2 tablespoons—with the herbs for a truly memorable taste.

24	zucchini flowers
1	tablespoon olive oil
2	pounds (900 g/6 medium-size) zucchini, minced
4	garlic cloves, minced or put through a press
	salt and freshly ground pepper to taste
2	large eggs, beaten
½ to ⅔	cup (125 to 165 ml) chopped fresh herbs such as parsley, basil, mint, chives to taste
2	tablespoons fresh lemon juice (optional)
6	tablespoons fresh bread crumbs, fine or coarse
¼	cup (62 ml) chicken, vegetable, or garlic stock (pages 127–30)
	basic tomato sauce (page 112) for serving (optional)

Gently pull the pollen-topped stem out from the center of each zucchini flower and discard. Set aside the flowers. Preheat the oven to 400°F (200°C). Oil a baking dish large enough to accommodate all of the flowers in one layer.

Heat the olive oil in a heavy-bottomed nonstick skillet over medium-low heat and add the zucchini. Cook, stirring, for about 5 minutes, until the zucchini begins to soften. Add the garlic, salt, and pepper. Cook, stirring, until the zucchini is tender and there is no liquid in the pan, about 10 minutes. Remove from the heat and allow to cool slightly.

Stir the eggs, herbs, lemon juice, and bread crumbs into the zucchini. Taste and adjust the seasonings. You should have about 3 cups (750 ml) of filling.

Gently stuff the flowers, using only enough filling so that you can reposition the petals over it. About 2 heaped teaspoons per flower should suffice. Twist the tops of the flowers together at the top and set in the oiled baking dish. Add the stock to the dish. Cover tightly with foil or a lid.

Bake for 20 minutes. Serve hot or cold, garnished, if desired, with the tomato sauce.

Note: One of the most successful versions of this dish I have ever made was with leftover risotto, which I mixed with fresh herbs. I wouldn't tell you to make a risotto just to fill the zucchini flowers, but know that leftovers make a great filling (fill and bake as directed).

ADVANCE PREPARATION: The flowers can be filled a day ahead of serving. In fact, you should fill the flowers the day you buy or pick them, or the petals will wilt (if they do wilt, you can still make the dish, but you'll have to be very careful not to tear the petals when you fill the flowers.) If they are to be served cold, they can be baked several hours before serving.

PER PORTION

Calories	81	Protein	4 G
Fat	4 G	Carbohydrate	8 G
Sodium	42 MG	Cholesterol	71 MG

PROVENÇAL SPINACH GRATIN
Tian d'épinards

SERVES 4 AS A SIDE DISH OR STARTER

A typical Provençal vegetable dish, *tian d'épinards* is traditionally a long-baking dish in which the spinach is cut into chiffonade and baked for an hour or more. I've tried the traditional method a few times, but I'm never satisfied because the spinach tends to be overcooked for my taste. So I wilt the spinach first and bake the *tian* for only 20 to 30 minutes, enough to brown the top. It's a delicious dish, either as a starter or as a side dish.

2¼	**pounds (1 kg) fresh spinach, stems removed**
	salt and freshly ground pepper to taste
2	**tablespoons olive oil**
1	**tablespoon unbleached flour**
¼	**cup (62 ml) milk**
½	**cup (30 g/1 large bunch) chopped parsley**
1 to 2	**garlic cloves, to taste, minced or put through a press (optional)**
2	**tablespoons fresh or dry bread crumbs**

Preheat the oven to 425°F (220°C). Brush a 1½- to 2-quart (1.5 to 2 l) gratin dish with olive oil. Cook the spinach briefly in a large pot of salted boiling water or wilt in a large, nonstick skillet over high heat in the water left on its leaves. This should take no more than 2 minutes once you hear the water beginning to sizzle.

Transfer the spinach to a colander and gently press against the sides of the colander to squeeze out water. The spinach does not have to be squeezed dry. Chop and toss with salt, pepper, 1 tablespoon of the olive oil, the flour, milk, parsley, and garlic. Transfer to the gratin dish. Sprinkle on the bread crumbs and drizzle on the remaining olive oil. Bake for 20 to 30 minutes, until the top is beginning to brown and the *tian* is sizzling.

ADVANCE PREPARATION: The *tian* can be prepared hours or even a day ahead of baking and held in the refrigerator. It can be baked an hour or so ahead of time and reheated.

VEGETABLES, GRAINS, AND BEANS

SPINACH AND RED PEPPER GRATIN
Tian d'épinards au poivron rôti

SERVES 6

Every once in a while I'll buy spinach on impulse, especially in the spring, when local spinach is so sweet it's almost as though it has sugar in the leaves. I developed this beautiful red pepper–studded gratin after just such an impulse buy, when I couldn't resist the mountains of rich green leaves when I saw them in my Paris market. Paris notwithstanding, this is pure Provence and as healthful as you can get. It makes a gorgeous first course and could also be the main attraction.

1	**large red bell pepper, about ½ pound (225 g)**
	salt to taste
3	**pounds (1.35 kg) spinach, stems removed**
1	**large egg**
⅓	**cup (85 ml) skim milk**
3	**garlic cloves, minced or put through a press**
	freshly ground pepper to taste
1	**teaspoon fresh thyme leaves or ½ teaspoon dried**
2	**tablespoons fresh or dry bread crumbs**
1	**tablespoon olive oil**

Preheat the oven to 400°F (200°C). Roast the pepper in the oven for 30 to 45 minutes, turning it every 15 minutes, until puffed, slightly brown, and soft. Transfer to a bowl and cover tightly. Allow to cool for 20 to 30 minutes. Reserve any liquid that accumulates in the bowl and peel and seed the pepper over the bowl so that you catch any additional liquid. Cut into thin strips and set aside.

While the pepper is baking, bring a large pot of water to a boil and add 2 tablespoons salt. Blanch the spinach, immediately transfer to a bowl of cold water, drain, and squeeze out as much liquid as you can. Chop coarsely.

Brush a 10½-inch (26 cm) ceramic tart pan or a 2-quart (2 l) gratin dish with olive oil.

Beat together the egg with the liquid from the roasted pepper and the milk. Toss with the spinach and stir in the garlic, salt, pepper, and thyme. Turn into the prepared baking dish. Sprinkle on the bread crumbs.

Arrange the pepper slices like the spokes of a wheel over the spinach if you're using a round baking dish. For a gratin dish, arrange the peppers in a crisscross pattern. Drizzle the olive oil over the top.

Bake for 30 minutes or until set and the top is just beginning to brown. Serve hot, warm, or at room temperature.

ADVANCE PREPARATION: This will hold for several hours, in or out of the refrigerator. If you're serving it at room temperature, you can make it a day ahead of time and refrigerate it until an hour before serving.

SPINACH AND RED PEPPER FLAN: For a flan, reduce the amount of spinach to 2 pounds (900 g) and add 1 large egg and 2 egg whites. Use ⅔ cup (165 ml) milk and omit the bread crumbs. Proceed as directed.

PER PORTION

Calories	93	Protein	7 G
Fat	5 G	Carbohydrate	9 G
Sodium	152 MG	Cholesterol	36 MG

If you are lucky enough to be in Provence during the month of June and to have a kitchen to cook in, you will be amazed by the garlic. At this time of year the thick-stemmed bulbs are huge, the juicy cloves covered with several layers of tender, easy-to-peel, almost leafy skin. This freshly harvested *ail nouveau,* "new garlic" or "green garlic," is in season from late May until the end of June. The cloves are sweet and fruity, pungent but not overpowering. Working with this garlic is sensuous and pleasing; I love removing the many layers of skin from the fat cloves and using it, either raw or cooked, in Provençal recipes.

Provence produces 10,000 to 11,000 tons of garlic a year. There are two types: *ail de moyenne conservation* (garlic that keeps for a moderate amount of time) and *ail de longue conservation* (long-keeping garlic). *Ail de moyenne conservation,* the first garlic to arrive on the market in the spring, is the ail nouveau. After being harvested in late spring, it keeps, with all of its aromatic virtues, until the end of the following February, when it is at its most aromatic. There are two varieties: one is white, the other, *ail violet,* is violet. The bulbs of both varieties are large and the stalks thick.

There is one variety of long-keeping garlic, *ail rouge.* White on the outside, with pink-skinned cloves, this garlic is harvested between mid-June and the end of July and keeps until the following June. The bulbs are not as large as the other varieties, and the cloves are smaller. Because it keeps for a year, this is the type that is most often used for braids. Garlic lovers prefer it to the other varieties because it is stronger and keeps longer.

No matter which kind of Provençal garlic you buy, it is always strongest in midwinter. My friend Lulu Peyraud, at the Bandol winery Domaine Tempier, says she never eats raw garlic between the end of February and the end of May. But the question has become slightly academic, because in the last decade Argentine garlic has become a big import, to the chagrin of the Provençal producers.

If you grow your own garlic, you can pull it at four to six weeks, before the cloves have formed separately—this very new garlic is exceptionally mild and sweet. You can find it sometimes at farmer's markets. Otherwise, look for fresh green garlic at Asian markets.

Sian au mes d'Abriéu
Que lis ai d'abrivon
See how in the month of April
The garlic quickly comes to life

Juliet porto l'aiet
July brings garlic

Quand li veno d'aiet soun marrido à pela,
es la marco d'un marrit ivèr
When the garlic is difficult to peel,
it's the sign of a hard winter

Aiet prim de pèu
Ivèr court e bèu
Garlic with thin skin,
Winter, short and fair

Carnava s'en vai
Fau se metre à l'ai
Carnival is over
Time to eat garlic

Aiet e pan, repas de paisan
Garlic and bread, the peasant's repast

Uno ensalado aiet-croustet, vous n'en licas lou bout di det
Salad with garlic croutons, finger-licking good

L'aiet es l'especarié dóu paure
Garlic is the poor man's grocery store

Quu se fringouio au rest d'aiet
póu pas senti la girouflado
He who rubs his collar with garlic
cannot smell a carnation

Vai t'en manja d'aiet! (Go, eat your garlic!)
Be a good soldier!

Es acqui l'ai (Here is the garlic)
That is the question

Demandon de cebo, e respond d'aiet
You ask him for onion, and he responds with garlic

Lou mortié sent l'aiet
The mortar smells the garlic

OVEN-ROASTED GARLIC
Ail rôti au four

SERVES 6

Oven-roasted garlic, like simmered garlic, loses its pungency and becomes sweet-tasting and heavenly. In Provence it is traditionally served with roast lamb and pork. I think it makes a luxurious side dish with almost anything—poultry, rabbit, seafood, vegetables.

8   **heads of garlic**
1   **tablespoon olive oil**
    salt and freshly ground pepper to taste
    a few fresh thyme sprigs
    a few fresh rosemary sprigs
¼   **cup (60 ml) hot water or more as needed**

Preheat the oven to 400°F (200°C). Oil a covered baking dish or casserole. Toss the heads of garlic with the olive oil, salt, and pepper in the baking dish. Add the thyme, rosemary, and water.

Cover and bake for 45 minutes. Check the water from time to time, and add a few more tablespoons if it has evaporated.

To serve, either squeeze out the puree and mash in a bowl, moistening with a small amount of liquid in the pan if any remains, or serve the whole heads of garlic and allow guests to squeeze out the puree themselves.

ADVANCE PREPARATION: You can bake these a few hours ahead of serving if you're going to serve the puree in a bowl. Reheat gently in a medium 350°F (180°C) oven.

PER PORTION

Calories	122	Protein	4 G
Fat	3 G	Carbohydrate	21 G
Sodium	11 MG	Cholesterol	0

GREEN GARLIC AND SPRING VEGETABLE RAGOUT

Ragoût à l'ail nouveau et aux primeurs

SERVES 4

This incredibly sweet ragout can be made only in the spring, late May to the end of June, when newly harvested green garlic is in season and the carrots and peas are marvelously sweet and tender. The fresh herbs are very important. Make sure that at least one of them is sweet, either tarragon or basil. I especially like the way tarragon marries with the sweet flavor of the carrots and garlic. Serve this delicious ragout as a main dish with pasta or as a side dish with fish or chicken.

1	tablespoon olive oil
2	heads of green garlic, cloves separated and peeled
¼	pound (115 g) baby carrots, peeled, quartered, and cut into 1-inch (2.5 cm) lengths
½	teaspoon sugar
2	pounds (900 g) borlotti (cranberry) beans, shelled (2 heaped cups)
2½	cups (625 ml) garlic or chicken stock (page 130 or 128) or enough to cover the vegetables
	a bouquet garni made with a bay leaf, a few fresh thyme sprigs, and a few parsley sprigs
	salt to taste
1½	pounds (675 g) fresh peas, shelled (1½ cups)
2	teaspoons slivered fresh sage
2 to 3	tablespoons snipped fresh herbs such as chives, tarragon, parsley, basil, to taste
	freshly ground pepper to taste

Heat the oil over medium heat in a lidded large heavy-bottomed casserole or saucepan. Add the garlic and carrots and cook, stirring or shaking the pan, for about 5 minutes, until the garlic begins to color slightly. Add the sugar and continue to cook, stirring, for another 2 to 3 minutes, until the sugar is dissolved. Add the borlotti beans, stock, bouquet garni, and salt. Bring to a simmer, reduce the heat, cover, and simmer for 30 minutes. Stir from time to time and add a bit of stock if the vegetables begin to dry out.

Add the peas and sage. Stir together, cover, and simmer for another 10 minutes. Stir in the herbs and pepper. Taste, adjust the seasonings, and serve.

To serve with pasta: I think wheels or penne, the shapes that peas are likely to get lodged in, work well with this. Cook 10 to 12 ounces (285 to 340 g) pasta, drain, and toss with the ragout.

ADVANCE PREPARATION: The ragout can be made, up to the adding of the herbs, hours before serving and reheated.

PER PORTION

Calories	325	Protein	18 G
Fat	5 G	Carbohydrate	55 G
Sodium	314 MG	Cholesterol	0

WHEATBERRY PILAF WITH WILD MUSHROOMS

Epeautre aux champignons sauvages

SERVES 6 GENEROUSLY AS A MAIN DISH,
8 AS A SIDE DISH OR STARTER

Epeautre, the Provençal wheatberry, lends itself to deeply aromatic risottolike pilafs. (Wheatberries are whole-wheat grains, available at natural foods stores.) This one is a perfect fall or winter dish. If you can't get fresh wild mushrooms, use a mixture of dried porcini (cèpes) and cultivated mushrooms. Eat this as a side dish with fish or poultry or as the main attraction. Obviously the soy sauce in this recipe is not Provençal but my own whim.

1	ounce (30 g/approximately 1 cup) dried cèpes (porcini)
2	cups (500 ml) boiling water
3½	cups (875 ml) chicken, garlic, or vegetable stock (pages 127–30)
1½	tablespoons olive oil
2	shallots or 1 small onion, minced
1	pound (450 g) fresh wild mushrooms such as chanterelles, cèpes, oyster mushrooms, horn of plenty mushrooms, girolles, or a combination
3 to 4	garlic cloves, to taste, minced or put through a press
	salt to taste
2	teaspoons tamari or Kikkoman soy sauce
1 to 2	teaspoons fresh thyme leaves or ½ to 1 teaspoon dried to taste
1	teaspoon chopped fresh rosemary or ½ teaspoon crushed dried
	freshly ground pepper to taste
2	cups (15 oz/420 g) wheatberries or *épeautre*
½	cup (125 ml) dry, fruity red wine, such as a gamay, Beaujolais, or Côtes du Rhône

VEGETABLES, GRAINS, AND BEANS

Place the dried mushrooms in a bowl or a heatproof glass measuring cup and pour on the boiling water. Let sit for 30 minutes. Strain into a bowl through a cheese-cloth- or paper towel–lined strainer and squeeze the mushrooms over the strainer. Add the liquid to the stock. Rinse the mushrooms in several changes of water, squeeze dry, and chop coarsely if very large. Set aside both the mushrooms and the liquid.

Heat the oil in a large heavy-bottomed skillet over medium-low heat. Add the shallots and sauté until tender and beginning to color, about 4 to 5 minutes. Add the fresh and dried mushrooms, garlic, and a little salt and sauté, stirring, until the mushrooms begin to release liquid, about 3 to 5 minutes. Add the soy sauce, herbs, and pepper and cook, stirring, for 5 to 8 minutes, until the mushrooms are cooked through and fragrant.

Add the wheatberries and cook, stirring, for a few minutes, until the wheat-berries are separate and coated with oil and the liquid from the mushrooms. Stir in the wine and cook over medium heat, stirring constantly. The wine should bubble, but not too quickly. You want some of the flavor to cook into the wheatberries before it evaporates.

When the wine has just about evaporated, stir in the stock. When the stock comes back to a boil, cover the pan, reduce the heat, and simmer for 1 hour or more, until the wheatberries are tender (they will maintain a chewy texture) and most of the stock is absorbed. If a small amount of stock remains in the pan, spoon it over the pilaf when you serve it. If you wish, you can uncover the pan and boil off whatever stock remains. Taste and adjust the seasonings. Transfer the pilaf to a warm serving dish and serve.

ADVANCE PREPARATION: Wheatberries do not get soggy as rice does, so you can make this a few hours before serving and reheat in the pan.

PER PORTION

Calories	343	Protein	13 G
Fat	7 G	Carbohydrate	62 G
Sodium	128 MG	Cholesterol	0

ASPARAGUS AND FRESH PEA RISOTTO
Risotto aux asperges et aux petits-pois du pays

SERVES 4 TO 6

The appearance of asparagus and peas *du pays* in the markets tell me that spring has arrived in Provence. The vegetables inspire dishes like this gorgeous risotto, which I make with rice from the Camargue when I'm in Provence and Italian Arborio rice when I'm not.

6 to 7	cups (1.5 to 1.75 l) vegetable, chicken, or garlic stock (pages 127–30) as needed
4	teaspoons olive oil
1	small onion or shallot, minced
2 to 3	large garlic cloves, to taste, minced or put through a press
	salt to taste
1½	cups (10½ oz/300 g) Italian Arborio rice
½	cup (125 ml) dry white wine
	pinch of saffron threads
1	pound (450 g) green asparagus, trimmed and cut into 1-inch (2.5 cm) pieces
1	pound (450 g) fresh peas, shelled (1 cup)
1	large egg, beaten
1	ounce (30 g) Parmesan cheese, grated (¼ cup)
¼	cup (about 30 g/½ large bunch) chopped fresh parsley
	freshly ground pepper to taste

Have the stock simmering in a saucepan.

Heat 1 tablespoon of the oil in a large heavy-bottomed nonstick skillet over medium heat. Add the onion and sauté until tender and beginning to color, about 5 minutes. Add the garlic and a little salt and cook for another 30 seconds, until the garlic begins to color. Add the remaining teaspoon of oil and the rice and continue to cook, stirring, until all the grains are separate, about 2 to 3 minutes.

Stir in the wine and cook over medium heat, stirring constantly. The wine should bubble, but not too quickly. You want some of the flavor to cook into the rice before it evaporates. When the wine has just about evaporated, stir in a ladleful or two of the simmering stock, enough to just cover the rice, and the saffron. The stock should bubble slowly. Cook, stirring constantly, until it is just about absorbed. Add another ladleful of the stock and continue to cook in this fashion, not too fast but not too slowly, adding more stock when the rice is almost dry, for 10 minutes.

Add the asparagus and the peas and continue adding stock and stirring the rice as you have been doing for another 15 to 20 minutes, until the rice is cooked al dente, and the vegetables are tender.

Beat together the egg and the Parmesan. Add another ladleful of stock and the parsley to the rice so that the rice is not completely dry; remove from the heat. Stir a ladleful of stock into the egg and cheese mixture and immediately stir this into the rice. Combine well, taste, and adjust the seasonings, adding salt and pepper to taste. The mixture should be creamy. Return to the heat and stir for a few seconds, then serve at once.

ADVANCE PREPARATION: All of the ingredients can be prepared hours or even a day in advance, but the risotto has to be served as soon as it's ready. However, you can begin the risotto an hour or so before dinner and remove from the heat before adding the asparagus and peas; then reheat and finish the dish shortly before serving.

PER PORTION

Calories	294	Protein	9 G
Fat	6 G	Carbohydrate	51 G
Sodium	99 MG	Cholesterol	39 MG

TRUC

SOAK BEANS IN BOTTLED WATER IF YOUR TAP WATER IS HARD

One of the most consistent lines running through all of the Provençal gastronomic literature I have read is "Don't soak or cook your beans [chick-peas, lentils, haricots] in well water." This is country, and here the water is hard. If your water is hard, soak your dried beans in bottled water. If it is extremely hard, cook them in bottled water too. They will soften much more quickly and be more digestible.

BEANS FOR GOOD LUCK

France has southern traditions too. Just as American southerners eat black-eyed peas on New Year's Day for good luck, the Provençaux eat chick-peas or lentils to guarantee a prosperous year.

TOMATO AND BEAN RAGOUT
Ragoût de haricots à la provençale

SERVES 4 AS A MAIN DISH, 6 AS A SIDE DISH

You can make this hearty dish anytime with dried beans and fresh or canned tomatoes. In summer, when fresh borlotti beans come in, there is nothing like them. I'll give you versions for both here. This ragout can also be transformed into a marvelous gratin.

1	pound (450 g/2 heaped cups) dried navy, Great Northern, or small white beans, washed, picked over, and soaked for 6 hours or overnight, or 3 pounds (1.35 kg) fresh borlotti (cranberry) beans, shelled (4 heaped cups)
2	quarts (2 l) water
2	onions, 1 peeled and stuck with a clove, the other chopped
6	large garlic cloves, minced or put through a press
1	bay leaf
	salt to taste
1	tablespoon olive oil
2	pounds (900 g/8 medium-size) fresh or canned tomatoes, peeled, seeded, and chopped
	pinch of sugar if needed
2	teaspoons fresh thyme leaves or 1 teaspoon dried
	freshly ground pepper to taste
3	tablespoons slivered fresh basil or more to taste, or 2 tablespoons low-fat pistou (page 109)
	thick garlic croutons (page 83) for serving
1 to 1½	ounces (30 to 45 g) Parmesan or Gruyère cheese, grated (4 to 6 tablespoons) (optional)

For dried beans: Drain the beans and combine them with the water, the whole onion, 2 of the garlic cloves, and the bay leaf in a large soup pot or Dutch oven. Bring to a boil, skim off any foam that rises, reduce the heat, and simmer for 45 minutes. Add 2 teaspoons salt or more to taste and continue to simmer for 45 to 60 minutes, until the beans are tender but not mushy. Remove from the heat and drain over a bowl. Taste the liquid and add salt if necessary.

For fresh beans: Combine the water, onion, 2 garlic cloves, and the bay leaf and bring to a boil. Add salt and the beans. Turn the heat to medium and cook for 30 to 45 minutes, until the beans are tender and the broth fragrant. Remove from the heat and drain over a bowl.

Heat the oil in a large heavy-bottomed flameproof casserole over medium-low heat and add the chopped onion. Cook, stirring, until the onion is tender, 5 to 8 minutes. Add half the remaining garlic and cook, stirring, for about 30 seconds, until the garlic begins to color. Add the tomatoes, the remaining garlic, a generous pinch of salt, and the sugar if the tomatoes are not sweet and fresh. Turn the heat up to medium and cook, stirring often, for 10 minutes, until the tomatoes have cooked down a bit and smell fragrant.

Stir in the beans, 2 cups (500 ml) of their cooking liquid, and the thyme. Bring to a simmer, taste and adjust the salt, add pepper, reduce the heat to low, cover, and simmer for 15 to 30 minutes, until the ragout is thick and fragrant. Stir often to prevent the ragout from sticking to the bottom of the pan (it helps to put the pot on a Flame Tamer). Stir in the basil or pistou, continue to simmer for a couple of minutes, and serve over thick garlic croutons, sprinkling the cheese over each serving if desired.

ADVANCE PREPARATION: This gets even better overnight and will keep for 4 days in the refrigerator. It will thicken in the refrigerator, so you might want to thin it out with a small amount of water or bean stock when you reheat it. It can also be frozen.

Leftovers: Make the stew into a gratin. Spoon it into a lightly oiled 1½- to 2-quart (1.5 to 2 l) baking or gratin dish, sprinkle with 2 tablespoons bread crumbs and 2 to 4 tablespoons grated Parmesan or Gruyère cheese, drizzle on a tablespoon of olive oil, and bake in a 425°F (220°C) oven for 20 minutes or until the top begins to brown.

PER PORTION

Calories	428	Protein	22 G
Fat	5 G	Carbohydrate	77 G
Sodium	235 MG	Cholesterol	0

VEGETABLES, GRAINS, AND BEANS

PANISSE GRATIN
Gratin de panisses

SERVES 6

Panisses are standard fare in Nice, sold in pasta shops everywhere, then cut into sticks and fried at home, or cut in half, sprinkled with cheese, and broiled. The mixture of water, chick-pea flour, salt, and olive oil is cooked as is cornmeal polenta, on top of the stove, stirring constantly with a wooden spoon until the *bouillie* is thick and smooth and you have a blister on the inside of your thumb. Then it is spread on oiled saucers until it cools. Mireille Johnston, in her marvelous book *The Cuisine of the Sun,* says families save their chipped saucers to make *panisses.* At this point the fragrant, now solid mixture is cooked, using one of the techniques just mentioned above—unless I am the cook. I cool the mixture on two dinner plates (it's fun to use the saucers, which give them the traditional shape; but that does leave you with lots of dishes to wash), then I cut them into 2-inch disks, sprinkle them with Parmesan, and brown them in a gratin dish. Serve this delicious gratin as a side dish with fish or chicken or as part of a vegetarian meal.

1	quart (1 l) water
½	pound (1¾ cups/225 g) chick-pea flour, sifted
5	teaspoons olive oil
¾	teaspoon salt
	freshly ground pepper to taste
1	ounce (30 g) Parmesan cheese, grated (¼ cup)

Brush 2 dinner plates, or 6 saucers for traditional *panisses,* with about a teaspoon of olive oil.

Combine the water, chick-pea flour, 2 teaspoons of the olive oil, and the salt in a bowl and transfer, in 2 batches, to a food processor fitted with the steel blade (you can do this in one batch if you have a large food processor bowl). Process for about 1 minute, until the mixture is smooth, and transfer to a large heavy-bottomed saucepan.

Stir constantly with a long-handled wooden spoon over medium heat for about 15 minutes. During this time the mixture will thicken and suddenly begin to lump, then it will smooth out. The mixture is ready to spread on the plates and cool when it has the consistency of very smooth pureed potatoes. It won't come away from the sides of the pot as polenta does, or it shouldn't, because if you cook it that long it will be difficult to spread the mixture neatly onto the plates.

Remove the pan from the heat and, if you perceive any lumps, stir vigorously with a whisk. Spoon onto the plates in an even layer and allow to cool. This should take about 20 minutes.

Preheat the oven to 425°F (220°C). Lightly oil a 3-quart (3 l) gratin dish. Using a 2-inch (5 cm) round cookie cutter, cut the cooled *panisse* dough into disks. Where the dough is thick—in the middle of the plates—cut the disks in half crosswise so that they are only about ⅓ inch (1 cm) thick. Place them in the gratin dish, slightly overlapping. Sprinkle the pieces of dough from between the disks here and there, top with lots of pepper and the cheese, and drizzle on 2 teaspoons of olive oil.

Bake for 20 to 25 minutes, until the cheese melts and the *panisses* begin to sizzle and brown slightly. Serve hot.

VARIATIONS: The delicious gratin can also be topped with a tomato sauce—either of those on pages 112 and 118—and baked as directed. You can also combine cooked vegetables, such as wild mushrooms or broccoli, with the chickpea disks in the gratin.

ADVANCE PREPARATION: The panisse dough, cut or in one piece, will keep for a few days in the refrigerator.

PER PORTION

Calories	196	Protein	9 G
Fat	8 G	Carbohydrate	23 G
Sodium	359 MG	Cholesterol	3 MG

CHAPTER 10

POULTRY AND RABBIT

For a population that has subsisted on an essentially vegetarian diet for centuries, the people of Provence have come up with a surprising number of delicious ways to prepare chicken and rabbit. And for a cook who began her career as a vegetarian, I am incredibly enthusiastic about these dishes. They may be higher on the food chain, but their fat content is low, and that's what concerns me.

Most of the recipes here are stews. The chicken or rabbit is simmered in stock or wine or both, along with those other wonderful Mediterranean ingredients, such as garlic, onion, herbs, tomatoes, and olives. These are heady meals. And because they're no-fuss, simmered affairs, they make good dishes for large or small dinner parties. Much can be done in advance, and most of these dishes can be reheated.

The Provençal people are frugal, as all country people must be, and when meat of any kind is served, every shred that isn't eaten is recycled. Daube, a long-simmering beef stew, is ground up and mixed with chard and herbs for Niçois ravioli and stuffed vegetables and is used in sauces. I don't have a recipe for beef daube in this collection, but I've often used the leftover rabbit and chicken from these dishes for stuffed vegetables (page 394) and ravioli.

Now a word about rabbit. I know that many of my readers won't have anything to do with it, and I don't aim to try to change your feelings. But some of you who don't have an aversion to eating this animal may never have been exposed to it, since rabbit has such a small market in the United States. I never really felt one way or another about rabbit and can't even remember the first time I ate it. I know it was in France, where rabbit is widely enjoyed. What I love about this meat is its depth of flavor and its leanness. There doesn't seem to be any fat, yet the flavor is much richer than that of chicken. Rabbit is raised for eating in France, and when you buy it there is some visible fat that is easy to remove. Then it's a pleasure to cook, because there's hardly any grease. Because rabbit is so lean, I always cook it in a liquid medium—stock, wine, or tomato sauce—until it's practically falling off the bone (this takes about 40 to 45 minutes). The simmering stew makes the kitchen smell marvelous.

STEWED CHICKEN WITH PASTIS
Poulet au pastis

SERVES 4 TO 6

This is one of the most wonderful-tasting chicken dishes I've ever eaten. The chicken pieces are marinated in and cooked with a small amount of anise-flavored liqueur, be it pastis, anisette, or Pernod (or even Greek ouzo, for that matter). There's just enough to perfume the dish, which also contains lots of garlic, saffron, tomatoes, and onions, without overpowering it. Serve the chicken in wide bowls with some of the broth and don't be shy about eating the pieces with your hands. It makes a wonderful, gutsy meal with a crisp green salad and fruity dessert.

1	3-pound (1.35 kg) chicken, cut into pieces and skin removed
2	tablespoons olive oil
½	cup (125 ml) pastis, anisette, or Pernod
½	teaspoon plus a pinch of saffron threads
	salt and freshly ground pepper to taste
2	medium-size onions, sliced
1½	pounds (675 g/6 medium-size) tomatoes, peeled, seeded, and chopped
6	large garlic cloves, minced or put through a press
1	dried fennel branch or ½ teaspoon crushed fennel seeds
1	large bunch of flat-leaf parsley, chopped (about ½ cup/30 g)
2	cups (500 ml) boiling water or chicken stock (page 128)
1	pound (450 g/4 medium-size) waxy potatoes, sliced
4	thick garlic croutons (page 83)
1	recipe spicy garlic puree (page 103)

Combine the chicken, 1 tablespoon of the olive oil, the pastis, ½ teaspoon saffron, and salt and pepper in a bowl, toss together, cover, and refrigerate overnight or for several hours, stirring every once in a while.

Heat the remaining olive oil in a large heavy-bottomed flameproof casserole over medium-low heat and add the onions. Cook, stirring, until tender, about 5 minutes. Add the tomatoes, garlic, and salt and pepper. Cook, stirring often, for 15 minutes, until the mixture is cooked down and fragrant. Add the chicken and its marinade, the fennel branch, and half the parsley. Stir together and add the boiling water or stock. Cover and cook over medium heat for 10 minutes. Add the sliced potatoes, turn down the heat, and simmer for 20 minutes, or until the chicken and potatoes are cooked through.

Raise the heat and bring the bouillon to a boil. Add the remaining pinch of saffron and the remaining parsley. Taste and add salt, pepper, or garlic if desired. Boil for 5 minutes and remove from the heat.

Serve over croutons in wide soup bowls and pass the spicy garlic puree in a bowl.

ADVANCE PREPARATION: The dish can be cooked until the chicken and potatoes are cooked through several hours before serving and held on the top of the stove. The spicy garlic puree can be made a day ahead.

PER PORTION

Calories	434	Protein	31 G
Fat	10 G	Carbohydrate	56 G
Sodium	406 MG	Cholesterol	76 MG

CHICKEN IN ONION, WINE, AND CAPER SAUCE
Poulet en capilotade

SERVES 4 TO 6

Capilotade, a lusty Provençal sauce containing lots of capers and onions, is wonderful with chicken. In this easy dish the sauce is made with white wine and chicken stock as opposed to the red wine and fish stock in the salt cod version on page 202. The dish makes a nice family dinner served with rice, wheatberries, pasta, or potatoes.

1	3-pound (1.35 kg) chicken, cut into pieces and skin removed
2	quarts (2 l) water or enough to cover the chicken
	a bouquet garni made with a bay leaf, a few fresh thyme sprigs, and a few parsley sprigs
4	black peppercorns
3	medium-size onions, one quartered, the rest chopped
2	medium-size carrots, peeled and coarsely chopped
6	garlic cloves, 4 peeled, 2 minced or put through a press
	salt to taste
1	tablespoon tomato paste
½	cup (125 ml) dry white wine
2	tablespoons olive oil
1	tablespoon red wine vinegar
1	tablespoon unbleached white flour
¼	cup (60 ml) drained capers, rinsed
1	teaspoon fresh thyme leaves or ½ teaspoon dried
½	teaspoon chopped fresh rosemary or ¼ teaspoon crushed dried
	freshly ground pepper to taste
3	tablespoons chopped parsley

Combine the chicken, water, bouquet garni, peppercorns, quartered onion, carrots, whole garlic cloves, and salt in a large soup pot or Dutch oven. Bring to a simmer and skim off any foam that rises. Reduce the heat, cover partially, and simmer until the chicken is cooked through—25 minutes for the white meat and 35 to 45 minutes for the dark meat. Remove the chicken and place in a bowl or serving dish. Strain the stock and reserve 1½ cups (375 ml) for the sauce and the rest for another use.

Stir together the tomato paste, wine, and chicken stock in a bowl. Set aside. Heat the oil in a large heavy-bottomed skillet over medium-low heat and add the chopped onions. Cook, stirring, until they soften, about 5 minutes. Add the minced garlic and continue to cook, stirring, until the garlic begins to color, about 30 to 60 seconds. Stir in the vinegar and flour and stir together for about 1 minute, until the mixture is just beginning to brown.

Add the wine mixture to the onions along with the capers, thyme, rosemary, salt, and pepper. Cook, uncovered, for 5 to 10 minutes, stirring often, until the sauce thickens slightly.

Stir the chicken back into the mixture, heat through, sprinkle with parsley, and serve.

ADVANCE PREPARATION: This can be made hours ahead of serving and can also be held overnight in the refrigerator. Reheat in a 350°F (180°C) oven for 10 to 15 minutes or stir over medium-low heat in a flameproof casserole to reheat.

PER PORTION

Calories	240	Protein	25 G
Fat	8 G	Carbohydrate	13 G
Sodium	266 MG	Cholesterol	76 MG

CHICKEN WITH TOMATOES, GARLIC, AND OLIVES
Poulet à l'ail et aux olives

SERVES 6

This heady, fragrant chicken dish is quick to make and great for dinner parties. It's another one of my brothy, rather than saucy, dishes, and everybody loves it.

2 tablespoons olive oil

1 3-pound (1.35 kg) chicken, cut into pieces and skin removed

1 medium-size or large onion, thinly sliced

10 garlic cloves, peeled and crushed

1 pound (450 g/4 medium-size) tomatoes, peeled, seeded, and chopped

2 teaspoons fresh thyme or 1 teaspoon dried
   salt and freshly ground pepper to taste

3 cups (750 ml) defatted chicken stock (page 128)

1 tablespoon tomato paste

1 bay leaf

¼ teaspoon saffron threads

¼ cup (1 ounce/30 g) imported black olives, preferably Niçoise, pitted

3 tablespoons chopped parsley

1 cup (7 oz/210 g) rice or ½ pound (225 g) fettuccine or wide noodles, cooked, for serving

Heat 1 tablespoon of the oil in a large nonstick skillet over medium-high heat and brown the chicken pieces in batches. Drain on paper towels.

Heat the remaining oil in a large heavy-bottomed casserole over medium-low heat and add the onion. Sauté, stirring, until the onion is tender, about 5 minutes. Add the garlic and sauté, stirring, for another few minutes, until the garlic begins to color. Add the tomatoes, thyme, salt, and pepper. Bring to a simmer and simmer for 10 minutes, stirring often. Add the chicken, stock, tomato paste, and bay leaf and bring to a simmer. Simmer for 20 minutes. Stir in the saffron and olives and simmer for another 10 minutes or until the chicken is cooked through. Taste and adjust seasonings. Stir in the parsley.

Remove from the heat and serve over rice or pasta in wide soup bowls. Place a piece of chicken over the rice or pasta and ladle in some broth with olives.

ADVANCE PREPARATION: This can be made several hours ahead of time and reheated.

PER PORTION

Calories	352	Protein	27 G
Fat	10 G	Carbohydrate	38 G
Sodium	159 MG	Cholesterol	76 MG

CHICKEN WITH 50 CLOVES OF GARLIC
Poulet à l'ail

SERVES 4

You've heard of chicken with 40 cloves of garlic. How about 50? In most of the recipes I've seen and used, and the one I included in *Mediterranean Light* (Bantam, 1989), the chicken is cut up and sautéed with the garlic, then cooked slowly on top of the stove. Not here. In this recipe, based on the one in Andrée Maureau's *Recettes en Provence* (Edisud, 1991), the chicken is filled and surrounded with unpeeled garlic cloves and baked in a covered dish. The bird comes out succulent, falling off the bone, and aromatic with the garlic, which is served on the side, to be squeezed onto croutons and onto pieces of chicken. An added advantage, for our purposes, to cooking the chicken this way is that it's very easy to remove the skin before serving the chicken.

1   **3-pound (1.35 kg) roasting chicken**

1   **tablespoon olive oil**
    salt and freshly ground pepper to taste

3   **heads of garlic, 40 to 50 cloves, cloves separated and crushed**
    a few fresh thyme and/or rosemary sprigs

2   **slices of baguette or country bread, plus additional bread as desired for serving**

1   **cup (250 ml) chicken stock (page 128)**

Preheat the oven to 350°F (180°C). Brush a lidded casserole large enough to accommodate the chicken with olive oil. Salt and pepper the chicken inside and out and rub with olive oil.

Fill the chicken with garlic cloves and the herb sprigs. Rub the slices of bread with garlic. Stuff the openings of the chicken cavity with the bread. Place the chicken in the casserole and surround with the remaining garlic. Add the stock to the baking dish and cover tightly.

Bake for 1 hour. Meanwhile, toast the remaining slices of bread and rub them with a cut clove of garlic.

The chicken is done when the juice runs clear when the chicken is pierced with a knife. For the best effect, take the covered casserole to the table and only then remove the lid. The aromas will intoxicate your guests. Remove and discard the skin, which will be loose around the chicken, carve, and serve with the garlic cloves, which should be squeezed from their skins onto the croutons and/or pieces of chicken.

ADVANCE PREPARATION: The chicken and garlic can be prepared for baking hours ahead.

PER PORTION

Calories	284	Protein	37 G
Fat	9 G	Carbohydrate	13 G
Sodium	133 MG	Cholesterol	114 MG

CHICKEN WITH SAFFRON RICE
La risoto
Le rizotto

SERVES 6

When I came across this recipe in a book of old Provençal recipes, I thought it must be for a risotto made with rice from the Camargue, which resembles Arborio rice. The traditional dish turns out to be a simple simmered chicken dish in which the chicken is served over fragrant saffron-hued rice. But I take liberties and cook the dish as a risotto, because I love the way rice tastes when it's cooked slowly in the saffrony chicken stock. If you cook the chicken a few hours before making the rice, you will be able to cool the stock, and it will be easier to skim off the fat.

1	3-pound (1.35 kg) chicken, cut into pieces and skin removed
2½	quarts (2.5 l) water
1½	cups (375 ml) dry white wine
2	medium-size onions, 1 quartered, the other chopped
6	garlic cloves, 3 peeled, the rest minced or put through a press
2	large carrots, sliced
2	pounds (900 g/8 medium-size) fresh or canned tomatoes, half seeded and quartered, half peeled, seeded, and chopped
	a bouquet garni made with a bay leaf, a few fresh thyme sprigs, and a few parsley sprigs
4	black peppercorns
	salt and freshly ground pepper to taste
1	tablespoon olive oil
1	medium-size green bell pepper, sliced
1	teaspoon fresh thyme or ½ teaspoon dried
1½	cups (10½ ounces/300 g) Arborio or Camargue rice

1 teaspoon saffron threads or ½ teaspoon powdered saffron

¼ cup (about 15 g/½ large bunch) chopped parsley

Combine the chicken, water, 1 cup (250 ml) of the white wine, the quartered onion, the whole garlic cloves, the carrots, the quartered tomatoes, the bouquet garni, peppercorns, and salt in a large heavy-bottomed soup pot or Dutch oven. Bring to a simmer. Skim off any foam that rises, cover, and simmer for 20 to 25 minutes, until the white meat is cooked through. Remove the white meat (breast and wing) pieces and transfer to a bowl. Continue to simmer the rest for another 20 minutes, until the dark meat is cooked through. Transfer the dark meat to the bowl and strain the broth through a cheesecloth-lined strainer. Skim off any visible fat. Moisten the chicken with a ladleful of broth while you cook the rice. Return the remaining broth to the stove and bring to a simmer.

Heat the oil in a large heavy-bottomed nonstick skillet over medium heat and add the chopped onion. Cook, stirring, for 5 minutes, until the onion has softened and is beginning to color. Add the minced garlic and green pepper, cook for about a minute, until the garlic begins to color, and add the thyme, chopped tomatoes, salt, and pepper. Turn the heat to medium-low and simmer for 5 to 10 minutes, stirring often, until the tomatoes have cooked down a bit.

Add the rice and stir together for a couple of minutes, until the grains are separate, then add the remaining ½ cup of wine. Cook, stirring, over medium heat, until the wine has evaporated, and add a ladleful of chicken stock and the saffron. Cook, stirring, until the stock is just about absorbed; then add another ladleful. Continue to cook in this way, adding more stock when the previous ladleful has just about been absorbed, until the rice is cooked through but still firm to the bite. Stir in another ladleful of stock, the chicken pieces, and the parsley. Taste and adjust the salt and pepper. Heat through and serve.

ADVANCE PREPARATION: The chicken can be cooked and the stock strained up to a day ahead of time. Refrigerate the stock and skim off any fat from the top before reheating. If you are making this for company and want to get a head start, cook the rice, following the recipe, for about 10 to 15 minutes. It should still be hard in the middle, and the last ladleful of stock should be absorbed. Turn off the heat. You can come back to it an hour or so later and proceed with the recipe without harming the texture of the rice.

PER PORTION

Calories	405	Protein	29 G
Fat	7 G	Carbohydrate	57 G
Sodium	115 MG	Cholesterol	76 MG

PAN-ROASTED QUAIL WITH QUINCES AND FIGS

Cailles aux figues et aux coings

SERVES 4

As September gives way to October, the colors of the Provençal markets change to the yellows, oranges, burgundies, and browns of fall. Figs stay around until November; quinces, pears, and apples abound. These fruits go wonderfully with game and poultry, as you will see when you taste this delicious, easy dish. I think couscous makes a perfect accompaniment to the quail.

4   quail, about ¼ pound (115 g) each

8   medium-size figs, cut into halves or quarters

2   medium-size quinces, peeled and diced

     water acidulated with the juice of ½ lemon

1   tablespoon canola or olive oil

     salt and freshly ground pepper to taste

2   shallots or 1 small onion, chopped

¼   cup (62 ml) cognac

1   garlic clove, crushed

1   cup (250 ml) dry red wine

2   teaspoons unbleached white flour

Stuff each quail with 1 to 1½ figs, whichever will fit. Prepare the quinces and keep them in a bowl of acidulated water while you brown the quail.

Heat the oil in a lidded saucepan big enough for all 4 quail over medium heat and add the quail. Brown on all sides, about 5 minutes, and drain on paper towels. Salt and pepper lightly.

Add the shallots to the pan and sauté, stirring, for about 3 minutes, until it begins to brown. Return the quail to the pan and add the cognac. Light with a match and flame.

When the flames die down, add the remaining figs, the drained chopped quinces, and the garlic. Whisk together the wine and flour and add to the pot. Turn the heat to medium-low, cover, and cook for 15 minutes, stirring occasionally, until the quail juices run clear when the quail is pierced with a knife. Transfer the quail to a warm platter or plates. Taste the sauce and adjust the seasonings. If you feel that it needs thickening, turn up the heat and reduce by about a fourth, then pour over the quail. Serve hot, with couscous, rice, or other grains.

ADVANCE PREPARATION: The ingredients can be prepared hours ahead of time. It's best to serve this at once, but the dish will be acceptable after being reheated.

PER PORTION

Calories	376	Protein	21 G
Fat	16 G	Carbohydrate	29 G
Sodium	60 MG	Cholesterol	N/A

RABBIT DAUBE (RABBIT AND RED WINE STEW)

Civié de lapin

Civet (ou daube) de lapin

SERVES 4 TO 6

To my palate this light rabbit daube provides all the satisfaction of a long-cooking beef daube, but it requires only an hour's cooking, and it has very little fat. It's warming and satisfying, a great meal on a cold winter night.

- 1 bottle of dry, fruity red wine, such as a Côtes du Rhône
- 2 bay leaves
- 3 fresh thyme sprigs or ½ teaspoon dried
- 6 large garlic cloves, 4 crushed, 2 minced or put through a press
- 1 leek, white part only, well washed and coarsely chopped
- 1 celery rib, coarsely chopped
- 1 carrot, coarsely chopped
- 1 3-pound (1.35 kg) rabbit, cut into pieces and trimmed of fat
- 2 tablespoons olive oil
- 1 ounce (30 g/¼ cup) unbleached white flour
- 1 medium-size onion, chopped
  salt and freshly ground pepper to taste
- 2 wide strips of orange zest

The night before: Combine the wine, one of the bay leaves, the thyme, crushed garlic, leek, celery, and carrot in a bowl or casserole. Rinse the rabbit pieces, pat dry, and add to this mixture. Marinate overnight in the refrigerator.

The next day: Remove the pieces of rabbit from the marinade and pat dry. Heat 1 tablespoon of the olive oil in a large heavy-bottomed casserole over medium-high heat. Dredge the rabbit pieces in flour and brown on all sides, about

1 minute per side. You will probably need to do this in 2 batches. Heat 2 teaspoons of oil after the first batch. Drain on paper towels.

Add 2 tablespoons of water to the pan and scrape the pan to deglaze. Pour off and discard.

Add a teaspoon of olive oil and the onion to the casserole and sauté, stirring, for about 30 seconds to a minute, until it begins to soften and stick to the pan. Return the rabbit to the casserole and pour in the marinade with all the vegetables. Add the remaining garlic and bay leaf and 1 scant teaspoon salt. Bring to a simmer, cover, and cook over low heat for 30 minutes. Add the pepper and orange zest, cover, and simmer for another 30 minutes or until the meat is tender and comes away from the bone easily. Stir from time to time to make sure pieces of rabbit don't stick to the pan. Taste and adjust the seasonings, adding salt and pepper to taste. Remove the bay leaves and serve hot with pasta, steamed potatoes, or rice.

Leftovers: Shred leftover meat and mix with any leftover sauce. Use as a topping for pasta or in a filling for ravioli or stuffed vegetables.

ADVANCE PREPARATION: This will hold for several hours, in or out of the refrigerator. Reheat gently before serving.

PER PORTION

Calories	338	Protein	36 G
Fat	14 G	Carbohydrate	14 G
Sodium	422 MG	Cholesterol	98 MG

POULTRY AND RABBIT

RABBIT STEWED IN ROSÉ WITH TOMATOES AND OLIVES

Lapin sauta eis oulivo

Lapin sauté aux olives

SERVES 6

I'm stretching it here by giving this dish the traditional Provençal name. In Provence they would sauté the rabbit with bacon and use lots of olive oil. I prefer stewing the rabbit slowly in tomato sauce and wine. In Provence the dish is usually made with green olives, but I love it with small Niçois olives or the meaty black olives from Nyons. This can be a summer or a winter dish, made with canned tomatoes in winter.

1	large rabbit, about 3 pounds (1.35 kg), cut into 6 to 8 pieces and trimmed of fat
1	bottle dry rosé wine, such as a Bandol or Côtes du Luberon
1	tablespoon unbleached white flour
2	tablespoons olive oil
1	medium-size or large onion, chopped
4 to 6	large garlic cloves, to taste, minced or put through a press
2	pounds (900 g/8 medium-size) tomatoes, peeled, seeded, and chopped
2	teaspoons fresh thyme leaves or 1 teaspoon dried
	salt and freshly ground pepper to taste
1	bay leaf
¼	cup (62 ml) imported black olives, preferably Niçois or Nyons, pitted (about 12 Nyons olives)
3	tablespoons chopped parsley or fresh basil
1	large egg yolk, beaten (optional)

Marinate the rabbit in the wine overnight or for several hours in the refrigerator. Remove the rabbit pieces from the wine and pat dry with paper towels. Strain the wine and discard the last ⅓ cup (85 ml) or so at the bottom of the bowl, which will be slightly cloudy. Mix the flour with ½ cup (125 ml) of the wine and set this aside along with the rest of the strained wine.

Heat 1 tablespoon of the oil in a large heavy-bottomed casserole or nonstick skillet over medium-high heat and brown the rabbit pieces in batches. Drain on paper towels. Deglaze the pan with a few tablespoons of water and discard this mixture.

Heat the remaining oil in a large heavy-bottomed casserole over medium-low heat and add the onion. Sauté, stirring, until the onion is tender, about 5 minutes. Add the garlic and sauté, stirring, for another minute, until the garlic begins to color. Add the tomatoes, thyme, salt, and pepper. Bring to a simmer and simmer for 10 minutes, stirring often, until the tomatoes have cooked down a bit. Add the rabbit, wine (including the wine mixed with flour), and bay leaf and bring to a simmer. Simmer for 45 minutes, until the rabbit is tender and falling off the bone.

Stir in the olives and simmer for another 5 minutes. Taste and adjust the seasonings. If you wish to thicken the sauce, stir a spoonful into the beaten egg yolk and then, off the heat, stir this back into the hot sauce. Stir in the parsley. Remove from the heat and serve on plates or in wide soup bowls, with rice, potatoes, or pasta.

Leftovers: Use leftovers for Niçois-style stuffed vegetables (page 394), as part of a ravioli filling, or toss with pasta.

ADVANCE PREPARATION: The dish can be made hours ahead and reheated.

PER PORTION

Calories	325	Protein	37 G
Fat	14 G	Carbohydrate	12 G
Sodium	140 MG	Cholesterol	98 MG

RABBIT COOKED IN PROVENÇAL
TOMATO SAUCE WITH SAGE

SERVES 4

Fresh sage and a hearty tomato sauce combine to give this rabbit dish a rich, savory earthiness.

1	small rabbit, about 2 pounds (900 g), cut into 8 pieces, or 4 large rabbit thighs
1	tablespoon olive oil
2	cups (500 ml) La Mère Besson's tomato sauce (page 114)
½	cup (125 ml) water
1	large garlic clove, minced or put through a press
2	tablespoons fresh sage leaves, slivered
	salt and freshly ground pepper to taste

Rinse the rabbit pieces and pat dry. Remove any visible fat.

Heat the olive oil in a lidded heavy-bottomed casserole over medium heat and brown the rabbit pieces on all sides. Add the tomato sauce, water, and garlic, stir, cover, and simmer over medium-low heat for 45 to 60 minutes, stirring occasionally until the rabbit is tender and falling from the bones. Stir in the sage, taste, and add salt and pepper if desired. Serve hot, with a steamed green vegetable and steamed potatoes.

Leftovers: Shred the rabbit and toss with pasta (page 290) or use in ravioli or vegetable stuffing.

ADVANCE PREPARATION: The tomato sauce can be made up to 5 days ahead and kept in the refrigerator.

PER PORTION

Calories	340	Protein	37 G
Fat	15 G	Carbohydrate	13 G
Sodium	344 MG	Cholesterol	98 MG

NIÇOIS-STYLE STUFFED
VEGETABLES
Farcis à la niçoise

SERVES 6

Stuffed vegetables are a Niçois staple. You see them in charcuteries and restaurants
all over the city. Typically they're stuffed with a pork mixture or a pork and veal
mixture. I developed my meat version with the leftovers of the preceding recipe.
The same filling could be used for ravioli. I have also used leftover Thanksgiving
turkey for this recipe, with terrific results. Like so many Provençal dishes, it's a great
vehicle for using up *restes*. Give yourself plenty of time for making this dish.

For the Stuffing:

2 to 2½	**cups (10 to 12½ oz/285 to 360 g) shredded cooked rabbit, chicken, turkey, or a combination**
	salt to taste
6	**cups (9.5 oz/about 270 g) Swiss chard leaves or spinach, stems removed**
1	**tablespoon olive oil**
1	**large onion, chopped**
2	**garlic cloves or more to taste, minced or put through a press**
½	**cup (125 ml) coarse fresh bread crumbs**
1	**cup (30 g) parsley leaves, chopped (½ cup)**
½	**cup (125 ml) cooked tomato sauce, such as one of the sauces on pages 112–18, or peeled and pureed fresh tomatoes**
1 to 2	**tablespoons chopped fresh rosemary or 1 to 2 teaspoons crushed dried to taste**
2	**teaspoons fresh thyme leaves or 1 teaspoon dried**
	freshly ground pepper
1	**large egg, beaten**

For the Vegetables:

12	small or 6 medium-size tomatoes
	salt to taste
6	small to medium-size zucchini, ends trimmed
6	small red bell peppers, or a mixture of red and green, ends cut off, membranes and seeds removed
3	small or medium-size white or purple onions, peeled, ends trimmed
	freshly ground pepper to taste
½	cup (125 ml) bread crumbs
2	ounces (60 g) Parmesan cheese, grated (½ cup)
1 to 2	tablespoons olive oil as needed

Make the stuffing: Finely chop the cooked rabbit and/or chicken in a food processor. Transfer to a bowl. Bring a large pot of water to a boil, add about a teaspoon of salt, and drop in the Swiss chard; cook for a minute or two. Transfer to a bowl of cold water, drain, and squeeze out all the excess water. Chop finely in a food processor—you should have about ¾ to 1 cup (185 to 250 ml)—and add to the chopped meat. Heat the oil in a heavy-bottomed nonstick skillet over medium-low heat and add the onion. Cook, stirring often, for about 5 minutes, until tender and beginning to soften. Add the garlic, cook for another minute, until it begins to color, and remove from the heat. Stir into the meat and chard mixture. Add the remaining stuffing ingredients and stir together well.

Bring a large pot of salted water to a boil. Meanwhile, cut the tops off the tomatoes, about ¾ inch (2 cm) down from the stem. Place a strainer over the bowl holding the stuffing and gently squeeze out the seeds and juice over the strainer. Using a small sharp knife, cut away the pulp from the inside of the tomatoes; chop it and add to the stuffing. Sprinkle the tomatoes with salt and turn them upside down on a rack or baking dish while you prepare the remaining vegetables.

When the water comes to a boil, add a teaspoon of salt and the zucchini, peppers, and onions. After 5 minutes, remove the peppers with a slotted spoon or deep-fry skimmer and rinse with cold water. Drain the zucchini and onions after 10 minutes and cool in a bowl of cold water.

Cut the zucchini in half lengthwise and, using a spoon or a small sharp knife, scoop or cut out the inside flesh, leaving a ¼-inch-thick (.75 cm) shell. You can chop the flesh and add it to the stuffing or set it aside for another use. Cut the onions in half crosswise and remove the inner layers (save for another use). Lightly salt and pepper all of the vegetables.

Preheat the oven to 425°F (220°C). Oil 1 or 2 gratin dishes, enough to accommodate all of the vegetables. Taste the stuffing and adjust seasonings if necessary. Fill the hollowed-out vegetables with the stuffing; don't fill them completely. Mix together the bread crumbs and Parmesan and sprinkle over the tops of the stuffed vegetables. Drizzle on a small amount of oil.

Bake for 30 to 40 minutes, until the topping is browned and the peppers have softened. Serve hot, warm, or cold.

ADVANCE PREPARATION: The stuffing can be made a day ahead of filling the vegetables. The vegetables can be stuffed and refrigerated a day ahead of baking and serving. You can serve this cold, so you can do the entire dish hours ahead of serving.

PER PORTION

Calories	367	Protein	27 G
Fat	14 G	Carbohydrate	38 G
Sodium	427 MG	Cholesterol	83 MG

POULTRY AND RABBIT

CHAPTER 11

DESSERTS

Dessert is fruit in Provence. There are some traditional sugary pastries and candies, *"les douceurs de Provence"*—the famous *calissons d'Aix,* made of sweet almond paste; fruit beignets; *nougat;* Niçois *ganses,* which are the closest thing to doughnuts I've ever had in France. But these are special sweets, not everyday desserts. Fruit is the perfect finish after an intensely flavored Provençal meal, and in Provence this can take many forms. It can be baked into luscious clafoutis, tarts, and dramatic soufflés, cooked down into comforting compotes and purees, poached in wine or syrup, or transformed into refreshing sorbets and granités. Just as often fruit is served as it is, *au nature;* one leans back after a meal and leisurely peels a peach, nibbles on an apricot, one sweet-tart half at a time, or slowly works one's way through a bunch of succulent cherries.

I have an indelible memory of eating a Provençal peach on my first trip to Europe. We were picnicking on a canal somewhere in southern France, having bought provisions in a nearby village. It was a huge peach, yellow, juicy, messy, sweet. That peach, and sleeping badly on the pebble beach at Nice, are the two things I remember about my first trip through Provence, when I was 15.

Cherries and Cavaillon melons dominate more recent memories, of the months of June and July spent at a rented house near Bonnieux. Late May and June are the height of the cherry season. Orchards line country roads, and the dark red cherries that weigh down the branches at this time of year tempt passersby. There were cherry trees all around the house, and that summer we put up so many jars of the fruit, in eau-de-vie and in vinegar and honey, that I still have some jars today, ten years later. And they're still good!

When the cherries are just about over, Cavaillon melons begin to reach a peak that is sustained throughout the summer. These sensuous, juicy melons are present at every meal during the summer. In the middle of my summer stay in Bonnieux I drove up to Paris to cater a big Fourth of July party given by the *International Herald Tribune.* Watermelon baskets filled with melon balls were on the menu, and as I made my way from Bonnieux to the autoroute I stopped at a roadside stand to buy my Cavaillon melons, just harvested and about a quarter of the price I knew I'd pay in Paris. I must have bought about 15 of them, and I can still remember vividly how their strong perfume took hold in the car.

After the cherries come the peaches, nectarines, and apricots, then the figs and the plums. Pears and apples of all kinds abound through the fall, winter, and spring. Quinces have been my big fruit discovery in Provence. They have a short season in the fall. Everybody seems to have quince trees in this region; all the small farms sell the tart, funny-looking, slightly furry pearlike fruit at the autumn markets. The fruit is cooked up into delicious compotes and made into a sweet, dense jelly called *pâte de coings.*

The first time you come to Provence, you may be struck by the amount of honey you see for sale in markets, shops, everywhere. Provence is the home of many proud, hardworking beekeepers, and the honey here is particularly good. At the markets the honey sellers always have a supply of small plastic spoons for tasting the different varieties lined up on their tables—*acacia* (acacia), *toutes fleurs* (mixed flowers), *lavande* (lavender), *thym* (thyme), *romarin* (rosemary), *tilleul* (linden), *châtaigne* (chestnut), *bruyère* (heather). Their colors range from pale and clear to dark brown. Some honeys are solid, some not. Lavender (my favorite), rosemary, and acacia are the mildest and the kind I use most often in cooking.

Honey sweetens many of my fruit desserts, and it goes into some of the crunchy biscottilike cookies I've included in this chapter. The cookies are nice to have on hand; they go well with sweet wine and marinated fruit, and I love to eat one or two with my afternoon tea. A glass of Muscat de Beaumes-de-Venise, that marvelous Rhône wine that tastes exactly like muscat grapes, accompanied by a lemony croquette (pages 437–38), makes a perfect dessert at any time of year.

MELON ICE WITH FRUIT
AND MINT GARNISH
Granité au melon

SERVES 8

The small round melons from Cavaillon, light green on the outside with bright orange fruit, are one of the great delicacies of Provence. They were so highly esteemed by the writer Alexandre Dumas *père* that in 1864 he made a deal with the municipal council of Cavaillon: in exchange for a set of his complete works for the library, he would receive an annuity of 12 Cavaillon melons for the rest of his life. Today Dumas's descendants still receive the annuity, and the first ripe melon of the year is sent to the president of France.

This granité is unbelievably simple, pure melon. Cantaloupe will do fine, but your melons must be juicy and ripe for the dessert to work. If they are at all bland, the granité will be even more bland. Make the granité at least 10 hours before serving. It will hold for weeks in the freezer.

For the Granité:

2   **large ripe cantaloupes, about 2½ pounds (1.25 kg) each**

2   **tablespoons lemon juice**

For the Garnish:

1   **large ripe cantaloupe or ½ cantaloupe and ½ honeydew**

½   **pint (4 oz/115 g) strawberries, trimmed and sliced**

3   **tablespoons slivered fresh mint leaves**

8   **fresh mint sprigs**

Make the granité. Remove the seeds and rind from the 2 cantaloupes and chop coarsely. Puree in a food processor or blender until smooth. Stir in the lemon juice. You should have about 4½ cups (1.12 l) puree or a little more. Freeze in a sorbetière according to the directions or transfer to a bowl or ice cube trays, cover, and place in the freezer.

When the mixture is just about frozen, after 2 to 3 hours, break it up once more in a food processor and freeze once more in the bowl or ice cube trays until just about frozen. Break up one more time and transfer to individual ½-cup (125 ml) ramekins. Cover each ramekin with plastic wrap and foil and freeze.

Make melon balls with the cantaloupe or cantaloupe and honeydew and toss with the strawberries and slivered mint. Refrigerate until ready to serve.

Thirty minutes before serving, transfer the granité to the refrigerator. To serve, unmold into dessert bowls and garnish with the fruit mixture. Decorate with a sprig of mint and serve at once. The granité will slowly melt into the fruit, which is the way it's supposed to be.

ADVANCE PREPARATION: The granité can be made at least a week before you serve it.

PER PORTION

Calories	81	Protein	2 G
Fat	.66 G	Carbohydrate	19 G
Sodium	20 MG	Cholesterol	0

MUSCAT DE BEAUMES-DE-VENISE WITH . . .

The Rhône Valley is famous for its sweet muscat wine, which tastes exactly like muscat grapes. This is one of the most distinctive grape flavors I know, and I have a weakness for both the grapes and the wine. Beaumes-de-Venise is one of the Côtes du Rhône-Villages. Muscat is not the only wine from that village, but it's probably the best-known one. With good reason. If you have Muscat de Beaumes-de-Venise on hand, you will always have dessert, for it *is* a dessert. I usually serve it with fruit or cookies (such as the hard biscottilike cookies on pages 437). Sometimes I toss the fruit with it, as in the case of the muscat grapes on page 403.

MUSCAT DE BEAUMES-DE-VENISE WITH MELON

SERVES 4 TO 6

1   large or 2 medium-size cantaloupes or a mixture of honeydew and cantaloupe

2   cups (500 ml) Muscat de Beaumes-de-Venise

Make melon balls and toss with the wine. Chill until ready to serve. You can also serve the fruit and wine separately (see note in the following recipe).

PER PORTION

Calories	156	Protein	.84 G
Fat	.26 G	Carbohydrate	17 G
Sodium	16 MG	Cholesterol	0

MUSCAT DE BEAUMES-DE-VENISE WITH MUSCAT GRAPES

SERVES 4 TO 6

2   pounds (900 g) green muscat grapes, washed, removed from the stems, and, if desired, cut in half and seeded

2   cups (500 ml) Muscat de Beaumes-de-Venise

Toss the grapes with the wine and chill until ready to serve.

Note: Here's another way to serve this dish: Cut the grape bunches into smaller clumps, but don't take the grapes off the stems. Serve the wine in small dessert wineglasses and the grapes on plates.

PER PORTION

Calories	226	Protein	.96 G
Fat	.84 G	Carbohydrate	35 G
Sodium	10 MG	Cholesterol	0

MUSCAT DE BEAUMES-DE-VENISE WITH COOKIES

Serve the chilled wine and pass a plate of Provençal almond cookies or honey almond cookies (page 436 or 437). Guests should dip the cookies in the wine.

LEMON SORBET
Sorbet au citron

SERVES 6

Lemons are such a cause célèbre along the Côte d'Azur that there's a lemon festival every winter in Menton on the Italian border. They seem always to be in season, or maybe it's just that I'm usually in this area at the same time of year, early spring, when the piles of lemons from the *pays* that I see in the markets inspire me to make dishes like this tart sorbet. It's an easy, refreshing dessert.

1   **cup (250 ml) water**
1   **cup (200 g) sugar**
2   **cups (500 ml) fresh lemon juice, from 8 to 12 lemons, depending on size**
    zest of 2 lemons
    fresh mint leaves for garnish (optional)

Combine the water and sugar in a saucepan and bring to a boil. Reduce the heat, stir to dissolve the sugar, and simmer gently for 10 minutes while you squeeze the lemons. Remove from the heat and allow to cool to lukewarm.

Stir the lemon juice and zest into the syrup and let sit for 1 hour.

Strain the mixture and freeze in an ice cream freezer or in a baking dish or bowl. When the mixture is frozen, allow it to soften for 15 minutes in the refrigerator, then break up the ice crystals in a food processor. The mixture will then be smooth and white. Freeze again and repeat this process or transfer directly to individual ramekins (if you repeat the process, transfer it to ramekins after breaking up the ice crystals a second time), cover with plastic wrap, and freeze at once.

Allow to soften for 10 to 15 minutes in the refrigerator before serving. Garnish each serving with mint leaves.

ADVANCE PREPARATION: Unlike most sorbets, this will lose its fresh flavor after a week or two in the freezer. But you can certainly make it a few days before serving.

PER PORTION

Calories	150	Protein	.32 G
Fat	0 G	Carbohydrate	41 G
Sodium	1 MG	Cholesterol	0

The thirteen desserts are the grand finale to the *gros souper,* the traditional Christmas Eve dinner. A *repas maigre,* no meat is served at this meal, but it is a feast nonetheless, where every dish is traditional, and each detail filled with symbolism. The table is set with three tablecloths and three candles to symbolize the Holy Trinity, and is not changed during the three days of Christmas (December 24, 25, and 26). When the family leaves for midnight Mass they do not clean the crumbs off the table, but leave them for the souls of their ancestors, who are believed to visit the house on Christmas Eve. The long corners of the tablecloth are knotted, to prevent bad spirits from using the tablecloth to get into the family.

The meal usually begins with a soup, perhaps *aigo boulido* (page 132), or in the Alpes, a clear soup with pasta (*creusets*). Fish follows, salt cod or grey mullet accompanied by snails and vegetables in an *aïoli monstre* (page 232). Cardoons are traditionally present, as well as artichokes, cauliflower, root vegetables such as parsnips and turnips, and greens—spinach or Swiss chard. After this there may or may not be a salad of winter greens—chicory, endive, frisée, and cheese. And then the famous thirteen desserts.

These desserts are innately Provençal—simple and unadorned, and for the most part, healthy. The number probably symbolizes Christ and his twelve apostles. As for what these thirteen desserts consist of, there is some variation throughout the region, and if you really stop to count, you might not come up with thirteen. *Pompe à l'huile,* the olive oil and orange flower-scented bread on page 84, is always served, as are dried fruit and nuts, and oranges or tangerines. We move swiftly toward thirteen here, because each dried fruit and nut is one dessert. Many are symbolic: almonds, hazelnuts, raisins, and figs are referred to as *Li pachichoi* in Provençal, *les 4 mendiants* (the four beggars) in French, because their respective colors evoke the robes of the mendicant orders—Carmelite, Augustine, Dominican, and Franciscan. Prunes, dates, and oranges or tangerines, quince jelly (*pâte de coings*) and other candied fruits from Apt are a big treat at the Christmas table.

Both white and black nougat, the Provençal candy made from almonds and honey, number among the thirteen desserts. A kind of winter melon may appear or not. You may see roasted chestnuts, other types of sweet fougasse, and rooster-shaped pastries called *cocoricos d'Auriol*. Other desserts—chocolates, fondants, candied chestnuts—have been finding their way onto the *gros souper* table, but their authenticity is disputable.

CHERRY CLAFOUTI
Clafouti aux cerises

SERVES 8

Cherry clafouti is actually a dish that originates in the Limousin, in central France. The word comes from a patois word from that region, *clafir,* which means to fill. But because cherries are a major crop in Provence, clafoutis have become part of the repertoire. The dish is like a cross between a flan and a cake, filled with unpitted cherries. The pits add flavor and aroma, and because they're there, you eat the dessert slowly, savoring each cherry. Cherries are the first spring fruit in Provence. Large, juicy, dark, and irresistible, they're ubiquitous.

I don't sprinkle powdered sugar over the top as traditionalists do; I prefer the fruit unembellished.

1½	**pounds (675 g) cherries, stems removed**
3	**tablespoons kirsch**
6	**tablespoons (75 g) sugar**
3	**large eggs**
1	**vanilla bean or ½ teaspoon vanilla extract**
⅔	**cup (100 g) sifted unbleached white flour**
¾	**cup (185 ml) plain nonfat yogurt**
	pinch of salt

Toss the cherries with the kirsch and 2 tablespoons of the sugar in a bowl. Let sit for 30 minutes. Meanwhile, preheat the oven to 400°F (200°C). Butter a 10½-inch (26 cm) ceramic tart pan or baking dish.

Drain the liquid from the cherries and beat together in the bowl of an electric mixer or with a whisk with the eggs, the seeds from the vanilla bean, and the remaining sugar. Slowly beat in the flour. Add the yogurt and salt. Mix together well.

Arrange the cherries in the baking dish. Pour in the batter. Bake for 25 minutes or until the top is browned and the clafouti is firm. Remove from the heat and cool on a rack. Serve warm or at room temperature.

ADVANCE PREPARATION: The dish will hold for several hours at room temperature. Leftovers are great for breakfast.

PER PORTION

Calories	178	Protein	5 G
Fat	3 G	Carbohydrate	33 G
Sodium	61 MG	Cholesterol	81 MG

TRUC

USING PHYLLO DOUGH FOR FRUIT TARTS

Using phyllo pastry, the paper-thin sheets of dough used in Greek pastry and sold in imported food shops, for low-fat dessert crusts is a really good idea. You need only 2 tablespoons of butter, and it's so easy! The crisp, flaky pastry is very tasty, and it makes fruit tarts a cinch. The only thing you have to be careful about is not making the tart too far ahead of serving, because the phyllo underneath the cooked fruit will become soggy if it sits for too long. However, you can crisp up the dough by reheating the tart in a 325°F oven for about 10 minutes. See individual recipes (pages 409, 415, and 422) for instructions.

APRICOT TART IN PHYLLO PASTRY
Tarte aux abricots

SERVES 8

This apricot tart is terrific; even dull-tasting apricots sweeten when they bake.

2	tablespoons unsalted butter
6	sheets of phyllo dough
1	large egg white, beaten
1½	pounds (675 g) apricots, cut in half, stones removed
1	tablespoon mild honey, such as clover, acacia, or lavender

Preheat the oven to 375°F (190°C). Melt the butter in a heavy-bottomed saucepan or a double boiler.

Brush the bottom of a 12-inch (30 cm) tart pan with a small amount of butter. Layer a sheet of phyllo dough in the pan so that it covers about two-thirds of the bottom of the pan and overlaps the sides of the pan. Brush it lightly with butter. Layer another sheet of phyllo dough over the first sheet so that it covers the part of the pan left uncovered by the first sheet. Layer the remaining 4 sheets in this way, turning the pan a little after each sheet and brushing the phyllo lightly with butter. Be sure to brush the part of the dough that goes up the sides of the pan. Now take the edges of the dough and roll them up, twisting gently, into an attractive lip. Press this into the edges of the pan, and brush the surface with butter. Brush the dough with the beaten egg white and bake for 5 minutes. Remove from the heat.

Arrange the apricots in the crust, cut side up. Heat the honey in the saucepan with the remains of the melted butter. Very lightly brush the apricots with the honey (you should use only half the honey for this, if that).

Bake the tart for 30 minutes or until the pastry is lightly browned. Remove from the heat and brush the edges of the crust with the remaining honey. Turn off the oven, return the tart to the oven, and allow to cool. The pastry will continue to crisp. Or serve hot.

ADVANCE PREPARATION: This will hold for a couple of hours but is best eaten soon after baking. The bottom will become slightly soggy, but the sides will remain crisp. You can reheat this in a low oven to recover some of the crispiness.

PER PORTION

Calories	116	Protein	3 G
Fat	4 G	Carbohydrate	19 G
Sodium	77 MG	Cholesterol	8 MG

FRESH APRICOT PUREE

MAKES 2 CUPS (500 ML)

In Provence the apricots are juicy and sweet, and that's what you'll need for this incredibly simple puree. The puree has all kinds of uses. My friend Lulu Peyraud in Bandol serves it plain or with yogurt or melon for dessert. I like to toss it with sliced peaches. I also keep it on hand when apricots are in season, to use as a luscious jam for toast.

2 to 2¼   pounds (900 g to 1 kg) fresh apricots

Bring a large pot of water to a boil. Drop in the apricots and boil for 20 seconds. Drain and run under cold water. Remove the skins, cut in half, and remove the stones.

Place the apricots in a noncorrosive saucepan (enamel, copper, or stainless steel) and bring to a simmer over medium-low heat. Simmer for 10 to 15 minutes, stirring every now and again, until the apricots have broken down into a thick puree. Remove from the heat and cool.

Store in a clean, dry jar in the refrigerator. It will keep for up to a month.

PER PORTION

Calories	108	Protein	3 G
Fat	.87 G	Carbohydrate	25 G
Sodium	2 MG	Cholesterol	0 MG

DESSERTS

APRICOT AND STRAWBERRY SALAD

SERVES 4

You need really good, ripe apricots for this if you use fresh fruit. If you can't find them, use good-quality apricots in syrup and drain off the syrup.

1   **pound (450 g) apricots, stones removed, sliced**
½   **pound (225 g/1 pint) strawberries, hulled and sliced**
1   **tablespoon mild honey, such as clover or acacia (optional)**
      juice of 1 orange
      juice of ½ lemon
      chopped fresh mint for garnish

Combine the fruit with the honey if you're using it and toss with the juices. Refrigerate until ready to serve. Sprinkle with mint just before serving.

ADVANCE PREPARATION: The fruit, without the mint, can be prepared several hours before serving and refrigerated.

PER PORTION

Calories	77	Protein	2 G
Fat	.64 G	Carbohydrate	18 G
Sodium	2 MG	Cholesterol	0

PEACH AND LAVENDER HONEY SOUP
Soupe aux pêches

SERVES 4

Fresh peaches, either white or yellow, are blended into a coarse puree and garnished with sliced peaches and mint in this refreshing, thirst-quenching summer dessert. The lavender honey gives it a special depth. For a bright splash of color you can garnish this with red currants.

2	**pounds (900 g/6 large) white or yellow peaches**
4	**teaspoons lavender, clover, or acacia honey**
3	**tablespoons fresh lemon juice or more to taste**
3	**tablespoons peach liqueur (*crème de pêches*)**
2	**tablespoons fresh mint leaves, cut into slivers, plus 4 attractive sprigs for garnish**
¼	**cup (60 ml) fresh red currants (optional)**

Bring a large pot of water to a boil and drop in all but one of the peaches (2 if you're using small peaches). After 30 seconds, drain and transfer to a bowl of cold water. Peel off the skins, remove the pits, and cut the peaches into quarters.

Puree the peaches coarsely in a food processor along with the honey, lemon juice, and liqueur. The mixture should be like a slightly chunky soup. Transfer to a bowl.

Pit and thinly slice the peach or peaches that you set aside and stir into the liquefied peaches. Cover and chill for several hours.

Shortly before serving, stir in the slivered mint leaves. Serve in dessert bowls, garnishing each portion with a sprig of mint and a tablespoon of red currants, if desired.

ADVANCE PREPARATION: This will hold for several hours in the refrigerator, but stir in the mint shortly before serving.

PLUM CLAFOUTI

SERVES 8

Plums hit the Provençal markets around midsummer and last well into the fall. There are large red ones, and the smaller purple plums called *prunes,* and greengages, or *reines-claudes.* The clafouti is best made with small plums, either purple plums or greengages.

2   tablespoons mild-flavored honey, such as clover, acacia, or lavender

2   tablespoons plum brandy or kirsch

3   large eggs or 1 large egg and 3 egg whites

1   vanilla bean or ½ teaspoon vanilla extract

¼   cup (50 g) granulated sugar

⅔   cup (85 g) sifted unbleached white flour

1   cup (250 ml) plain nonfat yogurt
    pinch of salt

2   pounds (900 g) plums, halved and pitted

2   teaspoons powdered sugar (optional)

Preheat the oven to 400°F (200°C). Butter a 10½-inch (26 cm) ceramic tart pan or baking dish.

In the bowl of an electric mixer or with a whisk, beat together the honey, brandy, eggs, seeds from the vanilla bean, and the granulated sugar. Slowly beat in the flour. Add the yogurt and salt. Mix together well.

Arrange the plums, cut side down, in the baking dish. Pour in the batter. Bake for 30 to 45 minutes or until the top is browned and the clafouti is firm. Remove from the heat, dust the top with the powdered sugar if desired, and cool on a rack. Serve warm or at room temperature.

ADVANCE PREPARATION: This can be made hours ahead of serving. The leftovers are wonderful for breakfast.

PER PORTION

Calories	187 (175)	Protein	6 (6) G
Fat	3 (2) G	Carbohydrate	35 (35) G
Sodium	67 (72) MG	Cholesterol	82 (28) MG

Note: Amounts in parentheses relate to the use of 1 egg and 3 egg whites.

GREENGAGE OR PLUM TART IN PHYLLO PASTRY

Tarte aux reines claudes ou aux quetsches

SERVES 6

My favorite Provençal plums are the green *reines claudes,* which are juicy, smaller versions of greengages. Use one kind or a mix for this low-fat tart.

2	tablespoons unsalted butter
6	sheets of phyllo dough
1	large egg white, lightly beaten
1½	pounds (675 g) greengages, plums, or a mixture, cut in half and stones removed
1	tablespoon mild honey, such as clover, acacia, or lavender

Preheat the oven to 375°F (190°C). Melt the butter in a heavy-bottomed saucepan or a double boiler.

Brush the bottom of a 12-inch (30 cm) tart pan with a small amount of butter. Layer a sheet of phyllo dough in the pan so that it covers about two-thirds of the bottom of the pan and overlaps the sides. Brush it lightly with butter. Layer another sheet of phyllo dough over the first sheet so that it covers the part of the pan left uncovered by the first sheet. Layer the remaining 4 sheets in this way, turning the pan a little after each sheet and brushing the phyllo lightly with butter. Be sure to brush the part of the dough that goes up the sides of the pan. Now take the edges of the dough and roll them up, twisting gently, into an attractive lip. Press this into the edges of the pan and brush the surface with butter. Brush the phyllo dough with the beaten egg white and bake for 5 minutes in the preheated oven. Remove from the heat.

Arrange the plums in the crust, cut side up. Heat the honey in the saucepan with the remains of the melted butter. Very lightly brush the plums with the honey (you should use only half the honey for this, if that).

Bake the tart for 30 minutes or until the pastry is lightly browned. Remove from the heat and brush the edges of the crust with the remaining honey. Turn off the oven, return the tart to the oven, and allow to cool. Or serve hot.

ADVANCE PREPARATION: This will hold for a couple of hours but is best eaten soon after baking. The bottom will become slightly soggy, but the sides will remain crisp. You can reheat this in a low oven to recover some of the crispiness.

PER PORTION

Calories	163	Protein	3 G
Fat	6 G	Carbohydrate	27 G
Sodium	102 MG	Cholesterol	10 MG

PEACH AND BERRY CLAFOUTI
Clafouti aux pêches et aux fruits rouges

Here's another idea for the sweet, juicy summer fruits of Provence. I've taken the liberty of adding blueberries, which are not Provençal (blackberries, however, are; they grow everywhere). I love the mix of primary colors.

1½	pounds (675 g) peaches, peeled, pitted, and thickly sliced
1	cup (250 ml) blueberries
½	pound (225 g) strawberries, hulled and cut in half (about 1½ cups)
2	tablespoons fresh lemon juice
2	tablespoons peach liqueur (crème de pêches)
1	tablespoon mild-flavored honey, such as clover or acacia
3	large eggs or 1 egg and 3 egg whites
1	vanilla bean or ½ teaspoon vanilla extract
¼	cup (50 g) granulated sugar
⅔	cup (85 g) sifted unbleached white flour
¾	cup (185 ml) plain nonfat yogurt
	pinch of salt
2	teaspoons powdered sugar (optional)

Bring a large pot of water to a boil and drop in the peaches. After 30 seconds, drain and transfer to a bowl of cold water. The skins will peel off easily. Slice and toss with the berries, lemon juice, liqueur, and honey. Let sit for 30 minutes. Pour off the liquid into a measuring cup.

Preheat the oven to 400°F (200°C). Lightly butter a 10½-inch (26 cm) ceramic tart pan or baking dish.

In the bowl of an electric mixer or with a whisk, beat together the eggs, seeds from the vanilla bean, and granulated sugar. Slowly beat in the flour. Add the yogurt to the juice from the fruit to measure 1 cup (250 ml) plus 2 tablespoons and stir this into the egg mixture along with the salt. Mix together well.

Arrange the fruit in the baking dish. Pour in the batter. Bake for 30 to 45 minutes or until the top is browned and the clafouti is firm. Remove from the heat, dust the top with the powdered sugar if desired, and cool on a rack. Serve warm or at room temperature.

ADVANCE PREPARATION: This can be made hours ahead of serving. It holds well for a day, and the leftovers make a wonderful breakfast.

PER PORTION

Calories	170 (157)	Protein	5 (5) G
Fat	3 (1) G	Carbohydrate	31 (31) G
Sodium	63 (68) MG	Cholesterol	81 (28) MG

Note: Amounts in parentheses relate to the use of 1 egg and 3 egg whites.

RHUBARB AND STRAWBERRY SOUP

SERVES 6

This sweet-tart puree is perfect after a robust Provençal meal. Serve it very cold.

2 to 2¼	pounds (900 g to 1 kg) rhubarb stalks, sliced
⅓ to ½	cup (85 to 125 ml) mild-flavored honey such as clover or acacia, to taste, plus 1 tablespoon for the strawberries
¼	cup (62 ml) water
1	pound (450 g) strawberries, hulled
2	cups (500 ml) fresh orange juice
	fresh mint sprigs for garnish

Combine the rhubarb, honey, and water in a large nonreactive saucepan and bring to a boil. Reduce the heat and simmer until the rhubarb begins to soften, about 10 minutes. Add half the strawberries and continue to cook, uncovered, stirring often, until the mixture is thick and compotelike, about 25 minutes. Remove from the heat and allow to cool slightly.

Transfer the compote to a blender or food processor and puree until smooth. Pour into a bowl or container and chill for several hours or overnight.

A few hours before serving, slice the remaining strawberries and toss with a tablespoon of honey. Shortly before serving, stir the orange juice into the soup.

Ladle the soup into bowls and spoon in sliced strawberries and some of their juice. Float a sprig of mint in each bowl and serve.

ADVANCE PREPARATION: The soup can be made a day before serving, but add the orange juice no more than a couple of hours before serving.

PER PORTION

Calories	175	Protein	3 G
Fat	.74 G	Carbohydrate	43 G
Sodium	9 MG	Cholesterol	0

FIG AND HONEY CLAFOUTI
Clafouti aux figues

These figs are brushed with honey and become as luxurious as confiture as they bake.

2 pounds (900 g/20 medium-size) fresh figs, cut in half lengthwise

⅓ cup (85 ml) mild-flavored honey, such as clover, acacia, or lavender

3 large eggs or 1 egg and 3 egg whites

1 vanilla bean or ½ teaspoon vanilla extract

¾ cup (110 g/3.75 oz) sifted unbleached white flour

½ cup (125 ml) plain nonfat yogurt

2 tablespoons fig eau-de-vie (optional)

grated zest of 1 orange

pinch of salt

1 tablespoon raw brown (turbinado) sugar

Preheat the oven to 400°F (205°C). Butter a 10½-inch (26 cm) ceramic tart pan or baking dish. Place the figs cut side up in the baking dish and brush each one with honey.

In the bowl of an electric mixer or with a whisk, beat together the eggs, seeds from the vanilla bean, and remaining honey. Slowly beat in the flour. Add the yogurt, eau-de-vie if desired, orange zest, and salt. Mix together well. Pour over the figs. Sprinkle the brown sugar over the top.

Bake for 25 to 35 minutes or until the top is browned and the clafouti is firm. Remove from the heat and cool on a rack. Serve warm or at room temperature.

ADVANCE PREPARATION: This will hold for several hours at room temperature. I like to eat the leftovers for breakfast.

Calories	213 (201)	Protein	5 (5) G
Fat	3 (2) G	Carbohydrate	44 (44) G
Sodium	58 (63) MG	Cholesterol	81 (28) MG

Note: Amounts in parentheses relate to the use of 1 egg and 3 egg whites.

FIG AND ORANGE GRANITÉ

SERVES 6 TO 8

A granité, the same thing as an Italian granita, is a fruit ice. It's like a sorbet but has less sugar and more ice crystals. This simple, subtle fig-orange ice is unbelievably easy to make.

½ cup (125 ml) water

⅓ cup (85 ml) mild-flavored honey, such as clover, acacia, or lavender

3 cups (750 ml) orange juice (fresh or from frozen concentrate)

1 pound (450 g) fresh red figs, stems removed

1 tablespoon fresh lemon juice

Combine the water and honey in a saucepan and bring to a simmer. Cook until reduced by about one-fourth and remove from the heat.

Combine the orange juice and figs in a blender and blend at high speed until smooth. Stir in the honey syrup and the lemon juice.

Transfer the mixture to a bowl, cover, and freeze until just about frozen solid. Transfer the mixture to a food processor and blend (in batches, if this is easier) until smooth. Return to the bowl, cover, and freeze.

When the mixture is frozen solid, transfer to the refrigerator for 30 minutes. Now cut into large pieces and blend in a food processor fitted with the steel blade until smooth. Transfer to individual ramekins, a mold, or a container, cover, and freeze.

Transfer the granité to the refrigerator 30 minutes before serving. Serve alone or with a ladleful of the compote in the following recipe.

Note: This can be frozen in an ice cream maker according to the manufacturer's instructions.

ADVANCED PREPARATION: This will keep for several weeks in the freezer.

PER PORTION

Calories	126	Protein	1 G
Fat	.34 G	Carbohydrate	32 G
Sodium	2 MG	Cholesterol	0

A COMPOTE OF FRESH FIGS AND GRAPES IN RED WINE WITH HONEY

SERVES 8

Serve this sweet, heady mixture with the preceding recipe for granité or as is. It's great with a hard cookie like a biscotti.

2   cups (500 ml) fruity red wine, such as a gamay or Beaujolais

⅓   cup (85 ml) mild-flavored honey, such as clover, acacia, or lavender

1   pound (450 g) fresh dark figs, cut in half lengthwise

½   pound (225 g) green grapes, preferably muscat, cut in half, seeds removed

Combine the wine and honey in a large nonreactive saucepan and bring to a simmer. Add the figs and grapes, simmer for 5 minutes, and remove from the heat. Allow to cool. Serve at room temperature or chilled.

ADVANCE PREPARATION: This can be made several hours before serving.

PER PORTION

Calories	144	Protein	.73 G
Fat	.30 G	Carbohydrate	28 G
Sodium	5 MG	Cholesterol	0

FIG TART IN PHYLLO PASTRY
Tarte aux figues

SERVES 6

This tart is almost Middle Eastern in character. Maybe it's the phyllo, maybe the figs. I think it has something to do with the tart's delicacy and simplicity.

2   tablespoons unsalted butter

6   sheets of phyllo dough

1   large egg white, lightly beaten

2   pounds (900 g) fresh figs, cut in half lengthwise

1   tablespoon mild honey, such as clover, acacia, or lavender

Preheat the oven to 375°F (190°C). Melt the butter in a heavy-bottomed saucepan or a double boiler.

Brush the bottom of a 10½- or 12-inch (26 or 30 cm) tart pan with a small amount of butter. Layer a sheet of phyllo dough in the pan so that it covers about two-thirds of the bottom of the pan and overlaps the sides. Brush it lightly with butter. Layer another sheet of phyllo dough over the first sheet so that it covers the part of the pan left uncovered by the first sheet. Layer the remaining 4 sheets in this way, turning the pan a little after each sheet and brushing the phyllo lightly with butter. Be sure to brush the part of the dough that goes up the sides of the pan. Now take the edges of the dough and roll them up, twisting gently, into an attractive lip. Press this into the edges of the pan and brush the surface with butter. Brush the phyllo dough with the beaten egg white and bake for 5 minutes. Remove from the heat.

Arrange the figs in the crust cut side up. Heat the honey in the saucepan with the remains of the melted butter. Very lightly brush the figs with the honey (you should use only half the honey for this, if that).

Bake the tart for 20 to 25 minutes or until the pastry is lightly browned. Remove from the heat and brush the edges of the crust with the remaining honey.

ADVANCE PREPARATION: This will hold for a couple of hours but is best served not too long after baking. The bottom will become slightly soggy, but the sides will remain crisp. You can reheat this in a low oven to recover some of the crispiness.

PER PORTION

Calories	215	Protein	3 G
Fat	5 G	Carbohydrate	42 G
Sodium	103 MG	Cholesterol	10 MG

PEAR CLAFOUTI
Clafouti aux poires

SERVES 8

In the fall all kinds of pears replace peaches and apricots in the Provençal markets. The first ones to come in are the smallish yellow Williams pears, which are firm and sweet and lend themselves to this simple, delicious clafouti. Boscs will be fine, too.

½   cup (125 ml) pear eau-de-vie or liqueur
2   tablespoons mild-flavored honey, such as clover, acacia, or lavender
2   pounds (900 g/6 medium-size) pears
3   large eggs
1   vanilla bean, or ½ teaspoon vanilla extract
¼   cup (50 g) sugar
⅔   cup (85 g) sifted unbleached white flour
½   cup (125 ml) plain nonfat yogurt
    pinch of salt

Combine the pear eau-de-vie and honey in a bowl. Peel, core, and slice the pears into the bowl. Toss and let sit for 30 minutes or longer.

Preheat the oven to 400°F (200°C). Butter a 10½-inch (26 cm) ceramic tart pan or baking dish.

In the bowl of an electric mixer or with a whisk, beat together the eggs, seeds from the vanilla bean, and sugar. Slowly beat in the flour. Add the yogurt and salt. Drain the pears and add their marinade. Mix together well.

Arrange the pears in the baking dish. Pour in the batter. Bake for 30 to 35 minutes or until the top is beginning to brown and the clafouti is firm. Remove from the heat and cool on a rack. Serve warm or at room temperature.

ADVANCE PREPARATION: This can be made hours ahead of serving. It holds well for a day, and the leftovers make a wonderful breakfast.

PER PORTION

Calories	196	Protein	5 G
Fat	3 G	Carbohydrate	40 G
Sodium	56 MG	Cholesterol	81 MG

QUINCE COMPOTE
Compote de coings

SERVES 4

One of the things I've always liked about France is that people who sell produce in the market will almost always tell you how to cook it. After I'd been in Provence for a few weeks one fall, I figured it was time to do something with the quinces that were pouring off people's trees and into the markets every week. "How do I prepare them?" I asked the vendor. "You make a compote; in syrup with vanilla." So I took them home and made this wonderful compote. The fragrance comes from the combination of the tart quince and the highly perfumed vanilla.

1	**quart (1 l) water**
	juice of ½ lemon
2	**pounds (900 g/2 large) quinces**
⅓	**cup (65 g) sugar**
½	**teaspoon ground cinnamon**
1	**vanilla bean, cut in half lengthwise**
¼	**cup (45 g) raisins (optional)**

Combine the water and lemon juice in a large nonaluminum saucepan. Quarter the quinces and place the pieces you aren't working with in the water while you peel, core, and slice each quarter.

Add the remaining ingredients to the saucepan and bring to a simmer over medium heat. Stir, reduce the heat, cover, and simmer for 1 hour, until the syrup is reduced by about half and the quinces are tender and pinkish. Serve hot or cold.

ADVANCE PREPARATION: This will keep for a week in the refrigerator. Leave the vanilla bean in with the quinces.

PER PORTION

Calories	146	Protein	.56 G
Fat	.13 G	Carbohydrate	38 G
Sodium	6 MG	Cholesterol	0

QUINCE AND APPLE OR PEAR SOUFFLÉ

Soufflé aux coings et aux pommes ou poires

SERVES 6

A soufflé is a marvelous vehicle for quinces, which have such a fine tart flavor but can have a difficult texture. Use either apples or pears in conjunction with the quinces for a fabulous dessert.

1	**pound (450 g/1 large) quince, peeled, cored, and diced**
1	**pound (450 g) tart eating apples or ripe pears, peeled, cored, and diced**
	a bowl of water mixed with the juice of ½ lemon
½	**cup (125 ml) water**
¼	**cup (50 g) plus 1 tablespoon sugar**
1	**vanilla bean, cut in half lengthwise**
½	**teaspoon ground cinnamon**
¼	**teaspoon freshly grated nutmeg**
	juice of 1 lemon
	butter for the soufflé dish
6	**large egg whites**
	pinch of salt

Quarter the fruit and keep each quarter in the bowl of lemon water as you peel, core, and dice the rest. Put the fruit back in the bowl of lemon water as you chop it.

Combine the quince, apples, water, all but 1 tablespoon of the sugar, the vanilla, spices, and lemon juice in a large nonaluminum saucepan and bring to a simmer. Reduce the heat and simmer for 30 to 40 minutes, stirring often, until the fruit is tender and beginning to stick to the bottom of the pan. Remove from the heat, remove the vanilla bean, and puree in a food processor fitted with the steel blade. You should have about 2 cups (500 ml) of puree.

Preheat the oven to 400°F (200°C). Butter a 2-quart (2 l) soufflé dish and dust with the remaining tablespoon of sugar.

Beat the egg whites until they begin to foam. Add the salt and continue to beat until you have stiff but not dry peaks. Stir one-fourth of the egg whites into the fruit puree and gently fold in the rest.

Spoon the mixture into the soufflé dish and bake for 20 to 30 minutes. The soufflé should have risen, the top should be brown, and the sides should be wobbly. Remove from the oven and serve at once.

ADVANCE PREPARATION: The ingredients for the soufflé can be prepared hours ahead of baking the soufflé. The fruit puree can be made as much as 2 days ahead, and the egg whites can be beaten up to 2 hours before being combined with the fruit.

PER PORTION

Calories	129	Protein	4 G
Fat	.89 G	Carbohydrate	28 G
Sodium	85 MG	Cholesterol	2 MG

PEAR AND APPLE SOUFFLÉ
Soufflé aux poires et aux pommes

SERVES 6

This is a marvelous winter dessert, especially after a filling meal. It tastes mainly of pear; the apple adds body and tartness. I first surprised guests with this at one of my aïoli dinners. While friends cleared away plates and platters, I disappeared into the kitchen, beat the egg whites, folded them into the pureed pears and apples, transferred the mixture to soufflé dishes, and shoved them all into a hot oven. Everyone was delighted when I presented the beautifully risen, ethereal soufflés just 10 minutes later. Don't be afraid of making these; the trick is a hot oven and a good timer. If you overcook them, the egg whites will harden.

1	pound (450 g) tart apples, peeled, cored, and sliced or coarsely chopped
1½	pounds (675 g) juicy pears, peeled, cored, and sliced or coarsely chopped
	juice of ½ lemon
¼	cup (50 g) plus 1 tablespoon vanilla sugar (page 431)
8	large egg whites

Prepare the apples and pears, putting the pieces directly into a bowl of water acidulated with the lemon juice as you peel and slice or chop. When all the fruit is prepared, drain and transfer to a large heavy-bottomed saucepan. Add all but 1 tablespoon of the sugar and bring to a simmer over medium heat. Stir together, turn the heat to low, and cook, uncovered, for 30 to 40 minutes, stirring often. The fruit should cook down to a puree and begin to stick to the bottom of the pan. Remove from the heat and puree until smooth in a food processor fitted with the steel blade. Allow to cool.

Preheat the oven to 425°F (220°C). Lightly butter a 2-quart (2 l) soufflé dish or 6 individual soufflé dishes. Dust the dish or dishes with the remaining tablespoon of sugar.

Beat the egg whites until they form stiff but not dry peaks. Stir a quarter of the beaten egg whites into the fruit puree. Gently fold in the rest. Transfer to the soufflé dish or ramekins. Place on a baking sheet and bake individual soufflés for 10 to 12 minutes, until puffed and brown. Bake a large soufflé for 15 to 20 minutes. Serve at once.

ADVANCE PREPARATION: This is actually a very convenient dessert. Although a baked soufflé can't wait, the puree can be made several days ahead of time and refrigerated. Allow it to come to room temperature before mixing with the egg whites. The egg whites can be beaten 2 hours before you mix together the soufflé.

PER PORTION

Calories	167	Protein	5 G
Fat	1 G	Carbohydrate	36 G
Sodium	80 MG	Cholesterol	2 MG

VANILLA SUGAR

MAKES 1 CUP

Vanilla sugar is exactly what it sounds like: sugar infused with vanilla. In France this is as much a household staple as baking powder is in the United States, for use in pastry and desserts like the clafoutis on pages 407, 413, 416, 419, and 424. Every time you despair at the price of vanilla beans required for a given recipe, remember that you can reuse the dried pods to make this fragrant sugar.

1 cup sugar
   the used pods of 1 to 3 vanilla beans, or 1
   vanilla bean, split down the middle

If you are reusing vanilla bean pods, make sure the pods are completely dry. Lay them on paper towels and allow to dry for several hours or overnight. Submerge in the sugar and cover tightly. If you are using a fresh bean, simply split it open down the middle and submerge in the sugar. Add more sugar and add used vanilla pods regularly. You can keep vanilla sugar on hand indefinitely.

CHRISTINE'S BAKED PEARS
WITH HONEY
Poires au four de Christine

SERVES 6

I felt immediately warm and optimistic one cold, rainy November night when I walked into my friend Christine Picasso's house and saw a big gratin dish filled with caramelized baked pears sitting in an inviting syrup. It's impossible to resist making pear desserts during the fall months in Provence, when there are so many beautiful kinds to choose from in the markets. Use a large, firm pear, like a Bosc or Comice, for this dish. The pears bake for two hours in a moderate oven, and as they do their skins shrivel and caramelize and the fruit becomes infused with the scent of honey and cloves. The tender, juicy pears literally melt in your mouth.

6   large ripe but firm pears
2   tablespoons honey: a strongish flavor like orange blossom is fine (Provençal lavender and *toutes fleurs* are great)
2   tablespoons raw brown (turbinado) sugar
12   cloves
    water as needed

Preheat the oven to 400°F (200°C). Cut a small cone out of the bottom of each pear and place a teaspoonful of honey in each one. Set the pears, bottom side down, in the baking dish. Sprinkle a teaspoon of the sugar over the top of each pear. Add the cloves to the baking dish and pour in enough water to cover the rounded bottoms, or about one-third of the pears.

Bake for 10 minutes, then turn down the oven to 350°F (180°C). Using a spoon or a baster, baste the pears with water from the baking dish and bake for 2 hours, basting every 15 minutes and turning the pears on their sides from time to time so that they cook evenly. Remove from the oven and allow to cool.

If there is more than a cup (250 ml) of liquid remaining in the baking dish, transfer it to a saucepan and bring to a boil. Reduce by half. Serve the pears at room temperature, moistened with a bit of syrup.

ADVANCE PREPARATION: These can be baked hours ahead
of serving and held at room temperature.

PER PORTION

Calories	161	Protein	.82 G
Fat	.84 G	Carbohydrate	42 G
Sodium	2 MG	Cholesterol	0

A DAY IN THE LIFE OF
A PROVENÇAL BEEKEEPER

Claude Jeanne gets stung by bees every day. Lots of them. He's as
used to bee stings as a chef is to nicks and burns. On the day I
accompanied him on his afternoon rounds I asked him how many
times he'd been stung since the morning. "Oh, I don't count.
Otherwise it would be too *décourageant.*"

The stings are a small nuisance in what is otherwise a very
fulfilling and very demanding *métier.* Beekeepers in Provence
probably know more beautiful nooks and crannies off tiny, bumpy
back roads than anyone else in the region. *"C'est dans la nature,"*
says Claude Jeanne, who lives and makes honey in a charming
village near Gordes and goes as far afield as the Ardèche, about
60 miles to the northwest, with his beehives. "I go to the Ardèche
for the chestnuts in June and July and for the heather in the fall."
That is, his bees go for the chestnuts and the heather. In August the
flavor of the month is lavender, and Claude and his bees can stick
closer to home.

The hives are large wooden boxes filled with wood-and-wax
frames where the bees, under the tutelage of one very fertile queen
who lays her weight in eggs every day (about 20,000), build their
honeycombs and feed themselves and the larvae. You notice the
ruches all over the place, set out in isolated spots, near enough to
the orchards or meadows or lavender fields for the bees to get the
scent of the flowers then in bloom. Set atop cinder blocks, the
boxes are empty on the bottom (that's where the bees fly in and
out), and their tops—wooden or metal "boxtops"—are held
down against the *mistral* with large, heavy stones. The *mistral* is the
beekeeper's enemy, for it scatters the scents that the bees rely on to
feed themselves. When a colony is at its height, there will be

50,000 to 60,000 bees, producing 15 to 20 kilos of honey (33 to 44 pounds) in a good year. Those bees *eat* a kilo of honey a day! (Well, it *is* awfully good here.)

At this time of year, early spring, the bees will produce honey called *toutes fleurs* from the nectar of various flowers, including dandelions, alfalfa, and clover. Claude's work consists of transporting hives to carefully selected spots—at night, when the bees are quiet—and, most important, checking the hives to see how the bees are doing. They have only begun to reproduce after a sleepy winter clumped up in the hive, and it is crucial that they get off to a healthy start.

We go to a wooded spot where there are about 35 hives. Claude gives me a netted safari hat, puts on his overalls and hat, and stokes up his most important tool, a small "smoker," which is a little metal canister with a leather bellows on one side, where the beekeeper burns a mixture of dried, crushed olive pits and pine needles. With the bellows he blows smoke out of a nozzle at the top of the can, and the smoke pacifies the bees so that he can work. He taps the outside of the box and listens for a buzzing sound; if there is no sound, the hive is no good, and he will take it back to his workshop to refurbish it. But most of the hives buzz. Claude sprays some smoke around the hive, lifts off the cover, sprays some more smoke, lifts off a plastic or metal flap between the frames and the cover, and sprays again. The smoke really works.

It's early in an already tardy spring, so the hives that are producing lots of bees are still only partially active—only the middle frames are covered with bees. It looks like a hell of a lot of bees to me, but in three weeks, when the eggs the queen is now laying have hatched, the entire box will be swarming. Claude takes out a "good" frame and shows me the honey that the bees have produced and the larvae in the honeycomb cells. "Those big humped shells are queens; when they hatch, they will fight it out, and the fittest will rule a colony." He moves the fuller frames farther apart so that the bees will not be so susceptible to disease (the biggest menace to beekeepers; certain parasites can wipe out a colony overnight and spread easily from hive to hive) and so that they will have room to produce more wax, eggs, and honey. He takes away the frames that have neither bees nor honey and replaces them with new ones, whose combs contain honey. Then he puts the top flap back on and ladles on a solution of honey and egg yolk powder; he is feeding the bees! They need the extra food for themselves and the larvae because it's a slow spring. Afterward

Claude lifts the 10 hives that aren't producing into the truck—it's heavy work—puts the tops back on the "good" hives, and goes on to another check spot.

None of this honey will be harvested. At this point the bees are producing only enough to feed themselves. In about three weeks, when the colonies are full (*"après les cerisiers"*—after the cherry blossoms), Claude will put a smaller box over the hives, with half-frames for the honey that he will sell. He has all the machinery for extracting, filtering, and bottling the honey in a small shed next to his house, his *mielerie*. His daily hive inspections will help him determine the moment for putting on the upper boxes.

After Claude collects his honey from the hives I saw today, he will lend the hives to a local apple farmer to help him pollinate his trees. This symbiotic relationship between farmers and beekeepers is one of the beauties of the business. The *apiculteurs* need the farmers for their land and crops, and the farmers need the bees for fertilization. When the farmers see that the moment is right, they will call people like Claude, who will be at the designated zucchini field or apple orchard before the next dawn with the bees.

As if all this didn't seem like enough work, there is also the selling. Those nice honey sellers at the colorful Provençal markets, who seem to have all day to talk to you about their honey, all "go out with their bees" every day like Claude Jeanne. But the markets—Jeanne does the Apt market on Saturday, Saint-Rémy-de-Provence on Wednesday, Bedouin Friday, and Coustellet, this last from November to May, on Sundays—are also part of the business. A lucky thing for us.

HONEY ALMOND COOKIES

Croquettes au miel et aux amandes

MAKES 60 COOKIES

Many of the wonderful honey sellers in the markets throughout Provence also sell cookies. They aren't too different from the honey biscotti I've been making for years: hard, not too sweet, wonderful for dipping.

½ **cup (3 oz/90 g) almonds**

2 **large eggs plus 1 egg white**

½ **cup (125 ml) mild-flavored honey, such as clover, acacia, or lavender**

1 **tablespoon orange flower water**

1 **teaspoon baking soda**

¼ **teaspoon salt**

2¾ **cups (13 oz/370 g) whole-wheat pastry flour or unbleached white flour, or a combination**

Preheat the oven to 375°F (190°C). Place the almonds on a baking sheet and roast them for about 10 minutes, until light golden and toasty. Remove from the oven and chop coarsely.

In a mixer, blend together the whole eggs, honey, orange flower water, baking soda, and salt. Gradually add the flour. Scrape the dough out of the bowl onto a lightly floured surface. Press out the dough and scatter the almonds over the top. Fold the dough over the almonds and knead gently until the almonds are distributed evenly through the dough.

Divide the dough in half and shape into 2 long logs, about 1½ to 2 inches (4 to 5 cm) wide and 1 inch (2.5 cm) high. Place them on a buttered and floured baking sheet, not too close together. Beat the egg white until foamy and brush it over the logs. Bake for 20 minutes, until golden brown and shiny. Remove from the oven and turn the oven down to 275°F (135°C).

Using a long serrated knife, cut the logs into diagonal slices about ¼ inch (.75 cm) thick. Place the cookies on 2 baking sheets and bake again for 30 to 40 minutes, until dry and hard and golden brown. Remove from the heat and cool. Keep in a covered container.

ADVANCE PREPARATION: These keep for weeks in a covered jar.

PROVENÇAL ALMOND COOKIES
Biscuits de provence aux amandes grillées

MAKES 60 COOKIES

You find hard, biscottilike almond cookies throughout Provence. Often they have a lemony flavor; sometimes they're seasoned with fennel; other times they're just plain, nutty almond. Here are a few recipes.

½   **cup (3 oz/90 g) almonds**
2   **large eggs plus 1 egg white**
½   **cup (100 g) sugar**
1   **teaspoon baking soda**
¼   **teaspoon salt**
10   **ounces (2 cups /285 g) whole-wheat pastry flour or unbleached white flour**

Preheat the oven to 375°F (190°C). Place the almonds on a baking sheet and roast them for about 10 minutes, until light golden and toasty. Remove from the oven and chop medium-fine.

In a mixer, blend together the whole eggs and sugar. Add the baking soda and salt. Gradually add the flour. Scrape the dough out onto a lightly floured work surface. Press out the dough and scatter the almonds over the top. Fold the dough over the almonds and knead gently until the almonds are distributed evenly through the dough.

Divide the dough in half and shape into 2 long logs, about 1½ to 2 inches (4 to 5 cm) wide and 1 inch (2.5 cm) high. Place them on a buttered and floured baking sheet, not too close together. Beat the egg white until foamy and brush it over the logs. Bake for 20 minutes, until golden brown and shiny. Remove from the oven and turn the oven down to 275°F (135°C).

Using a long serrated knife, cut the logs into diagonal slices about ¼ inch (.75 cm) thick. Place the cookies on 2 baking sheets and bake again for 30 to 40 minutes, until dry, hard, and lightly browned. Remove from the heat and cool. Keep in a covered container.

ADVANCE PREPARATION: These keep for weeks in a covered jar.

PER PORTION

Calories	35	Protein	1 G
Fat	1 G	Carbohydrate	5 G
Sodium	34 MG	Cholesterol	7 MG

VARIATIONS   *Lemon-Almond Cookies:* Add ¼ cup (62 ml) fresh lemon juice and the grated zest of 1 lemon to the eggs. You will need about ½ cup (2 oz/60 g) additional flour.

Fennel or *Anise Cookies:* Add 1 tablespoon crushed fennel or aniseed to the eggs.

SWEET SWISS CHARD TORTE
Tourta dé bléa
Tourte aux blettes

SERVES 8

This popular Niçois specialty seems a rather strange idea, but I like it. Not only is this a fine dessert, but it's also good with tea or served as an aperitif with white wine (add the optional cheese if you're going to serve it as an aperitif). But dessert is what it is in Nice.

1 recipe yeasted olive oil pastry (page 259)

For the Filling:
½ cup (90 g) raisins

½ cup (125 ml) rum or enough to cover the raisins

1 pound (450 g) Swiss chard leaves, about 2½ pounds (2.25 kg) with stalks

   salt to taste

3 large eggs plus 1 egg, beaten, for brushing the pastry

2 tart apples, peeled and finely chopped

¼ cup (62 ml) lightly toasted pine nuts

3 tablespoons mild-flavored honey, such as clover or acacia

¼ teaspoon freshly grated nutmeg

1 tablespoon powdered sugar (optional)

Prepare the filling while the pastry dough is rising. Soak the raisins in rum to cover until they swell. Separate the chard leaves from the stems and put the stems aside for another purpose, such as the gratin on page 342. Wash the leaves thoroughly and place in a bowl. Salt fairly heavily and briskly rub the leaves between your hands. This brings out some of the water in the leaves. Now wash again and dry thoroughly. Chop finely in a food processor. Season to taste with salt.

Beat 3 of the eggs in a large bowl. Drain the raisins. Stir in the chard, raisins, chopped apples, pine nuts, honey, and nutmeg.

When the pastry has risen and softened, punch it down gently and divide it into 2 pieces, one slightly smaller than the other. Shape into balls and lightly cover the smaller piece with plastic wrap while you roll out the larger piece. Butter a 10- to 12-inch (25 to 30 cm) tart or cake pan and roll out the larger piece of dough to fit the dish, about ⅛ inch (.5 cm) thick. Line the dish, cover loosely with a kitchen towel, and let rest for 20 to 30 minutes. Meanwhile, preheat the oven to 400°F (200°C).

Brush the pastry bottom with the additional beaten egg and spread the chard mixture over it in an even layer. Roll out the other piece of dough and place on top of the chard mixture. Join the edges with the bottom edge of the pastry. Cut a few slits in the top piece of dough and brush with beaten egg mixed with a little water to give it a bright golden brown color.

Bake for 40 minutes or until the pastry is a rich brown color. Remove from the heat, dust with powdered sugar if you wish, and allow to cool.

ADVANCE PREPARATION: The dough will hold for a day in the refrigerator, wrapped in plastic wrap. The chard mixture can be assembled hours before baking.

PER PORTION

Calories	307	Protein	9 G
Fat	12 G	Carbohydrate	45 G
Sodium	333 MG	Cholesterol	108 MG

PRUNE AND RED WINE COMPOTE
Compote de pruneaux au vin rouge

SERVES 6

There is a town in the Var, about 31 miles east of Aix, called Brignolles that is famous for its plums and prunes. But oddly enough, you don't see too many desserts made with prunes in Provence. I think of these luscious dried fruits whenever I drive by the town on my way from Aix to Nice. Although this refreshing compote is not particularly Provençal, all the elements in it are. It's one of my favorite desserts. Serve it with one of the hard cookies on pages 437–38 and dip the cookies in the wine.

1	pound (450 grams) prunes
1	quart (1 l) water
1	bottle of red wine, such as a Côtes du Rhône
¼	cup (50 g) sugar
1	3-inch cinnamon stick
2	slices of orange, seeds removed
4	strips of lemon zest

Place the prunes in a bowl. Bring the water to a boil and pour it over the prunes. Let sit for 5 minutes, then drain.

Combine the wine, sugar, cinnamon, orange slices, and lemon zest in a large nonreactive saucepan and bring to a simmer. Add the prunes, stir the mixture, simmer for 5 minutes, and remove from the heat. Allow to cool and chill or serve at room temperature.

Note: You can add other fruit to the mixture once you remove the prunes from the heat. Try sliced peaches, apricots, pears, or strawberries.

ADVANCE PREPARATION: The compote must be made several hours before serving. It will keep for several days in the refrigerator.

PER PORTION

Calories	306	Protein	2 G
Fat	.40 G	Carbohydrate	59 G
Sodium	10 MG	Cholesterol	0

PROVENÇAL TOAST

Que se lèvo dòu vin e dei fremo
Se lèvo de le fè de Diéu, diesien lei Rière.
Dins nosto Prouvenço
Lei fremo soun bello
E lei vin soun famous,
Sian i ped de Diéu!
A la bono vosto!

He who keeps wine and women at a distance
keeps faith in God at a distance, so say our ancestors.
In our Provence
the women are beautiful
and the wines are famous.
We are at God's feet!
To your health!

PROVENÇAL WINES

*. . . I realize that no matter how inspired, articulate, precise,
enthusiastic, or vivid I may attempt to be, this prose, by any standard
of measure, is wholly inadequate in portraying the magic and
experience of . . . a Châteauneuf-du-Pape from Beaucastel, a
Gigondas from Les Pallières, a Coteaux des Baux from the Domaine
Trévallon, or a Bandol from the Domaine Tempier, to name just a few
of the extraordinary wines that transcend normal wine vocabulary and
establish new tasting parameters for even the most advanced wine
enthusiast.*

ROBERT PARKER, *THE WINES OF THE RHÔNE
VALLEY AND PROVENCE*

It's not surprising that the wines I love and know best are the wines of Provence,
including the wines of the southern Rhône. I must admit that I have been terribly
spoiled: my initiation into wine in general and the wines of southern France in
particular began at Domaine Tempier, in Bandol, where the finest reds and the best
rosé wines of that appellation are made. Domaine Tempier reds are long-living and
robust, with rich, fruity, spicy flavors. The rosés are elegant, long in the mouth, dry
and rich with fruit. These wines, made within sight of the Mediterranean, are
meant to be drunk with Lulu Peyraud's fantastic Provençal food.

That goes for all of the good Provençal wines, of course; they can stand up to
garlic and the other robust seasonings that characterize Provençal cooking, yet they
won't be lost on fish or vegetarian meals. Hints of the herbs that grow wild in the
countryside are present in the bouquets of the wines, and their immediate fruity

flavors are often accompanied by spicy and more subtle vegetal tastes and aromas. White wines can be floral and robust or dry and elegant, and the well-made, fruity, dry, refreshing rosés can open up a new world to you. Like the people and the cuisines of Provence, its wines are open, accessible, sunny. Most can be appreciated soon after they are bottled, although top wines (such as those from the best wineries of Châteauneuf-du-Pape, Gigondas, Bandol, Palette) can age for 10 to 20 years.

Here are the better wines of the southern Rhône and Provence. Alas, not all of the wines produced in these places are good; some are downright poor. So it's important that you learn who the good producers are, and for this there is no more reliable, eloquent source than Robert Parker's *The Wines of the Rhône Valley and Provence.*

THE SOUTHERN RHÔNE

GIGONDAS: Robust, chewy, full-bodied, red wines. A small amount of quite good rosé is produced here as well.

CHÂTEAUNEUF-DU-PAPE: The reds are considered "the Bordeaux of the Rhône." They are full-bodied, round, long-lived, and often exceptional wines. Some are fruity and light, like Beaujolais. The small number of white wines produced here are floral, fruity, and excellent.

TAVEL: Rosé. The good Tavels (there are plenty of bad ones) are dry, floral, and excellent.

TOP CÔTES-DU-RHÔNE VILLAGES

BEAUMES-DE-VENISE: The famous dessert wine, Muscat de Beaumes-de-Venise, is produced here. It is one of the headiest, most fragrant wines I've ever tasted.

CAIRANNE: Red, white, rosé. Very fruity and earthy at the same time. The wines are supple and wonderful young. My favorite producer is Rabasse-Charavin.

RASTEAU: Dry red, similar to Cairanne.

SABLET: Mostly reds, very good to excellent.

ST-GERVAIS: Robert Parker writes of one top producer, Domaine

Ste.-Anne, which he says makes the best Viognier (a white varietal) in the southern Rhône and some good reds.

SEGURET: The village is near Rasteau, Cairanne, and Sablet and makes a similar style of very drinkable red wine. A major producer/exporter, Paul Jaboulet Aîné, whose wines you are likely to see in the United States, makes his Côtes-du-Rhône Villages from vineyards in this area.

VACQUEYRAS: Parker thinks Vacqueyras will have its own appellation some day and praises the "big, chewy, full-throttle" red wines made by the top producers here.

CÔTES-DU-RHÔNE

Ninety-nine percent of Côtes-du-Rhône are red wines, the rest rosé and white. Although most of the cooperative wine produced in the Côtes-du-Rhône is poor to adequate, some of the domaine production is excellent. One of my favorite red wines, full of soft, elegant fruit, is produced by Daniel Combes at Domaine de la Jasse in Violet, not far from Vaison-la-Romaine. Good Côtes-du-Rhônes that are widespread in America are produced by La Vieille Ferme, Paul Jaboulet Aîné, and E. Guigal.

OTHER UP-AND-COMING RHÔNE WINES

CÔTES DU VIVARAIS

COTEAUX DU TRICASTIN

CÔTES DU VENTOUX

PROVENCE

The viticultural regions of Provence begin south-southeast of Avignon. They include Bandol, Bellet, Cassis, Coteaux d'Aix-en-Provence, Coteaux des Baux-en-Provence, Côtes de Provence, Côtes du Luberon, and Palette.

BANDOL: The best red wines in Provence, and a great rosé, from Domaine Tempier.

B E L L E T :   This is a tiny appellation near Nice, producing one of Provence's best whites, a good rosé, and fair to good red.

C A S S I S :   Robert Parker says the white wines of Cassis are the only white wines he knows of that can stand up to bouillabaisse. I tend to agree with him (as I do on most wine matters).

C O T E A U X   D ' A I X - E N - P R O V E N C E   (I N C L U D E S   C O T E A U X   D E S   B A U X - E N - P R O V E N C E) :   Mostly reds. This area has "great potential" according to Parker and includes two outstanding producers, Château Vignelaure and Domaine Trévallon.

C Ô T E S   D E   P R O V E N C E :   Reds, whites, rosés. The rosés can be light and refreshing (as well as industrial and awful) and are better than the whites. The reds are getting better all the time.

C Ô T E S   D U   L U B E R O N :   These are also up-and-coming wines, with some light, fruity, fragrant reds and an excellent rosé from Château la Canorgue in Bonnieux.

P A L E T T E :   There is a truly great producer in this tiny appellation just outside of Aix-en-Provence, called Château Simone. It produces elegant, spicy, fruity reds, marvelous rosé, and particularly distinctive, long-living whites.

MENUS

Here are suggested menus for entertaining. For family dining, most recipes in Chapters 4 through 10 can be the focal point of a meal, with a salad and good bread. Some of the heartier salads, such as Main-Dish Salade Niçoise (page 26), Chick-Pea and Spinach Salad with a Chick-Pea Broth (page 35), Provençal Wheatberry Salad (page 41), and Warm Four-Bean Salad (page 43), can also make delicious, light main dishes.

ANY TIME OF YEAR

Tapenade on Croutons (page 56)
Quichets (page 54)
Aïoli Monstre (page 232)
Pear and Apple Soufflé (page 429)

Salade Mesclun (page 29) or Green Salad
Bouillabaisse "Dégustation" (page 166)
Saffron "Bouillabaisse" Bread (page 76)
Lemon Sorbet (page 404) or Melon Granité (page 400)

Ratatouille (page 312)
Socca Crêpes Filled with Brandade (page 199)
Salade Mesclun (page 29)
Christine's Baked Pears (page 432)

LATE SUMMER/EARLY FALL

A Terrine of Grilled Eggplant, Peppers, and Zucchini (page 46)
Mackerel Bouillabaisse with Fresh Peas or Zucchini (page 177)
Green Salad
Fig Tart in Phyllo Pastry (page 422)

Cold Zucchini Soup with Fresh Mint (page 158)
Whole Roast Fish with Garlic (page 218)
Tomato Gratin à la Provençale (page 346)
Potatoes with Sage (page 340)
Melon Granité (page 400)

Salade Mesclun (page 29) or Celery and Endives with Anchovy Paste (page 45)
Pan-Roasted Quail with Quinces and Figs (page 387)
Couscous
Winter Squash Gratin 1 or 2 (page 344 or 345)
Muscat de Beaumes-de-Venise with Muscat Grapes (page 403)
Provençal Almond Cookies (page 437)

Crespeou (page 251)
Salt Cod Bouillabaisse (page 175)
Green Salad or Salade Mesclun (page 29)
Apricot and Strawberry Salad (page 411)

Tomato and Basil Salad (page 52)
Tuna Steak Baked in a Bed of Lettuce (page 210)
Potato and Saffron Gratin (page 337)
Plum Clafouti (page 413)

Flat Onion Omelet (page 239)
Pappardelle with Tomato Sauce, Ricotta, and Shredded Rabbit (page 290)
Green Salad
Muscat de Beaumes-de-Venise with Melon (page 402)
Honey Almond Cookies (page 436)

Eggplant Flan with Tomato Coulis (page 320)
Grilled or Baked Sea Bass with Fennel (page 212)
Sautéed Horn of Plenty Mushrooms (page 329) or Oven-Roasted Girolles (page 327)
Steamed New Potatoes or Rice or Wheatberries
Green Salad or Arugula and Parmesan Salad (page 34)
Quince Compote (page 426)

FALL/WINTER

Spinach and Red Pepper Gratin (page 359)
Chicken with Saffron Rice (page 385)
Green Salad
Quince and Apple or Pear Soufflé (page 427)

Provençal Wheatberry Salad (page 41)
Whole Fish with Tapenade (page 220)
Basic Tomato Sauce (page 112)
Zucchini Gratin with Goat Cheese (page 352)
Prune and Red Wine Compote (page 441)

Arugula and Parmesan Salad (page 34)
Rabbit Daube (page 389)
Oven-Roasted Garlic (page 363)
Steamed Potatoes, Rice, or Pasta
Lemon Sorbet (page 404)

Celery and Endives with Anchovy Paste (page 45)
Chard Stalk Gratin (page 342)
Rich Fish Soup (page 170)
Sweet Swiss Chard Torte (page 439)

Salad with Warm Goat Cheese (page 37)
Fish Fillets Baked in Phyllo with Tomato Concassée (page 216)
Wheatberry Pilaf with Wild Mushrooms (page 366) or Winter Squash Gratin
    (pages 344–45)
Pear Clafouti (page 424)

Green Olive Tapenade (page 59) with Croutons and Crudités
Spinach and Red Pepper Gratin (page 359)
Stewed Chicken with Pastis (page 377)
Green Salad
Quince and Apple or Pear Soufflé (page 427)

Salade Mesclun (page 29)
Ratatouille (page 312)
Brandade and Spinach Gratin (page 200)
Christine's Baked Pears (page 432)

SPRING/SUMMER

Artichokes à la Barigoule (page 322)
Chicken with 50 Cloves of Garlic (page 383)
Panisse Gratin (page 373), Spinach Gratin (page 358), or Zucchini and Rice Gratin
    (page 354)
Green Salad
Rhubarb and Strawberry Soup (page 418)

Brandade (page 61) or White Bean "Brandade" (page 68) on Croutons
Spaghetti with Tomato and Clam Sauce (page 295)
Salade Mesclun (page 29) or Green Salad
Apricot Tart in Phyllo Pastry (page 409)

Stuffed Zucchini Flowers (page 356)
Rabbit Stewed in Rosé with Tomatoes and Olives (page 391)
Pasta
Green Salad
Muscat de Beaumes-de-Venise with Melon (page 402)

Artichoke and Potato Ragout (page 324)
Red Mullet with Tomatoes and Olives (page 222)
Steamed Green Vegetable
Green Salad
A Compote of Fresh Figs and Grapes in Red Wine with Honey (page 421)

Tomato and Basil Salad (page 52)
Quichets (page 54)
Chicken and Chard Ravioli (page 283)
Plum Clafouti (page 413)

Salade Mesclun (page 29) or Arugula and Parmesan Salad (page 34)
Grilled Tuna Steaks with Tomato Concassée and Pistou (page 209)
Roast Potatoes Filled with Slivered Bay Leaves (page 339)
Fig and Orange Granité (page 420)

Light Salade Niçoise (page 24)
Salt Cod and Herb Ravioli (page 276)
Greengage or Plum Tart in Phyllo Pastry (page 415)

VEGETARIAN MENUS

Mixed Provençal Hors d'Oeuvres:
>   Truccha (page 242) or Zucchini and Rice Gratin (page 354)
>   Oven-Roasted Peppers (page 50)
>   Salade Mesclun (page 29)
Soupe au Pistou (page 134)
Cherry Clafouti (page 407)

Salade Mesclun (page 29)
Ravioli with Ratatouille Filling (page 274)
Fig and Honey Clafouti (page 419)

Warm Four-Bean Salad (page 43)
Eggplant and Tomato Gratin (page 316)
Sautéed Wild Mushrooms (page 331)
Fresh Fruit

Tomato and Basil Salad (page 52)
Pappardelle with Asparagus, Fava Beans, and Ricotta (page 288)
Arugula and Parmesan Salad (page 34)
Peach and Lavender Honey Soup (page 412)

Salade Mesclun (page 29)
Socca Crêpes with Ratatouille and Goat Cheese (page 315)
Potato and Saffron Gratin (page 337)
Melon Granité (page 400)

Provençal Tabouli (page 32)
Tomato and Bean Ragout (page 371)
Provençal Spinach Gratin (page 358)
Lemon Sorbet (page 404)

Asparagus and Fresh Pea Risotto (page 368)
Arugula and Parmesan Salad (page 34)
Tomato and Basil Salad (page 52)
Muscat de Beaumes-de-Venise with Cookies (page 403)
Fresh Fruit

Mini Aïoli (page 49)
Fresh Pea "Bouillabaisse" (page 140)
Green Salad
Pear and Apple Soufflé (page 429)

Eggplant Flan with Tomato Coulis (page 320)
Pissaladière (page 304)
Salade Mesclun (page 29)
Peach and Berry Clafouti (page 416)

White Bean "Brandade" on Croutons (page 68)
Tomato and Basil Salad (page 52)
Ricotta and Herb Ravioli (page 281)
Melon with Apricot Puree (page 410)

Spinach and Red Pepper Gratin (page 359)
Pumpkin Ravioli in Garlic Broth with Parsley and Sage (page 280)
Green Salad
Christine's Baked Pears with Honey (page 432)

A Terrine of Grilled Eggplant, Peppers, and Zucchini (page 46)
Niçois Potato Gnocchi with Spicy Tomato Sauce (page 299)
Green Salad
Fig and Orange Granité (page 420)

BIBLIOGRAPHY

Baratier, Edouard (directeur). *Histoire de la Provence*. Toulouse: Editions Privat, 1990.

Bertrand, Régis; Bromberger, Christian; Martel, Claude; Mauron, Claude; Onimus, Jean; Ferrier, Jean-Paul. *Provence*. Paris: Christine Bonneton Editeur, 1990.

Besson, Joséphine. *La Mère Besson, Ma Cuisine Provençale*. Paris: Albin Michel, 1977.

Bonnadier, Jacques. *Cantate de l'Huile d'Olive*. Avignon: Editions A. Barthélemy, 1989.

Borelli, Irene. *La Cuisine Provençale*. Paris: Solar, 1975. `

Chanot-Bullier, C. *Vieilles Recettes de Cuisine Provençale*, 4th edition. Marseille: Tacussel, Editeur, 1988.

Clébert, Jean-Paul. *Le Livre de L'Ail*. Avignon: Editions Barthélemy, 1987

Davidson, Alan. *Mediterranean Seafood*, 2nd edition. England and New York: Penguin Books, 1981.

Escallier, Christine, and Musset, Danielle. *Pétrir, Frire, Mijoter: les Cuisines des Alpes du Sud*. Salagon: Les Alpes de Lumière, 1992.

Fisher, M.F.K. *A Considerable Town*. New York: Alfred A. Knopf, 1978.

Johnston, Mireille. *The Cuisine of the Sun*. New York: Random House, 1976.

Jouveau, René. *La Cuisine Provençale de Tradition Populaire*. Nîmes: Imprimerie Bené, 1976.

Maureau, Andrée. *Recettes en Provence*. Aix-en-Provence: Edisud, 1991.

Médecin, Jacques. *La Cuisine du Comté de Nice*. Paris: Julliard, 1972.

Mistral, Frédéric. *Mémoires et Récits*. Raphèle-les-Arles: Marcel, Petit, CPM, 1992.

Morard, Marius. *Manuel Complet de la Cuisinière Provençal*. Marseille: Lafitte Reprints, 1984.

Mutualité Sociale Agricole de Vaucluse. *L'Alimentation Provençale et la Santé*. Avignon: Editions A. Barthélemy, 1989.

Nazet, Marion. *Misé Lipeto: le calendrier gourmand de la cuisine provençale d'hier et d'aujourd'hui*, vols. I and II. 63340 Nonette: Editions Créer, 1982.

Nazet, Marion. *Cuisine et Fêtes en Provence*. Aix-en-Provence: Edisud, 1992.

Olney, Richard. *Simple French Food*. New York: Atheneum, 1974.

Parker, Robert M., Jr. *The Wines of the Rhône Valley and Provence*. New York: Simon & Schuster, 1987.

Poulain, Jean-Pierre, and Rouyer, Jean-Luc. *Histoire et Recettes de la Provence et du Comté de Nice*. Toulouse: Editions Privat, 1987.

Proverbes et Dictons Provençaux. Paris and Marseille: Rivages, 1991.

Reboul, J. B. *La Cuisinière Provençale*, 23rd edition. Marseille: Tacussel, Editeur, 1988.

Rey-Billeton, Lucette. *Les Bonnes Recettes du Soleil; la cuisine Provençale simple et facile*. Avignon: Editions Aubanel, 1989.

Rocchia, Jean-Marie. *Des Truffes en Général & de la Rabasse en Particulier*. Avignon: Editions A. Barthélemy, 1992.

Serguier, Clément. *Pour un Panier de Figues*. Avignon: Editions A. Barthélemy, 1992.

70 Médecins de France, revision by Prosper Montagné. *Le Trésor de la Cuisine du Bassin Méditerranéen*. Editions de la Tournelle, c. 1930.

Shulman, Martha Rose. *Mediterranean Light*. New York: Bantam Books, 1989.

Vergé, Roger. *Les Légumes de Mon Moulin*. Paris: Flammarion, 1972.

Wells, Patricia. *The Food Lover's Guide to France*. New York: Workman Publishing, 1987.

Wells, Patricia. *Bistro Cooking*. New York: Workman Publishing, 1989.

INDEX